A RELIGION FOR ONE WORLD

BOOKS BY KENNETH L. PATTON

PROSE:

Beyond Doubt
Man's Hidden Search
A Religion for One World

POETRY:

Hello Man
Strange Seed
The Visitor
Man Is the Meaning
Readings for the Celebration of Life
Recognition
The Ground of Being

A RELIGION FOR ONE WORLD

ART AND SYMBOLS
FOR A UNIVERSAL RELIGION

by Kenneth L. Patton

Charles R. McCormick, Photographer

BEACON PRESS: BOSTON
MEETING HOUSE PRESS: BOSTON

Library of Congress Catalogue Card Number 63-18732
Copyright Kenneth L. Patton 1964
All rights reserved
Published simultaneously in Canada by
S. J. Reginald Saunders and Co., Ltd., Toronto
Printed in the United States of America

Permission was kindly given by the publishers to quote from the
following:
Harper & Row
    A. Eustace Haydon, *The Ques of the Ages,* 1929
    A. Eustace Haydon, *Man's Search for the Good Life,* 1937
    A. H. Maslow, *Motivation and Personality,* 1954
    A. H. Maslow, *New Knowledge in Human Values,* 1959
    R. M. MacIver, *Integrity and Compromise,* 1957
Yale University Press
    John Dewey, *A Common Faith,* 1934

*To the members and friends
of the Charles Street Meeting House
whose labors and support have
created one possible version of
a religion for one world.*

Contents

Preface

This book is the description of an idea and the attempt to make it into a reality as a temple structure and a religious fellowship. It is divided into four sections, the first outlining the philosophy involved, the second describing the attitudes and methods inherent in the experimental process, the third describing the project itself, and the fourth presenting the plates and notes on the art collection and the symbols.

The Charles Street Meeting House, the home of the project, is at the foot of Beacon Hill in the historic part of Boston. It has been remarked that if one sat down on Mt. Vernon Street in back of the State House on an icy winter day, one would wind up right in front of the Meeting House. The building is under the protection of the Society for the Preservation of New England Antiquities.

Beacon Hill is a denizen of little old ladies. Three of them have stated their views regarding the Meeting House at various times. One of them, the veteran religious news editor for a Boston paper, attended one of our services when we had been opened for only a month or two. Upon leaving she remarked to one of our members, "This church is simply not in step."

The second attended the Meeting House for a couple of years, with evident ambivalence. One morning after the sermon she passed me on the way to the coffee hour, and remarked in a *sotto voce* that could have been heard fifty feet away, "Hog-wash." Later she betook herself to the evangelical fundamentalism of "Brimstone Corner."

The third incident occurred recently, when a new family was entering the Meeting House on Sunday morning for the first time. This little old lady, probably on her way to the Church of the Advent, and probably with complete good will, said to them, "I am so happy to see *somebody* going in there."

The reception of Bostoniana, proper and improper, to our efforts in the creation of a religion for one world, has run the full gamut of antagonism, enthusiastic approval, and utter disregard. This book is presented to elicit the estimation of the rest of the world surrounding "the hub of the universe."

It would be impossible to name the hundreds of people who have been associated with the Charles Street Meeting House in the last fifteen years, and who have contributed in one way or another to the projects described in this book. Our constituency has been afflicted with two kinds of transiency. There is the geographical transiency of people moving into the suburbs and to other parts of the country and the world. There is the motivational transiency of shifting enthusiasms and convictions. Both are heavy in an institution located in the center-city of a large metropolitan area. Therefore we have chosen to name only that small core-group of people who have had long and continuous involvement in the project, and who are either still associated with the Meeting House, or who have died or retired to live elsewhere. Without the loyalty and continuity of effort of these people, our projects would have been simply impossible. Many of these people have worked at literally dozens of different tasks over the years, making immense contributions in time, energy, ability and money. It would be impossible for me to adequately express my personal gratitude and devotion to them. They are as follows:

Dr. W. Frank Ames, Mrs. Rosamund Baldwin, Rev. Edna Bruner, Mrs. Helen Cushing, Miss Charlotte Edlund, Mr. and Mrs. Ralph Edlund, Miss Una Ford, Mr. and Mrs. Joseph Fish, Miss Bertha Houston, Mr. Roland Hueston, Mrs. Ethel Lockwood, Miss Mary Lillie, Mr. and Mrs. Wilson Lyons, Mr. and Mrs. Charles R. McCormick, Mr. and Mrs. Walter McDougall, Mr. Merrill Nearis, Mrs. Viola Pease, Dr. and Mrs. Clinton Lee Scott, Rev. Peter Lee Scott, Miss Charlotte Smith, Miss Anne Bradstreet Stedman, Mr. and Mrs. John Swenson, Miss Ruth Vickery.

The project has had three photographers, all of whom worked without compensation. They are Dr. W. Frank Ames, now deceased, Mr. Peter Rossiter, now of Texas, and Mr. Charles R. McCormick, whose labors on our behalf have been massive and of long duration. The photography of all three men is to be found in the sections of *The Plates* and *The Symbols*, the majority by Mr. McCormick.

Some of the projects have demanded special contributions, some of which are noted in the chapters that follow. Many members and friends of the Meeting House contributed funds and art works to the art collection. We cannot list them all. We are especially indebted to several major donors, to Mr. John G. Greene of Boston for art works, the pipe organ and a fund for its installation; to Prof. Samuel Eilenberg of New York for an extensive collection of Hindu and Buddhist art; to Mr. Corliss Lamont of New York for support of the art collection and Meeting House Press; to Mr. and Mrs. J. Ray Shute of Monroe, N. C., for their collection of American Indian art and funds for further purchases; to Mr. Wempo C. Wang of New York for a collection of Chinese paintings. On every hand we received special considerations and cooperation from art dealers. Here again we can mention only those with whom we have had long dealings and who were most generous in their cooperation. From Boston: Mr. Abraham Bornstein, Mr. Edward Brodney, Mr. Hy Fields, Mr. Ellis Levinson, Mr. Boris Mirsky, Mrs. Marika Raisz. From Cambridge, Mass.: Mr. Paul Bernheimer, Mr. Joseph Gropper. From New York: Mr. Frank Caro, Mr. Julius Carlbach.

In the production of this book I would like to thank Mrs. Viola Pease, Mrs. Gobin Stair, and my wife, Mitzi Anderson Patton, for their perceptive and critical reading of the mss., Mr. Armstrong Hunter and the staff of Hunter Press, and Mr. Gobin Stair and the staff of Beacon Press for their collaboration; and the people of the Meeting House who worked patiently in the gathering, folding and collating of these pages.

Some of the material has been re-written from articles that have appeared in the following periodicals: *The Humanist, The Crane Review, The Liberal Context, The Unitarian Register, The Universalist Leader,* and *The Edge.* We are grateful for permission to reprint it in this work.

Above all we wish to express our gratitude to the Massachusetts Universalist Convention, and the Universalist Churches of Massachusetts which composed it, for bringing the Charles Street Meeting House, Unitarian Universalist, into being, and for the subsidy that made the writing and publishing of this book possible. I would like to declare my personal gratitude to Dr. Clinton Lee Scott, Superintendent of the Massachusetts Universalist Convention when the project was initiated under his leadership. Without his foresight and courage and staunch liberalism we would never have come into existence nor have survived the difficulties of the first years of this venture.

And finally I wish to thank my wife, Mitzi, for her encouragement and forbearance and partnership.

K.L.P.

Leave your journeying to build temples,
and adorn them with intimations of longer
journeys you cannot take, and images of
countries you may never enter.

In far-off times others will put their
carvings beside yours, and light candles
where long ago yours burned away.

In their celebrations there will be a
lingering of your questions and your
solicitations.

The rafters and the pillars will remember
your dreams, and your children will
discover the beauty of your ancient hands.

Ground of Being
KENNETH L. PATTON

PART I.

THE POINT OF VIEW

CHAPTER 1

A Letter to Japan

(Adapted from an article published in a
liberal religious journal in Japan)

A universal religion cannot be built in any one culture, nor can it find its resources in any one culture. If the dream of a universal religion arises and flourishes in only one country it will remain but a dream, not a significant reality. For a world religion must be located in the whole world, and it must draw upon all the peoples and all the cultures of the world for its literature, philosophy, arts, and aspirations.

A few generations ago the barriers of distance and language would have made such an ideal romantic. Today a universal and international world religion is no more an impossibility than is the United Nations in the political world. It will have small beginnings, but those beginnings are already starting to emerge. It will be the work of the liberals in the various cultures, for internationalism and universalism are liberal sentiments and disciplines. Orthodox and conservative religions are isolationist, or else rely upon religious imperialism and colonialism. Liberalism, like science, is tolerant and inclusive in its outreach. It seeks to receive teaching, not to proselytize. It seeks to join, not to conquer and submerge others.

The enemy of universal religion is provincialism. Those who live within the confines of one faith or culture take its precepts and customs as normative and all-sufficient. Inherently prejudiced toward their own ways and creeds, they cannot give

1

objective appreciation to the ways of life and belief elsewhere. Prejudice plays into the hands of ignorance. Limitations of imagination and lack of sympathy for other religions and cultures are consolidated by dogmatic aversions to any opinions but their own.

The immorality of provincialism is pride, which masquerades in the dress of a self-deluding humility. Provincials claim to be the humble servants of the will of a universal god, whereas they are in practice the purveyors of their own religious bias. The Christian West has a notorious record in this regard, since its religious missionaries followed the builders of empire and attempted to fasten their creeds upon all the world. Many Christians still look upon the missionary movement as their deepest religious dedication. Some of us who once were part of it now blush at its presumptions.

In each nation and culture there is a mixture of attitudes. Side by side will be found the narrowest provincialism and the most cosmopolitan universalism. Both of these attitudes characterize the people of Japan, of the United States, and of any other nation. Religions are clearly ambivalent in this matter. They profess universalism and inclusive acceptance and love. There is an incipient universalism in the missionary movements of Islam, Buddhism, and Christianity, but it is so confused by the provincial and exclusive assumptions of these religions as to be rendered useless as an ideal leading to a world religion. Paradoxically, these are three claims of universal truth and power competing with one another. Thus rival universalisms based upon creeds and uniquely inspired prophets stand as barriers to the development of any effective religious universalism.

But an increasing number of people are dissatisfied with any religion or world view that establishes one tradition as supreme. In the West they have disassociated themselves from Christianity. They do not deny that Christianity possesses many virtues, but they no longer wish to be named Christians or to be limited to Christian beliefs. They call themselves liberals and "universalists." They have instigated some rethinking and redefinition of terms in liberal fellowships such as those of the Unitarians and Universalists.

2

Within the Unitarian Universalist Association there remain many who call themselves Christians and who wish to maintain their fellowship and affiliations in Christendom. The major argument within the Association centers on whether Unitarian Universalism shall be a world religion or the liberal wing of Protestant Christianity. The "universalists" desire a fellowship that will include liberals who have developed from Confucian, Hindu, Taoist, Buddhist, Shinto, and Islamic religious backgrounds, even as we have come out of Christian and Jewish traditions. None of these people would seek to identify themselves with the religion they had outgrown, the religion whose dogmatism and provincialism they had repudiated. They would declare themselves to be members of a universal and world religion which included the religious ideals and traditions of all peoples.

At present this goal is empty-sounding, for contact between the liberals in various parts of the world is scant. There are very few people of African and Oriental background in Unitarian and Universalist societies, since most of the people in America are of European Christian or Jewish background, or Negroes who have long since been Americanized. Thus we find it difficult to convince the few people from other cultural areas who may live among us that we are sincere in what we profess. We make use of the literature, music, symbols, and art of the world religions, but we are poorly educated in world culture, owing to the provincialism of Western education. We are limited by spotty self-education from inadequate resources. We are held back from realizing our goals by the provincialism of the people of other traditions in America, which at least equals that of the westerner. Only a small minority of the people from any land have sufficiently matured to become citizens of one world and members of one humanity.

But we cannot let this submerge our ideal. We shall seek these liberals wherever they are and build our fellowships with whoever is available. We can contact the liberal and universal groups that are emerging in all parts of the world, and with them seek to establish a world-wide fellowship of religious liberals. If we had sister societies in Japan of Buddhist and Shinto background, societies in India of Hindu background,

3

and in Turkey of Moslem background, we would present a more convincing demonstration of our ideal. If we could publish an international journal, hold conferences, exchange leaders, we would begin to achieve a social reality.

The experiments at the Charles Street Meeting House, Unitarian Universalist, in Boston, Massachusetts, attempt to combine the art, literature, idealism, philosophies, music, and symbolism of all the world's religions into a religion for one world. Although we are ill educated and naïve, our intentions are creative and honest. In an experimental venture we become educated as we proceed.

These reachings toward a world religion are not overly optimistic or utopian. We sometimes find ourselves closer in understanding and sympathy to liberals from Japan than we are to our near neighbors. Relatedness of ideas and convictions can flourish between people of widely separated traditions. The earth has become one neighborhood, and we have brothers in thought and attitude everywhere. We hope to bring this potential fellowship into communication and cooperation, whereby a universal religion, with organization in all countries, on all continents, will one day come into being.

CHAPTER 2

A Religion for One World

Several thousands of years of human culture have passed, and humanity has yet to create and establish a religion for a united human family. Instead the human scene is decorated with a multitude of faiths, local and exotic, and the major divisions break up into hundreds of small sects. Some of these religions believe that they have created a universal religion. Buddhism moved out of its native India into most of Asia and the East Indies. Islam probed deep into Africa, into Asia and the Islands. Missionary Christianity, in its many forms, has attempted to convert the world to the gospel of its Saviour.

None of these "universal" religions is likely to become the religion for one world. There is no hope for the establishment of any universal religion, to any extent, in the foreseeable future. An attempt to estimate how long it will take would result in the wildest of conjectures. A reaction toward supernaturalism and provincialism might push the date millennia into the future. A world crisis or wave of enlightenment might bring its accomplishment within a century.

The practical approach is to tackle the problem of creating a religion for one world on an experimental and "model" basis. Some people are convinced that a religion, in order to satisfy the inherent longing and idealism of our age, must be universal in its scope and outreach, at least in its intentions. We have

5

accepted this alternative and challenge to attempt to create a universal religion in miniature.

Since there is no possibility that such an experiment, regardless of how theoretically adequate it might be, will have any wide acceptance in our generation, some success other than popularity must be found. We can conceive of two basic aims. First, our religion must be a satisfying answer to our personal and group need for a means of communication and belonging. It should afford us the instrumentality whereby we can creatively explore and accept the multifarious human family. Through it we should be able to open our personal and group windows and doors to the rest of humanity, whether they respond by entering into our midst or not. At least we shall be able to go out through our doors to them, and we shall be able to bring the arts, symbols, literature, history, and strivings of all the race of man into our own purview and be enlightened and encouraged in our participation in the human venture. In this first aim we shall have ready tests of adequacy at hand, for in our own experience of becoming more universal in our sympathies and appreciations of the people of other times, cultures, and beliefs, we shall know immediately and intuitively whether our experiments are "working" or not.

In the second aim we cannot have such certainty. This aim will be to make, through our trials and errors and possible successes, some contribution to the philosophy and methods whereby a universal religion may some day unite the human race into one family in aspiration and endeavor. Here our standards and tests will be those of logic, historical relevance, intuition, design, internal consistency, and prophetic sense. One consideration will override any easy confidence we might be tempted to acquire, namely, the awareness that the future condition of humanity will be so radically different from anything that we can now envision that any experiment made in this age can have only an incomplete and suggestive importance to the ages to come. Future men will look back at our present fumblings as our modern astronomers now regard the astrologers of only a few centures ago.

This is an insight that our accumulating knowledge of the

6

inevitable evolution of human culture has given us. One who has studied the progress of man's meandering journey to knowledge and civilization is no longer able to congratulate his own generation as being anything more than a transient phase of a development of his species that *should,* if we do not misuse our rising power for self-destruction, be in its beginnings. We are not at the end of the play; we have declaimed only a few words of the prelude.

But even so, we must live out our lives within the limitations and opportunities which our era affords us. And it seems to some of us that the peculiar challenge of our age lies in making the first attempts to bring the human race into a state of brotherhood and cooperation. We have seen the development of world organizations in health, commerce, and communication. In the League of Nations and the United Nations we have the first attempts to give a working unity to the world's governmental structure. In Unesco and other U N agencies the problems of unifying world culture and welfare are being faced. Several great private foundations have taken a world outlook in the development of their programs of assistance. Universities, libraries, and museums are meeting the challenge by becoming institutions with a global scope.

We whose peculiar focus of interest lies in religion would also try our hand in this new adventure of bringing a world which in fact *is* one, because of the advances of science and technology, into the creative unity and function that the living organism of human society is capable of developing. Thus we are led to attempt our trial runs in a universal religion, just as the League of Nations was scarcely more than a trial run in world government. To have any sense of confidence and realism in this venture, we must probe as deeply as our limited experience and wisdom will permit into the problems involved, to discover the basic principles at work in the structure of a universal religion.

The first of these, important as it is, is much too ramified for our consideration here, and we shall give it only passing consideration. Any experiment toward a religion for one world, to have a chance to lead in the direction of unity and universality, must be realistic. It must be thoroughly enlightened

7

and equipped with the most dependable knowledge that men have discovered about themselves and their history, and the nature of the universe of which they are a part. If we attempt to build a universal religion out of beliefs and world views that are accounted as superstitions by the informed persons of our own age, it will have little chance to be of enduring meaning and influence in future eras, which will be much better informed than we are now.

We will not stop to argue the point, but it is my conviction that any experiment toward a religion for one world must be thoroughly naturalistic and scientific in its approach to what it will tentatively believe about the human situation. Future investigations into "spiritualism," extra-sensory perception, immortality, reincarnation, and other related supernatural phenomena may bring these notions to the status of possessing supporting evidence of such weight that they will regain the sway over the minds and acts of man that they possessed in the pre-scientific world. But, until such a trend manifests itself, it seems evident that the wave of the future is with a naturalistic world view. This is where creative thinking and experimentation are going on in other fields in our time, and it would seem that any trial at a universal religion would have to take the same viewpoint to have any future relevance.

Our second basic consideration, and the one on which we shall dwell at length, while related to the first, is different in emphasis. It is operational. What kind of universal religion is likely to be effective? Why have the other attempts at founding a universal religion had such limited success? A brief look at the approaches that do not promise success will help us to fasten upon one that might at least launch us on the long way we have to go.

No "revealed" religion will have much chance to become a religion for one world. Revelation gives a special authority and truth to those prophets through whom the deity has seen fit to make his revelation. By its very nature, such revelation is a limited, even an individual, relationship between the prophet and the god. It must be accepted on faith by the believers. It cannot be shared and cross-checked by other investigators to substantiate its validity and workability. Because it is closed and private in its source, it does not lend itself to acceptance outside the company of the faithful. Conversion to the revealed scriptures and their unique wisdom is also a personal and unsharable experience, even as was the original revelation to the prophet.

Since the revelation is written in the language of the prophet, and is couched in the folkways and aura of his culture, it is difficult to share its special, esoteric wisdom with people of other lands. Whereas such supernaturalism did make an extensive penetration in the pre-scientific world, where supernaturalism was scarcely challenged as the source of wisdom and dogma, that age has passed, even though extensive areas of ignorance and superstition still persist on the human scene. Revealed religions will continue to have temporary and local success in moving out in a universal direction, as Islam is demonstrating in Africa, but I can see only failure and frustration for them in the long haul.

One reason is that there is not just one revealed religion; there are several. The Christians proclaim that Jesus *is* God. The Moslems say that there is but one God and Mohammed is his prophet. For many millions Buddha is the only truly enlightened one. Not only is there this competition between the "universal" missionary religions, which will cause them to stymie one another in their attempt to convert the whole of humanity to their one true faith, but the quieter, less evangelistic ethnic religions such as Judaism, Hinduism, Taoism, Jainism, Parsiism, and Shintoism are equally convinced of the supernatural and perfect nature of their scriptures and rites, which arm them against being converted in any large numbers to any one or all of the militant evangelistic religions.

It follows from this line of reasoning that a universal religion will not be tied critically to any single culture or tradition; it will not be based on any provincialism, as are all of the revealed religions. Just as future men will not be ready to admit that the prophet of any one time or place has the monopoly on truth, so they will not be willing to admit that any one culture, however it conceives its traditions, is to be the only source of the vision and unity of the future.

Just as the physical anthropologists have shown that all the so-called "races" of man are fairly equal in basic physical and intellectual potential, so a study of comparative culture and religion brings quick and overwhelming evidence that what wisdom and goodness the human race has possessed have been widely distributed in the human family.

By the same token, a universal religion will not be conclusively focused on any one of the spiritual heroes or saviors, be he Moses, Jesus, Mohammed, Buddha, or whoever. The peculiar flavor of unique greatness and enlightenment that the hero has to his own tribe is seldom comprehensible to another tribe, especially when it has a hero of its own to worship.

This brief survey would seem to indicate that the attempts toward a universal religion made in the past had certain inherent operational deficiencies that will prevent their ever accomplishing their dream of universal conversion, *unless* they evolve into something with an ideology and a program quite different from what they now offer.

The chances for survival and effectiveness of any experiment aiming toward a universal religion will depend heavily upon its basic attitude and world view. There must be a universalizing principle which permits acceptance of the goodness and beauty of all the previous and present systems of life and religion, and yet which also allows an objective examination of all sanctities and shibboleths with the cool eye of scientific detachment. Such an attitude presents the best hope for a universal religion in our time, and perhaps in that part of the future we can in any way forsee.

In this point of view religions are operational; they are methods whereby men and women have tried to satisfy the needs and desires of life, have sought dependable knowledge, moral principles, and the means of bending the forces of their environment to fulfill their wants. All the elaborate structure of mythology, ritual, magic, and institutionalism was designed basically to assist man in his "quest for a good life."

The best capsule statement of this basic viewpoint and attitude of which I know is given by A. Eustace Haydon in *Man's Search for the Good Life*. It merits quotation at length.

The understanding of religions is greatly simplified

10

when man's religious history is viewed as a phase of the age-long adjustment of human beings, in social groups, to the actual and imaginary forces and facts of the unfolding natural world. Seen through the eyes of science, man is a child of the earth mother, a product of the cosmic process, with his origin millions of years deep in the pre-human ages. He is one of the myriads of life forms organized as relatively stable patterns of interaction with the environment. Every organism is a terminal thrust of a long line of living forms reaching back into the unplumbed deeps of time. Each is a structure of desire drives making demands upon the outer world in order to maintain or complete its own peculiar mode of life. From the inorganic to the human this is the saga of the ages — the endlessly changing quest of living organisms for adjustment and fulfillment in relation to an environment of threat and promise. On the human level the pattern became confusingly complex because, in addition to the ancient drives of desire which man shares with all forms of animal life, he embodies also the social desires learned in group relations through unnumbered centuries. Man's ascendency over other forms lay in his development of intelligence as a problem-solving instrument capable of making adjustments where desire was thwarted because of a novel situation or because an earlier mode of adjustment had failed. If the environment had been perfectly made to meet man's wants he would have had no need of intelligence. So on the social level, religions were a sign that the world was unsatisfying — not good but to be made good. They were the continuation in a more complex social form of the struggle of organisms to secure from the natural world the values which make life good. Religions were from the earliest human ages vital, integral phases of the life process, creating in infinite variety the modes of idea and practice through which the families of man faced the future with assurance.

The panorama of world religions unfolds with perfect naturalness when the dominant motif is kept in view. All the complex patterns find their meaning and justification in the long quest of man for the values of a complete life. But when philosophic ultimates, theories of revelation, or ideas of god and the spiritual world are used to

11

interpret the meaning of religions instead of being taken for what they are — the creations of religions — the picture becomes distorted and confused. From the age of primitive man until today religions have created a multitude of diverse patterns of the ideal of human happiness. Philosophy, building with religious materials, erected splendid cosmic systems making the final fulfillment of human hopes the theme song of reality. All of it began in the brave blundering of our earliest ancestors, battling for life, and striving to impose their will upon the world. All the elaborate structures of thought and ceremony of the later ages are successive refinements of the original theme. When they are seen as the products of religion which is itself a function of the life of man, all the windows are open to understanding. No form or idea of any age or culture can be snubbed or ignored or scorned. But the religious drive is more important than all its products of theology and cult. It is simple and elemental. It is man's search through the changing ages for the values that may make our common earthly life glad and beautiful and good.

This is the only basic viewpoint I know that is capable of expediting the appreciation of all the world religions for any person (or group) regardless of where the accident of birth may have placed him on the human scene. It is the key whereby all of man's attempts at religion, all his writings, his ethical principles, his rituals, temples, arts, songs, can be enjoyed. We identify, not with the particular theology, magic, or ritual practice, but rather with the prevailing hunger and searching that led these people, through whatever means, to seek answers to their questions, and means for produce, security, beauty, and hope. Whether a man is worshiping the sun to secure its continuing warmth and blessing upon his fields, or bowing before a fertility god to cause his seed to sprout and his wife to bear child, or placating the imagined evil spirits to ward off sickness and calamity — no matter how superstitious, unenlightened, unscientific, even brutal the religious practice may seem to be, the intent, the drive behind the religious practice is something which we share and in which we can have full identity and participation. I do not share

12

with the Moslem his faith in Allah and the revelation of Mohammed in the Koran, when he kneels on his prayer rug and bows toward Mecca. But I do share with him his devotion to that which he believes is good and wise. I do share his unremitting quest to bring himself into a relation with his world as he sees it, a relation that will bring abundance and beauty of life to himself and his family and the race of man. No matter how we may vary in our techniques and philosophy, we are united in that we are all striving, each according to his own light, to realize the highest dream of human achievement and realization of which we are capable, projecting it into scriptures, rites, and institutions.

When it is the basic questing that is honored, rather than the particular and transient mode of the quest, we have a key to a universal appreciation of all religions. Then "no form or idea of any age or culture can be snubbed or ignored or scorned." The painting, sculpture, and architecture of all the faiths belong to us, for they are urgent and compelling with the longing and aspiration of the people who created them. We catch the spirit of their quest in their poems, songs, and dances. We know the hunger and fear that drive them to beseech the mercy and cooperation of their gods, even though like emotions cause us to turn to other means of support and sustenance.

On this natural and human basis, on this emphasis on the underlying function of religion, rather than on differences in method and trappings, we find a basis for making an experiment in the direction of a religion for one world. It may be that we are mistaken in our opinion that this is the most likely concept our stage of understanding provides. Mankind one day may unite about the vision of one god, as the majority of people believe, although they disagree about the definition of the deity, and the name of his true prophet. It may be that the quest for a religion for one world is futile, and each people should continue to practice its tribal faith, and cooperate in other areas without cross-breeding religions. Many things are possible, and only many centuries will decide these issues. We can only testify to our own urgency toward a religion for one world, which has developed in us as we have engaged in this

13

experiment. We can only affirm our judgment that the idea of humanity's universal quest for the good life is the key to the gathering of the nations and the bringing of mankind into one community of respect, appreciation, cooperation, and love.

There is one conception of a universal religion from which I would like to disassociate the considerations of this book. Some people have proposed that all one needs to do to create a universal religion is to gather together the essential and superior teachings from all the religious writings of mankind, to unify them in a "world bible," and the resulting religious viewpoint would be convincing to all members of mankind who are susceptible to religious concerns. Several such world bibles have been assembled. This whole proposition is peculiarly mechanical and academic in its tone and assumptions. It implies that all that is necessary to construct such a religion is an adequate library of books, a group of scholars, and a research grant. The product would be as dead as the procedure.

A religion for one world, although it would make use of the teachings of all the world religions of the past and present, does not slavishly worship them or depend solely upon them for its resources. The religion for one world that is here being proposed develops generically out of a liberal attitude and method. It seeks truth and evidence wherever they may be discerned, going beyond all ancient and primitive religious ideas and formulations and holding all the teachings of the past, religious and otherwise, up to the scrutiny and criticism of present knowledge and theories. The community of science has become a truly world-wide community, even breaching the iron and bamboo curtains to bring scientists into creative conversation and sharing of findings with one another. The liberal also is tied to no traditions, to no geographical areas, to no specially designated disciplines and sources for authority. He is skeptical of the adequacy of any of the evidence and insights accumulated in the past, even those called religious and revealed. He would not suppose that all the essentials for a universal religion were contained in the religions already in existence, and that if he could succeed in winnowing out the best from all the religions the perfectly adequate religion of man would be in hand.

14

The liberal is often the product of the process of re-examining one of these traditional religions, the one into which he was born, and discovering that because of its tribalism, traditionalism, and dogmatism it was inadequate to satisfy his intellectual and emotional needs. He is not likely to make the error of thinking he can find a satisfactory religion by taking superior parts of many religions and making a perfect whole from them, since all these religions share the tribalism, traditionalism, and dogmatism of the one from which he has painfully graduated. He quickly sees that all traditional faiths, sharing as they do their beginnings and development in primitive and parochial human societies, inevitably will share the same basic insufficiencies. One religion may have virtues that another lacks, but all will possess deficiencies that would render any possible combination of their teachings and attitudes quite inadequate for a religion for one world.

A religion for one world will have to grow out of a one-world situation, which is still in an incomplete state of evolution. But we have become "one-world" enough that even Republican Presidential hopeful Wendell Willkie could recognize the fact, and it is convincing to religious liberals also. In attempting to live in one world, we are attempting self-consciously to create a religious viewpoint capable of handling the problems and potentialities of this one world social reality.

The liberal looks to the sciences — to astronomy, geology, biology, archaeology, anthropology, sociology, and psychology — for his views of man and the universe, out of which his religious concepts will be shaped. He realizes that before Darwin, a mere century ago, there was no adequate understanding of evolution and the biological process. Thirty years ago we were not aware that the universe was "galactic centered." Twenty-five years ago we had very sketchy ideas of the nature of matter and energy. Psychology is an infant science, scarcely fifty years of age. Archaeology can be almost totally contained within the last century and a half, and anthropology is so young it is still framing its basic concepts.

When the liberal seeks to make up his religion for one world, he goes primarily to that world itself, and to the knowledge he can find about the nature, behavior, and history of the

15

human species, rather than to the mythologies, bibles, and divine revelations of the world religions. He also goes to the poets and dramatists, to the novelists and artists, the musicians and philosophers of the past and present, whether they accounted their works to be "religious" or not. He includes the religions of the past and present as part of the human scene that he must evaluate. He searches their traditions for insights of value, ethical vision, and mystical depth. But he is not prejudiced in their favor simply because they parade under the name "religion." He does not believe that their truths are inherently superior to the truths of the market place, or of science, or of the arts, or of philosophy. His long disillusionment with the "perfect revelation" into which he was born has taught him better.

Consequently, when he has constructed his religious position, from whatever sources have been available, he does not consider it sufficient and beyond amendment, or something which all other men should desire to espouse. He is, rather, eager to submit it to correction, for only by amending and redesigning it will he attain a religious instrument of ever more profundity and efficacy. He would never pronounce that the religion he has selected and created should be a universal faith to which all mankind should subscribe. He does not consider such unity of belief desirable, preferring a creative difference of religious opinion and practice on the human scene, rather than a dead uniformity. The "one-world faith" proponents are a hang-over from the religious presumptions of orthodoxy and dogmatism. Whenever the liberal is approached by such claims, he catches an odor of the occult.

What then does he mean by a "religion for one world?" His position is similar to that of a person who has been in and through several social class levels in his sociological "mobility." He will eventually belong to no class at all, yet will have real relationships in all social classes. He has resigned from membership in a particular class, to become a member of society as a whole.

The liberal who has moved through several changes of religious viewpoint and institutional association may eventually find that he belongs to no sect or movement as such. I can

16

testify to this in my personal experience. As a child I was a Methodist. When, after fifteen years of slow evolution, I ceased to be a Christian, I was not then disposed to join some other movement, to be a Jew, a Moslem, a Hindu, or a Buddhist. I belonged to no tradition in the old sense. I had left my cultural provincialism and "belonging" behind, even as I had left behind the "upper-lower class" into which I had been born. I believe that I am now free from both social-class and denominational parochialism. Nothing will satisfy me short of being a member of the human race and having a religion for one world.

What is the relation of the person in a religion for one world to the many religious traditions of the race? It is very simple. They all belong to him, as part of his human past, but he "belongs" to none of them. In the sense of understanding and appreciation, he will acclaim them all, rejecting none. The role of appreciation in the religious experience of the liberal is strangely neglected. We seem to think that "our religion" consists of just those precepts and attitudes that we ourselves accept, and that all the rest is rejected. Yet we can appreciate a great deal of human experience and many attitudes which we would never care to assume ourselves. I would try to appreciate *everything* in man's religious history. In this sense I would seek to be a complete universalist. I believe that my critical and intuitive selection from the human and natural scene of those elements that will become my *practicing* religion will depend on whether my appreciation has attained universal scope. Otherwise it will proceed from ignorance and prejudice and be worth little.

The liberal does not believe that he is caught in a particular religion or culture merely by the fact that he is born into it and reared within it. The adventure of maturing, of education, and of exploring the world consists in moving out from the locus and environment of his birth to encompass in his understanding and appreciation all of the world, human and otherwise, that he can reach. He does not believe that any of the ways and ideas and attitudes of the human family are closed to his comprehension and emotional response. His mood is that of Terence, when he wrote, "I am a man, and nothing

17

that is human can be alien to me." He is bolstered in this belief by the anthropologists' elaboration of the principle of diffusion, whereby the attainments and behavior patterns of cultures have penetrated one another all during man's long history. The age-old diffusion, once spread by men wandering about the globe on foot and sailing the seas in frail vessels, has in our time been immensely accelerated and intensified by all the inventions of commerce and communication of the industrial era. The vast international exchange of ideas, arts, produce, and people is the means whereby we can become citizens of one world and attain the scope of understanding and sympathy that make a universal religion a realistic ideal in our time.

Sometimes the liberal who has ceased to be a "child of his own tradition" does not join another tradition as such. He does not again relate himself as a partisan, as a "member," of another tradition. Rather he holds himself responsive to, belonging to, *all* human traditions. This is not as difficult as it might seem, since he gains the conviction that in its full perspective there is only one tradition, the human tradition. He will not espouse everything in the beliefs and behavior of the human race, any more than as a Methodist he espoused everything in the beliefs and behavior of Christendom. But it is humanity that he belongs to, just as once he belonged to Methodism. Nor does he relate any longer to any particular geographical area as his fatherland. The planet has become a geographical unity, and he would feel at home anywhere upon it. He feels that the people living everywhere upon it are his people.

For this reason at the Charles Street Meeting House in Boston we have gathered the symbols and art of the world's religions to adorn our place of religious celebration. Thus we declare that they all belong to us, but by the fact that they are all there, with all their mutual contradictions and identities, we declare that we belong to none of them, nor to any selection or combination of them. They do not signify a "one-world faith" but rather a religion for one world, and the difference between these two concepts is crucial.

What do we take from the great panorama of world religions? On the appreciative level we take all. On the practicing level we take that which we judge to be enlightened, ethical, wise, and intuitively profound. We can take only a fraction of some insight, or most of it. But this assembly of religious symbols and art, accompanied by the books and music of these cultures, declares that we are free to take, from any and all parts of it, whatever of beauty, wisdom, and relevance we may discover. We affirm that all of man's traditions are for us now one immense storehouse of religious insights and history. We envision one inclusive world of religion and belong to it; it is for us a religion of one world.

This attitude brings us into a continuous conversation with all humanity in all times and places. You may object: "But the members of other traditions often set themselves apart from and against such liberals and universalists. How can you have a conversation with them?" Even if they set themselves apart, the universalist does not set himself apart from them. If they will not engage in warm, mutually accepting, person-to-person dialogue, he will go to their writings, their art, their folklore and take these into himself.

The anthropologist does much the same thing. He seeks to comprehend the cultures of all the world's people in their profoundest dimensions, in fullest sympathy and empathy, whether the people of those cultures so comprehend him or not. He shares with them whether or not they will or can share with him. This is the attitude of the member of a religion for one world. He has joined the world and the fellowship of the human race. He lives in intimate communion with all the reaches and varieties of mankind; they are his family. All their traditions are his, and from them, according to his personal temperament, his intellect, his moral insight, he selects the religion that he personally practices. But he does not offer this as a perfect and universally practicable religion and recommend that all men subscribe to it. He is not interested in creating another orthodoxy. He is neither so proud nor so stupid as to recommend it as a "one-world faith."

CHAPTER 3

One World - One Humanity

Phrases of profound inherent meaning can quickly become clichés, sliding over the mind and off the tongue with scarcely any meaning. Such is the phrase "one world — one humanity." In its basic meaning it is not a new idea. Paul expressed the conviction that God had made of one people all the nations of the world. But except to rare individuals, who have become citizens of the world and brothers of all humanity, this has been little more than a pretty-sounding ideal. Mankind has clung with jealous pride to small localities and smaller loyalties. It has meant more to be a member of a tribe than to be a member of humanity.

Here we face the most critical issue in a religion for one world: Can men and women feel loyalty and "belonging" to a group as large and various and scattered as the human race? Can they conceive of the earth as their neighborhood, their dwelling place?

Another minister visited the Meeting House. After he had looked at the centers of world religions, I asked him whether he thought such an approach would work for himself and his parishioners. He doubted, he said, that they could feel any compelling relationship to so many different traditions, symbolisms, and art forms. He thought people needed to relate to a single tradition, their own, and in his case liberal Christianity.

20

I protested that there was only a single human family, one human history, one human culture, and one human religion, that the differences among peoples, in their ideas, practices, arts, and ethics, were much less striking and significant than were their similarities and identities. He admitted this was factually true, but still felt that men could not relate intimately, religiously, to something so vast and diverse.

Evidence supports his conclusion, for the majority of people in our country and in other countries about the world, feel attached to "their own," to their own land, their own people, their own history. There is a growing nationalism in Asia and Africa. On these continents the people are taking new pride in their traditions and religions, recovering their cultural identity and power after centuries of European domination. This is necessary, for the dignity of the human race depends on the dignity of individuals and groups and nations. All the peoples of the earth must be free, self-governing, culturally creative, and self-respecting before the human race as a whole can be healthy and progressive. Some lands have a great deal of catching up to do, and they intend to have their rightful share of well-being and attainment.

But even so, those who place their hopes for a peaceful world in the United Nations and in a growing awareness of the meaning of world citizenship are disturbed by the divisiveness and bitterness between the national and racial groups of the human species. Slowly a new kind of human being is arising. Woodrow Wilson was one of the first great exemplars of a world view. Those who believed in and worked in the League of Nations, and those associated with its successor, the United Nations, are the pioneers of a new kind of human loyalty, loyalty to the race as a whole. Their idealism and commitment to the goal of world unity, world law, and world brotherhood increase one's faith that humanity can grow into such character and imagination as will be needed. If these comparatively few people can respond with an idealism that is nothing short of religious, then potentially all men can rise one day to attain the reality in the concept of "one world — one humanity."

Universalism as a religious movement began with an emphasis related to this. In the idea of Universal Salvation is the inherent idea of God as the Father of all people, who, in his loving-kindness, will see that all his children are at last saved for eternal life. None is to be damned to hell. Other theologies divided men into sheep and goats, into the saved and the damned, but Universalism affirmed the forgiving love of God and the unity of the human family both in this life and in eternity.

A century and a half ago, when this movement was coming into being, there was little need for the world view of today. Twentieth-century communication and transportation had not drawn the globe into a compact community. This "universalism" was little more than a theological concept. Some of us, quite aware that we are adding new dimensions to an old name and movement, believe that the name Universalism must expand to include these new "universals," such as universal brotherhood, universal peace, universal welfare, universal health, universal freedom, universal security, universal science and understanding. We are committed to "the truth known and to be known," and therefore we feel no hesitancy in demanding that the basic ideals and concepts of Universalism grow to meet the necessities of a later time. Nothing that we have believed can stand as barrier to what we must believe, if we are to keep pace with new understanding. No loyalty and denominationalism of another day can be allowed to bar us from the loyalties and identities that our own age requires of us, and these cannot be less than world-wide.

The term "one world" can have several meanings. In earlier times it was believed that there was only one world, that the earth was the center of the universe, and the stars and planets were merely smaller accessories to decorate "our" sky. This was *the* one world. Those who are acquainted with modern astronomy have long since given up this idea, at least intellectually. I wonder, however, whether emotional vestiges of the ancient idea of our world do not still linger. Do we not, in our religious ideas, still hold ourselves to be *the* children of God? And how could this be unless our world were also the apple of his creative eye? Religion has hardly adjusted to the understanding that this is *a* world, not *the* world. What is our relation to a universe, and whatever deity may or may not preside within it, when we are but one of many millions of planets where life systems have evolved? Life may be as lavishly strewn among the galaxies as these millions of galaxies are lavishly strewn about the universe.

A realistic attitude would seem to be that this is just *one* world, one among millions, and that we are *just* one species, members of *just* one evolutionary process, among millions of others. Perhaps there is no "importance" attached to us and our attainments in any cosmic economy. Perhaps such notions as "significance," "meaning," and "importance" are human concepts, and unrelated to other cosmic processes. Except, that is, for other creatures such as ourselves, wherever they may be. And, since we have no contact with them, we have importance only as a possibility in their imagination, as they do in ours.

If we are no longer *the* world, or *the* people, it is illogical to conceive of ourselves as the darlings of the universe. There may be no star boarders at all in the great rooming house of the universe. In fact, it seems that there is no landlord, and that we are all left to fend for ourselves as best we may. This is *just* one world.

The second meaning of "one world" could be that we have *only* one world. In spite of the predictions that in a few centuries we will be going to the moon for the winter, much as we now go to Miami, there is little prospect of our finding another handy planet for our excess population when we have bred the earth so thick that there is "standing room only." Some theorists have said that we might break up some of the other planets, say Jupiter, and bring the pieces into the same orbit as the earth, and thus create several new planets for ourselves. But I doubt that even the Army Engineering Corps will tackle this feat in our lifetime. As for migrating to another planet comparable to our earth, the nearest star to our sun is four light-years away. We would have to find the planet first, and with billions of stars in our Milky Way Galaxy, this might be worse than looking for a needle in a haystack. Even if we found one it might be hundreds or even thousands of light-years away. And if it was any good, another system of living creatures might already be occupying it, perhaps with a population problem even worse than ours.

There is a further caution regarding the notion that another world may be available to us. Hundreds of millions of years of evolution have subtly adjusted us to the environment of the earth. We are so delicately attuned that if we go up above sea level or below sea level a few thousand feet we are in dire straits. Our tolerances relative to heat, atmosphere, gravity, ultraviolet light, and other factors are quite narrow. Whatever other world we found might not be habitable, or might require such engineering to adapt it to our use as to be impracticable. Except for science-fiction addicts, we are stuck with *only* one world in the foreseeable future.

This raises an immediate question. In any large family if there is *only* one of anything, the question arises as to *whose* it is. The wise parent rules that it belongs to the whole family, that it must be shared. Share and share alike. How easily said and how hard to accomplish. The larger sibling will try to bully himself into a favored monopoly of the disputed item. That deadly quarrel about whose turn it is now is inevitable. And how the human family fights over this *only* one world.

The intellectual problem is not too difficult in this matter, but the emotional problems are monstrous. If there is only one world, then we have to limit reproduction for optimum living standards for all. Biologists have already calculated how many people the world can comfortably house and feed. But who can tell how to make a cantankerous humanity breed just so much and no more? We have little more concern for the earth and the future than a plague of locusts.

If we have only one world, then we must be its husband-men. We must assess all its resources and contrive their optimum usage. We must plan for succeeding generations, and not mine the earth insanely for the benefit of only a few generations, as we are now doing with such mineral fuels as coal and oil.

An even more profoundly ethical consideration lies in the distribution of the earth's wealth among the earth's peoples. Now it is divided ruthlessly on lines of national ownership. Those of us lucky enough to be born on this nearly untouched

North American continent, out of our generous hearts, "give" to the poorer Europeans and Asiatics. What a peculiar idea this is, really — that men own that part of the earth they happen to walk above. Shouldn't the produce of the earth be for them that need it? For example, if there is an epidemic anywhere in the world, now that we have a World Health Organization, the medicine and doctors from the rest of the world go immediately to the area that is endangered. Should not the same system work with food, with energy, metals, with all the earth's substance? Such a system works among our fifty states; why not among all the earth's nations and peoples? If we have any morality or religious sensitivity, should starvation, sickness, ignorance, slavery mean any the less to us, regardless of where it occurs in the human family? It should make us vomit in disgust at our pride and greed to want things for our own children more than we want them for the children of all humanity. And yet we sit among our rotting food surpluses, our luxurious garbage adding to our municipal budgets, while two-thirds of the earth's people have too little to eat. And we call ourselves a Christian country. There is *only* one world, and if all the people on it are to thrive, it must be shared among them all. The technical problems this redistribution will raise should be secondary to the insistence of the moral issue involved. For example, we condone the destruction of food because it would not be economically profitable to ship our potatoes to other parts of the world. When is economics morally uneconomical?

There is a third and deeper meaning to "one world." I know of no other way of expressing it than by saying that this *is* one world. The continents are all surrounded by one great body of water — not seven oceans, really, but *one* great ocean. There is only one atmosphere that blows about the whole earth, and the air that is over Boston now may be over Cape Town in a short time. The earth is one globe, one mass of soil and rock. How silly we are to think it is divided by the way it juts up above the surface of the one ocean. This *is* one world, so defined by the vast space of the universe that surrounds it.

The oneness of the world is an astronomical reality. No one can attain a sense of his relationship to the universe without getting the feel of the planet, as a unit in the solar system, as a unit in the galaxy, as part of a galaxy that is itself a unit of the universe. Out of the whole cosmos, *it is this one world that is our home.* Just as we get a cozy feeling about the people who live on the same block, so we should have this sense of neighborly identification with those who live with us on earth. It is such a tiny place in such a vast universe.

I think our feeling about this should be similar to our reaction when we look over a new house. There is a definite excitement to exploring the rooms, looking into the closets, peering out the windows to see the view, going into the corners of the attic and the cellar, roaming about the yard, looking for shrubs and perennials left by previous owners. This is where we are going to live, and we want to get the sense of it. And so is the earth our home, our house and garden. We have a sense of family identity with those who live in the same house with us, surrounded by the same walls, warmed by the same heat. So we should feel about all the other creatures who live with us on the earth, of whatever species they may be. All of the other animals are our "house pets," as it were.

When will we have the same emotions about "our world" as we have about "our native land"? What could be any more our native land than the earth itself? What could be any more our fatherland, our motherland? This *is* one world, *our* world.

Our sense of identity is a matter of the area of focus. We can identify in a meaningful way, with nature, with the universe as a whole. Coming closer in, we can identify with the earth. Sharpening the focus of identification still further, we identify as living creatures, with the life processes, and with all of animal life. In what is as yet a vague, almost quizzical sense, we identify not only with the life on this earth but with those other systems of life that we are told probably inhabit other worlds than ours. Do you not get an almost intangible sense of belonging when you think of other creatures in other solar systems? It is this sharpening of the focus of identity that brings Schweitzer to his "reverence for life" as possibly a more acute sense of relationship and moral obligation than would be reverence to the universe as a whole.

But nowhere is the focus more to be narrowed than to our

"one humanity." You may protest that it is far more limited than this, even to ourselves as individuals, to family, to clan, to nation. But I believe this is an irreligious and miserly affection, to the extent that such narrowness of loyalty shuts you off from fellow feeling for the rest of the human family.

Just as the idea of one world is an astronomical reality, so the concept of one humanity is a biological reality. On that level it is unarguable, even though the racists and fascists may disclaim it. We are a biological family, mutually fertile, intercommunicative, interdependent. We cannot escape this fact and the necessities it places upon us.

We have been taking somewhat of a cosmic stance, so let us look at this "one humanity" in its larger scope. What does it mean to be a member of a species? It means to be very much like all other members of that species, *very much alike.* Have you watched the crowds of children pouring out of a school building and been struck by how much your children are just like all the rest? We may not always enjoy the fact, but *we belong.* This belonging is the result of a continuous, interrelated process of evolution, in *one line,* that has been going on for hundreds of millions of years.

The opponents of evolution have loudly protested the idea that we "descended" from the apes. We did no such thing, of course; we proceeded in our own line of evolution, going back to a little tree lemur rather than to the monkeys. They have had their own line or lines. We are, really, not very closely related to any of the other animals, even the higher apes. During those millions of years, by the slow accumulation of mutations, we have taken on the shapes and proportions, the dimensions and potentialities that are ours. Slowly the realization is dawning, however, that *this is it.* We are what we are. Unless radically new knowledge and methods develop, it may take millions of years to effect any considerable improvement in the species. But, except for superficial regressions, there is no going back. Our evolution cannot be set back, even if we wanted it to be, so that we would rejoin the other animals. Each species moves out into its own being, and the area of its interbreeding defines the area of biological identity and all the countless other realities related to this.

27

In this sense of the evolutionary focus, we are biologically limited to our own species. We can appreciate, to be sure, the other flora and fauna, even have a feeling of belonging to them in a wider family sense. But when it comes to the profound and intimate sharing of kind with kind, *we are one humanity*. And I would conjecture that we are one humanity both on this earth and in the universe. Even if there are thinking creatures on other planets, what are the chances of shared, or "cultural," relationships with them? Look at the bizarre outbranching of life on this planet, the millions of strange creatures, living and extinct, all products of one earthly environment, and see how limited is our communication here, even with the higher animals. Let your imagination roam. Given other planets, with undoubted variations in soil, atmosphere, heat, chemistry, what are the chances of finding even in some distant age of space travel another species of creatures similar to ourselves? When we consider the barriers our biological differences place between us and the animals, how much greater are the barriers likely to be between us and creatures evolving on other worlds?

Why go into all this far-off nonsense? Just to underline the likelihood that there is only *one humanity* in the whole universe. We, as the human family, are alone in the universe. Our human brothers and sisters are all the family we have.

Franz Boas says that there is no such phenomenon as the so-called "primitive mind," that all the human species has basically the same thought structure and behavior, and that much of the thinking of so-called civilized people is just as superstitious, as mythological, as "primitive" as that of the bushman. How alike we are, all eating, sleeping, marrying, living, dying, like all the rest. But even more, all *speaking, working, farming, dancing, singing, painting, creating legends, worshiping*. We have been so struck with the differences in the ways we do these and other things that we have tended to ignore the much more important thing: *we all do these things*. We share the same basic needs and desires, we have the same basic environment and raw materials for their satisfaction, and we have evolved strikingly similar methods of communication, adjustment, art, and community living. This is nothing to be mystified about, now that we know how the diffusion of culture has taken place from most primitive times. Our separation by mountains, seas, distance has always been but a relative factor, and — given a racial history of a million years — of temporary and insignificant proportions.

We have always been but one humanity. We still are. It may even be prophesied that we probably always will be. Our great problem is, and has been for ages, how to live with each other, with our fellow human beings. Religion in its core is what Jesus and Buddha and Laotze and all the other sages have declared it to be: loving one another.

How can we fail, knowing the human situation? Yet we know that we have failed and can fail again. We have no special guarantee against disaster, whether from the elements without or from the human storms within; we have no more guarantee than did the dinosaur and the passenger pigeon against extinction; even less, since we are capable of inflicting it upon ourselves.

We can say the words: This is one world; you are one humanity. Live therefore in peace, and till the garden of the earth, and make your days and the years of your children a glad time upon the earth. We can say it, but will they listen? Will they respond? Will they *know?* Will they, and in time?

CHAPTER 4

Recovering the Past

Our lives are pulled in three directions. At times we are wholly absorbed in living in the present. At other times the present is like ashes, interest and delight burned out, and we yearn toward some dreamed-of goal. Some live so habitually in the future that present inconveniences or pleasures are discounted as inconsequential before the enticement of coming events.

The third direction in which our lives are drawn is toward the past. The present is brief; the future is problematical, unpredictable, and insecure. But the past is established and will endure. The men and beauties of the past will forever remain what they have been, regardless of our disappointment in our living companions. Unpredictable as Michelangelo may have seemed to his contemporaries, his genius and works are a constant possession to us now. The new play being introduced this season may be a trite failure, but Shakespeare will continue to be what he was.

The past stretches back in depth and thickness of texture for thousands of years, peopled by multitudes, an endless vista of history, legend, and art. Our lives are too brief to rehearse all the stories and excitements of the past. Some persons, lacking commitment to the present, spend their days mainly in the recovery of the past.

A productive life must contain a balanced distribution of

these three appeals. Without concern with and knowledge of the past any life is shallow, any personality is as thin as a paper cutout. Without an intense forward thrust into the future any life is without a driving purpose, without dreams and destination. Both of these interests must be concentrated in the present moment, investing it with richness, meaning, and absorbing labor. The whole man brings knowledge, techniques, and arts from the past in order to labor with concentration and satisfaction in the present for the accomplishment of a purpose whose adequate realization extends far into the future. The past is recovered to provide implements for building for tomorrow.

The past contains what we are; we are what the evolution of the past has produced. Without knowledge of what our past has been, we do not know what we ourselves contain and are. We must recover the past in order to discover the fullness of our own persons. This imperative applies to societies and nations as well as to people. Until we recover our past as the species of mankind evolving upon the planet earth, we will not comprehend our customs, institutions, and social frustrations.

We are born not only naked of clothing but naked of personality and knowledge. The world as it has been shaped by the past forms us into the kinds of creatures we become. Words and ways of thinking whose beginnings are so ancient we can only guess how they first developed are put into our mouths and minds; they become the equipment and substance of our thought. We do not understand how we think until we recover the past of our own language.

Our childhood days are burdensome with dos and don'ts. The moral history of the race is as old as the race itself. We become ridden with guilt, inhibited with convictions of moral responsibility. But we cannot know our own moral natures until we recover the historic development of moral principles and coercions. The same applies to our gestures, our laughter, our emotions, our games, our dwellings. The past is an immense and all-shaping structure around us. Self-knowledge and freedom are denied us until the past is known.

There are principles to be observed in recovering the past.

31

Often what passes for the study of history is the rehearsal of illusions. Men find in the past what their present inclinations move them to discover there, as was demonstrated in the general reaction to the theory of evolution. Men wished to believe that they had come into being by a special and spiritual creation, and that they were not a part of the animal kingdom. Many of the orthodox still will not accept the abundant evidence that supports the evolutionary hypothesis and makes it one of the best substantiated of all scientific theories.

People have convictions as to what they are, which are justified by opinions concerning their past. If they admit that their ideas about the past are in error, they will have to revise their definitions and descriptions of their own nature. Their writing of history is largely self-portraiture.

Religions venerate their sacred writings. The world in which the ancient poets and historians lived has long since escaped from the racial memory. The beliefs and superstitions, the world view, the moral customs, the rites and social conventions that underlie the writings are scarcely suspected, except by archaeologists. Believers memorize the scriptural texts from childhood. They mean something to them now, and they naively assume that they meant the same thing to the men who wrote them. This is the enduring illusion of the worshipers of holy books.

The twenty-third psalm is an example. It is prized as a reading for funeral services, for an assurance of immortality is found in the closing line, "And I shall dwell in the house of the Lord forever." Since there is little else in the Old Testament that even hints of immortality, this passage is specially treasured.

The editors of the new Revised Standard Version have set as their goal the elimination of all ambiguous and inexact translations. There has been rejoicing in some quarters that old favorites such as this psalm have been only slightly edited. The Hebrew word translated as "forever" means literally "as long as I live." The translators have included this reading as an alternate translation in a footnote, but they have left the sentimentally loaded word "forever" in the text. Thus the psalm will continue to be misread today, regardless of what it meant to the ancients.

The first principle in the recovery of the past is honesty. We must take from the past, not what we want to find there, but, as closely as can be determined, what actually occurred there. The integrity of the scientist must become our integrity as historians. It is often claimed that science has nothing to do with moral values. On the contrary, science rests on a foundation of scrupulous moral principles, the chief of which is an exacting honesty and objectivity. Religious folk could learn moral and religious lessons from the scientists, for religion often plays the loosest kind of cat-and-mouse game with honesty and evidence.

Geologists, anthropologists, archaeologists, researchers of all kinds have learned the pitfalls of self-deception. In confronting the cultures farthest removed from our own, such as those of so-called primitive peoples, we are looking at what we do not comprehend. We know very few facts about these people and the way they really live and think. Much of our assumed knowledge is made out of our own prejudice and the unadmitted fears that these people may be our equals and thus aspire to cancel the powers we hold over them. Thus the Europeans have discounted the complex cultures and civilizations of Africa and have denied that Africa possesses a history that they must reckon with.

Fear of losing our proud illusions brings us to concentrate on but a portion of our own past, excluding as insignificant the history of other cultures. Western education focuses mainly on Western civilization and scarcely mentions the equally ancient and significant civilizations of Asia. Many of our errors of judgment come from this foreshortened view of history. It substantiates the lies, whether intentional or not, that have justified colonialism, imperialism, slavery, exploitation, and genocide. It continues to rationalize the arrogance of white Christendom.

We must recover the past of the race, of all nations and all cultures, and the interrelations of all nations and cultures. The more of the past we recover, the plainer the realization that we are one race and that human culture is one culture and human history is one history. The only adequate history

33

is the history of the human race, and the only adequate education will encompass world culture. Anything less than this is a sham and a delusion which will fail to equip us to meet the problems of world trade, government, communication, and disagreement. We rushed into the task of understanding Japanese history after we found ourselves at war with Japan, and our armies deep in the Pacific. It was too little and too late. If we had bothered to learn about the Orient sooner, we might have avoided the war entirely. Justice Douglas and others have warned us that our ignorance of and unconcern with the nations of the hinterland of Asia may cause them to be lost to world communism. Ignorance has now become an extravagant folly.

The present is but the latest moment of the past. The barbarities of the past operate in continuous succession into this moment. We have not escaped the past; we are the past in its living continuance. The rites of our churches retain the barbaric splendor and superstition of five thousand years. Our myths and fears are close relatives to those that haunted man as he emerged into history. Witches were hanged at Salem and they are still hunted by our politicians. Ancient human sacrifice lingers in the victims of our state-operated gas chambers, gallows, and electric chairs. The mass murder of war now reigns with massive fanaticism and religious zeal, amazing and disheartening any who hope man may one day escape barbarism. No act of barbarity of any age ever compared to the use of the atomic bomb by our own government.

Cruelties and inequalities are visited upon the poor and on minority groups that no civilized people could stomach. Our children have turned to criminality, to the manias of speed and vandalism, to degeneracy and dope. New York City must hire hundreds of extra police, toters of clubs and guns, to deter children from theft, rape, and murder. These are the products of the barbarous deserts of our great cities. The worst comic books, movies, radio and television shows reek of sadism, cynicism, and lust. This is what we are.

Why are we this way? Only by studying how and why we have developed into this state will we uncover the measure of our sickness, the depth and tenacity of our social habits,

and the means for reconstruction and growth. Our only resources are in the accumulated experience of previous generations. If these resources are insufficient we must engage the
problems again where they leave off, and build further upon
their foundations. There is no beginning afresh. Only by
making new combinations of past ideals and techniques, only
by creating new inventions, based on insights afforded by
earlier inventions, can we inch forward. The past is the meaning of the present and the liability and asset of the future.

There is no easy method of reconstructing the past in order
to increase our understanding. To comprehend the significance
of any object of African art we must understand the whole
complex culture of the African tribal nations, their religion,
world view, customs, laws, and folklore. We cannot look at
a mask and intuitively comprehend it. Nor can we, innocent
of any understanding of the Semitic tribes of three thousand
years ago, memorize isolated verses from their anthology of
folklore, laws, and literature and assume comprehension of
the words glibly rendered.

We must rebuild the ancient world in our understanding in
order to appreciate any of its parts and products. This has
been called the socio-historical method, the reconstruction of
the social world of the past in order to gain insight into a happening of that world. It is a difficult task, never to be accomplished perfectly. We can never satisfactorily put ourselves in
the place of our ancient relatives and think and feel as they
once did. But we can appreciate our inadequacy, which will aid
our comprehension. Half of knowledge lies in comprehending
what we do not know. Regardless of whether we do this
task well enough, to do it at all will be of advantage.

Two novelistic ventures indicate what is possible when the
sincere artist, with the help of the scientific historian, attempts
to make the past alive. One of these is Waltari's *The Egyptian*.
In the last century thousands of students and scientists have
been busy at Egyptology, which activity has connotations of
amusement relative to the bizarre specialist. The novelist
combines this research and projects it into dramatic events and
personalities. We are taken on a journey to a strange land, into
another time. Our horizons of appreciation are widened. We

see connections between the happenings of the past and the problems of our own time. Several millennia of human history become a brief interlude of development.

It is not enough to recover our past within the brief span of the historical period. This is but yesterday, racially speaking. We must delve through hundreds of thousands of years, into the pitifully few remnants of the cave dwellers, into the charnel heaps of ancient villages, finding a bone, a tool, a spear tip driven into the rib of a mammoth. The archaeologists have already reconstructed a brilliant picture from the few clues that have been uncovered.

Vardis Fisher, gleaning these records and interpretations, has written a series of prehistorical novels called *The Human Testament*, beginning when the human animal was first developing marks of intelligence, language, tools, and twinges of moral sensibility. Fisher attempts to make our forebears come alive, to enable us to live imaginatively in the dawn of human life. No modern man understands himself until he knows that story, until he recovers the past which in accumulation is himself.

Our study of the Bible can work somewhat to liberalize and educate the people of Christendom, for it is one of the great source books of archaeological material, a mine for the scholar of human cultures. Growing knowledge of the cultures of Egypt, Assyria, Babylonia, Sumeria, Phoenicia, Crete, and Greece is enabling us to put the Bible in its historical context and to appreciate it as a document of human history.

Within the total human past, the Bible is but one narrow trail. But it is a trail back, a penetration in depth. We can learn much by following one line intensively, rather than by taking a smattering over a large area. If the Christians at length learn what the past was like, through the study of a few Semitic tribes, this may be an object lesson sufficient to motivate them to recover the whole of the human past. It is even possible to gain an understanding of the scientific method and attitude in the study of the research into the Bible in a divinity school.

Once a road has been built back into time, side roads can branch off from it, just as in digging a mine shaft passages are extended out from the shaft at various levels. The research of religious archaeologists is now indistinguishable from the field of archaeology in general. Those who began by digging back into the Twelve Tribes of Israel are now concerned to recover the past of the whole Mediterranean world, with side roads running out to encompass the globe. This development offers hope for the collapse of Christian provincialism and prejudice, working out from the seeds of science and objectivity within Christianity's own studies and educational institutions.

How shall we find time to recover the past? What about the urgent jobs of the present? Men must learn to busy themselves with "human work." Much labor is not fit for human nature, being mechanical, repetitious, requiring little imagination and intelligence. There is a protest that machines are taking man's work from him, but any work that a machine can do better than a man is not fit for men to do. The man must turn himself into a thoughtless machine in order to compete with the machine. Let mechanical gadgets do the mechanical things — add columns of figures, check measurements, tighten bolts. There is work which only men can do, work of thought, imagination and appreciation. Man must be the student, the interpreter, the philosopher, the teacher, the guide and critic of human affairs, and the recoverer and compiler of the past.

Our museums, libraries, foundations, research institutes, and universities demonstrate the people's increasing concern with these vocations. Men will be fully men when their interests and labors are concentrated on matters of thought, artistic creation and appreciation, the nurture and development of human personality, and not on the senseless manipulation of raw power. The minute explosions of energy in the synapses of the human brain are of greater significance and measure than the detonation of atomic bombs.

The recovery of the human past in any systematic and scientific sense has been attempted only in the last century and is as yet barely begun. This is the road to dependable knowledge and wisdom, not via divine revelation, but through patient digging, searching, collation, and integration of findings. The great storehouse of history will provide man with many of the understandings and tools whereby a mature civilization can be constructed.

Two main interests will occupy us. We will rehearse the tragedies of the race to learn how the mistakes of our ancestors may be avoided. And we will be concerned to thresh out the living seeds from the chaff of yesterday. The bulk of history consists of dullard repetition. But on occasion a seminal strain develops, some prophetic individual or minority begins to tread a new path. Some innovators declared ideals millennia ago that are still unrealized today. We must treasure the vitality of the past, the work of the inventors, creators, philosophers, and moral prophets, as well as the examples of simple dignity, honor, and self-sacrifice.

The vista is monstrous and quaint, charming and horrifying, noble and depraved, but vigorous, lusty, and alive. In it we shall discover the ranges and boundaries of our own natures.

During a visit to the Museum of Natural History in Chicago, one incident occurred that was more compelling than all the others. The museum has a diorama showing a site in France where megaliths mark one of the open temples of early times. Huge rough blocks of stone are lined up in long avenues, leading toward the rising sun. In the foreground stands one of our ancestors, a priest, a rapt expression on his powerful, bearded face, crudely clothed, his heavy arms lifted in praise to the sun. He is more tanned and rugged than we, but his body is the same as our bodies. Ten thousand years have left hardly a trace of evolutionary change. We have prehistoric faces and bodies, and no doubt prehistoric thoughts and emotions also.

Shivers crept along my jaws and down my back. Deep, deep within me I remembered. Our ways of relating ourselves to the earth and sun have changed scarcely at all. If his worshiping of the giant rising sun, the source of light and life, was superstitious, then we are superstitious still. What are our gods but the sun by other names? What is the sense of sustaining power that we feel in nature other than this same sense of identity and dependence upon the sun?

We feel quite modern as citizens of the mid-twentieth century. Much has happened in history of which we are the inheritors. We have come far, to a superiority high above our benighted ancestors. But this is true in the veriest surface of our lives, in that thin veneer of gadgets, science, dress, and manners called civilization. Underneath, profoundly bedded in the structure of our bodies, we are not modern at all.

We are the vessels of time, of millions upon millions of years of time. We are the past incarnate. We understand ourselves not in the slightest unless we know what this accumulation of time is within us, and how and why it has come about.

The intuitive realization of being vessels of time is the source of some of the fascination the sea has for us. We can somewhat modernize the land, deforest it, plow up the plains and civilize them into neat, packaged fields. We bisect and square off the land with roads and hedgerows, and set our houses in lines of sterile regularity. We make the earth mapable, adding to the landmarks of lakes, rivers, mountains, and shorelines the dots of our cities, the grid of railroads and highways, the divisions of states, counties, and nations. How simple a map seems when all of man's clutter has been removed from it.

Having thus civilized the land, we can ignore it. We walk for blocks and see nothing of the soil. It is the buried foundation of buildings and pavement. We live in rooms, artificially lighted and heated, air conditioned, experiencing nothing but man's artifacts. We are depressingly humanized. Where the earth does peep out around the edges of the asphalt and concrete, in yards and parks, the grass is evenly clipped, the wild weeds are pulled, and the plants man tolerates, god that he is, are lined up in dull, military files.

But there is one expanse man has not able to modernize: the sea. The land is ancient as soon as we get beneath our surface scratchings, but we forget this. The sea resists any permanent markings from the furrows we plow on her. Her tides erase even the scratches we make on her shores, and sometimes she invades the land and washes out our creations there.

The sea persists in her breadth and depth to remind us that the earth is a great vessel of time. Her waves, which we are powerless to detain, sweep endlessly like a ticking to mark time's passing. The sands heap into mountains to overwhelm us with the slow gnawing of her teeth upon the rocky lips of the continents. The welks, snails and fish we take from her are untouched, undomesticated. This modern time of man has not touched their deep homes at all. The underworld is unconcerned with our worried scramble on the planet's surface. The sea fascinates us with her casual but unarguable reminder of time.

Some of man's cultural creations are almost as impervious to change as the sea. Another exhibit at the Chicago Museum of Natural History drew my attention. In studying world culture and symbolism it has been a constant challenge to look for a masterful symbol of universalism. This symbol must indicate the inclusiveness, the wholeness of the human family, the oneness of the universe and its forms. It should stand for nature, man in nature, and man in community with his fellow man. We believe we have found the symbol in the circle, which is an ancient symbol of the universe, perhaps intimating a remote premonition of Einstein's verdict that space is curved. It has stood for the earth, the sun and the moon, for perfection, holiness, and unity.

It was with the excitement of discovery and recognition that we found the Chinese Pi disc, going back to at least 2000 B.C. Much has been written about this archaic jade object, and each variant interpretation serves to make it a richer embodiment of the principles and ideals which we seek to symbolize four thousand years later. Thus symbols too are vessels of time, carrying the worship and aspiration of our primitive forebears and linking us with them. Their symbols are quite suitable for our own use. We discover through them that we have not changed in our intuitions about man and the universe as much as we might think.

One case in the museum held stone artifacts from Stone Age France. How old were these objects — ten thousand years or more? The Stone Age covered an immense span. I looked at one of these objects unbelievingly. Here was the Chinese Pi disc, a flat stone disc with a hole in the center. Its resemblance was unmistakable; it had the same basic design and proportion. How long had this stone symbol been in use before it became the Chinese symbol for the heavens? How old is this idea of Universalism, which some consider so modern, radical, and heretical? Perhaps it is the oldest of all man's ideas. Man sits in a circle around a fire. He sees the circle, the disc, in the sun, in the moon. The horizon stretches in a circle all around him. Man strives for at-homeness, for oneness and belonging with his fellow creatures and with the fearful and wonderful nature on every side — what more is universalism than this? And our symbol is given us by Stone Age man from the very threshold of human history.

There is another indication in this stone symbol. Words are also symbols, made from sound rather than from stone, wood, or metal. Language is very ancient and embodies unacknowledged presumptions about the nature of the universe and experience. Our thinking is done through words and rhetoric, making these presumptions all-important to our beliefs, attitudes, and working myths. The very sense we make depends upon them. We are seldom able to think outside these tacit limitations and frames of reality. Through them we select the world of our experience in accord with their abundance and limitation, for they are a screen that admits to our eyes and our discourse only what we have the words to express.

Anthropologists have discovered that different cultures have dramatic differences in language, in thought structure, and consequently in their views of the world. Until we can enter and become at home in the language world of these peoples, to make their ways of thinking digestible to our comprehension, we understand them only superficially.

Our translation of the writings of other cultures is handicapped by these differences in basic thought patterns. In translating the words, we change the ideas into those of our own culture, thus erasing the unique quality and flavor of a different vision of reality. It is this latter that would be the most enticing to us, since it would bring us into another world through the thought and symbols of another people.

The languages of China, Japan, India, Africa, and the American Indians are vessels of time. They contain the intellectual and emotional history of their people, accumulated over thousands of years. One who earns admittance to the worlds they symbolize does something like finding a new self, for he learns to use his capacities for observation, feeling, and thought in ways he could never discover except by seeing life through the vast experience of other peoples. This is essentially what all education is, whether within our own culture or across cultural lines. We pour into the vessel of self the accumulated experience, vision, and interpretation from the cultural vessels of time, the traditions and lore and science of humanity.

The tools of Stone Age man are of an impressive design, functional rightness, beauty, and craftsmanship. They exhibit considerable technological skill, since they were made entirely by the use of other stone tools. To study these adzes, hammers, axes, knives, scrapers, mortars and pestles is to discover that each tool of mankind is a vessel of time. Each is an accumulation of a hundred thousand years of human labor and invention. The basic shapes have not changed for ten thousand years.

The same thing is true of most of the implements and goods of civilization. Weaving, pottery, agriculture, sports, painting, sculpture, architecture, sailing, transportation, communication — all are vessels of time, concentrations and saturations of history. Their meanings are the boiled-down, the winnowed dreams of millions of our forebears. The immensity of this treasure should cause every sensitive person to handle these cultural goods with awe and appreciation.

We make a token gesture at thanksgiving, but we are ordinarily crass, careless, unfeeling, and unaware, even brutal in our use of tools, language, ideas, clothing, and houses. Man is a creator of trash, a breaker, a despoiler, an ancient and perpetual vandal. Incalculable riches have been lost through his pillage, arson, spoliation, and stupidity. We get a bitter taste of cynicism for the human species, they have been such poor caretakers of the wealth in the vessel of time which is their own cultural accumulation.

There is a happier side to human history, for men are also collectors, lovers, treasurers of art and lore. They can develop a conscience, and archaeologists set out to rediscover the lost cities of the past. The cultures of Egypt and Babylonia, of the Medes, the Persians, the Cretans, of Sumeria, of Peru and Yucatan, long buried or forgotten, are being reclaimed, and are bringing our own past into our own consideration.

Our former learning, accordingly, must be differently assorted and related. The transcendental importance we have given to the Judaeo-Christian tradition has been possible only because we lost contact with the cultures of Sumeria, Babylonia, Assyria, Phoenicia, and Egypt, the older and often richer cultures among which Israel developed. Egypt and Sumeria had passed beyond their great periods by a thousand years before the little nation of Judea emerged. Much of the Old Testament is but a version of older Phoenician stories which in turn drew upon the past of Babylonia and Sumeria.

The Bible is a vessel of time, just how vast we are now learning. The literary genius of the Jewish people not only provides us with their own poetry, wisdom, and history but endows us with their uniquely beautiful version of a folklore, morality, and literature which was the general property of the whole of the Middle East, the Fertile Crescent in which human civilization was born. We now approach the Bible, not as divine revelation, but as a rich compendium of human history and culture, a valuable vessel of time.

Human history shrinks to almost superficial scope compared to the time factors in the evolution of life and of the cosmos. The astronomers have shattered our scales and proportions with their announcements of the universe as a vessel of time. The telescopes have gathered in light that left our neighbor galaxies two billion years ago. The universe seems to be a vessel of eternal time, moving self-creatively into a never-ending future.

We have not begun to cope emotionally with time in such dimensions. It is too vast for our comprehension, unmeasurable by the instruments of our few years. But this is the universe in which we live, in intimate contact, breathing its air into our bodies, walking and working in the light of its stars, deriving our food from its soil. All this is a saturate of time; we breathe, eat, and sleep history.

This knowledge is useful in many ways, to geologists, miners, and oilmen, to engineering and industry. Beyond such practicality the dimensions of time operate in the arts, in philosophy, in poetry and music, in the world of feelings and visions. The arena of time is the setting of our daily lives, the aura of our peace and tragedy.

The human body is an organic clock, a seventy-year clock, ticking its way to its ultimate running down. Through knowledge of evolution we have come to sense our bodies as parts of that one panoramic display of living creatures. Our breath and pulse are the continuance of an unbroken life movement that has endured for millions of years. All the many transformations are remembered in the present structure of our bodies, these vessels of time.

A single plant of red clover has 500 seeds. Weedy crabgrass makes 90,000 seeds on one plant. One orchid bears 3,770,000 seeds. Some forms of animal life are scarcely less fertile. The reproduction of mankind is geared to a million years of life when it was prey to the elements, wild beasts, unchecked disease, infant mortality, and early death. To survive, man needed to be marvelously fertile. We have checked many of the ravages of the Stone Age, but we still have the reproductive capacities of Stone Age man. We threaten to breed until the planet is choked with humanity, our standard of living is brutalized, wilderness areas are overrun, millions are dying of famine, and war is ravaging the exploding populations.

The source of this peril lies in the fact that we embody our biological history. Our bodies remember the dangers to life in the past; in our sex drives we remember and respond. Now these ancient habits are overdrawn, and power for survival turns into power for self-destruction. By conscious planning and discipline man has to adjust his Stone Age biology to the needs of these times. The uses of soil, minerals, food, all natural resources must be known in their history; their conservation must be planned. If we stupidly exploit this vessel of time it will punish us mercilessly. Man is a creature of nature; he cannot cross her ways and not be penalized.

Conversely, nature presents man with opportunities that he has not yet begun to inventory. Within himself are capacities not even tapped. The brain is an almost unexploited natural resource, even as are the oceans. Man and the world are vessels not only of past time but of future time also, empty vessels waiting to be filled. Billions of years of livable time await us on this planet.

Religion is a long-range view of life. The religious person has a background and perspective against which he sees his transitory acts, which are thereby composed into a web of cosmic meanings. His deeds point to and imply tomorrow. The religious man can endure present inconvenience and suffering for the chance of future goods. The acts and ideals that foresee the highest and farthest goods are the most religious. The acts and ideals that include the greatest number of people, and the greatest goods for each person, are the most religious.

We need a conditioned optimism. This is not an old and dying world, nor are we an old and dying race. We are not striving so much to save what we have as to build what we discern can be. It was the judgment of A. Eustace Haydon that we are in our very infancy as culture builders. The historian James Harvey Robinson wrote, "The human comedy seems to me now about to start."

In this time of atomic fear, it would be easy to believe that this is the end of the world. It is just the beginning. All that we have done as yet has been but the clearing of the land and the heaping of the stones. We have not yet laid the foundations of human society.

The Christian Bible encompasses a historical and cosmic framework for the human venture. All great religions do this. From its first phrase, "In the beginning," it moves to the picture of the New Jerusalem: "And there shall be no night there; and they need no candle, neither light of the sun; for the Lord God giveth them light; and they shall reign for ever and ever." The believer positions himself between the brackets of the beginning and the end.

Some of us are dubious concerning this framework; although poetry of grandeur, it is poor science. For the first time we have sufficient data to make a realistic conjecture about our place and role in the stream of time and history. Our fathers made brave and beautiful guesses, but we do not have to guess, or at least not as drastically.

45

The human comedy is about to start. The face of the earth has not yet been conquered. Millions still await freedom from drudgery and hunger. Science is a small child, the social sciences but babes in arms. Men have only begun to think in planetary terms. They complain that the frontiers are gone, but they stand before the widest frontier of all. The exploration of the globe, of the heavens, of the atom, of the person of man, of history, even when accomplished, will have but set the stage for the greatest adventure of all, the building of a world-wide human society.

With all their poetry, idealism, and moral earnestness, the religions of the past are but the spiritual totterings of an infant humanity. Hardly the first chapter of the Bible of Man has been written. Our religion can see back millions of years to the beginning of life; it cannot see forward to what New Jerusalem will be the destination of our growth. There will be no end eternally. The past is prelude.

CHAPTER 5

Religion and Symbols

THE FORMS OF LANGUAGE

It is intriguing to attempt to create phrases that exactly mirror reality, or as exactly as words can ever mirror reality. One such phrase might be "the prevalence of history." The past tends to dominate the present. We are reared into the meanings and manners of our forebears, and unless we exert nearly heroic efforts, we continue to speak and act as our fathers spoke and acted before us. The muddle of penalty and reward that this situation entails derives from the fact that we inherit both the strengths and the failings of our ancestors. By the prevalence of history the accumulated virtues and skills of a million years of the human past become our endowment, and the superstition, errors, and limiting antagonisms of the same million years become our handicap.

A fundamental issue of freedom lies in the capacity to escape the prevalence of the past, to free ourselves to choose that which we wish to become, and thus to escape the tyranny of the forms of the past. The free man is the one who can select that from the past which he wishes to prolongate, because he agrees with its factuality and worth; he can likewise reject that of the past which no longer satisfies the evidence at hand, his faculties of judgment, and his intuitions of necessity. Whatever of the past prevails into the present does so because the free man chooses that it shall survive. He is master over the past, not mastered by it. This man is a traditionalist within freedom, for he chooses which of the traditions he will sustain.

A man's relation to the past is ambiguous. What is his past, that of his family, of his village, of his country, or of his race? To a pertinent degree, what a man's past is depends on his opinion as to who his significant ancestors are. From the point of view of my family, there were many desirable and undesirable elements in the past of the small town into which I was born. My family wished me to adhere to just those religious and ethical ideals they espoused, and they firmly rejected the mores of other families on the same block. The past which was intended to prevail over me was the past of my immediate family, not that of my village. The world was divided by my family into Christian and pagan. My past was definitely determined to be the past of Christendom, and a small sect of that. Over the years my viewpoint has changed. I still relate to a past, but to a human past, not just a Christian past, and this has made all the difference.

Sometimes the personal interests and abilities of the individual lead him away from the traditions into which he was born. Often this divergence occurs on seemingly unrelated strata, but if the person seeks integrity and consistency in his life, he will attempt to bring these different strata into one focus, and then the conflicts will plague him, and radical departure from his traditional standpoint may result.

My own experience is relevant here because it is involved in the basic issue of the forms of language. I was born into a kind of Protestant Christianity wherein all the arts except the art of preaching were viewed with the abhorrence that is attached to heresy. Music, of an exceedingly dubious quality, was partially absolved. The dance was an enticement of Satan. The theater was lewd and suspect. Painting and sculpture as expressions of religion came under the proscription against graven images in the Old Testament. Ritual was associated with the Catholic Mass and detested. Religion was divided into the sacramental and the evangelical, and there was no mixing of the two.

There was almost no more art in the culture at large than there was in the Protestant churches of my youth, but what there was could be sought. My temperament was artistic, and soon I was involved with music, sculpture, painting, poetry, speech, and dramatics. The general culture, being mainly non-theological, permitted the full scope of artistic interest and endeavor, although it gave scant reward or encouragement to the arts.

The bite toward integration and consistency was in me, so the inevitable question was why the arts were not employed in the life of the church as I knew it. In the Old Testament I read about dance, ritual, and sacrifice. In the Episcopalian and Catholic churches I caught glimpses of elaborate sacraments, architectural splendor, rich music, the use of painting, sculpture, symbolism, lights and censers. It seemed to me that the arts which I studied in school and participated in in the theater and concert hall also belonged as agencies for the expression of religion. Were not all the arts but different forms of language? How could a person express the deepest meanings and overtones of life, which are his religion, unless he employed all the voices, all the arts, that are available to human expression?

A developing association with the arts quelled certain of the fears I had inherited from my family and sect. The world of the arts, all the arts, became an intimate province of being. I was more at home in the museum, the concert hall, the theater, finally, than I was in the church, blasphemous as the intimations of this experience might be. When you spend the preponderance of your waking hours practicing a musical instrument, painting at an easel, or scribbling poems, these labors become intimate, beyond question, and imbued with a confidence in the rightness of their declarative powers. If you are religious at all, the arts become the instruments of your religious meditation and utterance, whether their role is justified by the theologies and prejudices of your religious traditions or not. Your true beliefs, the faith of your very daily processes of life, involve the arts. The religion of your living practice in time overwhelms the religion of your parents' discipline and the verbalism of the creeds.

Here lies the reason why so many young artists turn away from the institutional practices of religion. They define and celebrate their living beliefs, anticipations, and mysticism continuously in their artistic activities. Their art *is* their religion, in that it is the way and the meaning of their lives. The church, especially when it eschews the arts, becomes an empty, a hollow institution and instrument to them. They neglect it, not so much because they no longer believe in its tenets as because it does not involve them and use them in their significant engagements with life, in artistic creation and expression. When you ponder upon how religion once engaged and employed Michelangelo and Da Vinci, this circumstance is cautionary.

There is an amusing, if sardonic, inconsistency in the church's rejection of the arts. It does not reject all of the arts, but rather prejudicially focuses most of its expression in one of them, the art of speech, to the practical exclusion of all the rest. This concentration can be traced to bibliolatry, the worship of the book, the Word of God. If God used words to reveal divine truth, then words must be all right. Music is not rejected, but the music that is mostly used is singing, where melody accompanies the word. In the chant we have a kind of musical speech. In the cantata the scriptural story is sung by soloists and choir. Music accompanies the reading of the Mass.

Perhaps it is because speaking is so everpresent and essential an element of daily life that we forget we are practicing the art of speech, like the man who was surprised to learn that he spoke prose. The practice of religion does not exist without art, but rather limits itself mainly to but one of the arts, one of the forms of language, speech. Even the Friends, when they are moved by the light within and seek to communicate with one another, must use the art of speech. When in their communal interchanges, they seek a consensus of opinion wherein they can find the loving agreement of their fellowship, they must use the art of speech. When the evangelical Protestant sets out to save souls, he must use the art of oratory and prayer.

Perhaps the best way to set forth the efficacy of the other arts to those who limit themselves to the art of speech is to interpret the other arts as also being forms of language. They are not essentially different from words, for they can be used well or poorly, to clarify or to befuddle, as clear, informative discourse or as propaganda, to tell the truth or to lie. They can be vague or explicit, scientific or superstitious, liberal or reactionary. For the very abuses which those in the Protestant Christian tradition fear they may be subject to if they allow symbolism, ritual, dance, painting, sculpture, and architectural splendor into their temples and celebrations can be and are as easily the abuses potential in the art of speech. And the other arts share with words the powers of evocation, of exposition, of information, of truthtelling, and of rigorous integrity. The other arts can be just as telling spokesmen for enlightenment, justice, equality, truth, and love as are readings, hymn verses and sermons, and discussion.

Furthermore, the things which mankind thinks, hopes, feels are many-sided, often subtle, often exceedingly difficult to render into speech. This is the reason why speech is almost always accompanied by another art, the art of gesture. We are all actors when we speak. The rude formalities of some classrooms inhibit this art. The child is asked to read or recite in class, and the product is dead, toneless, and almost meaningless. But let that child be released to the playground and his whole active body joins his voice in expressiveness. The art of the actor is mainly the highly skilled imitation of the natural art of expressiveness, of gesture, facial expression, and vocal intonation, which all people learn immediately and unselfconsciously as they learn to talk.

The spoken word is embodied in a fluidity of music, the music of human speech. Some operatic composers attempt to make the melody of the song extend the natural melodies of speech. Most people are not very successful masters of the art of speech, in that their rhetoric is poorly articulated, their vocabulary is insufficient to permit them to find the best words in the best order, and their powers of imagination are too limited for them to discover or create the images and metaphors that might enrich their speech and better enable them to communicate the complexities and subtleties of what they mean and feel. They can often supplement poor speech by a rich use of gesture, inflection, and facial expression, and do a substantial job of communication. When they must attempt to communicate by writing, and their words must stand naked of the accompanying arts, the poverty of their art of words is starkly evident. This is true of many professional users of words — speakers, preachers, teachers — as well as ordinary folk. They can be effective on the podium or platform, but if their manuscripts are published the result is flat and tasteless. Very few can compare with Emerson and William James, whose printed lectures read with the same warmth and aliveness that they possessed when spoken.

It is thus, by way of necessity, that the other arts creep into the art of speech. Protestants who would abhor drama in the church pull out a dozen theatrical stops in rendering their sermons and prayers. For the forms of language are facets, various dimensions, of one over-all art, the art of communication, which is the basis of the human community and its culture. The difference between man and the other animals lies in his arts of communication, which enable him to transfer learning and experience from one man to another, to accumulate it in libraries and museums, and to move out of the animal world of instinctive reaction and rudimentary teaching into the spacious elaboration and accumulation of experience and wisdom in civilization.

The interpenetration of the art of speech by the other forms of language does not end with gesture and inflection. Many Protestants and liberals have a mistrust of all symbolism. I wonder if any other single controversy has caused more church disruptions than the question of whether or not there should be a cross on the altar table. When one was already *in situ*, ministers have been known to hide it in a closet and put a vase of flowers in its place, hoping beyond hope that no one would miss it, but all in vain. Others have put one where none had been before, hoping it would be graciously accepted. One form of symbolic coercion takes place when a member of the parish gives an expensive cross in memory of the dead; then if the minister denies the symbol he is slighting the memory of the departed. Even if the removing or placing of the symbol is preceded by a long period of preparation in education and explanation, the technique is rarely successful for here the institution is involved in deep irrational aversions that cannot be clarified by mere lessons or diplomacy.

The strange thing about the antipathy of some people to symbols lies in the fact that words, which they use freely and without prejudice, are also signs and symbols. Words are symbols made out of sound, or out of abstract letter forms on a printed page. What inherent difference is there between the word "cross" and a brass or wood form of the cross? The cross is a brass or wood "word," if you will. If you protest that the cross is in the shape of the cross, it could be argued that this but makes it a more vivid word, and is akin to the phenomenon wherein some words actually sound like what they stand for, like the word "swish."

The argument is often raised that if you admit symbols into religious celebration the people will come to worship the symbol itself and not that which it designates. True, this is a danger, but it is not limited to brass and wood symbols. Words are probably even more liable to this misuse, which we indicate in such terms as "word-mongering," following "the word and not the deed," and the admonition in the Bible that men shall not "worship in word only." This is what is pointed out to us in the warning about "the tyranny of words." All symbols present the threat of their becoming a substitute for reality. The ancient Jews were most fearful of this possibility. They not only would not permit a painted or sculptural representation of God to be made; they also would not let him be given a name, for they saw that the spoken symbol was as dangerous as the visual symbol. God was to be designated as "I am," but no one was to attempt to picture what the unknowable and indescribable nature of God might be.

In one conference I happened upon a very violent reaction to symbolism of any kind. Some liberals boast that their religion does not need images or symbols but leaves each person free to think for himself and to relate to his world without such encumbrances. They have joined the free church in order to free themselves of symbols. I discovered in this one case that the persons reacting most strongly had been victims of the Nazi persecution. Their almost traumatic reaction to symbols became easily understandable, and I had a profound sympathy for it.

53

Even in the Nazi films the maniacal intensity, the demonic power of the Nazi rituals, their use of banners, symbols, parades, dramatic staging was overwhelming. To see how the people were captured by this display of propaganda struck apprehension in the observer, for it undermined any hope for sanity and discernment on the part of the mass of the people. Can the populace be taken in by such ancient flag waving, such obvious posturing, such solemn nonsense? The populace of Germany and of Italy was. The genocide, the persecution, the degrading brutality, the war and conquest that ensued from this Nazi ritualism would be sufficient to beget in anyone a loathing for ritual and symbolism in any form.

Those liberals who have grown up in the sacramental churches, and have experienced symbolism and ritual as the means through which what they believe is superstition prevails over the minds and the emotions of the adherents, have a similar fear and distrust of symbolism and ritual as such, and it is equally understandable. But their own reaction is also one of emotionalism and not logic. We should reject those uses of the arts that create the atmosphere and enhance the power of hatred, brutality, narrow pride in race and nationality, and religious superstition. But it does not follow that we must also reject those uses of the arts that create the atmosphere and supply the instruments for enlightenment, learning, communication, affection, and that world-wide fellowship of humanity which will one day make the earth a commonwealth of peace. The good works of the arts are as necessary, as indispensable to the good life, as the demonic uses of the arts are responsible for much of the power of the destructive forces in our society.

An illustration in miniature can be supplied within the province of words. A faddish use of certain words and phrases will often occur through advertising, slogan making, slang, and other spontaneous focusing on certain expressions. These words may come to stand for bad taste, quackery, or exploitation, and we may be in danger of turning against the words themselves, even as we have turned against their misuse. But they are often good words, words for which we have no adequate substitutes, and the loss of which would cripple the language. We cannot let misuse render good words unusable.

One example that comes home to us is the word "liberal," which we have long used to define our own general religious disposition and viewpoint. It is a magnificent word, in its specific meanings, in its music, and in its manifold overtones. But it has been badly used. It has been made to stand for distortions of truly liberal attitudes. It has been associated with looseness and lack of discipline in thinking. Many persons believe the word "liberal" has been hopelessly corrupted. When it is proposed as part of the name for our movement, there is always a vocal group that rises to oppose its use. Thus we come to have the same aversion to certain words as symbols as we do to symbols in the other forms of language.

In religion men attempt to conceptualize, to realize, and to express the greatest fullness of meaning and worth of which they are capable. Religion is composed of man's basic faith and hope, his aspiration to beauty and righteousness, his assessment of the meaning of existence. It is for this reason that the most prolific use of art has been in man's religious expression. No other group of buildings rival his temples. No poetry rivals his psalms and his mythical epics, his prophetic announcements. Nowhere has his sculpture and painting rivaled his depiction of the gods and the myths of his religious traditions. The dance has reached its highest forms in religious dance dramas, and the great dramas, such as the tragedies of Euripides and the Book of Job, bear upon man's religious fate.

Since religion is concerned with the concentrate, the magnificent, the eternal, whenever man's art reaches toward heights of greatness it takes on religious dimensions, regardless of what purpose the art sets for itself or what institutions foster its production. Broadly defined, religious expression and artistic expression inevitably merge.

As liberal religion seeks to become a universal religion, as it reaches out for its widest influence, its most profound realization, it cannot afford to reject any of the forms of language. It needs them all to express its fullness. Often a painter will be asked what his painting means. His rejoinder sometimes is, "If I could have said it in words I would have. I have said it in paint. The painting must tell you, or you must go uninformed."

55

There is so much for religion to say that it requires every form of language for its expression. If we spurn some forms, then we shall leave much of our meanings unexpressed, our declarations foreshortened and maimed. We shall leave those who might have understood us through the other arts un-reached. We shall not even realize some of our own meanings, which would have become clear to us only as we achieved expression of them through that form of language which was their necessity.

DOES RELIGION NEED SYMBOLS?

The answer to the question "Does religion need symbols?" can be given dogmatically. Religion cannot operate without symbols. The question is not whether we use symbols but what kinds of symbols we will employ. Many religions embody a prolific language of symbolism. Hinduism and Buddhism are extravagant in their use of symbolism of all varieties. Whether this attracts or repels depends on your canons of taste, whether your artistic palate is atuned to richness or asceticism. The cultures of China and Japan have created a great encyclopedia of symbolism, and not only of abstract and semi-abstract designs; every animal, bird, tree, and flower carries symbolic meanings. In the Christian world the Greek Orthodox, the Roman Catholics, and the Episcopalians cele-brate the Mass within a wealth of art and symbolism. In the Reformation the Protestants felt the need to protest against the symbolism and art of the Roman Catholic Church, as well as against its theology and institutional structure. And perhaps there was something natively austere in the personalities of the people of northern Europe, which received development in the German Pietistic and the Quaker movements and led to the plain forms of worship among such groups as the Cal-vinists, Puritans, Methodists, and Baptists.

The Quakers practice the extremity of the symbolism of no symbolism. Their central spiritual reality is the Inner Light, which works within the person, moving him to good works and, on occasion, to declaring his inspiration to his fellows. Any-thing which distracts the Inner Light from its free function must be eliminated. Enlightenment will come from the voice within, as the Holy Spirit speaks directly to and within the person. Art and symbols are not needed, to speak to him from without. The buildings and the assemblies of the Quakers are effective symbolizations of this faith, for their symbols are silence, the unadorned room, plain glass windows, the simple human presence of the fellowship, and the unpremeditated utterance of the members as they are prompted by the Inner Light to speak. The religious experience is essentially individualistic, but in their silent companionship, each listening to the voice within himself, they find their social bonds. They believe their religious experience should not be manifested in ritual but should express itself in acts of mercy and peace. Their good works assume symbolic dimensions, since their religious faith is characterized, given an image, through the acts which they perform. "By their deeds ye shall know them."

There seems to be some line of historical development between the non-symbolic trend in Protestantism and the ban of the ancient Jews against graven images. This originated in the aversion of a nomadic desert people to the lush imagery and ritual of an agricultural civilization in Palestine. Israel's desert asceticism continued into the Christian era among the Essenes. Because of this taboo, the Jews were deprived of the rich arts of painting and sculpture which flourished around them in Egypt, Babylonia, and Greece. They developed some architecture, now lost, but their main artistic glory was the great literature of their holy books. The scroll of the Torah became their major emblem, and its embellishment with covers, arks, shields, crowns and pointers provided an outlet for their thwarted artistic expression. Calligraphy became a major art.

Islam, stemming from the same Semitic desert background, also banned the graphic arts. Its architecture burst into a magnificence of abstract and floral decoration. The calligraphy and adornment of the Koran became the highest of arts, and the abstract and floral designs of their architecture found a companion means of expression in rugs. Pottery and metalwork also became high arts. Thus both Judaism and Islam, although they eschewed the graphic arts, found other areas of art and symbolism whereby they could enrich their religious expression. Protestant Christianity remained impoverished in all areas of art and symbolism. It even borrowed its literature from the ancient Jews, to such an extent that in many Protestant hymnals all of the responsive readings come from the Psalms.

An intriguing counterpart to the Quakers, at least ideologically, is to be found in Chang or Zen Buddhism in China and Japan. This movement protests that knowing and enlightenment are personal and cannot be communicated to others. They answer "foolish questions" with seeming nonsense and paradoxes. Their point of view roots back into Chinese Taoism, which also protested the futility of trying to put anything meaningful into words. But, paradoxically, especially in the Sung Dynasty and the succeeding period in Japan, the practitioners of Zen produced some of the greatest painting, poetry, ceramics and temple architecture in human history.

We should have reached an age of enlightenment in the twentieth century where ancient tribal taboos no longer inflict their prejudices upon us. But this is not the case, for even those who call themselves "liberals" still react with violent aversion to the use of symbols as such. They are simply one form of communication, a form of language, and they are good or bad only in terms of whether or not their usage is enlightened or corrupt. The symbols made of wood, metal, or stone, like the word-symbols made out of sound or calligraphy, are good or evil only as man's usage makes them so. Whatever evil they might have would lie in the motivation and practice of the individual or institution that employed them. In the hands of freedom-loving, undogmatic, truth-seeking liberals, they would be endowed with all the overtones and meanings of those who employed them. A poet uses the same words that the businessman, the gossip, the politician, the preacher, and the criminal do. Language is common; it is only the use made of it that is uncommon. The words of the poet become what the poet is; they partake of his sensitivity, his imagination, his love of beauty, sound, and imagery, his integrity, and his long discipline in their use.

The same can be said of all forms of symbolism and art, for when they are used to conceptualize and communicate the moral vision, the ideals, the love, the dedication, the sense of glory in life and the world which are the spirit of high religion, they take on the aura, the very spirit of the religion. This quality is implicit in the poetry of the Psalms, but it is also implicit in Sung Buddhist painting, in the Hindu sculpture of the ninth century, in the cathedrals of medieval Europe, in the symbolism of the lotus, and the cross, and the tantra. The Jews and the Moslems only impoverished their own religious expression when they deprived themselves of the graphic arts. Liberals who are averse to the use of arts and symbols simply shut off their own expression and communication through these media.

Religious meanings and feelings need to be communicated, not only to one's contemporaries, but to future generations. It may be sufficient for the Quaker to communicate to his contemporaries through silence, works, and inspired utterance, but how is he going to talk to the generations as yet unborn? The time will come when his voice, his presence, and his works will be forgotten. How will he bequeath his religious meaning and spirit to history?

The religions of Egypt, Sumeria, Assyria, and Babylonia had been forgotten for two millennia. The archaeologists have been busy for several generations exhuming the cities that lay buried under the mounds of Mesopotamia and the sands of Egypt. Whether or not the ancient people who lived in these cities wished to communicate with us, we wished to learn who they were, and what manner of religion they practiced. The only means of communication were the remnants of their arts and literature that lay buried. Their hieroglyphs resisted translation for many years, and some still have not been deciphered. Even when the languages are unlocked, we have insufficient knowledge of their meanings and overtones to make more than a rough translation. The pronunciation of their words is gone entirely. How much of the richness and suggestiveness of an ancient poetry can one recover when he can never hear how the poetry sounded, catch the inflections and melodies of the speech?

But the people of the cradle of civilization had more than one form of language. In their sculpture, paintings, engraved

59

seals, architecture, and pottery they left a record of their times, their mood of living, their ways of life. From the temples and the tombs of Egypt, in panoramic paintings and carvings, in a multitude of figurines that give a miniature reproduction of the people and their folkways, we can re-enter the ancient world of these people. Their literature becomes increasingly meaningful as we relate it to their other arts.

Where ancient peoples have had no written language, we must depend entirely on the arts to recover them to human memory. From stone tools and weapons, from rock and cave paintings, from the refuse heaps of cave dwellings and village sites, from the relics in their tombs we can work somewhat back into the world of their religious beliefs and practices. What is interesting for our present consideration is that the language of abstract and semi-pictorial symbols antedates the use of written language by thousands of years. The pictographs of the first writing are essentially symbols, and in China the calligraphy of the present day still bears a direct relationship to the symbols and pictographs of earliest times. Engraved in the stone walls and ceilings of the ancient cairns of the British Isles is a rich language of symbols. Man has turned to symbols from the very beginning in order to elaborate the mysteries and questions of his search. Whether or not we feel a need for symbols in our time, the men of all past ages have been drawn to them, for in them they have been able to indicate meanings beyond the powers of other forms of language, beyond the powers of painting and sculpture to pictorialize.

Whether or not we need symbols in our temples, when the Boston Public Library building was constructed, those responsible adorned the walls, the ceilings, the pedestals of the statutues, even the floors with a rich display of symbols of all kinds. John Singer Sargent reached back into ancient Egypt to recover its storehouse of symbolism for the mural decorations of this temple of learning. The buildings of museums and universities have been similarly enriched. The government uses symbols on its coins and stamps, the advertising arts resort to them, and the courts and capitol buildings of government make lavish use of them. If religion no longer feels the need of ritual, vestments, and symbols, the military establishment does.

Does religion need symbols? Yes, it cannot do without them if it wishes to say certain things in certain ways. Does liberal religion, which seeks to declare a new direction and clarity in religion, feel that it is able to discard them, regardless of the ages-old usages to which they have been put? The United Nations, which is also a pioneering, idealistic venture, made immediate and highly successful use of symbolism to help establish an image of its nature and purpose in the minds and emotions of humanity, circling a map of the world with an olive wreath of peace. Its founders said as much about the institution and its goals in the prose of the United Nations Charter, but the language of symbolism was also useful and necessary to promote its purposes. Nor was it feared that such use of symbolism would involve the organization in superstition and obscurantism. The symbol is as clear and explicit as any words could be.

Symbols are present not only in shapes of brass, wood, and stone. Rituals are a series of symbolic acts. The movements of the dance may by symbolic as well as descriptive. The titles and robes of positions of honor are symbolic. In all our behavior, what we do is not just what it rudely and immediately is; every gesture is overlaid with symbolic meanings. Each culture has what has been called a "hidden language" of symbolic meanings in its many forms and behaviors. So inherent is this symbolism in the very fabric of culture and meaning that what we know as civilization would be impossible without it. Whatever more or less it is, religion is a cultural reality. It partakes of symbolism whether it acknowledges it or not. Quakerism, with its seeming poverty of symbolism, is really as much manifested through symbols as is Greek Orthodoxy. Its symbolism is different but not absent.

Those of us who dwell in the open, non-supernatural world of naturalism will mistrust any symbolism that leans toward the occult. We will want symbols that have clear and definite denotata, even as we desire definite and determinable realities to lie behind our words and rhetoric. But we should not confuse the necessity of ridding symbols of their superstitious overlay with eliminating symbols themselves.

In the matter of symbolizing universal attitudes and values, an opposition of choices confronts us. In designing the meditation room at the United Nations, those responsible solved the problem of creating a room in which everyone would feel at home by eliminating all specific and tribal symbols. The room is bare except for a monolith, which is a universal symbol. Thus their solution was one universal symbol, the great stone, and the symbolic absence of all other more particularistic symbols.

An opposite solution to the problem of creating a universal symbolism is the choice of the Charles Street Meeting House in Boston which has universal symbols, such as the atom, the nebula, the earth, and the circle, but also includes the basic symbols of all the major human religions of all ages and places. The problem in this approach is to create a unity of design and interrelationship from these many symbols, so that their total presentation results, in its own way, in a unity as integrated and forceful as is that of the monolith in the United Nations. On a political level the United Nations also takes the path of a unity through diversity, in the array of the flags of all the member nations, just as in the United States we have symbols for each of the fifty states and one flag for the nation as a whole.

Symbolism operates on various levels. There is that of the overt, objective symbol, the object carved in brass, stone, or wood and placed in a position of significance in the temple or shrine. But symbolism also operates in manners that are undiscerned by most people. All the status positions within an institution, the orders and ways of the rituals, the architecture, with its particular forms and the uses which they imply, the time of meetings, the behavior of the people, the style of speech and manner of the leaders of worship, and the response of the assembly — literally everything that occurs in relation to the temple and the religious observances carries symbolic meanings as well as serving a functional purpose. Just as culture has its "hidden language," so does every religious community possess a corpus of tacit, unacknowledged symbolism in its behavior patterns and style of deportment.

62

Thus one who perceives the forms and uses of symbolism on its various levels finds the abhorrence of symbols on the part of liberals ironic to say the least. They reject the obvious symbolism that they can see, yet indulge in a plethora of less obvious symbolism in a dozen other modes. It is this hidden language to which the newcomer, "the outsider," reacts. He either likes or dislikes their ways, for if they have none of the clearly defined and concretely presented symbols, their actions speak clearly with many symbolic overtones. One might suggest that it would be more honest for the religious community to consciously realize the nature and meanings of its hidden symbols, and declare them in overt and visual forms, than to let them operate merely on the tacit and unadmitted level. In this way the congregation would declare to itself what its own themes and ideals were, enlightening its own internal conversations, and it would also make a clearly defined presentation of these themes and ideals to society as a whole, and to all who visit its assemblies.

We can only suggest some of the various levels on which hidden symbols operate in a liberal and universal religious fellowship. The structures and manners of the society itself are not simply functional. They imply philosophical, moral, and mystical presumptions. The congregational polity, which makes each individual society completely a self-sufficient and free unit, in no way directed or controlled by any hierarchical organization or authority, symbolizes a full assemblage of ideas and ideals about human freedom. The principles of freedom of belief for each member of the society follows upon the assumption of freedom for the society itself. The ideal of the full dignity and supreme worth of the individual personality is bound up in the other two related principles. The rules and bylaws of the society, its division into functioning departments, the annual meetings, the delegation of authority to the elected members of the board, their manner of meeting — all of these acts and institutions not only have functionality but imply and, in their way, symbolize the beliefs and ideals of the group. The position of the minister as an equal rather than as an authority, the manner of his dress, deportment, and assumption of titles add facets to this democratic complex. When discussion groups, seminars and forums, and all the implicit principles in the programs of child and adult education, plus new "shapes of assembly" adopted to facilitate the round-table, face-to-face confrontation of free and equal people, are added, the symbolism of this one democratic ideal is seen to be complex, many-layered, and yet a firmly integrated whole. Applied with thoroughness, it enables the principles of religious freedom to operate effectively.

When there is this amount of hidden symbolism in the very structure and behavior of the society, why should there be objection to adding certain overt and explicit symbols of this freedom? The torch of freedom, the clasped hands of brotherhood, the two pine trees in a circle (a symbol used by the cooperative movement), the United Nations symbol, the dove and olive branch of peace, the circle of unity and universalism are some that the Meeting House has chosen. In a sense, they are little more than a symbolic acknowledgment of an institutional and social reality already in operation. Are such symbols of freedom, cooperation, and peace threats to these very values themselves, as some seem to feel? Do they not rather offer a strengthening of the ideals themselves, since they stand for the shared commitment of the group to these ideals?

Another basic element in free religion is its experimental method, which is grounded in the scientific attitude. Here again activities and organizations have symbolic as well as functional influence. The fact that the fellowship has no creed, no profession of faith, no rituals of profession and submission such as prevail in orthodox religions, symbolizes the open and inquiring attitudes to belief. The prevailing dependence upon scientific findings by liberals for their views of the nature of man, of the universe, of life implies their reliance upon the method by which these opinions are created. The tentative and non-dogmatic way in which they hold their opinions does likewise. At the Meeting House the continuous use of new materials in the services, the "open hymnal" wherein a loose-leaf arrangement of materials is used rather than a bound hymnbook, the diversity of forms of the services, especially the festival services, all proclaim the experimental approach.

Another observation is that symbols themselves symbolize more than single ideas or viewpoints. For example, the symbol of the atom, the polar-projection map, the galaxy of Andromeda, the stellar globe, the spiral of growth and evolution, the cogwheel of technology, even the caduceus (an emblem of the physician), imply a reliance upon science, whereby these realities are explored and activities connected with them are sustained. Likewise, symbols for agriculture, labor, the atom, the cornucopia, the tree of life, the sun, the world stand for a naturalistic philosophy rather than a supernaturalistic one.

Perhaps the most important observation of this kind relates to the total symbol project at the Meeting House. Here we have assembled sixty-five symbols from the various world religions, and additional symbols relating to the various activities, concepts, and ideals of man and the processes of nature. Likewise the collection of religious art from the many cultures of the race, ancient and modern — although within these collections are hundreds of different symbolisms — comprises one single symbol: a symbol of one world. The entire auditorium, with all its symbols and artistic decorations, is a symbol of oneness, of one nature, one world, one fellowship of life, one human race, one human culture, and one human religion. These concepts are referred to in other disciplines as "the loom of language" and "the loom of art," wherein the unity of all language and all art is set forth. Underlying all the various sciences is the presumption of the basic unity of science. Even so, on a religious level, a universal religion must find a way to effectively symbolize the unity that prevails within all the diversity of the cultures, arts, ethical systems, and religious institutions of humanity. The temple, in all its detail, must have the ultimate integrity of a single symbol.

It is impossible to conceive of a religion that does not need symbols, since the very conception of a religion itself depends on the symbols whereby the conception is contained. The only question that is pertinent, when we set forth to create the setting, the architecture, the adornment, and the rituals of a universal religion, is what kind of symbolism will be most adequate for the task. The projects of the Charles

Street Meeting House embody our attempts to make one offering to a possible solution of this problem.

Liberal religionists lack appreciation of the aesthetic necessities in the development and motivation of human groups. Although their beliefs are highly principled and intelligent, they do not attract or stir any large numbers of people because they have not discovered and exploited their effective symbolism. Ideas and ideals need to be caught up in, to be enlarged and glorified in, symbols, rituals, and songs. The translations and restatements of ideals need not distort and sentimentalize them. The finest poetic images do not caricature the object or emotion portrayed, but enlighten and clarify it, enabling it to be discerned in a transparent and lucid reality. Thus seen, it carries an immediacy and solidity of impact that no intellectual abstraction ever possesses.

If we are to seek and create an adequate symbolism for ourselves, we are faced with a major problem in originality and inventiveness. Since we have made a basic break with the theological understructures of ancient religions, we cannot borrow or superficially modify the concepts, symbols, and rites of traditional religion. We must exploit the freshness and the power of our differences. To move from supernaturalism to naturalism, from magic to science, from miracles to human works, from immortality to the good life on earth, from salvation to character development, from a mysticism of "spirit" to a mysticism of man and nature, from concern with souls to concern for flesh-and-blood men, from emphasis upon heaven to emphasis on the reconstruction of the world through social action — this is to necessitate a wholly new framework of symbols, language, rituals, arts, and dramas. As John Dewey called for a "reconstruction in philosophy," so we must declare for a reconstruction in the arts of religion.

SYMBOLS AND SOCIAL ACTION

We must have symbols in order to engender social action, because all of man's thinking and motivation is symbolic. He can think only in and through the use of his language, arts, myths, and gestures, which are his cultural accumulation of symbols. His emotions are composed, directed, and touched off by the symbols of his reasoning and intercourse. Until he has dramatic and impelling symbols, and sets of symbols, for the brotherhood of man he will never be able to think, feel, and act in the ways that might bring it into reality.

Why do we persist in the destructive action of war, and delay the creation of a peaceful world? A major reason is symbolic. Our predominant symbolism is tribal and national. It directs and organizes our emotions toward provincialism, nationalism, a greater identification with the citizens of our own country than with those outside it, against whom we level such symbolic names as foreigner, alien, and enemy. When the nation goes into war it can marshal an entire equipage of symbols to effect its propaganda. Under its slogans of patriotism, with flags, uniforms and customs, it can regiment the people into armies and cadres and herd them like sheep toward mass self-sacrifice. Through symbolism it can institute the destruction of wealth, cities, and lives to fantastic proportions. The man who requested the privilege of writing a nation's songs was no fool. Control their symbols and you control a people and its destiny.

It is for symbolic reasons that the United Nations is of such transcendent importance to the human scene. Protest how we will about its slowness and its blunders and its compromises, we cannot do without the kind of symbol which it embodies. How are we to escape the self-destructive pitfalls of our national and tribal loyalties? Only by establishing another object of loyalty above them, conceived in and projected through its own symbols, which will enlarge and replace the narrower patriotism of caste, clan, sect, nation and culture.

The flag of the United States symbolically unifies the fifty member states into one federal body. The sense of identity and cohesion within this country is a powerful and tangible force. Some of us find it hard to imagine another civil war dividing our country as it did a century ago. What is it that enables 180 million people to live together peacefully? We live in and under a common symbolic framework, focusing on "one nation indivisible."

Without such a symbolic network, integrating all of mankind into one political, historical, and affectional unity, we shall never accomplish the brotherhood of man of the universalist vision. The establishing of the symbols for one world is a religious task. This ideal must have its feast days and holy days, its heroes and visionaries, of which President Woodrow Wilson is already one. Gathered under these banners will come the agencies of social work to lead from the ideal into the construction of realities. UNESCO shines forth among the world-wide services and is of special note in this context since it is concerned with world art, history, and culture. UNESCO attempts to assist the people of all cultures and notions to move into the symbolic world in which other people live. Until we can touch the reasons and realities of the lives of other peoples, becoming as familiar with their world views as we are with our own, we shall not have made the world our possession and home.

The great and conclusive issues in our struggle for survival in the atomic age are root and stock a matter of symbols. They are a matter of supplying the minds of men with the concepts and reasons why there must be a gathering of the nations. They are a matter of providing the symbols for the focusing of emotions and loyalties and dreams upon the image of one human family.

Social action consists not only of good deeds and the espousing of reformist causes. Social action is participation in the very construction of society and entails concern with elaborating the symbols whereby society thinks, feels, and is moved to act. Too much so-called social action is a matter of protesting prevailing evils, rather than of patiently and tediously reconstructing the institutions of society itself. Thus social action becomes a bit of lingo, referring to certain stereotypes of agitation about social action, rather than to creative and reconstructing procedures whereby society is renovated and rebuilt.

Especially when the activity relates to attitudes, to ideas, and to the matrix of commitments it is difficult to see where the term "action" applies. Yet action in the human sphere must be in the areas of ideas and emotions, even more than in overt and specific programs. The latter are tangible and often spectacular, but the former are more basic and more profound.

Some of the most pertinent arenas of "social action" cannot be classified under this name at all. A museum of science creates institutionalized symbols of the scientific quest and attitude. It helps to renovate the very minds of the populace — not by opposing anything but rather by espousing, elucidating, and illustrating the enlightenment and benefits of science itself.

The museums of fine art, also, which have now taken the arts of primitive peoples and the Orient into themselves, to become expositors of the art of humanity, without any sermons and agitation or legislative acts, slowly and positively give us new ways of seeing the unity of culture that lies beneath the diversity of man's arts. Subtly and pervasively, as we become better and better acquainted with the arts of the past and faraway places, we feel less and less alien to them. In time, without our realizing what has been happening, we discover that all these many arts belong to us, and that they are one. Thus the museum provides us the materials whereby we can experience the unity of human civilization, and experience is much more convincing than any preachment or committee action, than petitions and public rallies.

In models and idealistic projections, in minority demonstrations, a symbolic function can be exercised within the social body. In this sense the liberal and universal society performs an act of social relevance and creative change in and through its very existence, even though it may not engage in any programs of "social action" in the conventional sense. It is itself a laboratory experiment in a new form of social organization, and it demonstrates in its corporate manifestation a new ideal of human society. It creates its own symbols for one world, displays them, and, insofar as it is able, lives by them. Just so far as it does all this, it changes society, for it is itself a participating and influential segment of the social whole. If its difference is sufficiently creative and suggestive, it will become the traditional "leaven in the lump," and its ideals and symbols will issue from its own assemblies to alter the minds and the institutions of the world.

Immediate alleviation of ills must be one religious concern in social action. But this is not all. The religious society must also be concerned with prophetic and long-range solutions for pervading evils. It must find ways to so act now as to bring some influence to bear on the general direction that mankind is taking into the far future. The only way it can do this is to be profoundly idealistic and "impractical," and to attempt to conduct itself in its own institutional structures and relationships in the ways that man should espouse, rather than in the ways in which he lives at present. Thus, in a world divided into warmaking nationalities, we should live *now* in the idealism of world unity. Even as the temples of the orthodox sought to create within their buildings the image of the Kingdom of God, we must seek in our temples to create the image of the commonwealth of men.

THE MIGRATION OF SYMBOLS

Upon being introduced to the Meeting House project in collecting and integrating the art and symbols of the world religions, people have asked, "But isn't this eclectic?" The question seems to imply that something eclectic is superficial and less "real" emotionally and intellectually than the integral cultural practice of an ethnic group. The answer is no. We believe that the religions and cultures of humanity are one interrelated structure. Their uniting identities are more pervasive and enduring than their differences.

Archaeology and anthropology are recent sciences, but we already know enough to discern that all men in their thinking and behavior are one family unity. All start from the same branch of the tree of evolution. The paths of the earth's peoples cross and recross as they travel over the same plot of earth. For a million years men have been in constant interrelation and intermixture. The restless migration of the peoples, their trade, travel, and conquest, have brought about a continual inbreeding of language, mores, institutions, inventions, arts, and personality traits. Even where there has been comparatively extended isolation, as with the Australian aborigines and the Indians of the Americas, it has been only a matter of degree, not an absolute. The most extravagant variations known due to such isolation are not sufficient to alter the judgment of the anthropologists on the essential unity of human culture.

In gathering together in one setting the symbols, art, music, literature, and moral wisdom of the family of man, we are not trying to paste together inherently unrelated ideas and histories. We do not have to *join* these together, because they are one continuous fabric. We are merely tracing the existing connections of a structure that never has been destroyed. We do not call it eclecticism when a doctor examines the liver, heart, lungs, blood, stomach, and intestines in order to determine our state of health. They are all part of one organism, and the health of one depends upon the health of all. Even so, in history, culture, and religion mankind is one organism. The analogy cannot be carried too far, but we cannot appreciate the symbolism of our own group without knowing the symbolism of the entire human group. We cannot understand our own tongue without knowledge of the great network of tongues that comprise human speech. To explore the traditions of neighboring cultures is to explore our own culture, since they have grown with it in the same great matrix of human history.

The migration of symbols has not taken place in a vacuum. It is one aspect of the migration of man himself. Where man went, transporting his wares, his symbols went. The problem of the distribution of the racial stocks of the human species is of continuous fascination to anthropologists. The division of the human stock into what we have miscalled races is recent in the evolutionary time scheme, and we have not moved very far apart. Variations that in time might have led to several species of man, if they had developed in isolation, have not had time to work into anything significant. The human race is mutually fertile, and its cultural variations are serious only because of the ignorance and prejudice of the various branches of the family. Man's cultural differences would be inherently creative and fertile, were we to allow them to freely mix and stimulate each other. It is only man's fear and habitual stupidities and antagonisms that create dangers out of the cultural divergences that exist.

Man seems to have originated in south-central Africa, and to have fanned out from there. A great crescent drawn from there, through Egypt, Mesopotamia, India, and Indonesia, indicates his early home. Later he migrated to almost every corner of the globe. The Neolithic revolution, brought about by the introduction of agriculture and the domestication of animals, occurred in the Near East some eight to ten thousand years ago, bringing a dramatic increase in population and causing invasions and migrations that lasted some two thousand years. It is the very nature of new inventions in civilization to bring about population pressures and the movement of peoples, which movement carries the improvements with them. The spread of civilization outward from its area of origin is inevitable. Succeeding developments in the Bronze and Iron ages, with their further mixing of peoples, were but successive steps that have led through the industrial revolution to the atomic age. Now we are at the culmination of exploration, invasion, settlement, and amalgamation, with the last mountain and forest recesses and polar regions entered, and their people forced willy-nilly into mixing with the rest of us.

Beginning on the Persian plateau, in Mesopotamia and Egypt, about 3500 B.C., possibly coming to its first efflorescence in Sumeria, civilization as we know it spread out in all directions. It is here that we must look for the beginnings of developed religion and the migration of symbols. Somewhere in the third millenium B.C., civilization moved east into the Indus River valley and into China. Later China and India themselves became sources of this migration as it moved into southwest Asia, Indonesia, and the islands of Oceania, all the way to New Zealand, Easter Island, and the Hawaiians. The Negro people came into Africa from the East, forcing back the native Bushmen. The American Indians, in migrations that proceeded for thousands of years, trekked across the Bering Straits from the great cradle of Asia.

Anthropologists believe that many of the so-called tribal cultures, rather than being really "primitive," are the result of a disintegration of higher cultures in the past. Of one thing we can be sure: this movement and mixture of the people of the human race, which the anthropologists call "diffusion," was an immensely long and involved process. We have only begun to trace it. Without in any way minimizing the cultural differences of humanity, we may say that the outcome of this diffusion has been a universal sharing of basic cultural inventions which justifies our assertion that there is only one human culture. The differences are only variations within an impressive unity. It is because of this inherent unity of the human community that a people can move in one generation from an untouched tribal condition to an awareness of the need to live in the world community, as Margaret Mead's description of the Manus Islanders in her brilliant book *New Lives for Old* reveals. It is for this reason that the grandson of a cannibalistic Melanesian chieftain can win a Ph.D. in a great university. The differences between our cultures may seem to be vast, but the fact that the basis of all these variations is fundamentally the same allows movement from one cultural style to another within a generation or two.

Paul Hermann in *Conquest by Man* tells about man's travel, commerce, and conquest. Where did man get the wanderlust that served as the diffusing vehicle for his symbols? We are so distant in time from early man that we have forgotten his mode of life. We consider attachment to home, homesite, and village an inherent ingredient in man's nature. But man proceeded out of life as a beast, and for perhaps a million years he roamed as a hunter and gatherer, before settling down to agriculture a few thousand years ago. Only recently he became a home builder, and some nomads still pitch their tents for a while and then move on. Perhaps automobile trailers are again putting incipient nomads back into circulation. The vanishing gypsy still seems romantic, and travel is considered a pleasure in itself. Man is almost as much an animal of movement as are the migratory birds, and the fish and whales that roam the oceans.

The story of how flint mining and the manufacture of weapons and utensils led to widespread commerce, with trade routes through Europe and Asia twelve thousand to fourteen thousand years ago, opens new dimensions in our understanding of our ancestors. We have scarcely begun to evaluate religious ideas, symbolism, and practice in this framework. We still talk about unique centers of revelation, of purity and uniqueness of creed.

One of the first persons to apply a scientific method to the study of symbolism, and to bring it into the area of archaeological research, was Count Goblet d'Alviella, whose book *The Migration of Symbols* was first published over sixty years ago. Just as people, agriculture, and civilization went east and west out of Mesopotamia and Egypt, so religious symbols developed there and set forth on their involved migrations. Religious symbolism cannot be viewed in any sense as an independent evolution. It was carried back and forth across the earth just as were the arms of war and the goods of trade.

When entering the field of symbolism, one is confused by a myriad of forms and figures, a forest of symbols. Shortly one discovers that there are but a few basic symbols, and all others are an intermingling and outgrowth of them. The first signs related to the pervasive aspects of nature, to the sky and earth, to the sun and moon and the five planets, to the reproduction of vegetable, animal, and human life.

Why do we find the same symbols among peoples living far apart? Count d'Alviella says there are only two alternatives: Either they were conceived independently or they were borrowed by one country from another. There is a natural symbolism that resembles the omnipresence of certain implements of the Stone Age and does not seem to belong to any definite area or race. In this category he lists the representation of the sun as a disc or radiating face, the moon as a crescent, birds to symbolize the air, fish or wavy lines for water, the tree of life, phallic emblems, triangles, and the four directions of space symbolized by the cross.

The cross, all about us in Christendom, is an example of this type of "natural symbolism." Orthodox Christians have been concerned to explain why *their* symbol is found everywhere, often associated with the pagan religions they sought to supplant. It was found in Central America by the Spaniards, serving as a symbol for Tlaloc and Quetzalcoatl. Their assumption that it had been brought by earlier Christian missionaries cannot be substantiated. It represents the four quarters of the winds, bringing rain, and Tlaloc is the god of the waters.

The Assyrians used the cross with a circle in the center to designate the sun, to signify Anu, the god of the sky, since the sky is the space in which light radiates. The cross became a symbol of the sun in Chaldea, India, Greece, Persia, for the Gauls and the Indians of the Americas. In China the cross was put in a square, designating the earth. The Greek and Latin crosses were used in Egypt. As a symbol of the hammer or a boring tool, it was used as a hieroglyph, and "the Grinder" or "the Avenger" was often an attribute of Horus and other gods.

The T cross, St. Anthony's cross, was known among the Phoenicians as the *tau*. It has been found in Palestine, Gaul, Germany, in the Christian catacombs, and in Central America. Among the Celts and the ancient Germans it was the two-headed mallet, symbol of life and fertility. The Christians called it the tree of life, and in Central America it was called the tree of plenty. It is related to the crux ansata of Egypt, and the hammer of Thor, a symbol of lightning. The Christians adopted the cross because it was used by the Romans for crucifixion.

The cross is a symbol so old and basic, so connected with different meanings, that it is useless to talk of migration, except in certain specific situations, as when it was carried in the hands of Christian missionaries. It is one of the most ancient and common ingredients of man's communication. On this primary level, going back to that common past which we all share, we can assuredly speak of one human culture.

The migration of symbols as such appears at a later stage of history and involves the travel of, for example, the swastika, the winged globe, the caduceus, and the trisula. It takes d'Alviella some fifty pages to narrate the journeys of the tree of life. There may have been several beginnings for the symbol, for the tree is an impressive and important part of the environment. Since it grows out of earth into the heavens, it appeals to man as an agent between heaven and earth. He thinks of the rain as falling from its branches. It affords him shelter and shade, he eats of its fruits, its timber provides him with building material, and its juices are made into an intoxicating drink. D'Alviella traces it from origins in Mesopotamia, where it began as a simple stem-like affair and then related to the palm, the pomegranate, the cypress, the vine, and others. In time it became complex, being constructed of fragments taken from many plants.

The religious importance of the tree of life is manifest. It is found in association with many religious symbols and figures, and often in two settings, between two animals facing each other, or between two human or semihuman figures. Another version is the tree of paradise of the Aryans, known as the Tree of the Universe, the Tree of Life, and the Tree of Knowledge. The migrations of this symbol can be traced for three thousand years, and no one knows how many millennia it journeyed before that. It starts in Chaldea, with one line proceeding to Persia, the Arabs and Syria, to India, Indonesia, China, Tibet, Japan, and at some time to the Americas and to Mexico. Another line takes it to Asia Minor, Phoenicia, Greece, Libya, Byzantium, Italy, the Gauls, and contemporary Europe. The symbol is still very much with us. It is in constant use in India, Persia, and all over the world in Judaism. It is the root of sacred candelabra, and its latest use is in the diagram of the tree of evolutionary development. Thus science adapts to its use one of the most ancient of all religious symbols.

The day has come when the serious religious person, seeking to find avenues of understanding and fellowship between himself and other human beings, must leave the preconceptions and folkways of his tribal gods for a symbolism and a setting bearing the reality of our biological and cultural past. We exaggerate our differences and the local color of our regions. Variety we do have, but within a warm context of relationships and crossbreeding communication. We do not have to build roads between ourselves and the other peoples of the earth. The roads have always been there. Often they have been lost, but historians and archaeologists have been busy for a century and a half rediscovering them. They have been overgrown with superstitions, fears, rivalries, wars, and myths of racial superiority. They have been covered with ignorance and misconception. These too are being cleared away. The old roads wait for us.

We need not consider these roads of merely antiquarian interest. The paths of the migration of symbols, of the sciences and arts, of humanity, are to be used according to the needs of our time. Over these same paths will flow science, technology, engineering, medicine, learning, the arts, and philosophy. The wealth of any area of the earth can fertilize every other area of the earth. The science, lore, and religion of all the earth can supplement, correct, and enrich every part of the human scene. This is nothing new. It has been going on for a million years, gradually accelerating in recent millennia, as the stockpiling of culture and invention becomes more explosive. Now we have reached a zenith. But this zenith brings our greatest crisis, for these implements of wealth and growth, if misused, will become implements of our destruction.

Therefore the time has come for the migration of a new symbol, made like all the rest out of old symbols. It will be a symbol of one world, challenging the local and tribal symbols of the past. The migration of symbols is never finished. Now is the time for a more inclusive symbol than any before invented to start on its migration also.

CHAPTER 6

The Temple

THE UNIVERSAL TEMPLE

In countries that are predominantly of one faith, the temple in the village or city serves the whole community and belongs to everyone, not to some divisive sect. Those of us born into the atmosphere of denominationalism cannot easily conceive what the style and function of the true temple would be. A temple that contained the religious focus and activity of the entire community would not be in competition with any other religious institution for members and ascendancy. It would not be a missionary institution in this sense. The people would belong to it by birth, just as they are citizens of their nation by birth.

What would a temple be like if it were self-existent, if its presence and support were unquestionably accepted by the people? Perhaps it is impossible to build an authentic temple in this place and time. Divided as we are into major and minor sects and movements, any church building is the religious home for but a minority of the people. It means everything to them and little to those who belong to other denominations or to none at all. It may even be detested as the home of a presumed heresy.

This aspect of religion, which divides the community and culture rather than unifying them, is subversive of the religious spirit itself. The intentions of denominationalism are positive,

78

but the side effects are destructive of true community and of the most affirmative and creative facets of the religious experience. Instead of unifying the community it splits it. Instead of encompassing and unifying reality, it specializes the believer's viewpoint, so that he sees the world through the peephole of his sectarian concern and dogma. A premium is placed upon differences and idiosyncrasies.

There is an aura of self-consciousness, of egotism and self-righteousness in the stance of the denominational church. Much of the program and attitude is pointed at gaining converts, at public relations. The concern of church advocates that their particular cult be prosperous and popular is a denigration of the religious spirit. Yet our temples are built, as are department stores, to attract the buying public. Can this be the reason for a temple?

The reason for a temple is best seen, not in times of special services, but in the ordinary hours of the day and week. The Catholic Church, presuming universality in the midst of sectarian confusion, still functions as a temple should. The worshiper may go to the temple at an odd hour, to pray, to sit and meditate, to confess, or just to be quiet for a few minutes. He is not on display, since no one else may be there. He comes because in the temple he finds the symbolization of ideals and meanings. They are contained in the building, in its art, iconography, ritual objects, and atmosphere. He feels alone even though others may be there, for the temple is not performing a social or promotional function.

The reason for the temple turns on just this consideration, that it should be, not promotional, but presentational. It presents the known and felt reality of life and the world. It presents the definition and configuration of the accepted, often the unquestioned, realms of being. In these days of the explosion of knowledge, in the welter of rapidly changing reports about the nature of the atom and the galaxy and everything in between, we have lost the sense of a dependable and inevitable reality. There have been thousands of years when man's view of the world and the powers that move within it changed hardly at all. We are fumbling for a new vision of reality amidst the chaos of altered opinion. Perhaps the building of

79

great new temples will have to wait until humanity is fully at home and assured in the universe now being discovered by science.

Three views of temples in other times and places will give a contrast to our own position. In ancient China, with its naturalistic and agricultural religion, the temple, called the Hall of Light, was itself a symbol of the world. Its four sides stood for the four quarters of the earth. There were rooms in the center of the four sides and on each of the corners, eight in all. The officiating priests or the emperor, dividing the religious rites according to the twelve months and the changing seasons, progressed from room to room, facing in different directions, as the cycle of the year progressed. Through symbols of jade and bronze vessels and their use in rites and sacrifices, a conception of reality was totally projected. The religious celebration was a dance of the known world.

In India, from early Vedic times, the temples were built on the ground plan of a cosmic diagram, which was believed to be the mystical shape of the world. The temples were an architectural representation of the sky as a solid vault covering the world mountain, Meru.

Something of the same intent dominates the Gothic cathedrals of Catholic Europe, where the soaring arches presented visually the otherworldly view of the culture. Developing over centuries, Gothic architecture became so integrated and powerful in its symbolism and presentation that we cannot resist being caught up in its splendor, even though our view of reality has been basically changed.

Our temple is a place where sermons are preached, but these temples preach their own sermons. The temple is not just an enclosure of space, a shelter for meetings; it is a monument celebrating an ideal. Some temples in India have little or no interior. The temple is the exterior and its adornment. The architect and the artist acted as the creators and expressers of profound symbols. The temple is a work of consummate art, the enclosure of a vision, the universe in miniature. Our temples are ordinarily built to the image and size of man, but these temples are fashioned to the image and size of the known world, and to the size and shape of man's dreams of becoming. They do not mirror what man is; they point to what he can become.

Insofar as the temple presents a vision of life and the universe, its purpose is declarative, not argumentative and promotional. This presentational adequacy and integrity is found today in the planetarium. Architecturally, symbolically, institutionally, its purpose is to introduce us to the shape and behavior of the universe. Its programs are ritualistic in nature, and the projector in the center serves the purpose of an altar, and most dramatically. These are celebrations of the heavens.

Religiously we are midway in an evolution between a supernaturalism symbolically perfected in the Gothic cathedral and a naturalism best symbolized by the planetarium. Some day the naturalistic world view may seem the only sensible view to the people. Then we shall have new temples which will present that interpretation of reality for their acclaim and celebration.

To those of us caught up in the heat and controversy of this period of transit, it may seem that the lifeblood of religion is in its argumentation, its partisanship. We may be so inured to this that the possibility of a religion without opposition to other factions, a protesting minority set aganst the world and other faiths, may seem like a dispirited religion, something without toughness and point. Why have a religion unless there is a missionary, a teaching, a converting need? We sense our own definition only as we stand against other religious convictions. We gain a sense of virtue in setting ourselves apart and against. This is a war of the spirit, generating a morale similar to that of armies in combat. Can we have a religion of vigor and purpose that does not set itself against others, but is rather a religion for itself? Is it enough to be for a vision of goodness, and not to be pitted against an enemy of darkness?

A view that encompasses the world does not deny areas of growth, reform, and discovery within that scope. Many areas of labor and growth and idealism may be contained *within* a religious view and need not stem from a struggle *between* world views. Growth would then be constructive rather than controversial. We already honor this principle in practice in the non-controversial areas of idealism and reform that are common to the various denominations.

Massive identities and likenesses between the denominations are ignored, and the minuscule differences in verbal beliefs and ritual practices magnified. Party loyalties are so much constructed out of ignoring the common problems, struggles, and sympathies and exaggeratedly harping on the small differences that all party-line activities, whether religious, political, national, or whatever, seem irrecoverably nasty and degrading. They are of the very essence of prejudice and self-righteous self-deceit.

We can refuse to look at labels and dividing walls and look only at the behavior of the people. We are much more alike than we have thought we were. We all live in the same world, making fumbling attempts to come to terms with it. Change is occurring in all religious bodies, since they are all generically involved in the cultural matrix. In the Museum of Natural History in New York there is a magnificent documentation of the evolutionary theory. In just one hundred years Darwin's concepts have penetrated the marrow of our ideas about life and man, and every religious movement is affected by them.

Related patterns of change are occurring in all religions at once, but since we voluntarily and prejudicially segregate ourselves from each other, we do not share these parallel developments. They take place within different temples.

Is it possible, in our time and condition, for any religious group to build and use a temple with a strictly positive, creative, and communal purpose, and escape the insidious competitiveness, promotionalism, and fragmentation that dominate our religious life? Not perfectly, but surely to a meaningful degree. We can change our attitude somewhat by intentionally changing our behavior, by ceasing to promote, to compete, to proselytize, to boast, and to accuse. We cannot become in fact a community temple, where the whole neighborhood would gather, as did the villagers in the medieval church, and as do the villagers in a Hindu temple today. Even in India Moslem and Christian movements have split the cultural and religious homogeneity of Hinduism.

We can attempt to make a "local" and denominational temple, in its ideals and behavior, a true temple in its universality of acceptance and sympathy, even if it is used as such only by a minority of the members of the total community. It would be a strenuous exercise in religious discipline, but certainly an interesting one. The temple itself would have to present this universal orientation. We can affirm the findings of science and reason and love without prejudice and partisanship. We can be for the benefit and progress of all mankind.

The orthodox believer tells us that if we are not for him we are against him. Can we be for him even though we do not accept his doctrines? We can if we learn how to be for adequate evidence, for rational proof, for affectionate relationship, for artistic excellence, for moral achievement, regardless of their derivations. This attitude is already axiomatic in science, which is global and human-wide. We deplore attempts to nationalize science with programs of secrecy and closed borders. There are attitudes and virtues that are truly human, that transcend all national and cultural barriers. We can affirm these wherever they exist and operate.

Religion should be concerned about universal values, such as freedom, the dignity of the individual, honesty, integrity, purposeful and creative living. The paradox is that many religions do emphasize these values, but in the name of the sect, the prophet, the deity of a certain faith. They set themselves against other groups in announcing just those values that should work to draw men together.

If a temple could be devised to escape the denominationalism and divisiveness of religious architecture, symbolism, and practice in our time, a temple above "temples," a truly universal and communal setting, we would have the ideal. All we could then say would be, "This is where all men may come together in common seeking an aspiration if they will." They would not all come, but we can make a temple ready for them when they can.

THE MEETING HOUSE AND THE TEMPLE

Two general attitudes prevail in the building of temples. To one group the temple is a means for the salvation of their souls. They view it in a self-centered way. It is a tool whereby they seek to salvage their own lives. The worst example of this is the barren, often ugly gospel tabernacle, whose sole purpose is for the preaching of evangelical sermons and the baptizing of the saved.

To another group the temple is, in itself, an ultimate goal. It is their profoundest expression of apprehension and meaning in the face of the imponderables of life and the immensities of the universe of which they are a part. The existence of the temple is a continuous act of celebration of life and wonder on the part of the community which erected and maintains it.

Ours is an age concerned with consumer goods and services. We think almost automatically that buildings should *serve us* in some way. Man's various emporiums are grossly self-centered, and now church buildings are becoming mainly fitted to the human shape and to human service. Just as chairs are fitted to our bottoms and backs, our temples are shaped to the human image, and to the proportions and limitations of our present self-evaluation. The major considerations in planning a place of worship are how many people it will seat and how comfortably, and the acoustics. The considerations are predominantly utilitarian and materialistic. More important than the auditorium, and often the first parts to be built if the budget is limited, are the educational plant, the recreational rooms, parlors, kitchens, dining rooms, meeting rooms, and so on. Everything is designed to serve the needs of the people as we now estimate them.

Insidiously our churches are being remodeled to resemble other buildings of our time. Religion is thus acknowledging its unimportance, its secondary role to the worlds of business, education, sport, and entertainment. There was a time when the cathedral was the central architectural splendor of the town, set on its highest point. Then our cities had religious centers; now they have business centers.

Even the churches that still have non-utilitarian, symbolic steeples are runts among the city's buildings. In New York the great Catholic and Episcopalian cathedrals cannot challenge the dominance of the skyscrapers. They huddle among the stone canyons. Their upreaching spires, symbols of aspiration, do not reach to the upper floors of the temples dedicated to soap, oil, and sewing machines.

Is man only a user, a consumer? Does he have no purpose or function higher than the filling of his belly, the clothing of his back, and the transportation of his flabby legs? Churches are being crowded out of the center-city areas. Land there is too expensive for religion when it is needed for banks and department stores. The place for the church is in the residential area, where the kiddies are near the church school, and where the people live. Suburban churches are conceived as adjuncts to suburban homes, like carports or sun parlors. They are appurtenances to suburban life and have the same air of dullness that pervades the surroundings. The suburbs are removed from the business of uptown, from big affairs, from the theaters and concert halls. As the bedrooms of the city, they have a sleepy air about them.

Thus the churches of the suburbs resemble dwellings more than temples, as if the gospel they are intended to reflect is that of security, ease, and conservatism, and preaching is a divine neighborhood gossip. The center-city is given over to the depersonalized institutions of business. On a Sunday afternoon the center-city is deserted and cold, as if the buildings were part of a dead city from which all the people had fled. It is no place to live. Those who work and buy there during the weekdays might never come back, and they would have left nothing behind that they would miss. There the people are numbered and standardized replacement parts in a desert of steel and stone. One by one they drop out and others take their place, and no one is missed, not for long. He never really lived there; he just worked there.

Are these office buildings our temples? If so, then our worship is a strange, formless thing. When singing commercials are the anthems of your faith, what is your vision? On Sunday, the day of worship, the cold temples are deserted.

The two forms of religious buildings in severest contrast to each other are the meeting house and the temple. They most clearly represent the differences of opinion held as to the meaning of the temple. The meeting house in its simplest form among the Friends is simply a place of meeting. It is quite empty of symbolism and adornment. It is a shelter for fellowship. Its emptiness is to be filled with people and invites the

85

inner quietness of the worshipers. The building itself says nothing. If anything at all is spoken, it is by the people gathered in it. Its emptiness does not intrude an outer form or dictation upon the inner light of the attendant.

The temple is just the opposite. It has a central theme or meaning in its dominant architectural symbol, and it is often lavishly decorated with related symbols and art. There are temples that have no interior where people may gather; their meaning is that of a monument to an ideal or belief and they are to be appreciated from without. Other temples may be designed only to serve as a shrine where the people may pass through, where small groups may gather on special occasions, but not for "public meetings." Those which do serve to house a congregation for services are much more than just a housing like the meeting house.

The temple itself is an expression of a vision of reality and life. It is not something set apart from man's speaking, for it is a human art form, a way in which man preaches. But instead of being merely the bare room in which a sermon is delivered, the temple preaches its own sermon through architectural and artistic voices. Will not one preaching reinforce the other? If as the preacher gives his sermon the building that surrounds him is saying the same message in other forms, will this not create a symphony of voices, an orchestration of vision?

In tribal societies the sculptor holds an office of priesthood, since his carvings have divine powers and functions in the ceremonies. His work is as much an act of religious authority and power as is that of the dancer or the officiating priest. The architect is in a similar role in the building of a temple, for he is the creator and expresser of the profoundest symbols and meanings of the religious community. The creation of a temple demands as much religious sensitivity and knowledge of the architect as does the conducting of the religious ceremony of the priest. The architect cannot be just a designer, an engineer, hired to erect a building. He cannot express the religious motifs and intuitions if he is ignorant of the religion and stands outside its aura of convictions and emotions.

The temple is a great and consummate work of art in itself. It is the expression and the enclosure of a vision of the nature of the universe and man. The walls and adornment are the preachment. Such a temple is not built to the image and size of man, as is a meeting house, for it expresses all of reality — that within man and that which surrounds him in the world. It seeks to declare the image and vastness of known reality and to make a gesture of acknowledgment to the uncharted, the unknown, the infinite. A temple is the way in which men point beyond themselves, to indicate the size and shapes of their dreams of becoming. Temples do not mirror man, but rather demonstrate how man may outstrip himself, grow into new creaturehood and new knowledge.

There are other institutions that thrust man beyond himself, those of education, art, science, and government, but they do so in limited spheres. Religion attempts to assess the totality of life and experience and reality. We can expect only partial answers from fields of specialization. In free religion we express our own volition to face reality and to measure ourselves by the fullness of our ideals and our moral visions. This is symbolized in our temples, art, and rituals. Here religious celebration is free from political and commercial acts, and yet would underlie and penetrate all that we do.

Where apart from religion can we find a meaning, a unity that will bring all the parts of life into one whole? Can we create a religion which is capable of transcending all the tribalisms, nationalisms, controversies, and rivalries of the race? Only through ideals that deserve to be called religious will the coming unity of humanity bring peace without stagnation.

For some generations men have been copying the temples they created in the past, rather than designing new temples to declare a new vision of the world. We have not quite given up as temple builders. We are experimenting with new forms and materials, but as yet we hardly know what we are symbolizing, and too often our buildings end by saying very little, and that vaguely and badly. Too often we resort to ancient and outworn symbols, merely using new materials to give them a superficially new expression.

Temples evolve through many generations of experiment, invention, and accumulated lore and experience. We can expect a long evolution before temples are accomplished to express the nature of the world and man that has burst over our comprehension in the last few centuries. The problem is how to participate in that evolution creatively and patiently, for our dedicated efforts at temple building can advance the time when the new temples will be erected in all their fullness of beauty and meaning. This is our destiny, to wonder upon the temples of the past, to dream of the temples of the future, even as we are partly frustrated in our efforts to build great temples today. In our own Meeting House project we are symbolizing the general problem: attempting to turn a clear-paned, unadorned meeting house into a temple. It has become an assembly center of ideas, objects, and experiments, in an effort to formulate at least one answer to the dilemma of the meaning of the temple for modern man, an attempt to foresee the nature, symbolism, and meaning of the temples of to-morrow. For temple building can be, must be, as much an act of pioneering and prophecy as ever has been preaching and social action. For the temple declares all the meaning and goodness men have found, in the building that encloses and participates in the ceremonies and occasions of their lives.

A TEMPLE OF BEAUTY

One term is inclusive of the highest goods and indicates a definite standard of quality and achievement. This term is "beauty." It takes precedence over the other two terms in that threadbare trilogy of truth, beauty, and goodness. There may be truth that is not beautiful, and goodness that is not beautiful, but there cannot be beauty that is not true and good. Just insofar as beauty is without truth and goodness, it is flawed and incomplete.

The standard of worth that marks any achievement or labor as conclusive is quality. The quintessence of quality is beauty. Beauty is the name we give to that harmony of form, relationship, design, and completeness of expression marking the highest of all possible attainments and expressions. The only ultimate value of which we know is beauty. It is the name of the deepest stirring and response within ourselves upon the contemplation of the highest of all attainments. It is the name reserved for the best music in the most consummate performance. If there is a particularly fine play on the ball field, we say, "That was a beauty." We use "beauty" to characterize ultimate grace of body, gesture, and motion. The aim of the dance, with its striving for the most powerful and lyrical use of the body, is beauty. This is also the word we assign to the most sensitive and courageous acts of mercy and idealism. When any statement of fact is set forth with utmost lucidity, proportion, and imagination, it strikes us as not only factual but also beautiful. The final solution to a problem has aesthetic satisfaction. The scientist upon achieving a solution to his equation often has a feeling of heightened perception and response similar to that of an artist finishing his painting. His answer is not only true; it is also beautiful.

John Dewey somewhere remarked that perhaps more important to mankind than all the control over nature that comes through the sciences is the new revelation of the images of the world which we have come to see through science. Science not only reveals facts but gives a deeper and more extensive vision of the face of the world.

The ultimate worth of beauty is known to him who has experienced it. Each person proves his own case. The final value of beauty is a felt reality, and it cannot be communicated to another. Each must discover it for himself, and prove it to himself.

The emphasis of religion, especially in Protestantism and liberal religion, is superficial, incomplete, even misdirected. In both, true values of art and beauty are mainly ignored and denied. We tend to acclaim the means as if they were the ends themselves. We strive for a general good, but it is incomplete. Freedom, but for what? Social concern, but to what end? Justice, but to what issue? Understanding, but to what purpose? Kindness and consideration in human relations — but these relations are not abstractions. What are the human beings to be in association to achieve? An end to discrimination and prejudice, to be sure, but then what? Where are we going?

The orthodox have an answer: to heaven. But if we are to make this life an end in itself, then we must have a basic criterion of value whereby we can measure how the good life is good. If living is an end in itself, then the living experience must be lifted to a height of immediate and known worth. In only this way can living become a goal of religious striving. It is not enough to be fighting a rear-guard action to hold evils in check, girding on the sword of righteousness to do battle against war, exploitation, crime, disease, and ignorance. All this we must do, and in a measure we have scarcely attempted. But it is not enough.

Not only must we be against what is wrong in the world; we must be for that which could and should be the most right in the world. This decision in its culmination is beauty, where all human strivings and achievements reach their noblest and completest dignity, grace, and power.

We who seek to establish a religion for one world have declared that the whole of human society is our province, the whole of humanity our brotherhood. This is our tremendous gain, for it means that all the arts of man are ours also. The orthodox, since they identify with only one tradition, wall themselves off from all other religions. As universalists we are members of the human race. There is only one art, the art of humanity. All the aesthetic and religious strivings of mankind are ours, since they embody the related strivings of the race to achieve a satisfactory way of life. Here is where we can, if we have the wit, rectify our impoverished artistic state. We have no considerable arts of our own. If we are going to achieve a religious art, how better can we start than by identifying ourselves with the finest religious art of the race, ancient and modern?

As we assemble and appreciate the religious art of humanity, something will happen to us. We shall discover the peculiar and enduring symbols of our own liberal and universal movement in history. These will be suggested by the matrix of world culture that we are exploring and digesting. We shall discover what artistic messages our own artistic creations must project. The drama of one world and one race will demand its own statements, as has been significantly demonstrated in the photographic show "The Family of Man."

The glory of man is in his arts. Where else? What makes the bibles of humanity the inspirational sources they are, if not the fact that they contain the most intense and profound poetry of the race? Where are the records of the histories of the faiths embodied except in the arts? The most powerful and complete way to picture the universal dream of the race and the world is to be found in demonstrating the unity of the arts of humanity. We can adorn our buildings with the greatest imaginable wealth of art, creating temples of beauty in which we assemble and work together, and at the same time can make the most convincing preachment of our identification with the whole of the human venture.

The arts of the past and present are alive. This is the wonder of a work of art, that it never loses its life force. It is as if the passion of the artist is frozen into the stone and pigment, to be melted and released into life under the warm gaze of appreciation and love.

The temple should be the central structure of the community. It will be protested that the central structure is the home, or the school, or the bank, or the center of trade, or the sports arena. And to some persons each of these will be the temple of their lives, in that they seek and find the highest values of their lives in this place. Perhaps a note of smugness can be detected when we say the temple *should* be the center of the community life, but the assertion can be defended.

The purpose of the temple is to declare the fullness of meaning and mystery to be found in all the various aspects and activities of the community's existence. All other buildings declare the meaning and purpose of their specialized function, whether trade, money-changing, entertainment, healing, dwelling, or education. The temple has no utilitarian purpose, but is rather the place where all activities and values are celebrated and glorified. It is a monument which the community has erected to the dreams and ideals of its common life.

One way of attempting to make this point is to contrast the temple with two other institutions, the home and the museum. The home of no one family can be the central edifice of the community, unless it is the palace where the aristocratic overlord lives. Since democracy and equality are replacing superiority and aristocracy as basic values in human relations, the palace is vanishing from the community scene and where it

91

remains is being turned into a museum or other civic building.

The home is central for the family living in it and should be a place of warmth, beauty, security, convenience, and nobility. The home should, in its own way and uses, be as beautiful and noble as the temple. Too often in history the temple has been ennobled and the home debased, as in Mayan cities where the temple was a magnificent stone monument and the homes of the farmers were rude thatched huts. The home is a temple for the family it houses and should contain a shrine to the gods or the values that the family worships.

But just as the individual should live in a scope larger than himself, so should the family live in and for a larger world than that encompassed in the concerns and activities of the home. The home is temporary, and the children will soon leave it to make homes of their own. Its members each day issue from the home to their occupations in the larger world. Thus the home cannot be ceremonially, symbolically, sufficient for the imagination, the celebration of the individual. Witness the life of the Jews, who have their home ceremonies, in which the home becomes a temple for the Seder supper, but who also must go to the temple to join other Jewish families in more inclusive ceremony.

Each family can and should provide its store of beauty in the home, but the home is also utilitarian, and even though the tools and furniture of life should have beauty, they somewhat frustrate us when we try to make them point to eternal and ultimate meanings. The home should point to the temple, and be an adjunct of the temple, but something is lost if we try to make it a substitute for the temple.

For one thing, since the temple is a joint enterprise of the community, it is a symbol of a larger family of which each individual family is but a segment. When the temple becomes, in a religion for one world, a symbol of the whole human family, it is the place where each of us tries to relate to the whole race, making the planet a homestead, one dwelling place.

Since the temple is set aside from menial concerns, it can have a size, a splendor, a symbolic richness that would embarrass the humble confines of the home. Indeed, when such grandeur was achieved in the palace, it became perverse, for these are not the dimensions in which the individual and the family can live in modesty and mutuality. To build a palace for one's family is arrogance, but to help build a temple for all the community has no personal penalties of pride. Our homes should be good; our temples can be magnificent.

Before Western man came to Japan, the Japanese had no museums. Their art was to be found in the temples and monasteries, and in collections of individuals. In Japan the art was all alive, in use, as decorations in home and palace or as ritual objects in wayside shrines and the many temples of the land. But we counseled the Japanese to "save" their treasures, and under the direction of Mr. Fenollosa of Harvard they became museum builders as well as temple builders.

What is the weakness of the museum as against the temple? Its weakness lies in its concept of art as an end in itself. In a temple the art is gathered to make a declaration of a dream; its function is to speak. It is the setting of religious celebration. But in a museum the art is uprooted from its use in the temple and put on display as an end in itself. Those of us who flock to the museums to see their collections of beautiful things are grateful, but we can still lament that the museum marks the passing of the temple in all its splendor, and judge the museum to be a poor substitute for the temple.

The Boston Museum of Fine Arts houses many wonderful objects that once were in temples all over the world. The doorway of a Christian temple is there, and the interior of a chapel from Spain. An imitation of a Buddhist temple from Japan is filled with Buddhas that crowd upon one another. Temple statuary from Egypt, Babylonia, Greece, and Rome fills the galleries. And yet, even though the art of a thousand temples is gathered into one building, that building is still, in an important way, less than one temple with its own architecture, symbols, art, and congregation. For art that is uprooted and set apart is less than art that has its roots in community life and works its medicine of health and loveliness and significance in the daily acts and gatherings of the people. The art does not come to the museums until the temples in which it once was gloriously alive and working have died. We esteem our museums, probably because the world outside them is so lacking in great art, but they are mainly grave-yards in which we bury the art that once lived intimately and powerfully in the daily lives and worship of the people.

Two young artists came to me to be married. They had been associated with the Boston Museum of Fine Arts and had received permission to be married in the Spanish chapel. There was a wine ceremony in the service, and I brought a chalice from the Meeting House for the purpose. It looked quite in place on the altar in the chapel. I wondered as we conducted the service in this lovely setting how many wed-dings had taken place in it back in Spain, before it had been moved into a museum. The young man had been told, when he made his request of the museum, that his would be the first marriage ever performed there. Thus for a few moments a portion of the museum again became a temple and served its rightful purpose.

The pity of our condition is that some temples come to imitate museums in their disposal of religious art. Ancient communion services and collections of Judaica, for examples, are put on display in cases in the foyer.

The temple for a religion for one world attempts to correct this neglect and misuse of art. The art is again part of the temple, there to speak to the gathering of the people and their meditation, to their declarations of brotherhood and consci-ence. We hope one day that every village, every neighbor-hood will have its temple as is true in India and Japan today. We have substituted meeting houses for temples, and the sign of their poverty lies in the fact that they have no attractive-ness, no significance, unless they are filled with people. Who goes to a meeting house unless there is a meeting in it? When the people are gone, it is locked, for who would come to sit among the empty pews within the empty walls? Now that we have assembled the art of the world religions within our building, our historic name of Meeting House is ironic indeed unless we can make it mean something more, such as the place where people meet beauty, symbolism, and art, and in them confront the best, noblest, and most ideal visions of themselves.

For when people meet they should not just meet each other.

They should meet one another amidst the assemblage of a myriad visitors and speakers from the thousands of years of human history. They should meet, by way of their art and dreams, all the other families of wonderers and seekers among all the races, nations, and eras of history. Men are not made less, thus to congregate in a temple of beauty, which pictures all the ages of man, all the cultures of their fellow creatures. Rather is their meeting overshadowed and enriched by the echoes and overtones of many speaking voices, even as the home is warm when the speaking of one child finds the hum and background of the other members of his family.

We should put great works of art into living relationship with one another. In their interplay and integration they will spell out the many-branched but interrelated quest of humanity for beauty and life-goodness. They will not tell just one story. They will tell of our universal involvement in humanity in all its phases, all its cultures, myths, and manners. They will also tell of our love for beauty. They will declare as our gospel that the final good of human endeavor is the experience and creation of beauty, that the life of man himself becomes an art as it is dedicated to the creation and appreciation of beautiful things and ways.

The temple of beauty will declare that the end toward which we strive in preaching about decency and love in human relations is not just barren moralism but beauty within the association of human beings, as harmony and design and color combine to make a painting an ordered and expressive whole. It will declare that when we crusade against social evils we do so not just to eradicate pain and misfortune but because we are also repelled by the ugliness of hate and greed, poverty and crime. We wish to make a beautiful social order in which our cities will be flowering structures of loveliness. A city is ugly only if the people who create it and live in it are ugly in their lives and ways.

"A thing of beauty is a joy forever." This is the only eternity that transient human beings can know. Our days slip by and our powers wane, but in these escaping years we can fashion beauty, investing our days in enduring shapes of grace and meaning. As we live in beauty we will forget how brief and treacherous is our estate, for we will be caught up in great and lasting harmonies, movements, and culminations. Our lives will become an art, a dance in time, having their own proportions, themes, and fulfillments. Then, even though we pass, the beauty of the ways in which we lived, and the beauty we have shaped with our passing hands and speaking and love, will live after us.

CHAPTER 7

The Human Image

THE FULLNESS OF COMPANIONSHIP

Moral verbalisms are a delusory commodity. We have not fully divested ourselves of the primitive illusion that "saying makes it so." Our ancestors believed that uttering a curse would put into operation a cause-and-effect reaction that would inevitably bring the issue of the curse into being. In regard to personality development, we seem to believe that expressing pious moralities with words actually makes us the kind of person our speaking defines.

Religion, as well as whatever it was that Hamlet was reading, is mainly "words, words, words." In the sacramental churches the priest utters the sacred formula in order for the blessing and the forgiveness to be manifest. The speaking itself may be hurried and almost meaningless; it is the magical repetition of the formula that is efficacious. In the professional churches it is the profession of belief and repentance by the layman that has magical potency. If the devotee believes and professes his belief, he will be saved, regardless of whether the life he has lived has been righteous or unrighteous.

We may consider ourselves exempt from such folkways, characteristic, we say, of simple and superstitious folk, but let us not be so superior and self-righteous. The highly educated and the liberals are, if anything, more easily deluded by the seeming reality and potency of words than any other group.

97

Being intellectuals, they believe in words, have more of them, and use them better than the less well read. Since their education is primarily from books and couched in words, their susceptibility is compounded. They consider that if they know the verbal formula for an experience or a performance they are initiated into it. In actuality they may know many words about something without knowing anything significant or practical about it at all.

When the educated liberal has mouthed a conviction about democracy, or freedom, or the scientific spirit, or world brotherhood, he seems to think he has thereby demonstrated that he embodies and practices these ideals. Quite the opposite may be the case. Liberals are the ones who most often shout for the great, inclusive, yet strangely bodiless ideals such as the brotherhood of man. Why are they so ineffective in promoting it in active flesh-and-blood relationships? Prate of the ideal as they may, they are inept and embarrassed when they leave their small social group and try to deal with workers, farmers, tradesmen, and others in society. The causes they promote — political, religious, educational, or otherwise — seldom win a popular following, even when they verbally announce their concern with the welfare of the larger populace.

Brotherhood and companionship are delicate, complex, and baffling relationships. Few of us are strikingly successful at being satisfactory brothers and companions to those in our own families, to our close friends and associates. Many who profess to love the whole of humanity fail to live generously and creatively with the associates with whom they eat, sleep, and work every day.

Although it is difficult to have a full companionship with those near to us, it is not impossible if we work diligently to expand our understanding and sympathy for our fellows. An advantage lies in the face-to-face nature of these associations. Full companionship penetrates beneath the surface into the many strata of our persons. Close friends know much about us that we try, voluntarily and involuntarily, to conceal. They catch and interpret the minute telltales of our moods and motivations. When husband or wife complains that the spouse does not understand, it is likely that the spouse understands all too well.

It is a problem in close associations to maintain respect and affection for one another in spite of and because of knowing much about each other, both the pretty and the unpretty. Although familiarity does breed contempt, on even more occasions it breeds acceptance and boredom. The trial of loving is to maintain a warm acceptance of another when we are privy to his weakness, contradictoriness, and perversity.

The face-to-face relationship does provide the matrix, the enablement, for attaining to understanding love. When two persons are able to observe each other, listen to each other for many years, they learn to read that which the other is unable to write, and to hear what he is unable to speak. We are inept in expressing ourselves, logically or emotionally, but our very confusion and wordlessness can reveal the meanings and feelings that are inexpressible. What we are unable to declare intentionally may be revealed unintentionally. When we live with another, he tends to be unaffected at times by our presence, and we see him when he is "just being himself." No longer inhibited by our accustomed presence, he expresses himself unself-consciously through his own native being. We can also become so intimate with someone else that we are able intentionally to communicate experiences too personal and painful to be revealed to an outsider.

Although we may seldom attain to a full companionship with those with whom we live, our intimacy does make such a companionship possible. But what about the billions of human beings whom we shall never meet? Sensitive moments bring an overwhelming feeling of nostalgia and finiteness as we contemplate the numberless people, dead and living and still to be born, whom we shall never know. Having known a pitifully few persons in depth, we have some estimate of the richness of fellowship that the brevity of our lives and the paucity of our energies remove from the scope of our attention and participation. Absence, removal, busy-ness make only a fraction of the lives of our family and friends available to us.

A kind of shorthand of fellowship is possible for those who

live in the same culture and community, since they share the same language and folkways and manners, what someone has called the "silent language" of culture. And relationships with our compatriots have, as it were, exchangeable parts, since their ways are similar to the ways of others we have known. But what about the people who live on other continents, within other cultures, whose languages, customs, and religions may vary strikingly from our own? Here the silent language becomes a barrier rather than a door. Is it "globaloney" to talk about the brotherhood of man in view of the seemingly insurmountable obstacles that the different manners of communication and presentation offer?

Unless we are willing to work at the task of comprehension and appreciation with great wit and diligence, unless we are compellingly motivated to invest the time and energy to achieve understanding of the many tribes and civilizations of humanity, we might as well quit talking about one world and get on with the insanities of selfishness, provincialism, and militaristic suicide. To accomplish a full companionship with humanity, a person must be religiously motivated or he will not have the dedication and persistence to make the sacrifices necessary to fulfill the capacities of knowledge, wisdom, and affection that are his potential. In this sense, very few of us have religion.

There are several differences between liberal and orthodox religious attitudes and behavior, but in one essential they are the same. Without enthusiasm for the ends envisioned, neither position merits the name of religion. The orthodox person may expend his zeal in Bible reading, long prayers, and evangelism; he makes sacrifices in expenditure of time and strength and choices of satisfaction. The same is demanded of the person whose religious goal is a universal fellowship with humanity, who would be involved with the whole human family in its poignant quest for the good life. No religion is easily attainable or inexpensive.

Some people, such as Ghandi, Schweitzer, and Justice William O. Douglas, exhibit this dedication in high degree. They become, in effect, world citizens and spend their lives promoting brotherhood and understanding. There are thousands like them whose names are not so well known. Many young people seek a line of endeavor that will enable them to live with and for humanity, rather than being limited to the proud and antagonistic confines of a single country; they repudiate the kind of patriotism that is too often not just for one's own country but against all other countries. Some turn to the U N organizations, to international work camps, to the Peace Corps, to special areas of study in anthropology and world culture, and to any other outlet with universal scope. This is a new spirit abroad in the world. The documentary film *World Without End,* produced by UNESCO, illustrates that a powerful religious force of international goodwill and human brotherhood is developing, although its adherents are as yet comparatively few.

Once given a religious motivation in this direction, how do we develop and reinforce it? One way is through the arts of communication. It is impossible to do it on a face-to-face relationship with the peoples of the world, although William Douglas in his many trips about the world seems to be making a manful attempt to accomplish even this. But not even he can travel to enough places, or live in them long enough, to become at home among all the lands and neighborhoods of the race, to see and experience at firsthand everything he would have to share. We might well take advantage of all the travel possible, all the firsthand acquaintance we can, but in any case this would have to be supplemented by extensive study and appreciation through the varied arts of communication, fine and otherwise.

When we can live closely and long with other people they can communicate with us artlessly. But when communication is from one side of the planet to the other, and from one millenium to another, the arts are indispensable. Those who would minimize them as impractical and useless occupations should read enough history to learn that most of what we know about our ancestors and how they lived has come to us from the remains of their arts, from literature, pottery, architecture, sculpture, painting, weaving, and toolmaking. It is through the arts that men express themselves, especially when communication must be across great distances of the earth or time. Because the arts are the very substance of our knowledge of history, we will become citizens of one world and achieve any profundity of human brotherhood only through an extensive course in art appreciation.

One writer tells of calling at the home of a Japanese gentleman, being graciously received, and learning later that the man's wife was critically ill in another room of the house. The host might have been thought lacking in ordinary feelings of grief and concern for his wife in not informing his visitor of the situation, and in acting as if everything were normal in the household. But the Japanese would have considered it impolite to burden his guest with his troubles.

One who is widely acquainted with Japanese poetry, painting, and sculpture would never make this mistake. Their arts reveal the Japanese to be a richly emotional people. The gestures and verbal inflections of their drama strike us at first as exaggerations, even caricatures of emotions, they are so pointed and violent. But when we remember how melodramatic our own style of acting was only a generation or two ago, we realize how much in the arts is a matter of taste and style.

Most of us in the United States will never be able to live in Japan for any length of time. But we can be sympathetic viewers of Japanese films and performances of touring Kabuki troupes and readers of translations of Japanese poetry, fiction, philosophy, and religion. We can be students of Japanese art in museums, in the art objects we personally own, and in publications. We can be acquaintances of a few Japanese people, albeit transplanted into our own country. By these means a considerable understanding and companionship with the Japanese is possible, mainly through their arts.

It is the intention, the special province of the arts to express emotion and personality. No art is happier than that of China and Japan. One of the happiest of all Oriental figures is that of Hotei, the Japanese God of Good Fortune, although he has competition from Kwan Yin, Laotzu, Fokurukujiu, and the Laughing Buddha, with whom he is often identified. Hotei is a fat, bald man, usually depicted with his naked abdomen protruding unashamedly. Rubbing the tummy of a statue of Hotei is supposed to bring good luck. An art dealer, discussing a statue of Hotei in his collection, told me that when it was exhibited in an antique show he would catch other antique dealers sneaking a quick caress of Hotei's belly to bring them good luck. Superstition is international even when brotherhood is not.

In the Charles Street Meeting House collection of the art of the world's religions is a wood carving of Hotei, its abdomen being unusually restrained, which wears one of the most contagiously humorous and happy faces I have ever seen. It was purchased from Mr. Takeda, a Japanese gentleman who earns his living restoring and selling objects of Oriental art. Whenever Mr. Takeda looked at this Hotei on his shelves he would break into a smile that was the equal of Hotei's in affection and goodwill, and he would say, completely without affectation, as if he were talking about a living person, "I just love him." He would have been quite happy if no one had ever purchased him.

But we were fortunate enough to do so, after several months of anxiety lest someone else also fall in love with the carving and acquire the purchase price before we had managed to promote it. When Mr. Takeda took him down to wrap for us, he kissed the top of his head and said good-by to him as if he were an old friend, as indeed he was. For this statue was no dead piece of wood. It was alive with the feeling, the humor, the sense of proportion, beauty, and delicacy of form within the sculptor and his artistic tradition, many centuries old in Japanese art. This Hotei embodies the spirit of its people, as it is revealed through their gods, through the mythological, symbolical, and artistic figures which they worship and with which they live, and no other people live more fully with their art, with their expressions of the beautiful, than do the Japanese.

The statue of Hotei tells us a great deal about the people of Japan, and what it expresses comes to us directly, through touch and sight. This is not Hotei at all; this *is* the people of Japan, revealing themselves through the image of a happy god, who is nothing if he is not the artistic projection and expression of their own happiness. It is this contagion of feeling in all the arts that makes them open roads into the minds and emotions, into the personalities, of all peoples of other cultures who have been artists, and all human beings *have been* artists in more or less extent, for the artistic dimension is never totally absent from any human personality.

The relation of Mr. Takeda to Hotei tells us much about him and his people. How better can we know any nationality than through the care, expense, and energy which they expend on beauty and the arts? Is this not one of the chief glories of civilization and of the human spirit?

There is a serenity, at times a passivity, to the East which is difficult for the Occidental to experience. This is consummately expressed in the face and figure of the Buddha. Here is no mere depiction of a great teacher or god, depending on which variety of Buddhism is involved. Through the Buddha's image we can touch and absorb the emotions and the thought of the people who have embodied themselves in it for thousands of years. If you will sit quietly and look into the face of a Buddha for a few moments, you will feel a serenity, a peace rise within you in response. The inner quietness of Buddha, as felt and expressed by the artist, as contained and purified in the forms of an ancient art tradition, takes possession of you.

This power of communication of mood and feeling is present in all successful art. Degas has a painting of some women at work in a laundry. One of them is yawning, and the whole aura around the yawn is so beautifully expressed that hardly anyone who looks at the painting can withhold a yawn in response.

In no art is emotion so compellingly and fascinatingly expressed as in the tribal art of Africa. Be it terror, power, force, or a quiet and secluded inwardness, the African mask gives it a magical realization. In the tribal world the art was not just a representation of a power or a deity. The object itself — the mask, the headdress, the statue, the stool — was the power, the life. When the executioner of the secret society wore the mask to carry out the judgment of the tribal law, it was the mask, not the man wearing it, that performed the demanded retribution. It was the mask that contained the power to promote the adolescent boy to manhood, and when the initiation ceremony was finished, the mask was exhausted of its virtue and discarded as useless, dead.

Because of the complete belief and dedication of the tribal artist in his creation, which can never be imitated by the sophisticated and detached artists who have left the tribal world, the African mask strikes us less as an object than as a presence. It is a creature in its own being. Anyone who possesses one of these masks senses it as a living presence in the house. The tribal artist has indeed put his own life, his own fervor and absorption, into the image he has created.

Although few artists can endow their creations as powerfully with themselves and with the aura of their culture as do these tribal sculptors, this is just what every artist does to some degree and in his own fashion. His art is his medium of expressing his most profound realities and experiences. The efficacy of art as a means of communication inheres in its capability of transcending the encumbrances of geographical distance and time. When I first walked into the room of the Oriental Institute at the University of Chicago, to be confronted by the great head of a bull from Persia, although I remained erect, I *felt* as if I had been forced to my knees.

Since there was a proscription in the tribal lore of the Israelites against the making of images, the creative and artistic energy of the Hebrews was funneled into their literature. Their scriptures comprise one of the most splendid poetic treasures of the race. Prizing the Bible as highly as they do, the people of the western world should have learned the lesson that communication, the instrumentation of companionship and brotherhood, comes powerfully through the arts, in this case the arts of poetry and prose. The joy of the psalmist, the erotic passion of the Song of Solomon, the pessimism of Ecclesiastes, the ardor of the prophets for righteousness and justice — these move us as we read, although they were written in the third millenium before our own, in an Oriental land halfway around the globe, and we read them in a translation far removed from the original Semitic language in which they were composed.

Through the arts, if we open ourselves to them, we can

communicate with the human family, past and present. Not all of the people we would reach have been artists and poets, but they need not have been. There were artists and poets among them who were sufficiently intuitive and profound to attain universality, and declared not only their own spirit but that of their people and their times. There are such universal artists in all branches of human society today. If we ignore their works and the healing they might bring to our pride and provincialism, we impoverish and imperil ourselves.

The problem is not so simple as the foregoing might seem to have made it, for the achievement of knowledge and sympathy through the arts of communication is difficult. Even when we are adept in these arts, without goodwill our knowledge will be an empty aestheticism. But let us assume that we have a latent capacity for goodwill. It has become a cliché to state that all the world's people really want peace. Our goodwill cannot be realized and made effective in isolation from our fellows. We must discover a matériel of companionship and brotherhood. The matériel is the experience of the living reality of the other members of the human family, from which *may* issue goodwill and love. We cannot love in a vacuum. The fullness of our feeling for and knowledge of those we may never greet in person, the billions of the human family we may never meet, can be attained only through the arts, which are our own human voices of communication with one another.

THE HUMAN IMAGE

Gordon Alport, the psychologist, has rendered the verdict, "Without images it is impossible to form attitudes." If we are seeking to create the attitudes requisite to a religion for one world, we must begin with the attitude, in the disposition of the individual and society, of being members of the family of man. The concept of "mankind," of the whole population of the earth, past, present, and future, gathered into one collective image and entity, is difficult to achieve. But we can have no universal religion unless men can consider themselves members of the brotherhood of man. Thus we must create the requisite image, the image of man.

In our language and imagination we utilize two kinds of images. First comes the specific image, the image of the particular reality. The world of the very small child is probably made up of specific images. The baby first becomes acquainted with the face of his mother or father, or the one who takes personal care of him. If any other than the familiar image presents itself, the baby may become alarmed and cry, and he may be impossible to placate until the familiar image that represents security and belonging returns to him.

Within a few months the baby seems to have made a beginning in the direction of recognizing the general image. A human face becomes something to smile at and respond to, whether it is a familiar face or not. He will still respond more to the familiar face than to any other, but he has learned that a face as such betokens a certain kind of reality. His response to a human face will be different from his response to any other object in his environment. This is probably the beginning of his recognition of the human image, which is not a specific image but a generalized one signifying the realm of the human, the symbol of his own species identity, his human kinship.

The small child, until he has been conditioned by his social group, makes no distinctions among the people he meets, except perhaps to sense whether they are friendly or unfriendly. Color, dress, hair, type of feature, language, ethnic manner — none of these affects him. A human is a human. The baby is much wiser in his acceptance of basic identities than are the adults. He discerns the common human attributes in all men that the adult has learned to discount, to reject. This innocent acceptance which is native to the child becomes a most difficult, even sophisticated attainment in maturity, after the warping and conditioning of the local culture has shaped him to its limitations and bias.

The human image, that is, the objective reality apart from any reaction to it, is created by two interrelated forces, the evolutionary or biological, and the cultural. Our confusion and disaffection relating to the human image is caused, at least in part, by something common to both lines of development, the presence of diversity within unity. The biological

107

differences among the branches of the human species can work to estrange them, and can be used as pseudo-reasons to rationalize separatisms. These physical differences, often matters of superficial appearance, are more spectacular than significant. Ignorant and perverse men have cited them to justify excluding their fellows of differing color and form from the family of the human. The Caucasian has so excommunicated the Negro, and both the Negro and the European have hunted the Bushmen for sport as if they were mere animals. But physical anthropology and biology clearly demonstrate the biological unity of the family of man as one species.

Similarly the varieties of custom and behavior among the various cultural groups have worked to confuse our comprehension that there is but one human culture, evolving from basic and shared cultural inventions, and again differing in dramatic but relatively superficial aspects. An easy method of assessing the cultural unity and homogeneity of the human species is to contrast the behavior of *homo sapiens* with that of any other animal species, even the higher apes. The simplest and most primitive human cultures, those of the Bushmen of Australia and southern Africa, have language, literature, mythology, rituals, use tools and weapons, have devised a highly complex method of surviving in a desert country where more highly civilized people would perish, possess family and social institutions and patterns of relationship, are affectionate and sensitive in human relations, have ethical standards, and exhibit high artistic attainments. The sculpture and abtract design of an Australian aboriginal shield or churinga have artistic elegance, similar to that which makes us marvel at the cave art in France and Spain and the Sahara. Other animal species exhibit none of these attainments; they are the characteristics of humankind.

The delineation and documentation of these two aspects of the human identity, the biological and the cultural, are the province of the physical and cultural anthropologists. They have now probed back to creatures much like ourselves who lived 1,700,000 years ago. When our earliest ancestors seem to escape the earmarks of what we now call the human creature, they are dubbed protohuman or hominids. Sometime, a million or more years ago, an animal began making "human" motions, exhibiting the beginnings of language and tool using, and the human image slowly rose into the focus of historical identity.

The history of this species is being rapidly accumulated and organized. This is the realm of objective fact. There is no doubt that the human image exists. Our problem is how to make this human image a matter of rich emotional and intellectural experience for people. Surely this is one of the most important images through which to form attitudes of world-wide fellowship and concern. The human image in all its interest, variety, and oneness is indispensable, and will underlie the basic attitudes of universal religion. The concept of one race and one culture is as necessary to a religion for one world as the concept of the oneness of God is to mono-theism.

The young artist must learn a fundamental lesson: how to see what his eyes are already looking upon. Without train-ing we look at but do not discern. To see shape, form, solidity, color, shadow, and light and dark values is a demanding self-discipline. The image of man is all about us, in a myriad of representations and details and intimations, but we must learn to discern it and comprehehend it.

Archaelogists are trained to look for the marks of man, for pieces of human bone, for evidence of man's presence, for man's tools and rubbish, for signs of his campfires, his dirt floors, his postholes, for scraps of cloth and shards of pots. The image of early man must be reconstructed from a few clues and telltales. The structure of an entire skeleton may be deduced from a few bones, and an artist then attempts to imagine the outer appearance of the creature. His way of life is deduced from the refuse in his caves. Scientists are avid for any and all of these ancient scraps, for only by the interrelation of all available clues will the most composite and complete portrait of primitive man be reconstructed.

When the concept of the human image enters the religious realm, it becomes the human image as a totality, the face of man in all times and in all conditions. The archaeologist may be content with the image of man as an objective, scientific reality. The man of universal religion is also concerned with objective truthfulness and fullness, but for him the human image is also a moral, humane, and even mystical reality. He might be said to be concerned with the human presence.

Farmers often turned up stone axes, scrapers, and points in their plowing before the science of archaeology developed. They had the evidence in hand but not the theories, viewpoint, or techniques to probe its meaning. Even so there is, in a city of any considerable size, all the suggestive evidence needed for discovering the human image. It is our ignorance, obtuseness, lack of imagination, unconcern that deter us from making this use of it. It isn't that we cannot know but that we do not care to know. None are so blind as those who will not see.

We discovered this abundant evidence when we set out to make the collection of the art of the world religions at the Meeting House. We knew of the collections of world art in the museums, and of the books in the libraries, but we had almost no idea of what was elsewhere in our city. Experience proved the old admonition that he who seeks shall find. It became a kind of game, an artistic scavenger hunt. Within a mile of the Meeting House, in junk shops, antique shops, art galleries, auction galleries, book stores, and print shops, was the religious art of humanity. We had thought that we might have to be content with reproductions in making our symbolic collection, but originals were available, often for less than the cost of a good reproduction.

Each piece of this art was a message, a communication, declaring the religious devotion, the world view, the concept of self and human values, of people everywhere upon the earth, from the Eskimo to the Australian Bushman, from Japan to Java to Arabia. There were artifacts from the Stone Age and a vase from Egypt 6,000 years old. Each of these pieces bore its contribution to the human image. They had been about us all the time, but we had not seen them; we had not sought them out. As our collection grew our eyes became sensitized. We saw these traces of a world-wide culture everywhere, in the windows of jewelry shops, in gift shops, in reproductions in department stores, in the homes of our friends, and increasingly in movies and the theater and books.

On the basis of this experience, we can judge that if people do not attain to the human image, and through it to a sense of one humanity, it is not because the material for the image is lacking but because they are not responsive to it. I have watched people walking through the immense collections of Oriental, Primitive, and Near Eastern art in museums, seeing none of it. One of the most frustrating of all experiences relates to the Meeting House collection itself. Here we have carefully selected the most significant symbols and art works to represent the various facets of human history and religious experience. They have been arranged symbolically to elucidate their interrelatedness, their common source and significance. People will visit the Meeting House, stand in the middle of the room, glance idly about them for a few moments, and then leave. The image is there for them to see, as plain as the nose on the face of man, and they will not and cannot see it.

What is this image of man? It could not be modeled or painted. You could paint a million faces of individual human beings, but these would not contain it. You can talk about it, but you cannot describe it. You can know it as one of the most burning and convincing realities in your daily life, yet never be able to show it to someone else. For it is the memory of a million faces coalesced into one image. It is not simply a visual image, for it is a recollection of everything that human beings have done, said, and been. In it is every page that you have read, every word you have heard spoken. Somehow out of all your experience of men and their doing has come a sense of man. This is the human image.

Although this may seem very generalized, since it relates to so many different people and places, it is actually specific and limited. For this image sets man apart from all the other creatures of the earth and the universe. This is the sense of human individuality, even idiosyncrasy. This image of man is not a unique image, except that it is uniquely human. We have a smilar image for tree, made up of all the sights and experiences relating to trees in our life. It is not like any particular kind of tree, elm, fir, or oak, yet it is the image of them all. There are many kinds and colors of roses, from the simple wild rose, to the large, many-petaled varieties, but there is an image of rose that covers them all.

A strange thing is that, although it is made up of many personal experiences, the resultant image comes as close to being a universal as human beings can experience. I can never separate the image of rose from the many, many kinds of roses my grandmother had in her garden, with which I lived as a small child, but the image of rose which I hold relates to every rose in the world, and the roses of a hundred thousand years.

Human sympathy, imagination, intelligence, and love combine to create a wonderful catalyst, which blends all the many images into one image. I can trace some elements of the making of the image of man in my own experience – the copying of muscles and skeletons from *Gray's Anatomy,* the reading of books on anthropology, psychology, and history, careful, cold analyses, abstract and analytical – and these have somehow melted into the faces and arms of my grandmother and grandfather, the children in the second grade in a small town, the strange people seen on a thousand city streets, and made one image. Once this sense is known, once we invite and respond to the making of this human image, rejecting nothing that reports and mirrors man, the image blossoms with amazing fertility and feeds upon everything in the human scene.

The image is composed, not only of what we see in the faces and activities of others, but of pictures and reports of how other men have seen us and themselves. This is the genius of the arts, for they permit us to see what other men see, to see in the way that other men see.

Some artists have given us a brilliant accounting of the image, have left us a series of self-portraits, wherein we see them as they saw themselves with both an outward and an inner eye, and they have also given us their reports of how they saw other men and the world. Three have done this with great profundity: Rembrandt, Van Gogh, and Kaethe Kollwitz. Kollwitz and Rembrandt painted long series of self-portraits, spanning long lives. Taken together these become a mute autobiography, yet a more poignant one than any written in words, for here it is a series of full, connected images that speak. We see that just as Rembrandt came to paint other people with more warmth and compassion and sensitivity, so did he read more and more in his own face. All the many faces of his models that Rembrandt painted are in some indefinable way part of his own face, and in his own face are the echoes and shadows of all the men and women who have ever lived.

Kollwitz also lived in and through people. The eyes in her self-portraits are not simply searching out the reality of one person, Kaethe Kollwitz, wife, mother, artist, and lover of mankind; they are seeking humanity within her own face, until her last self-portrait, which pitilessly depicts the collapse and exhaustion of old age, becomes the portrait of every aged human being, borne down with too many years and too much pain.

Whereas there is something persistent, patient, enduring in Kollwitz and Rembrandt, Vincent Van Gogh in his brief ten years of painting flares up like lightning in the night. His penetration and intensity are overwhelming. He seems to see everything in a flash of insight, and to catch the full vision in his brilliant pigments. His self-portraits print his image bold, many-colored, yet an everlasting loneliness and compassion lie under the tempest of brush strokes like bone under flesh. In everything Vincent paints he gives us a new image, the image of his eyes. Ever after we must see a flowering fruit tree as he saw it. And ever after we must see people as Vincent saw them, see the beauty in ordinary folk, the postman, the potato diggers, the man cutting wheat under the fiery sun.

The image of man is not just an outer image; it is an inner image. Its inward quality begins with each of us, for the human image begins with the self-image; it is seen from inside out. All of our own emotons, fears, elations, doubts, enthusiasms, sureties are part of it. But we are not limited to our own inwardness, for in the arts and literature millennia of humankind have left us millions of portraits of their inner selves. The inward image of the arts lends profound dimensions and contributions to the human image that can be created

113

within the comprehension of each one of us.

For this reason the arts are the handmaidens of universal religion. The head of a man from the Esmeralda area of Ecuador, the stucco head of an Eagle Warrior from Yucatan, a jade mask from Mexico, the masks of the Northwest Coast Indians, a thousand faces of the Buddha, the face of Krishna and his beloved Radha, the sinister face of Kali, the smiling, patient faces of Laotzu and Confucius and many other Chinese sages, happy Hotei, serene Kwan Yin, a forest of masks from the forest of Africa, demonic, quiet, human, animal, the stiff figures from Assyria and Egypt, which yet have so much movement and breath, the saints and gargoyles of Europe's cathedrals, the infant Jesus in Mary's arms, Brueghel's peasants and Velasquez's courtiers, El Greco's ascetics and Goya's madmen, the children of Renoir and Cassatt — all artists in all times have enriched the image of man. Today's artists show us man fractured, distraught, embittered, but the image of man is made not just of what is seen in man in this age but of what has been seen in man in all ages.

There is in the Meeting House collection a small Yoruba statuette from Nigeria. The wood from which it is carved glows with the patina of many years of handling as a fetish. This figure speaks with an infinite appeal and humanity. The face possesses a mute, almost piteous transparency. The arms and body are gathered into one human gesture. What this statuette tells is one of the most profoundly religious messages that we can ever receive.

We cannot fully love any one human being without loving in him all men; otherwise we love only a part of him. For we are incomplete unless in us is the intimation, the report of all humanity. Each word we speak, each gesture we make, each feeling that stirs in us rises out of the depths of human history, echoing and re-echoing down the centuries. This is not to say that we cannot love the individual in all his uniqueness; it is to affirm that this human dimension, this relatedness, is part of his particularity and singleness. These are the full inferences and overtones of the person. He is a man, and he is man.

By the same token, we can reject no other person except to the rejection of ourselves, for in that rejection we are re-

114

jecting man. Just insofar as we inflict evil on any human creature, we do violence to the image of man that is being created within us, and thus we do evil to ourselves and defile our most sacred altars. This is the source of man's sickness and corruption, the debasement of the human image. With it comes a loss of personal dignity, a loss of a sense of personal worth, a fouling of the wellsprings of love and joy. Whatever evil we do to one of our fellows we do to ourselves; our punishment is self-inflicted and inescapable.

Everything of beauty and honor we make, every true report, every act of affection and consideration, we give to ourselves as we give to others. For whatever image of man we attain becomes the image of ourselves. Only that mercy and wisdom we bestow upon the image of man will we bestow upon the image we have made of ourselves, and whatever goodness we have known in humanity we shall know in our personal lives.

MANKIND AS HERO

An intriguing problem relating to the development of a religion for one world lies in the field of myth. What will happen to the myths of the religions that have developed in the tribal and ethnic religions of the past? Will they become merely charming literary relics, without any potency to generate images or directions in human behavior? Undoubtedly many of the old myths will be outworn and will descend to this category. A number of them already have. But are there some that, transcending the regionalism and topicality of their place and time of origin, will become generative and creative myths for the whole of mankind? Are there some that suit the new role of man in a united world, and the new societal behaviors that men will evolve?

We cannot forsee the future sufficiently well to answer this. But we can ask whether one of these myths is beginning to assume such a function even now, as we move into the one-world relationship. Does mankind have a living, working myth? Many myths of the past still have some following among various portions of the human race. Is there one master myth that dominates the thinking and behavior of modern man?

If there is, it is unfinished; a myth that has been completed is already dead. As long as a myth is living in the behavior of people, it is still a source of elaboration and tale-making. In this sense, the myth we seek is still in the process of coming to be. It is so much a part of our current mode and expectancy that it will be hard to isolate and define. But since it sets the very mood of man's morale and rationality, nothing can be more pertinent to our self-knowledge than to establish the nature of this myth.

Our working myth must have a history as well as a future. If the myth here considered is the living myth of our era, it had its beginning, at least in the West, in the Greek myth of Prometheus, a Titan, one of those giant heroes who seem to stand halfway between lowly humanity and the gods on Mount Olympus. His relation to man is clear, for he is the great champion of humankind. In this role he is the projection of man the mythmaker, for Prometheus carries man's own resentment of the gods and his incipient rebellion to their rule.

Prometheus is credited with being the creator of mankind. He is depicted as being the wisest of the Titans and as having a close association with the goddess Athene, who taught him many skills and sciences which he then imparted to mankind. These included most of the arts of the ancient world, such as architecture, astronomy, mathematics, navigation, medicine, and metallurgy. The growing abilities and prowess of the race of men made Zeus, the head of the Greek gods, jealous and angry. He decided to exterminate the whole race, and spared them only because Prometheus pleaded their case.

It is clear that the ancient rivalry between man and his gods, the gods of his own imagination, a rivalry for dominance and self-regard, is inherent in this myth. Man's resentment of the gods is indicated in the fact that his hero, Prometheus, is pictured as a practical joker, who played tricks on Zeus himself. Zeus decided to punish Prometheus by taking vengeance on men, whom Prometheus was championing, by withholding from them the use of fire. Without fire man would have been doomed to living in unheated caves and eating his food uncooked.

Prometheus turned to his benefactor, Athene, who helped

him to gain entrance to Mount Olympus. Once there, he defied the command of Zeus by stealing the fire Zeus had withheld. He set his torch alight from the sun, which the Greeks pictured as a chariot of fire. He then hid a live ember inside a fennel-stalk, put out his torch, and managed to escape without discovery. This burning coal was his gift of fire to mankind.

Zeus, of course, had to triumph over the rebel. Prometheus became one of the great suffering heroes of mythology, chained to a mountain, with a vulture continuously eating away at his liver. Since Prometheus' liver was restored each night, his torture was to be renewed. This portion of the myth seems to embody man's own sense of guilt at taking powers away from the gods.

The figure of Prometheus is still a symbol of man's growing control over nature, and the myth has slowly evolved during succeeding millennia. We no longer need an intermediate figure to stand between us and the gods, for the gods themselves are no longer fearsome, if they are believed in at all. Becoming more psychologically astute, we no longer need a figure into which we can project our own desired self-image. We are beginning to acknowledge the portrait, the being, we have created for ourselves. We have replaced the ancient hero Prometheus with the myth of mankind itself as hero.

The image of mankind as hero is not that of an individual man, although individuals share the quality of heroism. It is rather a composite, generalized image. The learning, arts, and skills that the older myth assigns to Prometheus were human achievements. We realize that the slow efforts of earlier generations of mankind, extending over a period of half a million years and longer, enabled man to domesticate fire and to accumulate the basic tools of culture and technology. Many thousands of years ago men invented the ax, the knife, the scraper, the gouge, the mortar and pestle, the spearhead and arrowhead. Some of these tools were made with a beauty and proportion that would be the envy of any modern craftsman or industrial designer. The hero to whom we give credit is man the maker, not Athene or her favorite, Prometheus.

The death of the gods has brought concurrently the death

of the demigods, such as the Titans, who might serve as substitute heroes before the higher deities, whom man himself could not approach and defy. The ancient mythical setting has collapsed. Mount Olympus has been replaced by the world of nature, impersonal, magnificent, and incomprehensibly vast. Man has climbed all the mountains, Mount Everest included, or knows he can climb them. Height is no longer the eminence of divinity. What is "up" in the world of relativity? The spacemen are now riding the rockets higher than man once dreamed heaven itself to be.

Zeus hurls no more thunderbolts, but the stars shower us with light and warmth and penetrating cosmic rays. Man still respects the powers of nature, so much mightier than his own, but he no longer fears them as he did Zeus. For these powers, as far as we can see, have no will, intention, or intelligence. The sun shines on the just and the unjust alike, not because of the indiscriminate mercy of Jehovah, but because this is the purposeless physical operation of a great atomic pile. The respect man gives to nature is restrained, since in some ways he has more respect for his own brain than he has for the sun. His brain can think; the sun cannot.

There is a prophecy in the further elaboration of the myth of Prometheus. Prometheus was cleverer than Zeus, being able to play tricks on him, to outwit him by stealing the fire Zeus had forbidden to man. He could also permanently frustrate Zeus, win real victories over him, since Zeus did not take fire back from man once it was given him. Mankind as hero now has an even greater superiority over nature in intelligence than Prometheus had over Zeus. But the myth should give us caution. Zeus still had greater might and could condemn the Titan to endless torture. Nature is still mightier than mankind, and man's own activities may bring penalties upon man from nature that will make the torture of Prometheus look like a blessing.

We may be able to avoid reprisals from nature, since the older myth has been reversed in one fundamental respect. Prometheus was opposed to Zeus, and engaged with him in a contest of wills. But now mankind looks upon nature as a teacher. Man learns from nature and uses nature's powers, but he no longer looks upon himself as being against nature. In fact, through biological evolution from the earth itself (as Prometheus was also born from the earth-mother), man considers himself to be nature as much as is anything else in the world. Man as hero is not a hero against nature as much as he is a hero in nature, and perhaps even a hero of nature.

Man's gratitude to Prometheus as the heroic creator of mankind has no modern counterpart, for mankind is not the creator of itself. Gratitude for the creative process of biological evolution is hard to maintain, since the preferred theories of evolution credit development to chance mutations that happened to have survival value, rather than to any purpose or entelechy within nature. Since only one mutation out of many thousands results in an improvement of the species, while all the others are disastrous impairments, it is hard to justify gratitude to mutations as such.

Just what the feeling tone of gratitude and regard accompanying the myth of mankind as hero should be is still nebulous. Instead of feeling gratitude for receiving from nature, as man received from Athene and Prometheus, ours will be an emotion arising from a sense of participating within nature. It will be an emotion of community and collaboration, and will express itself in festivals celebrating our kinship with mature, rather than in rites and attitudes of supplication and thanks.

What is this element of the "hero" in the myth of mankind? Heroism is commonly defined as action that goes beyond what could be normally expected in the line of duty. The hero gives an overplus in his acts; he is more committed, more strenuous, more dedicated, more altruistic, more self-sacrificing than one would ordinarily expect. Man received much more attention and concern from Prometheus than from the other gods and demigods, so he was mankind's hero.

Here the role of mankind as the hero of nature becomes clear. It is not implied, of course, that the rest of nature will consider man its hero, although even this attitude seems sometimes to be expressed in the regard of a dog for its master. But mankind, as one species developed by the evolutionary processes of nature, sees itself as performing a greater func-

119

tion in nature's scheme of things than could be expected from an animal species.

Parenthetically, it is worth noting that mankind's interference in the natural course of events may turn out to be more destructive than beneficial. Man may destroy the whole experiment of life on earth. This is the demonic and dark side of the new myth. If man presumes to the role of hero, he accepts a responsibility that includes universal destruction as well as universal benefit. Already he threatens to annihilate many of the other species of life, and to turn the green earth into a cinder pile and a sewer. To ignore the satanic aspects of our heroism would be a fatal flaw in our living and working myth. Some of us, looking upon the wasteful and exploitative operation of business, the warfare of nations, and the overbreeding of the race, fear that this part of an adequate mythos has been ignored, and that mankind will be lucky to escape holocaust or even annihilation.

But most myths are essentially optimistic. They constitute man's rationale of expectancy. Mankind certainly aspires to be the positive and creative hero, rather than the malevolent destroyer.

No other species seeks to interfere with the grand course of natural events, except to build nests and hills and burrows for shelter, and to find food for survival. Once physically secure, they relax their efforts; survival is enough. In contrast, man presumes to go beyond the ordinary call of duty, even to rebuilding the earthly landscape, conquering the elements, learning the laws of nature, and aiming at the mastery of communication and travel between the planets and stars of the heavens. The correspondence to the Greek myth is striking. The control of fire is the symbol of man's control over nature. Once the process of taking control is begun, there is no foreseeable end to the possibilities of pioneering. Each horizon reached reveals another lying beyond it.

Heroism goes beyond the expectations of duty. Thus the hero volunteers, elects himself to the task. Humanity now is sufficiently aware of its own capabilities to know that it has elected to become the husbandman and the shaper of the world. The role of the hero has not been forced upon it. Just as Prometheus seems to have volunteered to create and endow humanity, even at the displeasure of Zeus, so mankind has chosen its task, discoveries, and responsibilities. The universe is helpless to deny man his will, for it has no will of its own.

A contrast between the new myth and the old is based on the concept of evolution. The notion of the development of civilization was peculiarly static in the Greek myth. The arts and sciences were regarded as pre-existing in the mind of Athene; they did not need to be discovered or invented. This is an interesting parallel to Plato's theory of the realm of ideas. According to him all things in the universe exist as pure ideas before they ever take imperfect material form.

But today social and cultural evolutions are seen to be as natural as the biological. It has been said that the greatest of all inventions was the invention of invention. The inventors, such as Edison, have assumed heroic stature in our industrial age. The genius, the beginner, the originator, has always been a hero; in religion he is the prophet, the seer. The full scope of the image of mankind as hero lies in the assumption by humanity of the responsibility, not only of attaining knowledge and executing plans, but of creating plans. Mankind must not only bring the ideal into actuality; it must create the ideal itself.

What does humanity not elect to itself in terms of function and responsibility? It does not make of itself a god; this must be clearly understood in the shaping of the new myth. Man is "hero," not "god." The hero is human, and can only reshape what is already given; the god brings reality itself into being, creating out of a void. Man creates new shapes with old materials; material itself he does not create. Man does not create the world, or the laws that pattern its behavior. Man does not create life, or the modes of its processes. Man does not create himself. Here his role is more modest than that of Prometheus, who was conceived as both man and god, and who was the creator of man.

The world of nature is given as the scene of man's adventure. It is the wilderness he must explore. It is the desert he must tame and bring to flower. Man is the husbandman, the domesticator. He is also the planner, the idealist, the purposer, the dreamer, the willer. But his creative role always presumes a stubborn raw material: the world itself, and the laws of nature. Hence the humility in a role that might otherwise seem arrogant. Prometheus was arrogant. The practical joke he played on Zeus had no purpose, except that of the cutup. Before man can learn the ways of nature, he must accept nature and submit his ambitions to the limitations and resources of reality. Only as he learns profoundly what nature is can he know what nature is capable of becoming. He must study how evolution has developed without human control before he can be wise enough to mold the processes of life and growth and bring them somewhat under human direction. Stupidity and ignorance can turn man from hero into devil, proudly presuming to know more than he does, to attempt more than he can do. He can emulate Prometheus, but not Zeus. The myth has no place for arrogance in the character of the hero. The penalties of ignorance and willfulness are too severe to let us conceive of the hero as brash, inconsiderate, stubborn, and violent. Pride there can be — pride in the satisfaction of achievement, of knowledge, of full use of one's powers — and dedication. But the pride is based on humility, sustained by the ability to learn, conditioned by the acceptance of reality.

The myth of mankind as hero is incomplete. It will undergo unceasing growth and clarification. There is evidence of the existence and content of the living, working myth in the daydreaming of humanity. In one form it appears in the hypotheses and plans of the scientists and engineers, in the nature of their projects, and in science fiction. Mankind is not willing to assume that there is any knowledge which it cannot discover. This has ever been the human mood. The artist strives for an excellence, even a perfection, that might have challenged the gods. Perfectionism in religious vocation drove men to asceticism and sainthood. In love and human relations man has, at least at times, sought to make real his own highest ideals.

Now that the twentieth century has opened vistas of space through astronomy, and offers the needed power in atomic energy, man labors to become the pioneer of space, a migrant to other worlds. Thus his myth makes him out to be, not just the hero of planet earth, but possibly the mind, the creative purpose of star system and galaxies. Just as the mythmaking of others ages brought visions of gods of perfect knowledge, perfect power, and eternity, so this later myth has brought dreams of infinity and limitless outreach. The myth is truly epic in scope.

But here again, this is a human myth, not a myth of deity. For man is cautious and realistic enough to assume that a universe in which he developed is surely one in which others like himself, perhaps greater than himself, have also evolved. The great ears of the new radio telescopes are tuned to outer space, hoping to catch messages from other tribes of life, attached to other stars, who themselves may be broadcasting in the hope that their messages will somewhere be received. Mankind as hero may have to share the stage of the universe with other species of heroic, thinking, dreaming creatures.

Always in the role of the hero is the element of self-sacrifice. Prometheus, chained naked to the mountain and eaten alive by a vulture, bore suffering equal to his daring and good deeds. Mankind is also a tragic figure, for tragedy seems to be built into his very nature, inherent in life itself. Any creature that rises to knowledge and power sufficient to enable him to play the role of the hero also knows the nature of his own being, and the fatal limitations that nature imposes.

And man, the creature capable of infinite dreams, and of conceiving and initiating projects that can be achieved only in thousands of years, finds his existence caged within the few years of his lifetime. His inevitable death is his tragedy and, as such, is the final measure of his heroism.

The hero is necessarily a human hero, and we can wonder whether there is any like situation anywhere else. Perhaps the other creatures on other planets have evolved a life system where they do not die, where the poignancy of death and oblivion is unknown. But this is the very stuff of the human myth. Even the Titans could die.

To turn to another ancient hero, mankind will always find itself, in each of its members, playing the role of Moses.

Always we will struggle to bring the Children of Israel into a Promised Land which we ourselves shall not be able to enter. We shall see it, each from the mountains of his own desert, lying beautiful and far off. Reports of it will be brought from those who forge ahead to explore. But we must be able to love our people, our children, enough to strive to bring humanity closer to that world, though we cannot share it with them.

This is the greatness of men and women, that they dream and work and sacrifice, even though they will die. For mankind as hero is a brief and mortal emergence of will and hope, like the youth who dies at the beginning of his first battle. How short is the longest life! How always it seems that we came here only yesterday! How can this brief creature dream of traveling the millions of light-years of space? How can he tackle problems that could baffle a thousand of his brief generations? How can he dare to love so much, to give so much, if he must forsake it all so soon?

This essay into the reinterpretation of one of the myths of the ancient Greeks is included here to give some suggestion as to how the myths of tribal and ethnic groups may be enlarged and expanded until they become myths of all mankind. A religion for one world will, by a process of selection, of trial and error, sift out those myths from the enormous library of man's mythology that continue to have relevance and suggestiveness.

All the myths of past religions have value in themselves, as part of human literature and religious interpretation, as cherished treasures of man's imaginative and idealizing history. But some myths will have the native vigor, the basic and enduring truth, to emerge from their local use to the world scene. They will take on new shapes, new interpretations, even more radical than those suggested for the myth of Prometheus above. But through this regeneration of old myths to interpret the new conditions and necessities of human development, that which is alive in the religious past will continue into the religion for one world. The ancient tribes are the seedbeds of man's future myth-making.

CHAPTER 8

Poets and Religion

When we cease ascribing the religious scriptures to the revelation of the gods, to whom then do we give credit for the bibles of humanity? There is only one possible answer: we must thank the poets of the human race. Religion is man's impassioned affirmation of life. When Jesus gave his definition of the core meaning of religion, he said it was to love God with all your heart, all your soul, and all your mind, and to love your neighbor as yourself. The emphasis is on the act of love. Our religion is our love affair with life, and no man who is not in love with life has a religion worthy of the name. Our religious scriptures, the basic ones and the most used and most influential of all the religious writings, are love poetry. They are love songs written to project our love of life, of humanity, of nature, of beauty, of wisdom, of goodness into expressions of power and celebration. A work of art is an act of celebrating a portion of reality. The art of religion is the most composite and consummate of all the arts, the art of life itself.

In more ancient times life and experience were not crudely divided, as we try to divide them in our times, into the sacred and the secular, the profane and the holy. Thus the anthology of history, myth, proverbs, stories, wisdom, prophecy, and poetry of the Jewish people becomes their religious Bible. Religion and life being the same essential matter, since the poet was concerned with life he was concerned with religion. It is this wholeness and integration of life and society that the naturalist and humanist is seeking in his religion. Life and reality are once again a unity for him, even as they were for his more primitive ancestors. And he is discovering that all the so-called secular arts of our time are the valid and necessary voices of the world of his religious intuitions.

Poets have been called the unacknowledged legislators of humanity. Since, except in China, poets seldom have been involved effectively in matters of lawmaking and government, what kind of truth can such a statement possess? Our answer lies in the relationship of the poets to religious literature. If Mohammed, or any writer, did not receive his words from God, as he was supposed to have done, whence did they come? From Mohammed, of course. If they were not received by revelation, then they came from the prophet's own insights and intuitions. The prophet-poet is the person who is able to ingest the experience and aspirations of his people. He embodies the most profound assumptions and hopes of his people. The questions and arguments of the community become his own interior conversation. The individual prophet-poet, through his powers of observation, appreciation, sympathy, and empathy, can take unto himself the many points of view and problems of his people. Thus he is representative of them all. He is not an elected representative, as are the members of the House and Senate, but by his own abilities, his fitness of identification and comprehension, he creates a valid forum within his own mind and emotions, wherein the debates of his people can take place. If in the churning processes of his integrative and creative imagination he can find answers to the dilemmas of his time, he becomes a new prophet. If he can find the right and powerful words in which to express the new aspiration of his community, which has arisen within himself, he becomes a new scribe, a new "revealer."

Insofar as the prophet-poet has discovered through his own intuition the preferable shape of the future, he is the effective legislator of his race. It makes no difference that he was not elected to this office. It makes no difference if his writings are spurned, even ridiculed, by his own generation. If his insights are adequate, necessary, by their inherent logic and imaginative power, they will write themselves indelibly upon the imagination and memory of the people, even as they attempt to reject them. In fact, the very violence of their rejection proves the power of their penetration and is the first step in the process of examination, argument, and growth whereby the people will convince themselves in time of the necessity of the prophet's adjuration.

Thus, in a naturalistic world view, for the term "revelation" we substitute the term "intuition," and instead of presuming God to be the source, we ascribe the ideas and images to the poets who utter them. It is not the all-knowing mind of God that is the source of the inherent wisdom of the scriptures; it is the enlightened intelligence and imagination and fervor of the self-elected members of the community itself that produce the bibles of the community.

We have been hearing much recently of the necessity of myth in religion and life. Through myths, say the philosophers and students of culture, man creates the images and expectations that enable him to adjust emotionally and effectively to his world. His stories of creation and the gods, his descriptions of the sources of power and sustenance, help him to feel comfortable and at home in the universe. They give meaning and direction to his life.

Perhaps it is not myth which man needs, but that of which myth is only a representation. Myth is a kind of poetry, and its creation and elaboration have been major tasks of the poets of the race. Not only are the myths told in and through poetry, the great epics of the world religions, but the myths themselves are poetic images and analogies. One of the most universal of these is the myth of the dying and rising god, who is a poetic analogy of the growth and decay of vegetation in the cycle of the seasons of the year. The vegetation of the earth becomes Adonis, a beautiful young god, who is born in the springtime, comes to his maturity in the summer, then dies a bloody death as the leaves of the trees turn scarlet in the fall. Through the cold winter he lives in the underworld of death, until he rises to a new life the next spring.

This is in itself a poetical image, which in turn becomes the basis for endless elaborations, a theme for the poets for thousands of years. And before he became scientific about the writing of history, what man recalled of his past was expressed in legend, which merged with myth, to become such epic poems as Beowulf, the Iliad, and the Odyssey, and the stories of Abraham, Jacob, Joseph, Moses, Samson, and David. Where does fact leave off and myth begin? The problem did not occur to primitive man, who made of his history a song to sing, and who was more concerned with giving an account of the spirit and fervor and dreams of his people than with statistics and accuracy of news reporting.

Not only was history turned into legend and myths and poems, but the account of persons was also. The great figures of the past, as they are described by early man, soon became not so much men who lived and walked the earth like ordinary folk but poetic dreams of greatness and heroism in human flesh. They embodied man's dream of his own possible strength and beauty. Thus we must turn to what purports to be description of these early leaders, less to learn what they were themselves, although much of that is also hidden in the legends, than to discover the people's ideals for themselves with which their hero-men were invested.

The heroes, then, are the embodiments of poetical, imaginary qualities. Rather than being the men that were, they are man's dream of his own potential goodness read back into the glamorized figures of the past, until early man cannot tell them from the gods themselves. They become half-god, half-man, or ascend as did Elisha in a fiery chariot, without dying, into heaven; or soon, like Julius Caesar, become a star in the sky; or, in Jesus' case, become the Son of God, and then a member of the Trinity, God of very God.

But might it not be that the need of early man was not so much myth as it was poetry, and myth happened to be the form that man's poetic drive used in those days? The world must pass through the alembic of the human imagination. There the realities of experience are warmed and colored over with man's own emotions; they become not just seen images but felt images. They reside no longer merely in the impersonal landscape, but in the inner landscape of man's memories

128

and dreams. This is no longer just the world; it is man's home, seen through the love with which he gilds that home. And who is to say that his feelings about the world are any the less real than the world concerning which he feels?

Without emotions, the world is not habitable to man as man. He lives by what we have come to call "felt realities," which might also be called realities of feeling. This is the truth that underlies the fancies and seeming absurdities of the myths. Myths are not true as scientific reports of events may be true, but they are true as dramas which embody and release man's feelings, his fears, his terror, his ecstasy, his sense of doom, his hope. They are the true stories of his emotions.

I believe the myths were useful, even necessary, to primitive man, not because he needed myths as such but because he needed vehicles, forms, whereby he could poeticize his experience and his world. It was the poetry of life he needed. Myth was only his verse form, if you will. We still need poetry; we are scarcely human without it. We may not, however, need that *form* of poetry that is myth. There are many other poetic devices. In fact, I believe that myth is a primitive poetic instrument which we have pretty much outgrown. But we have by no means outgrown poetry, nor have we outgrown the indigenous relationship between poetry and religion.

There are some who seem to think we have. They would make religion almost entirely a matter of social issues and social justice. They would make the materials of religious education dry, factual, and scientific. They would measure success in religion, not in poetic qualities, but in the quantitative dimensions of business, in the size and population of their institutions, in statistics of growth, in the amounts of the budgets raised. It is as vulgar to identify religious values with budget figures as it is to judge the worth of a painting by the sum it will sell for in a London auction. Religion has come to imitate the success standards of business, banking, and politics. It forgets that its own prophetic leaders have always stood scornfully apart from such goals and values.

Science and industry have reached certain limited goals by a process of depersonalizing, dehumanizing, depoetizing reality and human relations. Science must remove human preference,

129

prejudice, feelings from its considerations in order to see nature as it is, and not through a deforming mist of human feelings about nature. In order to get a standardized product, quickly and cheaply produced, the similar impersonalities of the machine and assembly-line procedures have made industry almost as dehumanized and cold as science. Automation goes the whole distance and removes man himself, body, feelings, and all, from the productive process. The ideal seems to be a spotless, uninhabited, gleaming factory, wherein no man tracks in either dust with his feet or emotions with his silly heart. We forget that, in order to get a cheap product, we must inevitably fatally cheapen the product itself. For, since we are men, the richness of any object lies in its human values, in its emotional and poetic richness, and these are eliminated from our products by the mechanical means of their manufacture.

All this has meant the degrading of the function and the reputation of the poet, not only in industry and commerce and culture in general, but also in religion, which is really the inward face of our civilization. Society decides that poetry is worthless in this mechanical world. A poem is obviously an inferior machine tool for boring out the cylinder block of a Buick. Rating it as inferior to processed cheese, Corn Kix, and nail polish, the buyers of poetry are so few it is no longer profitable to publish books of poetry. Thus less and less poetry is available to leaven the lump of our world, people read less and less of it, and it is still further debased on the market.

Religion, following meekly the lead of successful business, also cannot see where poetry is very important to its success. In religion, as in the world of Miniver Cheevy, art is on the town. Our own denomination gives this emphasis when it can find moneys for every day, prosy, organizational, promotional, and fund-raising activity but cannot pay a hymnal commission to gather a body of rich poetry and music for the vitalization of the movement's religious worship. Other denominations also expect unpaid commissions to develop their hymnals, but some do supply paid executives, editors and secretaries to carry the brunt of the labor. Except for proofreading, and some funds for expenses during commission meetings and for postage, our commission created the hymnal gratis, and the denomination simply paid for the publication. This is not just a write-off of poetry and songs; it is indirectly — and not very indirectly at that — a confession on the part of our fellowship, or at least of its leaders, that it does not consider the worship, the religious celebrations of liberal religion, worth wasting more than a pittance upon. When it comes to the religious arts themselves, we are out of business.

I would not be caught arguing against science, or industry, or commerce, or organized religion. I am only arguing that these are not the end-all and be-all of life, that indeed they may not be the most important part of life. I will claim that poetry, along with the other arts, now on relief, on the town, eating out of the garbage pails of society — that this beggar is the crown and the glory of life, and worth more ultimately than all these other wealthy and well-favored activities put together.

Some interesting publishing occurred a few years ago. Within a few months of each other, in large, definitive editions running to two and three volumes and up to fifty dollars in price, appeared the complete collected letters of the poet Keats, the poetess Emily Dickinson, and the painter Van Gogh. This constitutes an admission beyond an admission. How important were the poems of Keats and Dickinson, and the paintings of Van Gogh, who was surely a great romantic poet in canvas and pigment? They were so important that, after neglecting them shamefully during their living years, even spurning and abusing them, we now jealously collect every written word of the poets we can find, every letter and note written, and publish these in carefully edited editions, that they may not be lost to humanity.

But what is so important about a lot of old letters? In these letters we find the same poetic imagination, the same intangible sense of life, the same strength and tenderness of dream and ideal, the same inflammability of spirit, that was in the artists' formal works.

What is it that the poet or the painter does? He invents values and meanings, invents them not out of thin air but by rearranging, reconsidering, and pondering the world and life. New experience floods in upon us — now, in this avalanche of communication, science, and research, more than ever before.

131

We ask, "What does it all mean?" That is not the best question. A better one is, "What meaning can we make of it all?" For it may mean nothing until man sees in it potentialities for his own use, potentialities of images, analogies, overtones, relationships, vistas, that cannot be said to be in the material itself. These are there *when man sees them,* for then they are related to the human creatures who so see them, feel them, and use them.

Perhaps we can use the function of art itself as an analogy. A potter takes a lump of clay and forms a vessel out of it, decorating it with symbols and figures, rendering it with high artistic skill, coloring it beautifully, and firing it with a magnificent glaze. As material it is still just so much common clay and pigment. But man has shaped meanings, values, beauties upon this material, to make it a rich object in his eyes. Do these values exist in it without man?

The poet performs such a function upon the materials of the world, upon human experience, also, but he does it without shaping and firing the clay. That is, he does not mold it with his hands or with tools, or bake it in a kiln. But he does change the world: he changes the world *as man sees it and feels it.* He glazes the clay of the world with ideas, images, emotions, relationships, values. Just as the potter makes the clay *worth more* in his reshaping and glazing of it, so the poet makes the world *worth more* by showing us how to see more of worth in the world and in our relationships with the world.

There must have been a time when gold and diamonds went unnoticed, undiscriminated by primitive man. There must have been men who mused over these objects, became attracted to the soft yellow of the gold and the clear hardness of the diamond. In nature these two elements have no especial value, but they find value in man's eyes. How revealing that old construction is. The value they have is *in man's eyes.* Man puts value into them, through his act of appreciation. In this sense he creates values by giving values to things that had no value before, for no one had evaluated them before. It is like saying that no person is beloved until someone has come who loves him.

In the sense in which we are using the term, the men who

made gold into a *precious* metal and the diamond into a *precious* stone were poets; they gave emotional, imaginative, and poetical values to objects that did not possess them before, and then taught all other men to see these same values. Thus they added goodness to the human scene, this world, and to human lives, by initiating men into new realms of appreciation and value uncreated before them. Jesus said, "I come that you might have life, and have it more abundantly." In this he spoke as a poet, for the poet creates abundance, adds to the potential abundance in the felt realities of the world. For in extending the range and application of feelings, he increases the realms of realities that can be felt and the feelings we are capable of having about them.

But the poet not only creates or discovers new abundance in the world about us, as a moment's reflection will disclose. For he has not changed the shape of that world, as the potter does. What he has done, essentially, is to enlarge the abundance of intuitions, concepts, imaginative meanings, and associations within the human mind; he has elucidated and enlarged our capacities for feelings and made more subtle and delicate our perception of and evocation of feelings. He is primarily the explorer of himself and, by implication, of all the other men related generically to him.

How does he work? First he falls in love, or he discovers love within him, even as he discovers his own blood. He explores that love and then finds himself driven to seek words, images, rhythms, and rhymes to convey his feelings to others. He tries to make the poem *be* his feeling, to make the same feeling be in the structure, the existence of the poem, the painting, the sculpture, the song, that he knows inside himself. If he can do this, another man can sense the emotional, imaginative realities and dimensions in the poem and thereby see them for the first time. Through his art, the poet lends his sensibilities to another. In this way he can *show* his love, his dream.

And this is what religious revelation has always been about, some of us think. This is where creation, spiritual creation, is at work in the universe. In his own experience, his feelings, his image-making mind, that surprises himself in producing ideas he knows not whence (probably the poet himself was

133

the originator of the idea that they came from some outer source) — the poet in his introspection finds he is revealing himself to himself. This is a revelation in the sense of uncovering so that the eye can see. Then, having uncovered something new to himself, in his poems he uncovers it to other men. He reveals.

It should be a sobering thought in our materialistic, giant-production-minded world that the most meaningful and essential labor of man needs no machinery, no raw materials at all. For many poems have been completed wholly within the mind of the poet, needing not even to be written down. In fact, man had long and rich oral traditions in poetry, and in religion, its other name, before he invented writing. At best all he needs is pencil and paper. The best things in life are free? Free in material cost, but you cannot escape the expense of the spirit. The poets are at work today, paying the old price of neglect, of anguish and discipline to find the exact word, the apt image, the one rhythm. But do not pity them, for the poet is the last man you need to tell of the importance of his task.

Just insofar as each man is about his love affair with life, and seeking ways of making that love manifest, he is a poet, consumed in the art of life and its expression, and just to that extent he is also religious.

CHAPTER 9

The Celebration of Life

ART AND WORSHIP

Persons in the Protestant tradition living in the United States in the mid-twentieth century are, by the nature of their traditions and environment, more poorly prepared to appreciate the potential relationship between art and worship than any other people in history. The reasons are basically two: Protestantism, more than any other major religious movement, has been prejudiced against the use of art an instrument of religious life; and our society, based upon a highly developed machine technology, now moving into its automation phase, has depleted the labor and activity of the people of living artistic expression, religious or otherwise.

In order to understand the full potential of the relationship between art and worship, because of the negative attitudes of Protestantism we must turn to other cultural traditions than our own. The deformity of Protestantism in this regard is so atypical, even unique, in the entire cultural evolution of the race that almost any other religion chosen at random would serve our purpose better. Even Islam and Judaism, eschewing as they do the plastic arts, are still far more involved in the arts than is Protestant Christianity, from which liberal religion has inherited its basic characteristics. Islam has calligraphy, architecture, prayer rugs, metalwork, and pottery, and, inconsistently, even painting. The only painting I have seen of

135

Mohammed had his face covered. Judaism has calligraphy, the daily rituals of the observance of its laws, many menorahs, lamps, spice boxes, scrolls, scroll cases, arks and ark covers, Torah shields and crowns, and phylacteries, along with plates and vessels and special foods for the sacred meals.

Protestantism is now somewhat recovering from its anti-Catholicism, in which all crosses, robes, statuary, and ritual splendor were rejected along with Rome. It reached its nadir, aesthetically speaking, in the Friends' meeting, where even the art of speech is passed by in favor of silence. Almost as iconoclastic, artistically, are the services of the Ethical Societies and some humanistic Unitarians, where a worship service is made up of a lecture patted on each end by some piano music. The lecture itself must be delivered without heat and prejudice, foregoing even the art of oratory. There is little Protestant art of any kind worthy of the name. What architectural originality Protestantism has developed lies in the stark simplicity of the New England meeting house. The ungainly brutalities of the "barnyard Gothic" of the midwest should be eliminated by a sort of religious slum clearance project.

Liberal religion, in its beginnings, was but the Protestant Reformation carried to its inevitable conclusions, and Puritan Protestantism at that. I know of only one parish that had Episcopalian origins, although others have sought to assimilate them. I have often wondered whether any kind of social instrument was ever invented as resistant to aesthetic treatment and adornment as our "order of service." Even the name "order" has a cold, sterile tone to it. Most of these orders are rational, not aesthetic in conception, stringing together unrelated bits of readings, hymns, anthems, solos, collections, and announcements. If, by chance, some element of the service has artistic efficacy, you can be sure the service as a whole lacks artistic integrity and development and organic harmony, such as give the Mass its structure and splendor.

Even in those elements where we have laid stress our record is thin and spotty. A few prayers have literary merit. A rare minister carries preaching to an art. But how few sermons bear reading in print, where the lack of prose style cannot be masked by the resonances of the pulpit voice. Some hymns deserve the name of musical art, but seldom does the singing. Although there is a considerable body of great choral music, its performance is comparatively rare. Music is predominantly on the organ, the most mechanical and impersonal of all instruments. The great bulk of Protestant hymnody is trash, musically and literarily, and the product of the anthem factories is indescribable. Even so, music is the one art not entirely scanted, although a fanatical fringe of the Reformation did make out the innocent piano to be an instrument of the devil.

What are the arts, splendid in other religious traditions, that mainly go begging in our own? Architecture (we are mainly concerned with shelter and floor space for seating and classrooms), sculpture, painting, the dance ritual, drama, lighting (i.e., lamps, candelabra, rose windows), censers (where there is smoke there must be fire), torch processions (our imitations are febrile), ceremonial dances with masks and drums, ritual painting (sand painting of the Navahos), calligraphy and illumination of holy books, poetry (such as the Zen haiku), symbolism, gateways and shrines, processionals, myth-making, ritual arts of food, bathing, and daily ceremonials (Hindu daily rituals and prayers of Islam), religious decorations of beads, crucifixes, clothing.

It would seem almost impertinent for us, who have so massively denied the arts and their usage, to presume to judge what the relation between art and religious expression and appreciation can be. How could we know, since we have not attempted to find out? Which brings us to the second handicap we face: the nature of the technological society in which we live. The machine is the deadly enemy of arts of all kind. Art is the production of goods, enriched with style, with the creator's vision of beauty, imagination, and personality. Anything made by the person himself (handmade) can serve as a medium of that person's self-expression and creative development. The act of artistic making, of creating, is itself an act of worship, in my opinion the highest of all. Worship can take place in the studio and the workshop as well as in the temple. Which is the greater act of worship, thinking about the act (meditation), talking about the act (preaching), agonizing about the act (prayer), or doing the act itself? "In their handi-

137

work is their prayer." Perhaps when we turn making over to machines, in order to become mere consumers, in losing our own human function, the creative arts, we lose at once the combined values of both art and religion. Then our religion becomes talk and detached, unproductive "services" (without functional service) and our art become a piddling dilettantism. Art for the sake of art has lost its vital embodiment in the meaningful and daily activities of life. When we detach "self-expression" from the menial (that is necessary) labors of the self, there is little self left to "express."

Our inadequacy to estimate the relationship between art and worship is thus profoundly bedded in the fact that we have ceased to live by artistic means and sensibilities. The average person's relationship to the arts is more and more considered to be that of appreciator, not of creator. The "artistic" person is one who likes to listen to good music, look at good paintings, and read good literature. Only a few people need be creators, artists, since by reproductions, recordings, films, radio, television, printing, their products can be made available to endless millions. Thus, with the machine as dispenser, art becomes another form of consumership.

The church presumes to be the creative leaven in the dough of the world. All too often it is but a borrower, an imitator. Since the majority of the people seem to be content with the observer's role in the arts, even in living itself (watching movies and TV rather than living life), the church in its services continues to put the parishioner in the role of the fan, the onlooker. It is enough for him (or more often her) to submit to a service arranged by another, listen to paid singers sing, paid instrumentalists play, paid prayers pray, and paid preachers preach. Is there perhaps a special art of pew-sitting, a way for the churchgoer to be involved in the art of worship? Of course, some kind of creative exercise is supposed to be going on within the worshiper, but what kind of subterranean art is this?

My personal judgment on the relationship of art and worship is that ideally they are one and the same thing; their identity is total. The term "art" denotes the most profound dimensions of worship, and the term "worship" denotes the most profound developments of art. (I say "worship" only because it is in common usage to denote the activity of religious concern and sensibility, but personally I prefer the term "celebration of life.") As was said earlier, however, we must turn to other cultures for illustrations.

What is most impressive about tribal societies is the unity of their view of the relationship among the individual, the tribe, and the universe. There is no sacred and secular in the tribal world. Every act and thought has religious dimensions, since everything shares in the tribal mystique. Thus we can say that all the art of an African tribe is religious art, for nothing created escapes involvement in the network of myths and relationships that is the tribal view of the world.

The carver of masks and fetish statues in an African village, for instance, has a position of religious importance similar to that of a priest in our society. The statuary he carves has religious "being," sacredness. The carving of a mask is itself a ritual act, as is the dance and ceremony. The figures carved to represent ancestors are believed to contain the spirits of the ancestors. Living itself, in the tribal world, becomes an enlarged religious ritual. Every daily act — eating, dressing, hunting — has its ritual dimensions. The tribe develops an artistic style, an artistic personality, so that all Yoruba creations, for example, have one character. Here, without a doubt, the performance of the arts is the performance of worship. Art and worship are one.

It is this integrity, or oneness, that life and religion in our civilizations (so-called) have lost. Both art and worship are fractured, rifled, emasculated, because our culture no longer has a single unifying view of life and the universe. We have no vital, consuming religious vision, but rather a horde of fragmentary, competing religious visions. Where these generate deep religious convictions, they are more likely to produce partisanship and fanaticism than profound religious creativity. The splintery, disintegrated, jittery turbulence of much contemporary painting only reflects the disruption of religious wholeness in our society. The same characteristics are found in much of our music, poetry, drama, and fiction. Our art, rather than being religious art, is art produced by the decay

139

and disintegration of the religious vision.

The tribal societies, their religions, and their splendid religious arts are now part of human history. This phase of human cultural evolution is over. Are we moving toward a larger "tribalism," in which the earth is one tribal area and mankind is one tribe? Some "universalists" believe that we are, and that we are moving toward a new unity of vision, into another "one world," which will again produce that unity of art and worship signalizing the immediacy and vitality of both. If this vision can be attained by individuals and small groups now, however long it takes the majority of humanity to come to it, they may again be able to demonstrate the unity of art and worship in terms of modern knowledge and relationships, even as past cultures have splendidly exercised it.

The attribute that characterizes both art and worship at their profoundest levels is significance. I have coined a word in order to call it the "profundation" of experience, the deepening or "profunding" of meanings. This characterizes every serious effort of artistic creation and appreciation. The meaning seems to be tangibly, realistically determined only in the discovery of its expression. We know when we are able to say. Through artistic expression the inner vision is turned outer and becomes sharable, a basis of communion. The mystic seeks art in order that his unsayable vision can be declared. Poetry and painting and music are the languages of mysticism. I doubt there is any considerable religious activity and vigor without a corresponding activity and vigor in the arts. Religious power demands and seizes its requisite means of declaration, and these are the arts. Any religious movement which can be satisfied with secondhand religious arts is a secondhand religion, a borrowing from its betters.

Having lost a profound sense of significance in our times, we are driven in our secular arts to express our conviction of insignificance. And the religious arts, so-called, can only parrot the symbols, myths, and arts of those past ages when a sense of significance drove man to sing psalms of jubilation. But how weakly we sing them, thus removed from their sources of vigor. We could rationalize a separation between art and worship only when worship had become dead, because man

140

had no sense of the significance of himself and his world to give it life. In times like these we need no art because we have no valid worship to employ it.

This sense of religious significance is described by Dorothy Lee in *Freedom and Culture* in the traditional world view of the Hopis before outside invasion disrupted their tribal life.

Human society is a part of a larger structured whole, so an individual cooperates with even more than the members of his human group. Every aspect of nature, plants and rocks and animals, colors and cardinal directions and numbers and sex distinctions, the dead and the living, all have a cooperative share in the maintenance of a universal order. Eventually, the effort of each individual, human or not, goes into this huge whole. And here, too, it is every aspect of a person which counts. The entire being of the Hopi individual affects the balance of nature; and as each individual develops his inner potential, as he enhances his participation, so does the entire universe become invigorated. Not his behavior alone, but his entire unique being is significant.

Much of the time and energy of the Hopi goes into working at ceremonials. These are highly organized and form part of an established ceremonial cycle. Each ceremony "belongs to" a secret society, usually a men's society and only members of this society have the privilege and the responsibility of carrying out the ceremony. Each ceremony involves an exceedingly complex order of detailed acts: preparatory rites, acts of purification, gathering of materials, preparation of masks and sand paintings and medicine water, composition of new songs, rehearsal of dances. The women prepare food to be exchanged reciprocally. The ceremonials themselves last nine or seventeen days. Though only one secret society is charged with the responsibility of a specific ceremony, the entire group of "spectators" — all the villagers and visitors from other pueblos who come to the performances — eventually participate, through keeping a "good heart," through their wholehearted involvement in what they watch, through laughing at the burlesque and pranks afforded by the clowns.

Each main ceremony has reference to a phase of the

agricultural cycle, helping the universal order to become actual. . . Each main ceremony also has reference to the whole of life, to the entire cosmic system. The aim is the well-being of the universal whole, not of the individual. If the individual profits by the ceremonial, it is because he is an integral part of this whole which has become invigorated. The individual maintains harmony with the universe for the sake of the universal order, and only derivatively for his own sake. Eventually, through the maintenance of this harmony, the human group thrives, the sun moves along its established course from solstice to solstice, the thunderclouds gather and release their rain, the corn sprouts and roots and fills and ripens.

In such a world view, the being of each person, and each of his acts, is imbued with significance. "Every individual within the system has his unique role, and each role is different and indispensable." Thus all of the person's acts are considered as ritual and art, and this implication is only heightened and concentrated in the major ceremonials. The life of such people is profoundly artistic; we treasure their pottery, blankets, masks, and ceremonial dolls, and travel miles to watch their ceremonies. It would be utter nonsense to try to separate their art of song, dance, costume, drama, from their worship, for their worship is one long artistic performance.

But here art is ennobled with ultimate meaning. There is no isolated, lonely, neglected artist, attempting to create his own private symbolism and mythology and express it in his poems and painting. Here the artist functions meaningfully, indispensably, for his society and for his universe. It was when religious art had such import, in Egypt, Babylonia, Greece, China, India, in medieval Christianity, in the tribal societies of the Hopis and the Yorubas, that the profoundly great religious art was created. Our disassociated, individualized artists strive frantically, but hopelessly, to capture for their private symbolism that power and magnitude to be found in a Japanese Buddha, a dancing Siva, a Sung landscape, a great bull from Persepolis, a Mayan stele, a Gothic Madonna, and they fail. Such art is capable of being produced only when the artist is creating within the realm of ritual significance of a great religious culture. It takes more than a personal religion, which some of our artists have, to imbue such works. The artist must be the creative hands of the sense of religious significance of a people and a tradition. Thus he becomes more than himself, and the powers of the integral community, of many centuries, flow through him and into his work. Then his art is the worship of his people, their worship of their world.

What religious arts of worship there are among us worthy of notice are an inheritance from the past, a past that recedes farther and farther from the needs and sensibilities and convictions of the present and of tomorrow. Art and worship are divorced. The artist concentrates on his own umbilical emptiness, and his works are sterile. The church, having no creative arts, withers, becomes stale and trite with a triteness centuries dry. Our religious art lies in the exhibition of mummies.

But a new vision of the world is upon us, a universe new to man's eyes and understanding, a world-wide human community painfully gathering itself. New symbols, new songs, new dances, and new temples will come forth to declare it. For as this new vision of man and his world accumulates, clarifies, and comes into focus, men and women will have to portray it. They will need to celebrate it. When they know the significance of their beings and their deeds in this newly envisioned world, they will create new ceremonials.

For man the artist and man the worshiper are one man, and his arts are the words and gestures of his worship. Without his creations he does not create himself. His fullness is to make his every work both a work of art and an act of worship. Anything less defiles his person, foreshortens his exultation, and blasphemes against his dreams.

Art has become in our time a kind of consumership. With our many means of reproduction of music, paintings, sculpture, and literature, and with factory techniques for the manufacture of furniture, ceramics, jewelry, clothing, means of communication — even assembly-line houses — we tend more and more to identify art as a product, something to be consumed or appreciated.

But art is primarily the creative activity and experience of the artist, rather than the possession of the product. The artist's experience in conceiving, projecting, and rendering his insights and inspirations is the fundamental artistic experience. The appreciative experience of the non-creator, who must receive art as a finished product, without any participation in the process of production itself, is secondary.

Those who are involved in the creation of art, and who have experienced both the creative process and the appreciative process, cannot help comparing the two. Rewarding as art appreciation is, it cannot measure up to that experience in which the entire being of the artist is fulfilled in conceiving and creating his own artistic vision.

If we approach the religious experience — call it worship, or celebration, or what you will — from this point of reference, what is there to say about the experience of artistic creativity itself as religious experience? If we go to the experience of the artist himself, to see how he is involved in relating to the world about him, conceptualizing the world and his situation in it, we can say that all artistic creativity is a religious activity, not just that which produces the icons, temples, and rituals of what we especially designate religion.

All artistic creation involves certain formal, aesthetic, intuitional, idealistic concerns that are quite impractical and non-commercial. They are closely related to, if not identical with, what in religious parlance have been called "spiritual" values. Although the artist works with materials — stone, wood, cloth, pigments, sounds — his product, as art, is not "materialistic." Although he may make instruments that have practical usage, such as tools, their artistic, aesthetic proportions, their adornment, that which makes them works of art, is not essentially utilitarian. We must make one demurrer from this argument, to the effect that form does follow function, especially in tools, and the ultimacy of gracefulness and aesthetic value may be identical with the most perfect shape of utility. The streamlining of automobiles and airplanes is a case in point, as is the grace of a surgeon's scalpel.

But the artist is not primarily concerned with making materialistic products. The material out of which the work is made carries quite "immaterial" meanings through the structure, rhythms, and harmonies that invest it. The concreteness of a work of art is its most superficial aspect. The medium, whatever it may be, becomes a carrier of language, of meanings quite beyond the realm of wood, stone, plaster, sound, or whatever. The primary end or use of art lies in its expressibility. Its function lies beyond its material.

It is this aesthetic, ideal function of art that gives every act of artistic creativity and every artistic expression those values and meanings that we call religious. It gives art its place in religious worship and celebration. Works of art run the gamut of significance from trivial to profound, from silly to sublime, but then the celebration of life and the universe also encompasses the full range of reality and can find room for the full range of man's arts.

Is art something to be used in worship, or is the experience of creativity itself worship? The art work is only the end result of the process of creation. The art is the process of the painting; the picture is what remains when the creative process comes to a halt. If the artist is concerned to interpret the world about him, his creation will involve the opening of himself to the world. Much as a worshiper opens himself to the realities which he worships, the artist opens himself completely to whatever he addresses, invites the response of his total self to it. He engages the self-revelations of nature with his own imagination, intuitions, and meanings. In his works he renders his interpretation of reality and of his experience with reality and states something (never all) of the wonder of this encounter. The frustration of the artist is that he is never able, in his art, to declare all that he discovers in this state of openness.

The work of art is the way the artist communicates with his fellows. He is never more responsive, more open, more sensitive, more self-realized, than when he is absorbed in creation. Some artists become so preoccupied with the creative process itself that they have little interest in their work when it is done. The end is the act of painting itself, not the picture produced. Here is the most decisive indictment of our consumer culture. Man is not most himself when he consumes, even when he consumes works of art, but rather when he creates.

What then is the function of the appreciation of the works of other artists? If the appreciator is to realize the full potentiality in any work, he must relive the process by which it was created. The experience of the artist in its creation is the true message of the work. This is what it "says."

I once became so engrossed in hearing one of Schubert's symphonies that it seemed as if I were writing it as it was played. The experience was as shattering as any of my own creative experiences because, as far as I was able, I went through the emotional and intuitional experience of re-creating the music within myself. I have had similar experiences with paintings, sculpture, architecture, and poetry. Unless the appreciator has got everything, experientially, from the work that the artist discovered, expressed, and experienced in its creation, he has not fully known it. In this sense the meaning of the term "religion" or "worship" lies in that saturation of significance and beauty to be found in the most profound experience of artistic creation and appreciation.

One could object that art is very much a conscious discipline, a matter of exercising acquired skills. Art is also a matter of tedious practice. But these acquired skills are only agencies whereby the artist accomplishes something that skill and discipline alone cannot attain, that conscious planning cannot prefigure. A time comes when deep, unconscious motivations and intuitions take over the overt and conscious processes, and the carefully acquired skills are used to declare something that skill itself could not create.

At this point the artistic disciplines, acquired in long years of patient and often uninspired labor, become the means of expressing the religious experience. Those insights, "revelations," that are ecstatic and integrative take form and utterance in and through the language forms and mediums that the artist has mastered. Through his disciplines the artist can give expression to religious experience and communicate it to others. Through the images, symbols, and associations whereby he expresses his own experience he recalls and interprets for others *their* own experiences. If the expression is sufficiently powerful, it can evoke its own religious experience in the appreciator, even as it did in the artist during the process of creation.

146

There is a question whether man was capable of having such religious experiences before he acquired the means to express them. The limits of our capacity to experience run parallel to the limits of our capacity to conceptualize, symbolize, imagine, and express. There is no religious experience, on the human level, except through the cumulative agency of millennia of human culture and artistic activity. The artists, the poets, novelists and dramatists, create language, and language is the means whereby we think and dream, and, perhaps, love. If we have no creative religious arts ourselves, and in our own times, then we are capable of religious experience and celebration only because we have inherited the wealth and agency of thousands of years of artistic creativity in the richer generations that preceded us.

The great artists are persons who live in a profound unity with the world about them, and within themselves. Out of a continuous openness and response to the world, they bring forth their works, which are their side of a continuous conversation between them and reality. The person who has reached religious fullness always lives in this unity; it is the constant temper of his daily life. The Zen Buddhist calls this state enlightenment or satori. He no longer needs meditation or worship to establish this unity, for it is his constant province of being. The Chang landscapes of the Sung Dynasty are expressions of the continuius unity of man with his universe. The highest art of China and Japan was this expression of the Chang or Zen religious experience and philosophy. Here we find the full unity of art and worship, and the work of art becomes the most profound expression of the religious experience.

It may be that we will be able to develop forms of religious celebration which incorporate the act of artistic creation itself and do not rely entirely on the performing of previously created works. This spontaneity is so essential a part of Negro spirituals, for instance, that they are almost totally dead when sung as completely arranged and set pieces. In Hindu music the raga is an extemporization on a given scale, using the accumulated learning, skill, and tradition which the musician has acquired. The raga is thus a free creative experience

147

as well as a performance. Much of contemporary jazz has this openness and extemporaneous nature. It is of interest that in earlier periods European composers often extemporized when playing concerts, and that recitals of all kinds allowed much more freedom in interpretation on the part of the concert artist than would be tolerated today. Such composers as Lukas Foss have attempted to make arrangements for a kind of planned extemporaneity within their compositions.

Perhaps the ideal utilization of artistic creativity in religious celebration or worship would combine developed skills and disciplines with the openness and surprise of the act of artistic creation. It is just here that the Friends, who neglect most of the arts of worship, have excelled. Their services invite fresh creative utterance on the part of the worshipers, as they are prompted by the Inner Light to speak.

CELEBRATION OF LIFE

Man has an inherent need to celebrate. When we get a raise on the job, we rush home and tell the wife to dress up — we are going out to celebrate. We celebrate turning points in our national history, such as the Fourth of July. We celebrate the birthdays of great men and the anniversary of the day Columbus discovered America. Our seasonal celebrations go far back beyond the beginnings of historical memory to celebrations of the yearly solstices, of spring and harvest. We treasure the personal celebrations of birth, puberty, marriage, and death.

Religion is slowly changing its focus and attitudes, as increasing knowledge changes our views of ourselves and the world. Emphasis is swinging from the worship of a god or a savior myth to the natural world and the ideals of the human venture. It is the opinion of some that this reorientation eliminates the necessity of worship, that the purpose of worship was only to placate supernatural powers. We can now lie abed on the day of the sun, named for the sun worship of old paganism. Long before mankind worshiped a supernatural deity, he sought to find means of influencing the powers of nature, the sun, the moon, the elements, and the seasons.

Even though we may no longer need to worship the supernatural, there still may be value in celebrations, in meditations, in the use of the arts to extend and deepen our feelings, our sense of significance and meaning. The person who has no need of celebrations, whether sacred or secular, natural or supernatural, is a dull fellow. There are people who are simply not moved. Art, beauty, success, and tragedy leave them phlegmatically unresponsive, a sign of either lack of intelligence or emotional insensitivity, of deep inner conflict that inhibits a healthy release of feelings.

Most of us are born responsive and excitable creatures, but we are often stultified by our culture until we have no vital enthusiasms. The weight of mass culture has buried our native liveliness under a swamp of habits and routine. The Bill of Rights guarantees us religious liberty, but of what value is this if we have no religious enthusiasms to exercise? Of what value are the means to education, to the arts and music, to the theater and literature, if we are such stolid creatures that we are unmoved to capitalize upon our opportunities?

The person who has lost his orthodox religion but has no motivation to create and enjoy a free and liberal religion is in the same straits. He is liberated *from* the imprisonment of creeds, but he is not liberated *into* the creative enjoyment of the celebration of life, as an outflow of natural exuberance from human experience.

When I was twenty I went with a friend to visit his girl. When we left her house Duane yelled, "Wow," ran down the block, grabbed a light post and swung himself around in mid-air. That was a celebration of life. Daily events are common only because we degrade them in our attention and estimation. The stars when we get a chance to see them clearly, bright clouds on a summer afternoon, the animations of a child, a drink of cold water should stir us to the feeling of celebration. There is no moment of any day or night when the world around us and the flowing of life within us are not sufficient to provoke an exclamation of delight. No one is so pitiable as he who stands bored while the overwhelming universe pours down over his ears.

A truth is startling, for any event seen freshly is a violent experience. We are either strongly attracted or repelled. The same applies to the arts, whereby we communicate to each other the import of our experiences. If the art carries the meaning of the original experience to the hearer or viewer, it will elicit a reaction comparable to the original event. It will also have a "shock of rightness" as art relative to its capacity to evoke feeling and a conviction of verisimilitude.

Celebration is no new idea in worship. Ritualistic religions are busy with celebrations of divine events. Christmas celebrates the birth of Christ, Good Friday celebrates his martyrdom, and Easter his resurrection. The Eucharist celebrates the power of the Saviour to forgive and redeem. Sabbath worship is the weekly celebration of the presence and power of God. The sacraments celebrate specific efficacies of divine power. One speaks of "the celebration of the Mass."

The interpretation of worship as "celebration" was developed by Von Ogden Vogt in his *Art and Religion*. The book offers a key to the reinterpretation of the mood and attitude of religious services that is especially apt for the religious naturalist and the universalist. Celebration is an act of affirming and rejoicing in a significant object or event. It is an act of personal and social imagination, concerned with the recollection of past events and the anticipation of coming events. The act of imagination is projected through ritual and dramatic ceremony. Celebrations have a monumental function. They not only signify that to which they specifically apply but imply the overarching structure of the culture and reach out to connect with the continuum of the universe.

The quest for an inclusive object for celebration is the same as that of Schweitzer in seeking a locus for reverence. The unavoidable answer is the reverence for life and the celebration of life. Life is the richest and most suggestive word for what is implied in the background and presence of the living creature. It is a general and inclusive word, yet a word of sharply specific import. It carries a freight of meanings and implied emotions. In Chinese there is but one word for both "religion" and "life," and the best translation for the concept of the *Tao* is "the way of life."

The naturalist relates to the sustaining forces of his natural environment. In a religion for one world we are conscious of the life forces of the multitude of the human family. Each creature depends upon the cooperative activity of the other creatures of life, the elements, the soil, the sun and the heavens, and, in farthest range, the entire universe. Ecology attempts to comprehend the complex interrelationship of living organisms and their surrounding environments. To understand life we must understand the universe that supports life, which is but one small activity in the burning of the galaxies. To celebrate life we must celebrate the universe.

If our celebration of the universe is not to be a mawkish and occult affair, it must have a specific and realistic focus within the universe, a central theme. Beginning with that theme all nature may be implied, but without a dominant motif our celebrations will diffuse into a devotional fog. Although we are celebrating the entire universe, we are centering upon one aspect in the total behavior of nature, that localized and specialized development we call life. It is proper that we do this, for we are living creatures, and we cannot help seeing the universe from the point of view of living creatures. The universe is important to us because in it we have evolved and by it we are sustained. In our egoism we place more value upon life than upon other types of physical and chemical activity. We judge, with inevitable naïveté, that the rest of the universe is significant because it supports life.

This is excusable, since this is *our* celebration. We are celebrating the universe as our home as an expression of our needs and our emotions. Since our experience is human, anything in which men are involved is inherently humanistic. Our celebrations of life must always be most immediately the celebration of human life. We have sympathy for other forms of life, in what we call the fellowship of life, but this begins with and circles back upon the human situation. We may never prize any other creatures with the self-centered devotion we accord our own species. Since the survival of the species is of primary importance to us, it is just as well that we do not. We must be able to destroy some pests and bacteria to insure our own security.

With the maturing of the theory of evolution, we have come to appreciate the unity of life as well as its diversity. All life

151

is but the exfoliation of the one tree of life; the family of life is but one family. It is possible to view the entire evolution of life on the planet as a single event. In all its detail and variety, it is still microscopic as an event in comparison to the infinities of time and space in the universe. Seen in the perspective of universal dimensions, the entire panorama of life is a particular and definable happening which we can celebrate. It is worthy of our celebration. The orthodox are stirred to religious devotion by the myth of creation, and we can be as powerfully stirred by the drama of evolution. A museum of natural history is a temple to the celebration of life. When we are fully identified with nature, the events of natural history become our religious history. An understanding of them is religious education.

In the celebration of life we are celebrating the energy and structure of nature, out of and through which life evolves and is sustained. There is a fundamental difference between the celebration of life and the more traditional kind of religious celebration. The latter tends to honor a finality above and behind the flux of events. God endures as a perfect and unchanging figure. But in nature we can foresee no final shape to events. There is no heavenly destination to anticipate. We learn to prize and celebrate the movement, the energy, and the journey that is nature.

Flux and change of themselves are meaningless and uninspiring. They are chaos and madness. We must discern in them a theme and development, a continuity of meaning, some area of progress and increase of value. This we can perceive in tracing the chain of life's movement through the chaos of the universe at large. There is a directional drift, a nisus, in life's development. Smuts call it the "holistic" principle, the tendency in nature to develop into ever more complex wholes. Life grows from large molecules in the virus to single cells, then to many-celled and many-organed creatures, and up to man. There has been a gradual progression toward complexity, sensitivity, and finally intelligence. We have no reason to believe that the development of life will not go on for many millions of years.

In the celebration of life we move from the contemplation

152

of the fixed about which all change revolves to the contemplation of the stream of events that possesses stability only in terms of a constant movement toward an undefined goal, a goal that flees before the ability of the imagination of man ever to finally fashion it. The art that best expresses life is the art of movement, song, dance, and drama. These cannot be known apart from their fragile performance in time. They cannot be translated into other terms than those of their own flowing structure.

Our lives are such movement, our hearts the metronomes beating out the rhythm of the dance of life. Our breath furnishes the inescapable cadence. The phrasing of the day and night, the developing movements and themes of the seasons, the symphonic development of the ages of man, to the last dying fall and the echoes lost in the silence of death — it is the song of life that we celebrate.

The celebration of life issues from the discovery of the universe around us, and from social and shared experience. It is also something intimate, native to each personal experience, and ultimately unsharable. We can share with no one else the sense of our heart's beating, the constant savor of saliva on the tongue, the weariness of our bones. The sense of time working in and through him is each man's personal knowledge. To experience life is to be life. In celebrating life we are celebrating our most secret and incommunicable selves as well as celebrating the universe swinging over us. The universe beneath our skins is as immense as that whole of which we are the merest atom. Infinities of time and history are composed in our brief days. If we can escape in our imagination from our entrapment in flesh and time, we can comprehend our private histories as identical with the universe, our future life extending into the untouchable tomorrows.

Those who have been burdened by duty, forced to stay too long in one place, may have the chance to go on a journey. They have an urgency to see all they can. For centuries mankind has thought itself to be closed in a narrow locality. Now the release has come and the universe has been opened for our escape, through our imagination, understanding, and creative powers, into the immense auditorium of nature. A child taken from the small rooms of his home into the spaces of a public hall has an uncontrollable urge to run up and down its length; so we have been dashing about this great room. Shortly we will learn to move serenely in the expanse. Life will become a grand journey.

Persons on a journey often sing together, for the sense of travel is one with the movement of song. As we get the sense and rhythm of the journey of life, it too will bring us a need for song. Then what we have called worship will be named the celebration of the journey, the song of life.

CHAPTER 10

Mysticism and World Religion

Mysticism does not offer a sufficient remedy for the ills of the individual personality or a solution for world strife. It is a necessary element in both personal and social health, but by itself it is a formless and directionless surge of feeling and response. Like water, it has great power and usefulness, but it must be put in a container to have form and stability. And it tends to take on the shape of the container into which it is put. The containers of mysticism are the dominant ideas, myths, and expectancies of the culture in which it arises.

In this sense our powers of feeling are like our powers of thought. We can think only with and through the concepts, the language, the patterns of rhetoric, and the store of knowledge that our culture provides us. Our thinking is much more conclusively limited by the language and grammar of our culture than we had heretofore imagined. Perhaps we had taken our own language as a sort of norm or absolute system of concepts, which would enable us to move anywhere in the realm of ideas. This is not the case. We now know that language systems and cultural patterns can contain only certain ideas, and if we are to escape these boundaries, we must expand and renovate our words and their usage, for they are the very tools by which we think.

In less obvious ways, they are also the channels by which

we feel, by which we love, by which we possess a sense of belonging as against a sense of being set apart, of alienation. Since all the cultures, with their language, myths, and personality attitudes, are the outgrowths of tribal societies, they are by nature opposed to ideas and feelings of a world-wide scope. They serve the narrowness and antagonism of the tribe and the state much better than the inclusive and generous attitudes needed to make an international association like the United Nations operate creatively. This is why we can expect to have many centuries of lingering nationalistic and tribal dissension and enmity. We carry too heavy a baggage of local and regional sentiment and prejudice to be able to move swiftly into an authentic atmosphere of unity and acceptance of one world.

One might think the mystic, going as he does to reality itself for his primary reference, could overleap the tribal feeling and prejudice and lead the way to a warless and cooperative world. This does not seem to be so. A. Eustace Haydon made a lifelong study of world religion from a naturalistic and humanistic viewpoint. In *The Quest of the Ages* he makes some trenchant observations as to how mysticism operates in the various religious traditions. In discussing how persons attempt to prove the existence of God he observes:

A final resort lay in the assurance of mystical experience. For the mystic there was no need for external authority of Church, or Scripture or creed. But once more the proof failed to stand objective analysis. The knowledge given in the mystic's experience was found to be no greater than that of his social environment. Joy, peace, and an untroubled confidence are the qualities of the mystic state. There is a feeling of at-home-ness in the universe. This is true whether the mystic be atheist, theist, or polytheist. The experience has genuine religious value, but brings back no report from the unseen.

In other words, mystical experience surrounds the world as we know it with an aura of rich feeling, enabling a person to live fully, responsively, creatively in the world as it is given to him by his culture, but mysticism is not a method of knowledge that enables one to reach beyond the world as given, to break open new areas of comprehension and understanding. This is accomplished, not through feeling, but through study, research, science. Mystical feelings may participate in the objective and analytical study, as the reports of some scientists give testimony. But at other times the scientist must rigorously guard against the intrusion of his feelings upon his investigations and the generalizations he draws from his data.

Haydon gives a further elaboration of his conclusion:

> The authority of mystical experience appears at first glance to have a different value [from the authority of Scriptures]. Other authorities were public. This belongs to the solitariness of the personal life and has been all-sufficient for many individuals. The mystic in every age escaped the limitations of formal religion. He did not need to bow to the authority of the priest, or Scripture, or institution for assurance in his religious life. His methods of meditation or Yoga technique brought him into immediate union with reality and gave him an unshakable confidence and peace. He was perfectly at home in the universe, and in a way beyond all understanding or intellectual explanation, sure of the truth of his religious ideas. In India, the technique of the mystic experience was developed as a practical part of religious training. After the individual had been thoroughly instructed in the faith of the group, the meditation discipline, with its ecstatic sense of union, gave a final assurance of truth. In Buddhism this experience was the final step in the Noble Eightfold Path leading to salvation. The Sufis of Islam and the Christian mystics knew well the bliss of ecstatic union and the stages of the way. For all mystics everywhere the experience was the same. Treated purely as a psychological phenomenon, there is no difference. The unhesitating assurance of their interpretation of the reality they touch in mystic intuition is common to them all. But the interpretations are widely at variance. For mystics may be atheists, or pluralists, or theists, or pantheists. There are naturalistic mystics, and there are mystics who are trinitarians. The conclusion is inevitable. The truth the mystic finds is exactly what he has accepted from his social and religious environment. Mystical states are purely subjective. They bring no news from another

157

realm of reality. Their value lies only in giving a warm glow of security to whatever religious world view the individual may hold. So long as belief remains in a supernatural realm from which revelation may come, the mystic will be certain beyond all possibility of doubt, that his insight and joy flow from the divine word. But Gautama Buddha was content with the calm bliss of the experience itself, ignoring the existence of gods. The Hindu idealists found it in the true nature of the Self. Any hope that authority for modern religion might find a last refuge in mysticism has no foundation. The wisdom of the mystics is only the social wisdom suffused with emotion. The technique may be a powerful means of intrenching conservatism. It might even serve to yield aesthetic happiness in the experience itself. But man's quest for the good life must seek elsewhere for trustworthy guide and authority.

With this we may wholly agree, and yet insist, as I am sure Haydon would also, that a religion must be something more than guide and authority. As Haydon says, the mystical experience "has genuine religious value." We might question whether knowledge or belief is ever religious in its dimensions unless it is suffused and supported by mystical emotions. We might ask how the great religious innovators, such as Isaiah, Amos, Jesus, and Buddha, achieved their insights, which do seem to add new knowledge and viewpoint to their cultural inheritance. Is it not likely that these were men of high abilities in critical intelligence, united with profound mystical sensitivities, which enabled them to give us something whole, new ideas at once suffused with new and enlightening emotions? Perhaps this is just what religious insight is as differing from scientific and other kinds of insight: the insight is a full integration of both thought and feeling.

A religion suitable for the dimensions and needs of one world will be the most difficult and notable religion humanity has yet devised. There have been suggestions of a universal religion in the tribal and cultural religions of the past. Confucius acclaimed all the men of the four seas as his brothers. The Jews affirmed that God had made of one people all nations. But even the verbalism of universal brotherhood and love has been rare, and too often it has been couched in the terms of a universal missionary enterprise to convert all humanity to the one true faith.

Our problem is a dual one, on the levels of both thought and feeling. People must become able to conceptualize the human family, to understand it as a concrete, vivid actuality. Some would call such a term, "the human family," an abstraction. It certainly is not. Three billion people are a considerable and an exceedingly tangible and concrete reality. It seems like an abstraction only because it is difficult to conceptualize. It is real enough, but we do not have symbols that render this reality convincingly to our thinking. Somehow we must achieve such symbols, and a profound intellectual conviction of them.

Just as it is hard to think of humanity as a whole, so it is hard to feel any tangible emotion about it. We read that a thousand people have died in a catastrophe in Siam, but this does not seem to register upon our emotions. Can we ever truly love, have compassion, for the whole human race? And if we cannot, is it not silly to talk about world and universal religion?

A clue to an answer is found in the fact that there are a few people who do seem to have concern, affection, and conscience regarding the whole of humanity. Such scope of religious devotion has been attributed to Jesus, Gandhi, and Schweitzer, and it is undoubtedly a characteristic of other people less well known. If these persons can so think, feel, and behave, then we know that this universality is a potentiality of human nature, at least in its highest development. And religious idealism should be the apex of our striving as human beings, not some level of mediocrity.

In his study of psychologically healthy people, Abraham Maslow writes that they have this feeling for mankind about which we are concerned. "They have for human beings in general a deep feeling of identification, sympathy and affection. . . . Because of this they have a genuine desire to help the human race. It is as if they were all members of a single family. . . . These people *tend* to be kind or at least patient to almost everyone. They have an especially tender love for children and are easily touched by them. In a very real even though special sense, they have love or rather compassion for all mankind."

These are very exceptional people, of the highest intelligence and powers of imagination and healthiness of emotion. They are also realistic and unsentimental. Surely their feelings for humanity should be shared by all people. The facts of the human scene, the universality of loss, tragedy, illness, grief, and death cry out in justification of such universal compassion. Yet most human beings cannot find within themselves the imaginative and emotional resources to comply. Universal religion demands that we attain them.

Another psychologist, Gordon W. Allport, has considered this problem in an article bearing the unfriendly title "Normative Compatability in the Light of Social Science." He is seeking an ethical theory that will stand up when exposed to "social-scientific analysis." Allport observes that "in any form of human association, men wish to preserve their self-esteem — their self-love — and simultaneously wish to have warm, affiliative relations with their fellows. No one seems initially to want to hate. Hatred grows up as a consequence of blocked self-esteem and blocked affection."

If men desire warm relations with their fellows, how can we enlarge the circle of those they consider their fellows until it encompasses all humanity? Allport looks at desegregation in this regard. "On the social level it is a matter of bringing resistant provincial interests in line with more inclusive national and world values. On the personal level, it is a problem of enlarging the outlook of individuals who live now according to an exclusionist formula that secures for them self-esteem at the expense of dark-skinned people." Just what is the capacity of people to their areas of association, integration, and affection? How large a circle can we belong to meaningfully?

Allport cites an interesting study made by Piaget in Geneva relating to the process of enlargement in childhood. This study is so crucial to our considerations that it demands quotation in full:

> . . . These investigators find that the children around
> six and seven years of age, living in the city of Geneva,
> are unable to think of themselves as both Genevese and
> Swiss. Given a crayon and asked to draw a circle for
> Geneva and for Switzerland, they ordinarily draw two

circles side by side. And they insist if they are Genevese they cannot simultaneously be Swiss. As for foreign lands, the children suffer from even greater cognitive impoverishment. Considering Italy they know only that their father visited Italy, or an aunt comes from there. Even loyalty to the homeland does not yet exist. The child's affective reactions are wholly egocentric. "I like Lausanne because I ate chocolate there." "I like Bern because my uncle lives there." In Piaget's language, these children have not yet commenced the process of "decentering," that is, from the unit of self to any larger social unit.

Ages eight and nine are transitional. Although the child draws a circle for Geneva properly inside the circle for Switzerland, he still has difficulty translating spatial enclosures into terms of social enclosure. He may say, for example, "I'm Swiss now so I can't be Genevese any longer." True, the concept of the homeland is gradually growing, but in a self-centered way. The child says, "I like Switzerland because I was born there." As for foreign lands, he knows of their existence but commonly views them with scorn. The French are dirty; the Americans want war; and people living in other lands all wish they were Swiss, of course. The child of this age has taken bits of conversation from his home and school and fitted them to his own affective self-centeredness.

Only at the age of ten and eleven do we find that decentering has made appreciable progress. Egocentricity begins to give way to the principles of reciprocity and inclusion. The child of ten or eleven understands his dual membership in a smaller and larger political unity. He also gives fewer personal reasons for his affective attachment to his homeland. Switzerland now becomes the land of the Red Cross; it is the country without war. Further, the child understands that members of other countries are as attached to their own lands as he to his — this is the principle of "reciprocity." But cognitive reciprocity does not necessarily mean that the child is capable of seeing good in all the peoples he knows about. He may still despise them. Whether the child outgrows his affective provincialism along with his cognitive provincialism seems to depend largely on the attitudes he learns from his parents.

161

Now this study teaches us certain lessons. For one thing, it shows that maturation and time are needed to achieve a decentering from the unit of self to a progressively larger social unit. Further, this process may be arrested at any stage along the way, especially in its affective aspects. It is significant that Piaget gives no evidence that his children (at least up to fourteen years of age) discern the possibility of membership in any supranational grouping. Decentering has not reached the point where the child feels himself as belonging to the European region, to be a supporter of the United Nations; certainly none mentions his membership in the conclusive collective of mankind. Even if in later years such cognitive enlargement takes place, the chances are that the corresponding affective enlargement will be lacking. Using Piaget's terms, we may then say that adults in all nations are still incompletely decentered. Cognitively they may stumble at the threshold of supranational chambers, but affectively they fail to enter.

A study conducted in Belgium by de Bie shows how few adults are concerned with identification across national boundaries. Even those of a higher level of education have little sense of international relationships. Membership in any unit larger than the nation simply is not a psychological reality.

Many of us in liberal religion have a group of interrelated goals. We are trying to build a religion of freedom, of respect for persons, of the open mind, of the scientific attitude, and of humanism, whether this be a theistic or a naturalistic humanism. Our religion is directed toward the full self-realization of people, emphasizing the values of the arts and culture. We strive for social justice, mercy, charity and goodwill.

To some of us another dimension of liberal religion has been added: the welfare of humanity as a whole, citizenship in one world, the fellowship of all people — if you will, a religion of and for one world. In this we attempt to share the history, arts, devotions of all mankind. Instead of identifying with a Judaeo-Christian tradition, a Hindu tradition, a Confucianist tradition, we are seeking to merge them all in a human tradition.

What do we have to build upon, if we are to achieve this

162

world religion? Primarily the capacity within people to relate in compassion and understanding to the whole of the human family. Men have claimed this capacity in the past, for their gods challenged them to love all men and to seek the salvation of all the world. Our basic extension of religious meaning and devotion is no larger than this. But the way we relate to humanity is toward the others, whereas the tribal and orthodox religions try to make all others relate toward them. This is a drastic, a critical difference in religious orientation. The question is, are we capable of making it?

The article we have just quoted was ominous enough in its beginnings. But the last sentence quoted has a shocking impact psychologically and intellectually, equal to the physical reaction to having a brick dropped on your head from a fourth-story window. "Membership in any unit larger than the nation simply is not a psychological reality." If this is true, it makes our dream of a religion wherein men will have membership in humanity at large just a silly, utopian sentimentality. If this is true, we had better resign ourselves to the fact that such a religion is likely to be extremely unpopular, held by the merest of minorities, for a long, long time.

And yet, although this defines the magnitude and the difficulty of our task, it cannot discourage us, for mankind has no considerable prospect of a future, perhaps even of survival, unless it can become one compassionate fellowship. A future of never-ending war between the tribes of the human race, given modern weapons, is a prospect of such brutality and indecency that it is intolerable. One man, when he heard that his country had dropped the atomic bomb on Hiroshima, said, "I think that I have lived long enough." If what we would call world religion, or world fellowship and brotherhood, is not possible to our race, it would seem that Jehovah was ill advised to counsel Noah to build an ark for himself and his family. It would have been better to have had the dirty business of the human experiment finished a few thousand years ago, before human weakness and evil had been implemented by scientific weapons, than to have prolonged our slow suicide until now.

But some of us cannot give up so easily. If membership in the human family is not a psychological reality now, one day

163

it may be. At one time membership in any unit larger than the small, family-centered tribe was not a psychological reality for the human species. Now men can conceive membership in a nation of 180 million people. Thus we in the United States feel a membership tie to more people within our nation than there were on earth a few thousand years ago. Would it be inherently any more difficult to have membership in three billions of people than in 180 millions of people? I do not believe so. Then why is it so far from being a psychological reality for most of us?

Allport goes on in his article to consider this. He quotes R. C. Angell, who concludes "that interacting nations will enjoy peace only when they become parts of a social system that embraces them." Thus our fifty states, as parts of the social system of the United States that embraces them, do not prevent us from crossing state boundaries in our sense of fellowship and membership. The entire world is slowly developing, even in spite of iron and bamboo curtains, the beginnings of a world-wide social system. When this has become mature, we shall have something equivalent to a United States of the World, or so we dream.

Allport, in his professional lingo, affirms of the average adult that "cognitively and affectively he is potentially capable of considerable decentering." Or, in Sunday School language, a man is capable of loving all of humanity. Some people already do, although there are only a few of them. Allport says the root of the matter lies in "the posture of the individual's mentality." If prejudice can be learned, then brotherhood and universality can also be learned. Allport offers several suggestions for furthering this end. One points straight at liberal religion and could well provide us with a challenging and creative mission and task.

> . . . How can we develop symbols of inclusion that will assist children, and citizens, and statesmen to look beyond the confines of egocentricity? Without images it is impossible to form attitudes. Our symbols today are overwhelmingly local and nationalistic. We continue to view our fellowship circles, as did Piaget's children, as lying side by side, not as concentric. We have few symbols of inclusion, but even if effective supranational symbols ex-

isted, they would, of course, have no magic property. Men's choices can be only among sequences they have known, and so our problem of training involves also the giving of experience, especially in childhood, that will enlarge the cognitive style and turn the mind automatically toward the integrative mode of handling conflict.

Can our ministers and teachers translate this into preachments of urgency and prophecy? Can we make our church buildings, their adornment of symbolism and art, the shape and deportment of our assemblies, into instruments for so enlarging the minds and emotions of mankind that they may include all one another? Here is a task, of moral, aesthetic, sociological, and philosophical inventiveness: to create and apply the symbols needed, and through education and association to build in people that enlargement, those attitudes, that "posture of mentality," that will enable them to have compassion for all mankind, without which universal religion is but idealistic twaddle, true "globaloney."

And what has this to do with mysticism? Only when the mystic finds in his culture such universal symbols, such universal attitudes and convictions, will his mystical experience support and enwrap these ideals. Our mystical intuitions and sense of reality work intimately with our intellectual understanding and convictions. They work in and through the symbols, concepts, thought patterns, even prejudices of the culture within which they arise and develop. Even as man is composed of all the influences of his environment and culture, so the mystical abilities of man are inherently related to them. Man is not wholly free and creative until he is free and creative in all his activities. A free mystical and emotional power can exist only where there is a free mind, a free personality.

Thus the mystical, the emotional side of man is guided by his mind, and his mind in turn is guided by his feelings. And symbols and concepts and art are the structural fibers that weave the tough fabrics of his thinking and feeling. But there is only one weaving. Thought and science are the warp, and the emotions and mysticism are the woof, and together they weave a cloak to cover the shivering of humanity's alarm.

Can we find the symbols that will make each of our temples, standing on the corners of our city streets, adorning the hillsides on the edges of our cities, rising on the squares of towns, a bold, graphic declaration of universal brotherhood? Can we create the windows, paintings, sculpture, chalices, the songs, anthems, meditations, the shapes of assembly, the styles of group behavior and organization, that will declare our membership in humanity, our kinship to all living creatures, and our at-home-ness in the universe?

If we can, perhaps as artists of living and religious faith we can accept the analysis and challenge of the social scientists, and as living creative fellowships invent, fabricate, and then fulfill in our lives the prophecy of a free and peaceful and compassionate world. If we do, a new generation of religious mystics will arise, whose mystic vision will be the single family of man, living in the wide and sun-warmed world, husbandmen of the one large farm of the world, citizens of the commonwealth of man. And these mystics will find in themselves a fire, a vision, that will light their own minds and imaginations, and they will touch unto like fire all those upon whom their words fall, all those upon whom the doves of their compassion alight. Men will move in freedom amidst their dreams. Slowly their dreams will take shape upon the earth, and paths of further growth will be opened, and another and yet another vision of morality and splendor and strength will spring up in awakened minds and hearts.

180 MILLION

Knowledge has many dimensions, some of them so subtle, so intangible, as to be quite beyond our powers of communication. They may be difficult for even the knower to discern. We experience what we might call a process of "realization." We can know something as a concept, as a statement of fact, and yet have little comprehension of the fullness of reality implicit in the idea or object of concern. Even after we "know" something it can gradually become more and more "real" to us. For often what we call knowledge is removed from any tangible or sustained experience of that which is known. Literate man is peculiarly apt to get this kind of knowledge since he goes to books in order to learn, rather than to events or the objects which the books describe. He may think he knows something upon reading about it but find after he has experienced it at first hand that he had no "realization" of what he had read.

This past summer we drove across the northern part of our country, then down the west coast, and returned by cutting a path from the southwest to the northeast corners of it, with side excursions, some eleven thousand miles. We had known that we lived in a big country, but the bigness was not a reality to us until we had actually experienced it by passing across it. Of course all we did in our travel was to draw a thin line of observation, a path of vision, across it. The massive bulk of the country we did not, and never will, see; life is too short and too busy with other occupations than sightseeing. But we saw enough so that the country has come to a realization within us as never before.

A parallel experience was sustained in relating to the people of the country. We knew the fact that there were 180 million people in the United States before we began the journey, but as we passed through village after village, city after city, slowly the realization of 180 million persons, each different from the other, each with his own private world of life, each distinct and individual, began to gather in our feelings and comprehension. We began to realize two opposite things, how much they were like us in ideas, viewpoint, attitudes, and yet how few of them shared some of the distinctive religious and cultural convictions which we believed of momentous concern. We began to realize, in a way that transcended the impact of mere statistics, what it means to be a member of a small minority movement. The liberals in our movement do not yet number 180 thousand in our country, and we are scattered among 180 millions of our fellows. Slowly there grew within us the understanding of what it means to be insignificant in numbers and size.

Yet we feel that we have big, significant insights, relating to big problems, problems which concern the total population. And the sense of the overwhelming numbers of people of our own country forced us to ponder what the full realization of the number of people on the planet, some three billions, really means. We believe we have a world mission, calling ourselves

Unitarians and Universalists. We seek to relate to the oneness, the wholeness of the human family.

The town of Cass Lake, Minnesota, is near some Indian reservations. Many Indians are on the streets and in the stores. Some are clean, well dressed, obviously educated, and have become adjusted to the ways of life and ideas of the general population. But some are still mainly of the world of their tribal past. They wandered futilely about the town. They are not at home on the streets, but neither are they at home when they go to the reservation in the countryside. Their old world of nomadic, Stone Age life is gone, but they have not yet moved into the new world which has usurped it. They are spiritually, culturally homeless. Many of them will eke out their existence in an idle, alcoholic fog.

Some of my own ancestors came from an eastern tribe of these people, but I feel incomprehensibly remote from them, at least as far as being able to communicate with them is concerned. Even if I were to live with them for years as an anthropologist, to learn their world and ways until I could talk with them "as a native," they still would be unable to enter my world and talk to me, unless they were willing to move into my world. And this is just what they seem unwilling or unable to do. Why should they be so motivated? We forced the necessity of change upon them by invading and occupying their world, destroying their ancient way of life. They did not ask for it.

These are some of the 180 million people. For some years I was a member and minister of the Disciples of Christ, or the Christian Church. We were driving through the areas where they are thickest, and it seemed as if we came upon a sign for the Christian Church in at least every other town. These were people that for many years I talked with and talked at, but could I really communicate with them from this heretical minority religious viewpoint into which my thinking had developed? Could I communicate with them any more successfully than with the uprooted Indians — indeed, as successfully? It is dampening to realize how immensely unconcerned other people are with that which most concerns us. In minor matters this fact does not disturb us, but when the unconcern

168

relates to basic religious ideals and needs, the sense of isolation and powerlessness calls for all the courage and tenacity we have to oppose it. How can the small minority maintain its morale, its sense of mission, its hope of working some significant reform in convictions and actions? It must have a magnificent faith in the yeastiness of its leaven, confronted with such a mighty lump of dough.

Our purpose in making the trip was to meet with fellow religious liberals in several conferences across the country. Even though we were traveling among the great variegated mass of our people, we were seeking out those closest to us. Thus the journey sharpened two opposite kinds of comparison: how different we were from those most different from ourselves, and how alike we were to those most like ourselves. We were taking stock of the other members of our minority group, seeing where we stood in the small family as well as within the large family.

It was a warming experience to join the members of liberal religious fellowships on the west coast and find ourselves at home, indeed more at home with more people than we would have been in a similar conference on the east coast. We gained the conviction that our minority movement had considerable integrity and cohesion, that its members, scattered about a vast continent, were a mutually supporting and sustaining community. Our confidence in the influence which one-tenth of one percent of the population might exert on the rest of the people increased.

There is considerable variety, even controversy, within this minority. Its cutting edge is dulled because it seeks to cut in several directions. The weight of the argument of the fraction loses force against the majority when much of its argument is turned toward itself. Often the individuals and societies that make up the minority movement are themselves yet smaller minorities within that minority. We were concerned as to how we stood with these other members of our group. Would we find on the opposite side of the continent groups sharing our peculiar point of view and emphasis? Would they be doing so much the same kind of job that if we failed in our risks and experiments we could feel they would replace us and the general cause would not suffer?

169

The answers we found were both encouraging and discouraging. We were encouraged to discover other parishes engaged in the same kinds of projects that concerned us — not a majority but a significant number. We found evidences that some of the things we had been doing were having an impact thousands of miles from home. We met people who had once been members of the Charles Street Meeting House in Boston now working in and leading societies in the West. We found others doing some things differently and better than we were doing them, and we learned much.

But the main thing we learned was that no one else was doing our particular job, either well or poorly. Others were doing things similar, but none was doing just what we were, and in the way that we were doing it. We became convinced that what we were doing was indispensable in a certain way. Not indispensable in that the world could not do without it, or that some other experimental group would not undertake a similar project and submit closely comparable findings and contributions. But if we ceased operations the world would lose that particular congeries of activities and presentations that we are on the way to furnishing. We discovered that the Meeting House has a personality, a manner, a product that is unique. We were happy to find that others were doing their jobs well, and that they resembled our labors. There was also a kind of pleasure in finding that no one else was doing our work, and that we thus had our own mission and responsibility.

Thus our response was a doubled-barreled one, two barrels side by side and firing in the same direction. Our relation as a small fellowship to the 180 millions of the country and the 180 thousands of our denomination was a parallel one and demanded the same functions of us. We could do our task best by taking aim at one objective and firing both barrels at once. The institution or the individual of integrity wears the same face in all situations. The honest and effective person is not all things to all men, but rather one thing to all men. He may change his words to suit the understanding of different persons, but he does not change the essential import of his message.

A religious person, like a religious institution, has one charge for his life: to establish the highest and most inclusive ideals within the scope of his comprehension and imagination, and then to bend his efforts in one continuous and integrated effort to realize those ideals. Without singleness and direction a life or a movement, except in the most unusual circumstances, will not have sufficient impact or clarity of meaning to be of any significance in the giant movements of history. A hurricane has been known to drive a straw through a pine board; there is more than one kind of straw in the wind.

This was the conviction that came as we traveled among 180 million people, weaving through the sprawling welters that are Chicago, Los Angeles, St. Louis, and New York, and the vast prairies and deserts where the ranches are many miles apart. How can one send a message to all these people? What kind of message will reach them, or any of them? The rules, I decided, are not those of politics, or public relations, or salesmanship. The rules are those of art. The message must have clarity, style, force. The message will reach this many people not by mass, or repetition, or seductiveness, or pleasantness. The power must be put into the message itself. The expression must find its own way. One might better spend his life, not trying to shout it louder, but to say it better; to say is so clearly and so well that it will convince even when it is whispered; to declare it so well that the people will come seeking the expression of it — one cannot take it to so many.

Should not the declarations of religion have a directness and simplicity that is childlike? That is, should they not be without guile and conniving? Surely they will not be said to convince or to sell, but to make a complete statement of a truth. Their aim will be factuality and lucidity; if these are attained style and beauty of expression are their accompaniments. If anything is said perfectly it is said beautifully.

A lifetime is none too long to attain the requisite refinement whereby such a statement of religious ideals can be expressed. By "expression" we do not refer to verbal or artistic expression only, but also to acts, to a way and style of living that make the religion a living experience. To clearly express religious ideals in one's behavior, in an institution's behavior, demands

171

skill in the art of living, the most subtle and difficult of all the arts, for it is not successful until it has reached such heights of artistic realization as to be artless.

Prime ingredients in style are power and focus, as can be illustrated by a homely analogy. If you place a flat-bottomed chest on a floor, the weight will be equally distributed and no marks will be made in the floor. But if the legs of the chest are pointed, the weight of the chest over a long period of time will drive the legs down into the floor; through weight and pointedness they will make their mark. This observation is carried into the phrase "a pointed remark," and "his statement made its point." The opposite is stated in "his remarks were pointless."

What then can a religious group do? It can, working where it is, make as powerful and perfect a presentation of its ideals as it is able. It might as well stay where it is, for this world is so large that one spot is about as good as another. A church in the center of a great city can be ignored as easily as, perhaps more easily than, the church on a country crossroads.

We might make a suggestive list of ways in which it can declare its beliefs and convictions. It can build its temple, whether large or small, as a lucid and declarative symbolic expression of the religious ideal. Greatness in architecture and symbolism is not related to size. This is a challenge every small parish has and few acknowledge. Smallness in size does not necessitate smallness in conception. It can seek to make the songs and poetry and rituals of its services as full and perfect in their declarations as possible. Its members may seek paintings, statuary, dance, and drama to declare their enthusiasms and concerns. Where these are not to be found, they will set themselves to create them. Since they are few in number, they will seek to make their deeds and relationships specific in their idealism. They will live out their religion where they are, knowing their neighborhood is in the midst of the greater neighborhoods of the country and the planet, and that they do not need a more strategic locality for their religious work; indeed there is none. In order to get to the fields of need in far lands, one must first travel through the slums of one's own city.

172

Weight, impact of influence, has dimensions of time. Time is required to train and practice until one's powers of expression have adequacy and style, until the repeated demonstration of one's concern makes its meanings clear and discernible to his fellows. This lesson was taught to me by a young man who came up as I was leaving one parish to go to another. He said, "I have been listening to you for the last three years and I am just beginning to see what it is you are saying." Perhaps this indicates that I was not saying it well, or that he had a block against acknowledging the meaning, or that the meaning had to be approached from a hundred sides to be seen wholly, or all these things. But a lifetime is hardly long enough to make a full statement and expression of a religious concern and insight.

Another time dimension in religious expression relates to the time needed for the slow correction, improvement, and comprehension of a work. Petrarch spent most of his life writing one sonnet series. Some painters live with a painting for many years, growing with it, waiting for it to mature in conception and expression. Brahms waited many years before writing his first symphony, and then was content to produce only four in a lifetime. Saint-Saens waited until his old age and wrote but one. Some great works are done quickly, but if growth continues, time deepens and enriches the expression. The paintings of Rembrandt well into his thirties were polished, brittle, almost impersonal, but those of the latter half of his life gained another kind of virtuosity in simplicity, humanity, and compassion.

It isn't how many things are said, or how widespread the places in which they are said. A few statements made with consummate power will not need to be multiplied to make their point. As a local illustration, I can imagine spending a lifetime attempting to make a collection of the art of the world religions, such as we are making at the Meeting House, as perfect an expression as possible. Rather than trying to make several collections, or to make a big collection, it seems better to make a collection in which each piece perfectly bespeaks the religion of its culture, and the total collection fully covers the varieties and styles of man's religious quest and expression. One great collection will make the point of the unity and relatedness of man's religious endeavors better than a hundred careless assemblies.

For five years a few religious liberals have been working on a new hymnal. Our aim has not been to make a big hymnal, but to gather together the finest collection possible. Now that immediate task is done, but the finding and making of songs that sing our religious quest is not. A life would be well spent at this one task, unremittingly seeking for beautiful songs. Fifty great hymns that mankind could not resist singing might do more to convince the world of the precepts of free religion than anything else we could do.

In the last century liberal religion had several fine hymn writers, whose works are now found in the hymnbooks of many more conservative denominations. When a hymnbook commission sets to work, it gathers all the hymnbooks it can find, seeking new words and tunes. If you have made a lovely song, you need not sell it; others will seek it out. The songs will win their own converts.

Out there, all around us in this great country, are 180 million people. Around them in the planet are three billion people. How do we meet them? How do we come to terms with them? Do we go out and invade their institutions and lands, as did the empire builders and the missionaries? Do we wage war to conquer them, to force them to our will? Do we spread religion by the sword as did Charlemagne and Mohammed?

Should we let such a horde of people overwhelm us, until we lose our zest and confidence in the crowd and sulk in cynical silence? Do we try to go out and promote ourselves, and get big and prosperous, so that we can number our cohorts in the millions, instead of the thousands? There is no need of it.

The single voice, the voice of the few, if it speaks more clearly, more charitably, more reasonably, more universally, will be heard. Let our weapons of conquest be reason, integrity, diligence, patience, and love, and the multitudes of the people will seem like fields for the harvest of peace, and not a threat to our freedom and our habitations.

PART II.

THE METHOD

CHAPTER 11

Religion as Experiment

RELIGION — CRUTCH OR SPADE

Religion has been called a crutch. For the liberal it is a spade. But some people use a spade to lean on and make a crutch out of it. We might say, ironically, that in effect they put a pad over the blade so it will not cut their under-arm, and knock off the handle to make a better stump. Then they wonder why it doesn't still dig ground.

There is a type of reaction that is endemic among certain so-called liberals. Persons are attracted into the liberal church, show a good deal of enthusiasm for a while, and react affirmatively to the ideas in the addresses and discussions. But soon they cease attending. Word drifts back that, much as they agree with the ideas of liberal religion, they have decided they can get along quite well without belonging to a church. They say, "I do not really need it." They do not seem to ask themselves whether the church needs them.

A considerable assumption underlies their reaction. Basic is the idea that religion is something you involve yourself in because it gives something to you, and you stay in it only as long as you are getting something out of it. That is, the church fills what the psychologists call a "deficiency need." This theory of motivation has it that we do things largely because we lack something. We eat when we are hungry, drink to quench our thirst, study when we are ignorant, and join a church because it fills a painful need in our lives.

According to this assumption a church is a crutch, something to support us when we cannot stand up by ourselves, and something we are happy to discard as useless as soon as we can walk under our own power. The church would be put in the same category as the school, the hospital, a sanatorium, an asylum, places which restore us to health and sufficiency, but on which we do not want to waste time when we are well, or educated, or sane, or happy.

The church itself has done much to foster this conception of its function. A teacher of mine wrote a book on pastoral psychology called *Cure of Souls,* putting the minister beside the doctor as a healer, someone useful for the sick, but a nuisance to the healthy. Ministers are usually trained to consider their function that of saving or redeeming fallen persons. With the orthodox this means the saving of souls, and with the liberals it means pastoral counseling, saving personalities. I know ministers who spend the bulk of their time counseling people with problems. Perhaps it is only justice if these people feel no further need of the minister when their problems are solved.

The church as missionary, setting out to save the heathen and sinners, to rescue the derelicts in the skid rows, to raise funds for the needy, to conduct service and relief projects, demonstrates this ancient concept of the function of religion, defined by Jesus as giving a drink of cold water to the thirsty, visiting the sick, and befriending the widow and orphan. It is no mistake that churches express themselves by creating orphanages, hospitals, and old people's homes.

There is nothing wrong with religion as a crutch, when the crutch is what is needed. The problem arises when people consider it to be *only* a crutch, dispensable as soon as they can walk again. The church, both liberal and orthodox, should serve all the crutch functions it has assumed in the past. The religious society must be warm with mercy and offer succor to its cripples, its hungry, its dispossessed, its sick, its lonely, its ill and disturbed, its ignorant. But this should be only a portion, and a minor portion, of the activity of organized religion, just as such remedial activity is only a lesser function of a fully expressive and creative culture. These are recovery functions, not the main constructive and enlarging activities of whole and healthy people.

I would not say anything to lessen the importance of religious education. But I wonder sometimes if education has not been oversold to liberal churches in proportion to the total function of liberal religion. This is evidenced in our building programs. A church structure generally has two units, with a possible third. There is the sanctuary for worship, the church school building, and possibly a parlor, dining room, and kitchen for ecclesiastical feasting and sociability. But worshiping and teaching are the chief emphases, and in the liberal church the sanctuary is also largely another classroom, with the sermon a sort of aggrandized professional lecture, aimed primarily at education. It had better instruct, for it seldom inspires.

It is assuredly a function of the church to teach, but is teaching its main function, or merely preparatory to its main function? After the people decide they have learned what the church school teachers and the ministers have to teach them, are they not likely to consider the church a crutch they can now do without? Especially since the church does not seem to afford them an opportunity to do much more than continue to be perennial students of the word, and not doers thereof?

How would it be if our church plants had a fourth section, and that the largest of all — a workshop? Perhaps the church could then say, "The church is a crutch only to those who need a crutch. To all the healthy it is a spade. If you need a crutch, come to us. But after you are through with the crutch, we have a spade for you to use. And we are mainly interested in affording you a crutch so you can hurry and get on with your digging."

Perhaps we are getting farther away from this ideal than we were in our grandparents' time. It seems to me there was much more participation in the activity of the laymen in the churches in my childhood. I can remember a time when a lusty "Amen, amen," or "Praise the Lord," was regularly added to the preacher's utterance from the "amen corner." Clinton Scott tells of one such enthusiast getting into a Universalist church by mistake, to the consternation of the regular attendants. He said, however, that he enjoyed the unsolicited interpolations. For the first time in his memory he knew for sure that a member of his congregation was enthusiastic about the sermon.

I wonder if it is still the practice in orthodox circles to have laymen give some of the prayers. This spread the spadework of a Sunday morning about the congregation. Sometimes certain elders held forth too long, while hunger pains gnawed the gathering. One patriarch in one of my early parishes used his prayer to make a rebuttal of the arguments of the sermon. But at least some of the members came to church to do something, not just to be served.

Giving vent to amens and prayers may not be the first things we think of as the spadework of religion, but they did give the believers a sense of being of some use after they were saved. The church was a place where you practiced religion, as well as a place where you were taught, lectured, and provided with a free amateur analysis. But now our churches remind me of a notice that comes out of the loudspeakers at a baseball park. It goes something like this: "The American League has instructed the management of the Boston Red Sox to warn all spectators that they will be prosecuted by law if they go onto the field while the game is in progress. They are warned not to interfere with the players or the flight of the ball." The spectators are only spectators and must stay in the stands where good spectators belong. They should not try to get into the act. Playing the game is for professional players. It is enough for the people to sit and watch.

More and more of our life is given over to the role of spectator, via radio, television, movie, press, theater. Entertainment is endlessly multiplied by machine (now we have teaching machines, too), even as goods are cheaply and inanely multiplied by machines. It is enough for man to be spectator and consumer. Our churches have followed suit. And since they are mainly concerned with relieving deficiencies, as soon as the new enthusiast decides that he "doesn't need the church any more," he happily goes to the theater, the radio, resorts, books, records, and the idiot box. Does he fail to realize that he is only trading the crutch of the church for the even more insidious crutch of a consumer-oriented society? The crutch of the church at least helps him to walk again. The automobile relieves him of the necessity of walking at all, except around the house, and from door to the curb. Let the arms and legs atrophy. The machines will do our work and our loco-motion. Let the brain shrivel. The advertiser and the editor will think for us. Let the creative abilities rot. A few artists via the machines will sing, play, act, write for us all. Of course they too will succumb to the general dry rot of the culture and in time echo back to us only the stalest clichés. The debacle of television is full proof of the prevailing sickness. It is not even a crutch that is offered us, but a scented hog wallow.

When the transient enthusiasts aforementioned decide that they do not need liberal religion any more, I do not pursue them or try to argue them out of it. They are probably right. They don't need it. The key word here is *need*. I have noticed that these people seldom go from the church into some type of activity. Evidently they don't need to be giving themselves in labor that is dedicated to the upbuilding and correcting of the world they live in. Are they saying that it was nice to hear the ideals expressed in the services but that they have no need to apply them in their own lives? The preachments are challenging, but who wants to be challenged? There are so many more amusing things to do.

We might call the religious man, liberally speaking, the functioning idealist. The verbal idealist is satisfied to merely mouth idealistic platitudes. The functioning idealist must begin to put his ideals into acts, projects, and constructions. Let him be stirred by the presentation of an area of need, by a possible correction of a social ill, and his first reaction is "What can I do about it?" He goes looking for a spade. And if his church doesn't have a spade waiting for him, he will seek out some other institution or arena that does. Very often these liberal religionists will be active in a number of related agencies concerned with such issues as race relations, peace, birth control, prison reform, constructive legislation, juvenile delinquency, mental health, the United Nations, international relations, and civil liberties. Or they will be supporting the creative artistic and cultural efforts of the community, the theatres, choruses, orchestras, museums, adult education, libraries. To see possibilities of growth and improvement

181

engages them as persons; they cannot stay out of the work and the excitement of making things happen.

One definition of religion that accords with this attitude is given by John Dewey in *A Common Faith:* "Any activity pursued in behalf of an ideal and against obstacles and in spite of threats of personal loss because of conviction of its general and enduring value is religious in quality." According to this definition the religious process has only begun when the ideal end is envisaged, or when the educational job has been done. Once the religious man glimpses the ideal end, he must pursue it, he must engage in activity in its behalf. This engagement is dangerous, uncomfortable, costly. It brings him up against obstacles. It threatens sacrifice, personal loss. But these he endures for the sake of the envisaged long-range good, its "general and enduring value."

I believe this is the function of the church — not to be a crutch, not even to be an educator or mainly a preacher, the announcer of the ideal ends. The religious fellowship must be a workshop in which dedicated people are engaged in bringing these ideal ends into the realities of the structure and relationships of the world. Dewey calls this the "active relation between the ideal and the actual." Surely the church would not be judged unnecessary were it solidly and dangerously involved in battling for the highest ideals humanity has conceived. What person of religious disposition could "do without the church" if the church were "doing" its religious faith in this fashion?

Liberal religion has concerned itself with the considering and the framing and the announcing of ideal ends. This is mainly what its preaching does, or should do. In its highest form, this is the art of prophecy, the function of the religious imagination and conscience. It is no mean or unworthy task. Dewey says again, " . . . the ideal has its roots in natural conditions; it emerges when the imagination idealizes existence by laying hold of the possibilities offered to thought and action. There are values, goods, actually realized upon a natural basis — the goods of human association, of art and knowledge. The idealizing imagination seizes upon the most precious things found in the climacteric moments of experience and projects

182

them. We need no external criterion and guarantee for their goodness. They are had, they exist as good, and out of them we frame our ideal ends."

I can imagine no better definition of the educational and imaginative and intellectual sides of naturalistic, humanistic, and liberal religion than this. Here our goals and dreams emerge out the very stuff of our daily lives and our highest experiences. From the heat and struggle of our own lives we catch glimpses of a possible wise and good way of life that is attainable. This should concern our minds and imaginations. Our lessons and sermons should proclaim the ideals man has brought forth out his own mind and emotions, and they do. But this is only the awakening, only the beginning of the religious quest, the religious mission. For the end is not to see the ideal in some far-off utopian dream but to make it actual in the streets, the factories, the governments, and the homes of this world. You can't do that with crutches. You need spades.

In fact, the process of idealizing is itself rudimentary and abortive if it is allowed to remain in the realm of verbalisms, of preachments and teachings, where the church now mainly leaves it. Dewey's argument in this matter is irrefutable:

Moreover the process of creation is experimental and continuous. The artist, scientific man, or good citizen, depends upon what others have done before him and are doing around him. The sense of new values that become ends to be realized arises first in dim and uncertain form. As the values are dwelt upon and carried forward in action they grow in definiteness and coherence. Interaction between aim and existent conditions improves and tests the ideal; and conditions are at the same time modified. Ideals change as they are applied to existing conditions. The process endures and advances with the life of humanity. What one person and one group accomplish becomes the standing ground and starting point of those who succeed them. When the vital factors in this natural process are generally acknowledged in emotion, thought and action, the process will be both accelerated and purified through elimination of that irrelevant element that culminates in the idea of the supernatural.

183

There is the province of liberal religion, in "emotion, thought and action." Now we spend most of our time and energy on the first two, on emotion and thought, but these deteriorate into sentimentality and arid intellectualism when they are not ruggedly married with action. The spade is a handy tool, with a sharp blade to cleave the soil and turn it up, and the flat of the blade to thump the clod and break it down. An ideal *is* a spade for turning over real earth. It soon rusts if unused. And in use it will dull unless constantly sharpened with further application of emotion and thought. The religious experience and practice are a unity of these three things, emotion, thought, and action, and as long as liberal religious institutions withhold themselves from action, they stunt and smother themselves and their ideal ends.

How would the church fare as a workshop? Most people are morally lazy. Business is generally cynical about ideals that might disturb profits. Perhaps the church survives as a flourishing social institution only because it doesn't try to put its ideals to work. When Jesus advised action to the rich young ruler — to sell his possessions, give the money to the poor, and follow him as a disciple — he lost a big pledger fast. This is not how you run a special appeals campaign. Better lay low on the action stuff until we have canvassed the big givers.

The action of the vision of ideal ends is dual, in that it acts upon the actor as well as upon the world in which he acts. For the ideal glimpsed shows forth further developments of our own persons, as well as charges and improvements in the world about us. So we find that we must renovate and upgrade ourselves, even as we try to better the environment. As in charity, religious action begins at home. In fact, we see that we ourselves are part of the world, and the most immediate way to improve the environment is to improve that part of it which is our self.

The same is true of the church. The church is given a spade through its ideal not only to do digging in the world, but to do a digging job upon itself. For the church, as an institution, is a portion of that very world which it would right. To the degree that the church improves its own structure, behavior, and human relations, it improves that part of the world which it is.

The person and the church may have some excuse for failure to apply their ideals to the world, saying it is too big, too reluctant, too complex a problem. They cannot have the same excuses in the same degree for failure to improve themselves. How many of us exercise the freedoms this democracy gives us to make our own persons after the image of our own desire? How many churches take full advantage of the freedom of religion in our society to make the church itself the universal, enlightened, loving fellowship of the religious ideal?

We talk much about social action, but the church also is part of society. Surely one of the most effective ways of improving society lies in improving the churches, the professed agencies of idealism and reform within society. How the church bleats about the evils in the world, even as it slothfully and cowardly refrains from correcting the evils within itself.

Surely the social action with which humanity must be finally concerned, as the culmination of all human doing, is exemplified in the arts. For in the arts men try to express the most profound of their apprehensions, meanings, and perceptions of beauty. Yet one seldom thinks of the arts in terms of social action.

Religious worship or celebration is the most composite and complete of all the arts, being the full celebration of life itself. If ever spadework and creativity were needed, it is in the religious arts of liberal religion. As we create and shape our ideal ends, we should be able to project them into the friendly and demonstrative forms of poetry, song, dance, drama, and ritual. There they will have a powerful and affective life far more evocative than that of the prose of our lecturing.

When we look at the miniature society of the religious fellowship, and to the exploding, violent scope of the world-wide human family, and see all the stupendous tasks there are to do, if we are to catch up with even a few of the ideals of mercy, brotherhood, and health we can now see, how can we fail to catch fire, and be spurred on to the most strenuous action of which we are capable? If this is what the administration of religion can do for us, who can say that he can do without it?

But even above this, out of the ideals we now can see, new ideals are slowly, surprisingly emerging. To labor among the old ideals, that out of our striving to attain them the new and regenerative ideals of the next age can take form — surely this is the greatest work of all. For the last and best spadework that religion does is to turn up a fresh earth of idealism itself, to never let the vision of the good life become stale and infertile. Our religious vision is something we must be making and remaking in itself, even as we apply it to the remaking of the world.

THE IDEAL AND THE INDIVIDUAL

People who claim that their ideals are their own have been accused of arrogance and heresy. Ideals come to us as the property of the tribe, the state, and the church. The individual is expected to espouse the ideals provided him by the authorities.

Mystics are an embarrassment to established religion, for they claim to have their own sources of moral insight. Their ideals seem impractical, since they exceed the preachments of the church and the behavior of the priests. They create tensions with commerce and politics, through which the churches are supported. Paradoxically, they defy the authority of the church by insisting on ideals higher than those required by institutional religion.

Ideals, as living realities, must be the creation and possession of individuals. They achieve their finest definition and accomplishment in individual lives, rather than in society. Their creative power works mainly within the individual, born in his moral imagination, clarifying in the struggles of his conscience. An ideal grafted on the person from without as a law or command does not have the conviction of the ideal arising from his experience and insight.

An example of the conflict between the individual and society is the pacifist, to whom violence is abhorrent. Because he is committed to the ideal of the peaceful settlement of all differences, he refuses to bear arms for the nation. Since his personal idealism is higher than that of the nation, he is treated as a criminal.

In areas where racial prejudice is standard, persecution is visited on those who live by the ideal of equality. Where re-

186

ligious bigotry and orthodoxy is the norm, universality of tolerance and appreciation is punished.

People congratulate themselves if they live up to the idealism of state and church. If they stay out of jail and attain the moderate ethical standards of the law, they consider it an achievement; for some it is. They also try to live up to the letter of the law of the church, and moral perfection is complying with the commandments and the catechism. Acceptance of outside moral authorities is justified if they are superior to oneself. This would be supremely logical to those who believe in the perfect revelation of moral truth in religious authority and its transfer to the laws of the land of "God's" country. These views are still predominant; few accept the idea of the evolution and developing nature of all customs and institutions.

To the evolutionist, the established idealism is mediocre, since it is a middle morality. The law establishes a level of toleration of evil, not of good, setting the lowest standard of behavior to which we can fall without punishment. Where it sets levels of achievement, they are minimum, as in a driver's test, compulsory education, or pure food laws. Realms of excellence are beyond the province of government.

The same is true of organized religion. Denominations have their constitutions and laws. These profess to be superlative idealism as the civil law does not, but they are the result of group activity and tradition, and they too only set an average, a common denominator. The prophets and reformers that rise in the church, calling on it to mend its ways, are treated no better than is the conscientious objector in the institutions of government. Church and state share basic institutional structures and behaviors, and in a theocratic system they are one institution.

An ideal is a vision of unrealized good. It is a projection of the imagination, and man is the only creature we know capable of such imagination. Through concepts we can "put things into words," and then, using mental images, we can go beyond what the eye has seen, elaborating images of what we desire to become. The "practical" man sees what he sees and considers dreams to be illusions. Ideals are also realities;

187

they are *real* ideals, and they operate in tangible ways, causing us to rearrange our activities to make the ideal actual.

Ideals arise in individuals. Did you ever see a dream walking? They are the fruit of the imagination, and we do not imagine as committees, sects, and nations. The product of one man's imagination can stir the imagination of another; thus we are fed with images and ideas from our fellows. But each person takes the old ideas and images into himself, breeds them in the heat of his own mind and emotions, and creates his own personal dream.

The individual's ideal may not prove to be novel and original; it may be scarcely distinguishable from the ideals of the society in which he lives. It will be his own, nevertheless, for it will have the flavor of his personality, his idiom, and relate to the world he knows, to the stream of his unrepeatable history. He will apply his ideal to his own life and associations. The only human realities are those of the individual person; we suffer and understand, not as groups but as persons, and we dream as individuals. A nation is only what its people make it; if it cannot find its greatness in its specific men and women, it cannot find it at all.

All advances in idealism come from individuals. Groups do not make progress except by the agency of pioneering individuals within them. In our corporate-mindedness we forget this and give such abstractions as universities, churches, nations credit for progress. No ideal has emerged on the human scene until some one person conceived it for the first time. The fabric of goodness making up civilization is woven from innumerable threads of the idealizing visions of the people.

Each man must be his own prophet if he is to be a man. If civilization is the product of the pooling of the visionary struggles of millions of our fellows, we cannot deny the need to make our own contribution to the swelling stream. The most debilitating influence of the conception of divine power is that it deprives men of the assurance of their own ability and responsibility to create their own ideals.

What if every person on earth were convinced that he was an agent of prophetic vision, that through the crucible of his fervor new dimensions of being, new gains in life would be added to the race? This is the concept of a democracy of religious growth and participation. Life is complex. We need not only the ideals of a few creators that can influence all humanity but a multitude of daily ideals. Every care can deserve our attention, our concern for development, and the world be bettered in the improvement of its most humble parts. Thus would be eliminated the excess of slovenly labor, bad housekeeping, and laziness due to individuals who excuse themselves from standards of achievement.

Too often the person of complex intelligence, of much learning and little wisdom, does not find enlightenment but only confuses the issues. Much passes for reason that is rationalization, the justification for believing as he has before. The individual excuses himself from decisions by saying, "Who am I, one ignorant man, to question the judgment of church and country? Can one person discern a truth and morality superior to that of the powers and dignitaries?" Sometimes he can. The hope of democratic institutions is that the "common man" has a directness of understanding and insight often superior to that of the "informed expert." The man who knows much may bog down in a welter of detail, whereas one of simpler understanding sees to the center of the issue.

Amos, reputed to be a countryman, a trimmer of sycamore trees, analyzed the evils of Israel as no other priest or prophet before him. How could Amos see the injustices to the poor, the emptiness of official religion that overlooked civic abuses while it cared only for its sacrifices? Because he was a husbandman, and saw that the human orchards of Israel were badly cared for.

Ideals are a commonplace in human experience; we have ideas of betterment every day. Most of us do not trust our own judgment, discounting our own insights. "If it were that simple someone else would have thought of it before now," we say to ourselves, and pass it by. The most profound of ideals are so simple as to be obvious. The insight that slaughter is a stupid way to settle disagreements is something millions have seen, but the nations are not able to give heed. A child can see that all men are basically alike; it takes learning to be prejudiced. Amos saw the evil of the wealthy gouging the

189

poor. Amos became a prophet because he believed in his own idealizing insight and spoke his own judgment. The world would greatly increase in morality if each person heeded his own idealizing intuition and followed it to speak and act.

The ideal not only works to renovate society; it is the means whereby the individual creates himself. The imagination is the forerunner of the man, for he is not something finished but a continual becoming. He moves from what he was to what he will be. We are much; our imagination tells what we may be. The mind gives us an image of the future self. When we follow this lead and become this image, the mind, sighting from there, can set for us a further ideal. There is no foreseeable end to our becoming if we will believe in and follow our imagination. Progress is cumulative; we move forward one advance at a time, and we cannot foresee the second and third advances that will proceed from the first.

The person who gets into the habit of responding to his own visionary voice will increase its facilities and scope, just as he can exercise and increase any talent. We grow under the tension between the ideal and the real; growth is bought with unremitting discontent and endeavor. Unless the dream of becoming is more enticing than what we already are, we will remain in our present condition. The virtue of man is his incompletion, but being unfinished is a point of view. A man has to believe he is unfinished, or he is finished. His ideals are his announcement of incompletion.

The paradox in the excellence of past achievements is that they were good enough for the past but they are never good enough for tomorrow. We do something today — plant a garden, build a house, cook a meal, write a poem, paint a picture — and when we finish we say with satisfaction, "That is as good as I can do." We go to sleep with that satisfaction. When we awaken, we discover that we cannot live on yesterday's self-congratulation. We must earn it again the next day. Nor is it enough to repeat what we did yesterday; we must do it differently and better.

We are what we do. If we repeat yesterday's doing, we repeat ourselves. We cease to grow, which means that we begin to die. If we only make today as well as we made it yesterday, we are not making ourselves. It is less to repeat a thing than to do it the first time. Each thing we do suffers subtly by repetition.

This is the deep reason why everyone must create his own dreams. If we borrow someone else's dream, as a housewife buys a dress pattern, we do not make ourselves but a stereotype. Each of us has his own idealizing capacities. It is not enough that we become by doing our own acts; we must gauge and adjust those acts by our own ideals. Only the man who does this is an original, himself. And in thus becoming himself, he adds his singular contribution to the human scene. The first contribution he can make to others is the self he has within him to become. Not only is the gift without the giver bare, the gift is the giver.

The Metropolitan Museum in New York has a superlative collection of paintings by Rembrandt. Their dates reveal the story of how Rembrandt became himself. He was an early success at painting stylish portraits. They are formally posed and seldom probe beneath the surface appearance of the sitter. When he was forty his people became more human, with more depth of personality. The better painter he became, the less popular were his works.

Some people must have advised Rembrandt to paint as he had earlier, when he received more commissions, but he listened to himself and painted in his own way. In his fifties he was painting "Old Woman Cutting Her Nails" and other masterpieces. With each painting his vision becomes more profound, until it is hard to endure the beauty of his models. His later self-portraits have a sympathy and poignancy that is kept from bathos only by the immense dignity of the man who looks at us with immeasurable patience and wisdom.

No one else could have given Rembrandt the ideals whereby he became Rembrandt. No one before him had been over the road this painter traveled. His questions and answers had never been written. I have known people who did not paint their self-portrait, as did Rembrandt, but who like him became their self-portrait, in that their lives were a long drawing and redrawing of their own image, and each day they became more themselves.

191

What is this mirror in which we look to draw this face of ours? The mirror is our ideals, what we are wont to call our better self. It is that, but it is even more our becoming self. Our ideals are the self that we yet may be. We forsake them and fail them only to our own and to the world's poverty.

IDEAS AS SEEDS

In the panorama of cultural evolution we can trace back to the seed from which the tree of culture has grown. The indispensable seed is the idea. Some ideas do not come until the time is ripe for them to germinate, and they may come to several persons about the same time. But the dramatic changes in the course of cultural development depend on ideas. We can wonder how some ideas were born — the idea of the stone tool, the idea of hafting stones and making axes and spears and arrows of them, the idea of the wheel, the idea of taming fire, the idea of taming and utilizing wild animals, and the idea that started neolithic revolution, the orderly planting and tending of the seeds of the plants, rather than gathering the fruits of their wild and untended growth.

Sometimes ideas are born and lie idle, like unplanted seeds, for many centuries, before they are planted and multiply. Such an idea was that of the atomic structure of matter, which was the conjecture of early Greek philosophers but was not utilized and developed until two thousand years later. Here was a seed produced before the time was ready for its planting. Or perhaps the seed was planted soon after it was generated, but certain accidental circumstances prevented its growth. When are the times ready? The answer is difficult. It has been said that nothing can stop the growth of an idea whose time has come.

With the development of science, the concept of research and the use of the hypothesis, we have come to cherish ideas as seeds. Some men who have peculiarly fertile imaginations are set aside as "idea men" and given the task of thinking up possible answers, possible points of beginning. Ideas are intangible commodities. They are difficult to judge, for who can tell which idea will prove fruitful in long application? It may take lifetimes for some ideas to be judged true or false

192

by their application. Consequently, even though the idea men receive more encouragement and support than ever before, they are still largely neglected, even scorned as crackpots and radicals. If their ideas are at all revolutionary, and thus promising, they will deny the commonly accepted sense and practice of their times.

The idea men in the field of religion and morals have been called prophets. A good idea is a prediction of where to look for the answers to quandaries. A hypothesis predicts a solution. The scientist then tests out the prediction and discards it if it is a false prophecy. Without hypotheses (prophecies) the scientist would have no bases on which to set up his experiments. He must have something to try out before he can make a trial. In moral realms we must have ideas as to where the good lies before we can seek it.

Such a predictive moral idea is the one accredited to Jesus, that he who lives by the sword will die by the sword. The wars and violence that have engaged the nations since then have tested this now ancient prophecy. Perhaps only now, with the implements of total war, are we at the point of making a complete test of this idea. We are now told that both the United States and Russia have sufficient weapons to totally destroy each other, and all the other peoples of the earth. We have invented the term "overkill" to describe this unhappy preparedness for a surplus of death over that which is alive to kill.

The tragedy of the sufficient idea lies just here. If mankind had recognized the merit of this moral idea two thousand years ago, and ceased to live by the sword, unimaginable suffering and loss could have been avoided. If we heed it now, we will survive the peril of atomic and germ warfare.

The fullness of the present consists in living prophetically into the future. Two kinds of acts engage the future. There are those that we can fully accomplish now, which have foreseeable future utility, such as building a road or a bridge. But there are some future needs which we feel we must plan for but have not the engineering to handle. The needs themselves escape our powers of estimation; we cannot fully conceive and map them. One such need is for an adequate world government and world court, but what would its satisfactory form and constitution be? Our theorizing is done blindly, for we have no tested principles and procedures to guide us in this unexplored area of future problems.

The fact that we cannot solve these problems now does not relieve us of the responsibility of doing something about them now. We can sense some of the probable directions of development, frame ideals, posit necessities, issues, dangers, and rewards. We can theorize or work with ideas, hoping that these will function as seeds from which world law and government will some day develop.

The sowing of seed is a legitimate function. In farming seeding is an art, requiring special knowledge, skills, and machinery. Soils and seasons must be known, and science will treat the seeds against disease. There are large grain operations in the prairie states where sowers start in the spring in Texas and work their way north, sowing wheat fields all the way into Canada. Then they return south and start their seeding operations over again. They do no cultivating or harvesting; other crews follow after them to do their specialized tasks.

Is there a role in human evolution for those who can only plant seeds, who will be unable to live to harvest the crops that grow from them? Moses led his people to a Promised Land that he himself would never enter. Research scientists work on experiments that only future generations of scientists can conclude. Are there standards by which we can judge the success of seed-sowing, even though no prospect of crops appears likely for generations?

One concept of success involves immediate results, such as immediate profits and sales in business. In book publishing this philosophy seeks an immediate buyer response, hoping for a best seller. If a book does not sell in a few months, it is "remaindered," and the unbound copies are sold for paper. A university press, on the other hand, publishes books that it believes need to be published, whether they will sell in volume or not. They may sell at a low volume for many years. These books are often seed-books, tools for the specialists, for scientists and scholars. The books are seeds in the sense that

194

their ideas are germinative; they are judged, not by their present popularity, but by their future significance. You cannot judge a university press book by the success and failure standards of the commercial press. You cannot judge the seed-sower by the standards of the harvester.

There is an art in selecting seeds. William James speaks of live and dead issues. Some continue to sow seeds whose growth has already been accomplished. They are planted, not because they promise a new crop, but because of the attractiveness of the crops they have produced in the past. The ideas of traditionalism are such old seeds, and the crops they will produce are fully predictable, and fully repetitious.

It is another matter to select seeds that will produce novelty and progress. Such a collection of seeds was the Declaration on Human Rights of the United Nations. This has not been accepted officially, yet the seeds of the ideas of human equality and freedom are sown in the minds of humanity and will produce rich harvests in future generations. Our own Declaration of Independence and Constitution were not only political instruments within our own young republic. They were seed ideas that have taken root and borne fruit in the political institutions of many nations that came into existence after our own.

There is an art to keeping the seeds in the ground until they can sprout, to preparing and cultivating the soil, warding off pests, and protecting the unsprouted seeds from rot and mold. The seed must have its chance to germinate and to sprout. This can be a matter demanding great endurance for one who plants seeds that may need generations in order to sprout. Such, assuredly, are the seeds of a religion for one world. These are ideas which the world is advanced enough to have forced into man's consciousness. The time has come for them to flourish as ideas. But the world is not yet ready for them to germinate into influential institutions and movements. They will intrigue the loyalty and labor of but small minorities, whose function will be the tending of the seed.

There will probably not be a functional world government in several lifetimes, with world free trade and uninhibited movement of people between the continents. We will not live to see the breakdown of cultural barriers and religious antagonism, the dissipation of racial and ethnic prejudice. We will not see the commonwealth of man flourishing. Nationalism and regionalism will develop to new heights before the necessity of world unity will supersede them. One-world religious fellowship, where differences are accepted as valuable variations rather than as threatening heresies, a world liberalism, acceptance and cooperation in the religious sphere — this will be the last of the unities to come.

Any attempt to picture this necessity, to demonstrate it in miniature, can only be a seed. It may flourish in individual lives, to be the inner world of their contemplation and their idealism. It may prevail in minority group institutions, such as the liberal fellowship. Our hope is that it will become the concern of an international minority. But even the greatest development in our generation can be but a seed before the need of the world.

In the dust bowl, reclamation of the prairies is attempted by sowing clumps of sod across wide areas. These take root and begin to spread out, slowly filling in the gaps between the widely scattered clumps. Religious societies with a one-world orientation are today but such widely scattered seed clumps, growing in an unfriendly desert of opinion and prejudice. We can only hope that over centuries they will stubbornly extend their edges, until the tall grass of prosperity and peace and brotherhood grows over a united world.

THE RENEWAL OF CHANGE

Can we live by realities, or must we have resort to myth in order to cast the world in the shape of our desires? This is the question that underlies all religions. How far can religion be a simple realism, seeking to bring men into adjustment to things as they are? If there were not values in realism, we would not be the curious truth seekers that we are. But are these value enough, or must we have a further security, a faith to assure us, when our search for knowledge ends in the unknown and the unknowable, or when the facts force a conclusion not to our liking?

Underlying these queries is a question about human nature.

Can we live with reality regardless of what reality may be? When through science we set out to make the nature of the world known to us, we are putting ourselves on trial: Can we accept the world which our research will uncover? If it turns out that the world operates differently from the way our ancient faiths decreed, can we reshape our beliefs and expectancies, the essential ingredients of our morale, in order to be creative and happy persons in the world as we come to know it?

Haunting the poetry of all times and places is the theme of transiency. "This too shall pass away." The Hindus have looked unflinchingly at the never-ending flux and change of the natural world, but they have sought to escape its consequences by judging that all material things are only maya, illusion. The panorama of change is multiplied through reincarnations, for men have series of lives, each one conditioned by the one that preceded it. They do not look upon these successive visitations to life with anticipation but seek to escape the wheel of rebirth and maya into the world of the spirit, where there is no more life and death. Although they admit that flux and change are in the nature of things, they erase the demands of this knowledge by denying that the world of things is real.

Our intuition and knowledge find this world of change to be, not illusion, but the one and valid world. We have no other choice but to affirm the goodness in our lives even as they are passing. The living organism begins to die as soon as it is born. We must acclaim life, if we can, even though it is only a long dying. We must find good in working even though the products of our labor are fleeting.

Our potentiality for adjustment lies in the amorphous, unstructured nature of the human personality. Our moods are what our culture, in all its myths and expectancies, has made them. If we had been brought up with another view of the world, what now seems emotionally indispensable would concern us little. Cultural anthropology demonstrates that different peoples have different attitudes and needs, having been oriented to different world views, different kinds of reality and hope. Whether this cultural relativism might apply to

197

any and all extremities of viewpoint we do not yet know.

In the world of evolution there are no fixed creations and forms. All things grow out of the past and into the undetermined future. The unmoving stars move. The solid earth trembles and quakes as it shifts to new contours, and cities roll and tumble as the earth buckles. Our life process, having endured for hundreds of millions of years, may be snuffed out by radioactive poisons.

Insecurity is a consistent theme in neuroses and psychoses. Some people cannot endure it. They must know what they can count on or their minds grind to a halt. They flee the world of reality into the shades of an illusory world where they can huddle until they die. Change will go on, but they have refused to reckon with it any more.

If man is a creature of change, he should develop health and creativity when he accepts his own nature and the nature of the world. Change does not threaten man but challenges him. He can find in it his native emotional environment. If he pursues growth rather than fixity, he will be exploiting his own nature, and he can be well adjusted and happy. If the universe is in constant change, and man can accept and even glory in this, he will at last be able to be at home in the world.

Attitudes are embedded in language and folkways. It is onerous to shake off the patterns of feeling and behavior of past ages, for we live by the customs they established, and speak the language they devised to express the meanings of their view of the world.

If the universe is constantly self-creative, the theologians must adapt their attributes of the Creator to correspond with the nature of the world he has created. Several concepts of a struggling god, a god of growth and change, have been offered. The changeless being, the unmoved mover, is passing. He was relevant only when the universe was conceived as stable.

Man can endure and thrive in a world of change. Biologically he is as much a creature of change as anything else. The life process is unthreatened by the passing of individual creatures, for life is a continuity of the species through generations of perishing individuals. Life is not threatened by change, for life is change.

Our shift of emphasis must be simple but drastic. Instead of trying to *get* somewhere, we must try to *go* somewhere. We shift emphasis from the destination, as if it were a fixed resting place, to the going. It is not *what* we become that is important, but *how* we are becoming. What we do in the becoming is more important than what we become, because what we become is but a stage in a further becoming. There is no finality in life's achievements. If we attempt to stabilize something already done, it becomes our tomb.

If you put your hand on a surface, you have a sensation of touch and texture for a while, and then your hand accustoms itself and you lose the sense of feeling. You have to move your hand over the surface before the sensation is renewed. You feel, you live, only as you move. If you stay in one place too long, your hands and feet go to sleep. Inertia is death.

In the face of these commonplace experiences and what they imply, people still want changelessness. We make virtue out of steadfastness. The man who is always where we have come to expect him to be is the man we trust. The man who is always eluding us we mistrust. If in his undependability, however, he makes a discovery, this is the man we honor long after we have forgotten the dependable citizen.

Psychologists talk about the process of becoming as an essential concept of personality. A person is not so much what he has achieved as what he is in the process of becoming. Gordon Allport lays stress on what he calls "intentions." One is less that at which he has arrived than the direction in which he is going.

Most of us have a few dominant interests, and in pursuing them we take our shape and direction as persons. If we are to live satisfactorily in change, we must live wholly in change. We must be a powerful and directive current in the flow of events. The elements that will enable us to create meaning and substance in our lives in the flow of change will be strong intentions, which move us to future acts, which involve us in series of related and expanding efforts. The man is his doing.

This kind of person cannot be happy without change. Our

professed longing for a destination is sentimentalized myth. We would not want it if we achieved it. In this is the incipient evil of the society that structures itself toward the attaining of security for its members. It should seek to enable them to attain usefulness and growth. If salvation is anything, it is to live a life of continuing interest, involvement, and growth to the end. The life that has been saved is the life that has been well used. The goal is to stay in movement as long as we live. One doctor, engaged in research, learned that he was a terminal case of cancer. He kept on working steadily until two days before he died. He did not finish his research, but then research is never finished. He fully used his life in going where he chose to go.

We can find security only in the constant renewal of change, in the renewal of intentions and engagements. We have a stability that is found only in motion, the stability of the bicycle rider, who begins to fall over as soon as his forward motion is retarded. The hardest job I ever had was ushering in a movie theater. If the block I was working became filled, it was my task to stand at the head of the aisle, straight and motionless. After a few minutes every muscle would begin to protest. I would make every possible excuse to move — go down the aisle to look for empty seats, go out for a drink of water, talk to the doorman, anything to get away from stability. Nothing is harder than not moving.

The most insecure people are the retired, those out of work, those who can think of nothing to do. If a line of development becomes dull, if a goal is neared, then we must renew change. We must flee all finishes and make every ending a new beginning.

RELIGION AS EXPERIMENT

Once the liberal departs from the shelter of revealed truth, he finds himself in a welter of conflicting opinions, theories, and incomplete knowledge. This is the world of science. Science has only insufficient theories and incomplete knowledge. Improvement can be made over this incompletion only through research and experiment. When a religion develops with the attitude of science, with a dedication to scientific method rather than to revealed truth, it must reshape its methodology to fit its presumptions.

In some liberal churches the order of service has been in use for as long as the memory of the oldest communicant. It has become an orthodoxy of procedure. Any attempt to change it, to alter one of its basic ingredients, meets the same opposition one would receive in a fundamentalist Baptist church if he tried to eliminate the closed communion and baptism by immersion. In these churches there is very little opportunity for experiment and change of any sort, yet they would consider themselves quite liberal and scientific in outlook. The question is, Can a religious movement be scientific in its attitude toward dependable knowledge and belief, and not equally scientific in its methods, in its ways of association, organization, and forms of celebration? What then follows is the question, Is it possible to have a religion that is operationally conceived as an experiment, as a kind of trial and test, rather than as a final surety of faith? And further, is it possible that faith in a methodology, such as truth-seeking and science, can replace in the religious experience a faith in a fixed revelation?

For some people the excitement of science's unfinished quest for knowledge will be most appealing, and they could be satisfied with none other than a religion of experiment. For them it is sufficient. For others, who need surety (or who have been habituated to it), an experimental religion would seem worse than no religion at all. These seem to be in the majority, even in the liberal churches. What is appalling to anyone committed to an experimental approach is the immense capacity of the human animal for habituation, routine, and submission to tradition.

We must be realistic concerning human nature, for nothing but frustration and chaos ensue when an experimental approach is foisted onto a congregation that is resistant to it. Also, it is possible that the capacity for routine is so predominant in human nature that the appeal of experimentalism will never be sufficient motivation to keep a considerable congregation together. Perhaps experimentation is largely a matter for experts, specialized laboratories, and experimental institutes. Perhaps the great majority can be educated to accept, in time, the *results* of experimentation but will be little involved in the experimentation itself.

If anyone attempts to set up a religious center with an experimental approach, he will be involved in a compounded experiment. First, he will be attempting whatever experiments he and the group seek to prove out. Second, he will be trying to discover whether or not a group can be held together and grow when experimentation is its main concern and occupation, its main group activity. If the group does not thrive, its failure will not prove that under other circumstances, with different personnel and different organizational procedures, a religious group might not thrive with experiment as its basic motivation. It will indicate that such a success is unlikely, and it will also reveal some of the difficulties entailed.

Attempting to create a religious fellowship on the experimental presumption presents massive obstacles. There are four general reactions of people. Most of them have no interest in it whatever, fail to understand it, and see only that it is an outlandish, a bizarre kind of organization. The second group look upon it as a curiosity. It is something that one should visit once, like a wax museum or a flea circus. The third group join it and attend some of its functions, but they relate to it as they would to any other religious organization, showing no inclination to become involved in its experimentation and labors. They may like the unconventional materials and attitudes that they find, but their approach is that of the institutional consumer. They buy what is offered as a product and have no interest in the production. The fourth group, and they are the smallest of the lot, are the workers, who actively engage themselves in the experiments. The difficulty is that they are too few in number to carry the financial and labor load that is entailed. It is as if a manufacturing concern were to expect its experimental laboratory to support itself by manufacturing and marketing the results of its experiments. Perhaps it is an operational fallacy to consider the church as an experimental laboratory, and the whole concept is unsound. Just as a business supports the laboratory, putting its inventions and processes to use in the general plant, so religious movements may have to set up experimental laboratories as separate agencies from the congregations. We resist this conclusion because we are convinced that the experimental attitude is an inherent ingredient of liberalism. The only way liberalism can express itself is through experiment of some sort. A considerable element of experimentation must be present in the methods and program of a liberal church if it is to be liberal in reality rather than in pose.

There are two kinds of religious position. In one, religious knowledge is presented as revealed and final. Religious methods and behavior relating to such knowledge must consist in acceptance and commitment, obedience and faith. In the other, religious knowledge is presented as incomplete, human, faulty, and in process of continuous correction and addition. One cannot relate to this kind of knowledge as he does to the first. He cannot make a final commitment of faith to propositions that are faulty and incomplete. He cannot accept knowledge acquired by men through their own investigations without tentativeness and reservations. The only thing that merits his final commitment is the operation, the seeking for ever more substantial and encompassing knowledge. If we have engaged the scientific attitude in our religious quest, our religious zeal and labore are involved in truth-seeking. This necessitates our being engaged in experiment. The liberal is exercising his religious devotion only when he is actively searching for further truth. The orthodox can pray for their god to reveal the truth to them. The liberal must seek this truth for himself; his search becomes his prayer, his act of devotion or worship. The traditionalist will read his Bible faithfully to learn the truth. The liberal must turn to his sources with an equal diligence and devotion, and these sources are the studies and the sciences of man.

Tillich has said that religion must have a dimension of the ultimate. The orthodox can find this ultimate in the divine revelation. The only ultimate the free man knows is the unlimited beyond that always outstrips his most fervent striving. We cannot attain to all knowledge or perfect truth, but we can be striving for more knowledge, for a greater sufficiency of facts and techniques. We will diligently study all that mankind has learned up to now, but only in order that we may go on to probe the still unanswered questions.

The liberal churches have contented themselves with the first part of this charge. They are commendably avid to seek out the knowledge and theories so far attained, and they have a fair liberalism in keeping their minds open to new ideas and facts; but they are still mainly consumers. They seldom go on to become involved in searching beyond the limits of present knowledge and operational techniques. Thus they have developed a style of programming wherein they have endless forums and discussion groups, bringing in experts in this, that, and the other field, to learn the latest findings. This is very topical and praiseworthy. But it is not enough. They must develop their own areas of pursuit and discovery, conduct their own experiments.

The necessity for such action is so obvious as to be transparent. The search for knowledge and techniques has become highly specialized in our society. Research grants are being issued to specialists in many fields — medicine, all the various sciences, social studies, transportation, government, public health, urban renewal. But where is the research being done in the field of religion? The separation of church and state, which we prize, takes all federal funds and federal intervention out of the area of religion. Except for historical and biblical research, the theological schools show little interest or creativity in this realm. The theologians, for all their mountainous labors, bring forth mousy squeaks. Even those schools training the liberal ministry are more concerned with producing ministers who will behave successfully in churches as they now are than with producing bold experimenters who will make the liberal churches into the experimental outposts they might be. Experimenters are looked upon as dubious clerical material, since they may well disturb the ecclesiastical peace of the churches to which they would minister. Batteries of tests will ordinarily screen them from among the candidates before they are admitted to the preacher factories. They might be too enthusiastic, lacking in the dignity and the presence expected of the liberal ministry.

What are the experiments that need to be carried on in the area of liberal religion? They are of two general sorts. The first is the acquisition of new religious knowledge and theories, in the fields of cosmology, morality, ethical action, the nature of man, the meaning of life, religious education, the development of personality, the solution of pervasive problems, such as war, delinquency, alienation, decline in morale, and over-population. In this religious liberals must study and correlate the findings of other areas of specialized study and the sciences, and also conduct their own research from the peculiarly religious point of view.

The second area of experimentation covers the creation of new kinds of personal and group activity and relationship, wherein emerging religious knowledge is embodied in personal living, in group behavior in the church and community, and in the teaching, rituals, and celebrations of the religious society. In this area we must become creative artists in many of the arts — indeed in all — as well as seekers for truth.

It is here that the resistance of many liberal churches to changes in their orders of service is pertinent. It is disastrous, to both the contents and the containers, to keep putting new wine in old bottles. The possible avenues of experiment and creativity in the area of the arts of religious celebration are at once exceedingly exciting and discouraging: exciting because the use of the dance, music, drama, painting, sculpture, ritual, and architecture to express the new visions of man and the universe that are breaking open to our understanding presents opportunities of such a scope as to be overwhelming; discouraging because of the reluctance of the liberals themselves to capitalize on this opportunity.

What, at least theoretically, are the resources of the liberal churches for engaging in experimentation in religion? They are so vast as to make one jittery to contemplate them. For if liberals ever realized the resources they have, and effectively employed them, they would create a revolution in religious practice, behavior, and attitude that would echo down history.

Every liberal fellowship and church could be a laboratory in religious understanding and methods. If the immense amount of busywork we now engage in, from church fairs and bean suppers and card parties to men's and women's meetings, discussion groups, and religious education, and yes, Sunday services, were turned to creative and experimental uses, the facilities in buildings, equipment, funds, and personnel could produce staggering results. In fact, the facilities are so extensive that if only one church or fellowship out of every hundred became such a living laboratory the results would be revolutionary.

Why doesn't it happen? The answer is at hand: Anton Carlson was wont to observe that people are even now as far from living by the method and attitude of science as was the man in the Peking caves. The scientific attitude of openness, teachability, experimentalism, ruthless investigation, correction and replacement of disproved methods and ideas is a new thing on the human scene. It is understood by only a small minority of the people and is held by fewer still. And even among the small group of research scientists it is usually limited to one or a few areas of specialization. A research chemist may be quite unscientific and reactionary in politics and religion. The great bulk of religious belief and behavior is still pre-scientific. Most people can neither think nor feel as the scientific attitude demands. For this is an *attitude,* a direction of mind, personality, emotions, of one's whole being. In this attitude the human being throws off his immemorial and self-imposed shackles and becomes a free man, free in his thought and in his acts, free from tradition and the weight of past authority.

But the person of the scientific attitude does not thereby divest himself of responsibility; this is freedom, not license. He is committed to confront and to accept the findings of his research, and to live by them today, even as he seeks in further research to undermine them and to replace them by even more dependable concepts and programs in the future. An old Universalist bond of union says that we are committed to "the truth known and to be known." This is good, but it needs to go farther, to declare that we are devoted to the continuing and unrelenting labors and experiments whereby new truth is brought to man's understanding.

There is a dimension of religious commitment here that bears a disconcerting resemblance to the demands of orthodox religion. Some liberals may think liberalism is an easygoing religion, where the old compulsions and commitments are

206

relaxed, a genteel and an unsweaty faith. Far from it. The fundamentalists preach that one must be born again to be saved, and they expect, at least in their oratory, that the believers shall walk "in newness of life." The liberal has an equally demanding prospect, which has been defined by Henry Nelson Wieman as the attitude of holding oneself transformable before the discovery of new knowledge and the necessities in attitude and behavior inherent in new knowledge. The orthodox believer may achieve his new birth in one glorious burial of the old man, and the resurrection of the new, symbolized in baptism. The liberal has no such easy and once-over program. He must hold himself transformable as long as he lives to whatever new evidence the truth-seekers provide him. Since we live within an explosion of knowledge, this becomes a heroic, a religious responsibility.

For the liberal, growing up is not ended at twenty-one. He grows all his days as new experiences, new insights, new understandings enter his comprehension to change the dimensions of his world and his estimation of his own nature. This is the unrelenting frontier, and in it man is forever a pioneer, a discoverer. He invites the obligation of self-renewal in seeking to work in the experiments, whose results will make his self-transformation a necessity.

FELLOWSHIP IN CREATION

In most job situations a kind of security grows out of a continuity of expectancy and performance. The craftsman comes to know just what he must do to satisfy his own standards of excellence and to produce a product that pleases his customers. The amount of his labor is fixed by custom. He belongs among his fellow workers and his fellow citizens if he satisfies these known and accepted norms.

But when a person decides to depart from the social standards of employment and comportment, he loses both his social acceptance and the internal balance and security which come from meeting the ways of his fellows. Then he must find other means of measuring himself and his work and establishing his security of belonging to society and the universe. He must do this through his own imagination and evaluation, since he has departed from the forms that society has set up for him. He creates his own forms and values and justifies himself in his own eyes. What fellowship he can find will come from persons like himself who move out into new realms, and who are also looking for companionship outside the conventional institutions and associations. The fellowship he finds is a fellowship in creation.

Liberal religion, if it follows its own pronouncements and ideals, can scarcely be anything but a fellowship in creation. I would like to discuss this, using my own role, that of the minister, as a touchstone. Perhaps if we look at the minister in three of his manifestations, in the orthodox priesthood, the average liberal ministry, and the creative liberal ministry, we will get a sense of the contrasts and differences involved.

The orthodox priest is in a position of complete authority and security. Since he is the custodian and the purveyor of divine truth and law, his edicts and his functions cannot be questioned. Nor is there any occasion for him to question himself, except to check whether or not he complies perfectly with the dogmas and prescribed rites of the church.

The only creativeness required of him is that of the performer. As the reader, the actor of the rituals, perhaps as a chanter or cantor, or an expositor of the revealed word, he can be an expressive artist. Often he is not that, since his performance of the rituals is magical and not artistic, and the dullest run-through of the verbiage is all that is required. The arts of ritual have flourished in some periods, but they are also liable to fall into the most stolid of routines.

In any case, the orthodox priest has everything prescribed for him, even to the given rite and service for every Sunday of the year. His merit is in obedience and faithfulness to authority. If he attempts to innovate, to create, he stands in the position of being a challenger, not of just the higher authorities of the church, but of God, since God is the source of the creeds and rituals of the established institution. This is a fellowship in faith, not in creation.

The minister of the average liberal church is caught in an in-between role. Although he is supposed to be the minister and preacher of a "free-mind fellowship," in actuality his freedom has severe limitations. His training has not provided him with the body of dogma and the rites of the orthodox, but he has been given a body of learning strangely similar in form and content to that of the orthodox. He also has been taught, in general terms, what is suitable material for his sermons and his services.

When he leaves the school, he finds himself serving parishes which have a set of stereotyped activities and habits, orders of service, hymns, readings, and rituals. These do not vary in any considerable degree from parish to parish, except that there is something of a separation between the liberal and conservative sides of the denomination. In any case, he has to be a replaceable part if he is to have any job security. That is, his performance must be typical enough so that he can move from parish to parish and give satisfactory service. He can do this only if he is conventional and acceptable in the liberal way, a way that within its own prescriptions is hardly more flexible and tolerant of individualism and experimental divergence than is the orthodox. Thus, although what he is able to do in the liberal church might get him fired from an orthodox pulpit, there are other violations of the liberal *status quo* that will get him fired from the liberal pulpit also. If he finds himself at home within the boundaries of liberalism, all is well. But if he continues to be truly liberal and begins to break through into fresh fields of experimentation and change, the liberal parish will treat him with scarcely less tolerance and generosity than will the orthodox parish.

There has been a good deal of activity on the part of the ministry to establish its status as a profession, similar to the professions of law, medicine, and education. The professional is not ordinarily a creative operator. He is trained in his professional school into a tradition of information and practice, as in law and medicine, which he proceeds to apply after graduation. In medicine there is a clear separation between the research scientist and the practitioner. One creates and the other applies.

The professional has the security of the accepted tradition behind him. He has his degree and his license; he does things in the prescribed and legal manner. This is not true of the

209

experimenter, the creator, who is continually venturing into new fields, trying out untested materials and procedures, violating the accustomed ways of doing things. The creator, then, is a perpetual amateur, for his work is carried out where there are as yet no developed professional standards. He does not possess an accredited body of learning, but is rather seeking new information in areas of ignorance.

Religion has historically been the agency of tradition; the ways of religion seem to be inherently orthodox and traditional. It is for this reason that the priests have always persecuted the prophets, and probably always will. Religion has relied on surety, on faith, on divine revelation, on unalterable truths. It must alter its fundamental disposition in order to choose the opposite areas of concern, the uncreated, the uncharted. It must be willing to exchange perfect knowledge for ignorance, faith for doubt, pioneering uncertainty for the assurance of dogma.

This is a matter not only of theory but also of temperament. The experimenter moves in a frontier land where there are no guideposts. He has no time and usage standards by which to validate his findings and conclusions. He cannot be sure when he is succeeding and when he is failing. His most brilliant innovations may bring estrangement and rejection because of their novelty, rather than popularity and "success." He must be the kind of person who can rely upon his own judgment, taste, and intuition for his assurances, rather than upon the agreement and support of the populace.

The relation of the experimental minister to the people is revolutionized. Whereas his typical role enables him to substantiate his message with "Thus saith the Lord," as an experimenter he must admit that he does not have the answers, but is rather seeking them. In this role his position is not superior to that of all other seeking and ignorant men. He does not even know whether he is asking the right questions and is on the right tack. This is a far cry from the priestly assurance that "I am the way and the truth and the light, and none cometh unto the Father but by me."

It came as a pleasant surprise to enter graduate study in a university and discover that there were professors who were willing to admit that they did not know the answers. One had presumed that what equipped one to be a teacher was the possession of the answers. But the graduate professor is willing to say, in a context of equality, "We all know what has already been discovered. These are some of the unanswered questions. We will search for answers to them together."

In this setting democracy and equality have been restored to the educational situation. The student may not know as much as the professor, but he knows enough to share with the professor the remaining areas of ignorance. Their equality lies in their knowing enough to know what they do not know. Here degrees and professional titles are of no practical value, for in the areas of ignorance there is no authority for anyone to have. Here authority must be discovered by uncovering new information. Thus the only authority is functional; each person is measured by what he is able to produce in the future, not by what he has mastered or discovered in the past. In scientific research important new findings are often made by younger men.

In the experimental religious society the minister assumes no role relating to the parishioners other than that of being a fellow seeker after enlightenment. The mood of the fellowship is that of the graduate seminar, not that of the undergraduate lecture hall, where the mute mass of students submits to the authority of superior knowledge. What does the minister have to offer in such a situation, in order to justify his assuming the role of minister? Something similar to the qualifications of the graduate study professor. He has some advantage in full-time study and occupation, in longer application to this kind of experimentation. His education, if it did not make him an authority of divine dogma, has given him a background in which he can evaluate problems and estimate the possible worth of hypotheses and lines of investigation. What practice he has had, if he remains pliable, will enable him to discern new forms and questions growing out of the old, for knowledge is a matter of gradual evolution. New areas of interest are somewhat illumined by his old associations.

211

An example occurs in the concentrated study given to the Jewish and Christian traditions in theological education. If the liberal minister attempts to widen his understanding to include the study of other religions in the same depth to which he has explored these two, he will find that his knowledge of two of the world's religions, properly conceived, is of great advantage in helping him to appreciate the others, just as knowledge of his native language can help him in the study of other languages. Not only has he learned something about two distinct religious traditions; he has learned something about religion as a world-wide phenomenon. And the habits and methods of research that he applied to these two can be likewise applied to the others.

Above all the liberal minister, like the graduate school professor, has experience in organizing research projects, knowledge of library and research techniques, skills in examination and framing questions and evaluating evidence. He has no authority in the sense that he can predict what the conclusions will be, but he can serve as a trained leader, organizer, and supervisor. As a minister he is also a full-time employee in the experimental projects, working with others who can give only part-time work to them. In his full-time role he can keep projects moving, fill in gaps, pick up loose ends. He can give continuity and interrelationship to a group of projects. Since he has made this particular kind of seeking his lifework, by the continuity and persistence of his own interest and activities he can act as a bridge for the contributions of many other people in succeeding years. In the transiency of American life, people move rapidly in and out of a congregation. The minister can carry the contributions of those who have already moved elsewhere into the purview and participation of the newcomers. He becomes a synthesizer, a coordinator, a catch-all.

The minister, as its spokesman, as its public front, can give a certain identity and image to a project. This function can be easily corrupted if he becomes merely a front man. But he can carry the findings of the projects to other parts of the country, publicize them through his writings, and dramatize them through his zeal and commitment. Unlike the others

212

involved, who may have full-time commitments in other areas of occupation, he has no other functional identity than his relationship to the religious project. All the members of the group should be willing to commit themselves to it, but he can focus his commitment as they may not be able to do.

There is an intriguing mixture of individualism and group participation in creative collaborations such as this. The creative individual is willing to work in a group, and with others, but he must also be sufficiently motivated to continue alone, and under his own powers, if necessary. Creation with fellowship is fine, but if the fellowship ceases, the creativity must go on or the cause suffers. Therefore the morale and the motivation must inhere within the individual. There is a stubborn integrity to his disposition. He will not change his opinions or course of operation unless he has been convinced objectively that the change is justified. Once new evidence is marshaled, he must be infinitely flexible in readjusting his conclusions and his methods of operation, but he cannot be moved from his experiments simply by social pressure.

If society does not support him, he will go underground, or work on in isolation, as did Cézanne for most of his life. If pressure is brought on him to deny his finding, he may resort to subterfuge, as did Galileo, or defiantly refuse, as did Bruno, but coercion will not alter his convictions. He will endure persecution and even death before he will forego his integrity and his freedom of mind. He will labor for many years, take endless slights and disappointments, if he believes his labors are in the direction of enlightenment, justice, and the betterment of the human lot.

Which is to say that creative and experimental religion is a "religion," a way of life, a devotion and a dedication. Some of us believe it has a dynamic superior to that of religions based upon authority and revelation. The creator has a loyalty founded in an occupation, a loyalty to the search, an identification with that which is still becoming rather than that which has eternally been. The fellowship of the faithful is well known, and well proved. The fellowship of creation is the only fellowship that can be promised to those who dedicate themselves as pioneers to bring a new form of religion into being.

But it is assuredly not less of a fellowship on this account. Perhaps it carries some of the powers of group adherence of fellowships of the faith when they are small and persecuted minorities. It is certainly a religious way of life and association in its own right, more similar to the schools of prophets of the past than to the priestly congregations.

CHAPTER 12

The Face of Liberal Religion

Liberal religion has no clear-cut face to present to the world. We are more easily describable in terms of what we are not than in terms of what we are. We are somewhat like a cardboard figure with the face cut out in a photographer's booth in an arcade. Anyone can put his head through the opening, have his picture taken, and label the result, "This is a religious liberal."

If liberal religion does not have a face, it is because it is not consistently liberal, for liberalism is a definable, recognizable attitude and practice. If we were liberal personally and institutionally, we would have a liberal face to present to the world. The consistently liberal church is a *rara avis*. Ours is a fellowship where one can be a liberal if he can get away with it, which depends on luck, native wit, stupidly stubborn endurance, and sufficient agility to stay two leaps ahead of the guillotine. The institutions and people of liberal religion take as much delight in persecuting their prophets as has any orthodox movement, ancient or modern.

The liberal face is worn by a few churches and individuals. It is not a finished face, for it is still living and growing. It wears the evidence of its past struggles and prophesies the direction of its future shape. It is a face on its way to becoming a face, a face that predicts the face it will be.

215

I do not know whether a denomination can afford such a face. An individual can. A minority can. But can a continent-wide denomination? To live in terms of what the future will be, rather than in terms of what the past was and the present is, is to live in insecurity and peril of failure. Institutions are designed to survive and prosper. For an institution to hold itself expendable for the sake of ideals may be in itself too idealistic. Churches preach hypocritically, "He who saves his life will lose it, but he who loses his life will save it," but they seldom practice what they preach. Perhaps those that have done so *have* lost their lives and are forgotten.

The free church should be equipped to face its task in two perspectives. It should bring a long and profound look from the past experience of the race. What are the enduring values of life? How does our present problem relate to similar crises in history? Only if it has such wisdom can the free church sort out the peculiar dangers and discover the peculiar resources for improvement in the contemporary scene.

But along with using tradition and history, the church must also be the most modern and realistic of institutions. It should be daring and radical in its experimentation with the latest theories and discoveries. Further, it should itself be an inventor and innovator. It should be prophesying in its own behavior the way the race must go. It should be the foremost experimental laboratory in human relations of its time. Instead of designing its techniques to save men for an afterlife, it should be demonstrating its efficiency in saving for men the creative and moral goodness of the lives they are now living.

Obviously most free and liberal churches are failing at this task, and many so labeled are not even at the job. But I am sure that only the liberal church can and will tackle it. This is a safe bet for if any conservative church undertook the task it would make itself into a liberal church as it grew in its work.

The liberal church must be a free society. Even though this has been a traditional emphasis, because of the increasing infringement of freedoms and civil liberties in the larger community the religious society must prize and emphasize and define the ideal freedom of its miniature community. Obviously such a society will not be an accident; it will come into existence and sustain itself only through the people who compose it. These people must comprehend the nature of freedom, and they must have an abounding love for freedom. Too many of our Unitarian and Universalist churches, far from accomplishing this ideal, have a real mistrust of the free man.

Since this church is free, it may not exclude any from its membership. But it will have a built-in mechanism for sorting out its kind. This mechanism will be its own practice of free ways, which will become a test of fire for anyone who seeks to join the company. Such a society is immediately and painfully rough on any incipient Hitler or dogmatist. He will not be expelled or excommunicated from the body of the free, but after testing the climate he will remove himself to more congenial temperatures. This treatment may seem ruthless and inhospitable, but it is an irrevocable necessity if the free church is to stay free and increase in freedom. If it is not resorted to, then many will join the church who neither love freedom for others nor desire it for themselves, and soon they will smother all venturesomeness of the free spirit.

This is just what has happened to many of our churches. They have wanted to have new members, but persons of the free temperament are always scarce. The temptation is to belittle our uniqueness and invite in the congenial Protestants and others who are merely looking for a neighborhood club and a place to put the children in Sunday School. Their attendance is prized and their pledges pay the bills. The temptation, nay, the habit, is to hush up controversy, muzzle the radical, and minimize differences of opinion in order to make the immigrants more comfortable. Freedom cannot survive such adulterations.

On the other hand, the wide open and continuous practice of freedom will not lose you the real converts you seek. If the newcomer has the taste and zest of freedom in him, he will come back, if only to continue the argument. The ones you lose you should lose, for the free society must be selective in this world of slaves and mannikins. The free men winnowed out of the chaff of the conformists will be the church's strength and life. If this means that you must continue to be few, so be it. Your value is in your quality, not in your bulk.

Fundamental to this freedom is a respect for oneself and for others. I was once asked if I requested a statement of belief from someone joining the church. To me this is an incomprehensible insult to the dignity of a free man. Each man must have the inalienable right to create his own beliefs and hold them as he will. To partake of the free society a man only need love freedom. Other than to believe in freedom as a principle and a process, he need not subscribe to any particular dogma. When we respect men and women in their capacity to think, judge, and choose for themselves, a too consistent agreement will become suspicious and disagreeable.

The task of the free church is to encourage its members in their independence. It does this by nurturing and supporting their attempts to stand on their own feet. In the free-for-all, conducted with no loss of affection and no anger, wherein the most violent disagreements are cause for rejoicing rather than lament, and where a man is loved the more, the more ably he defends his opinions, and where the man is loved the most when he proves that he can readily change his viewpoint when he is proved in error — in this society persons can become mature in judgment and in the exercise of freedom. When they go into the wider world, where they no longer are upheld in their freedom by their compatriots in liberalism, these men and women will be able to stand alone against all tyranny and all servility if need be. They will have the courage and the conviction of those whose liberty is their faith.

The world needs such men and women today. How abhorrent is the spectacle of entertainers, teachers, public servants fawning and groveling before the investigators. Thought control and political orthodoxy can be fastened only upon slaves and cowards. Free men are the salt of the earth and the leaven of the lump of the democratic nation. My grandmother used to keep some of the dough from each baking, in which the yeast would work, and which would be used to leaven the next batch of bread. The free church must be such a lump, where the yeast of freedom is always working and increasing, for it is our task to be the carriers and breeders of freedom in the world.

The only authority for the free man lies in the consistency

and adequacy of evidence in any proposition. Authority does not inhere in the man, but in his demonstrations of competence. Thus no title or position of itself gives a man prestige and power. The free man bows to no office or throne. Without awe for the official, the free man never accords an automatic respect to any man, regardless of his position. He recoils from self-importance and pose. Above all he is not deluded that a man's ability to get elected to office assures that he has any sense of decency. Even after being installed in office he may continue to be a crass and petty politician. Thus the free man can never come to worship the state and its officers. No one becomes anything more than a man in his eyes. To encourage this insouciance and disrespect of officialdom is the task of the free church, for it is the only sure bulwark against statism, the worship of nationalism and totalitarianism.

The minister in the free church has a unique significance above the value of what he may say or do; this is the inherent value in his performance as a free man. The members of a free church in a real sense purchase freedom for their minister. He is answerable only to them. If they support him, then relative to his income he cannot be touched by the rest of society. He will not lose his job for acting as a free man. Thus he is free to be the goad and gadfly of the community. He can accuse and criticize wherever he believes evil is in operation. Around his position our society has drawn a King's X.

He plays a useful function to his congregation. He can do tasks for them which might bring to them heavy reprisals. I partook of this relation with one of my members. He did not feel that he could criticize the labor policies of the company for which he worked, because of penalties that the company could lay upon him. He brought me the material and I became his spokesman. But this cat's-paw function of mine lasted only a short time. Soon he gained in confidence, and in a few years he became a labor leader in open opposition to his company's policies. As his union gained in power, so he gained in security and in protection of his rightful freedoms.

To hear a man speak who you know is as close to being a wholly free man as is humanly possible is a value in itself. Whether what he says has any great profundity, his freedom is itself a profound manifestation, and a symbolic demonstration of the ideal freedom of the religious fellowship. The free pulpit is something that the congregation should prize not just for the benefit of the preacher; it is of itself a kind of functional shrine to the ideal of freedom, and its use each Sunday morning is a practical ritual in a religious faith.

Will the time come when the people of the liberal church realize how magnificent the free pulpit is, regardless of the stature of the man who occupies it? Just as the sacred altar of the orthodox has for them a meaning in itself apart from the priest officiating at the mass, so the free pulpit should be elevated as a symbol in the veneration of the free congregation. And they should use it themselves more often than they do, asserting their privilege to themselves to be the free preacher.

Is there anything more noble in the human community than a man standing before his peers and declaring to them the most urgent and disturbing thoughts he has? Communication is the foundation of community and the structuring fabric of society and civilization. Those church members who punish and persecute a minister for speaking against their beliefs and prejudices, those who do not prize his free voice even when they dislike the things he says, have desecrated a central shrine of their faith, and they have betrayed the faith and spirit of their fellowship. If the salt has lost its savor, wherewith shall it be salted?

The free society of the liberal church operates as something near to an idealistic anarchy. Here, for the sake of the creative uses of freedom, we are willing to remove all rules and laws from our fellowship and let men be what they are and declare what they think. The free man must, ultimately, be a law unto himself, for the pioneering outreaches of his probing will reach beyond the boundaries staked out by law and custom. He must be allowed to move out and forward into the unexplored without penalty if the race is ever to advance and progress. His must be the privilege to doubt any credo, to pursue any skepticism.

The exercise of the free society demands maturity. Just as the doctor and the psychiatrist cannot afford to be shocked by any human sickness, aberration, or mania, even so those who explore fearlessly in the realm of ideas cannot be squeamish. One's range of understanding, appreciation, and liberality can be measured by his capacity not to be shocked and offended. Such reactions are not the marks of virtue so much as of immaturity and impractical "delicacy." Vigorous freedom demands a strong intellectual stomach. Freedom has only those uses to which the people are capable of putting it. Most churches, even the liberal ones, are like the parlor of bygone days where few things could be touched by the children. To make our churches open, fearless, exploratory, places where the real problems are attacked with candor — that should be our task. And there is no area of human concern, no occupation that can be placed outside the moral criticism of the religious fellowship.

It is the task of the free church to open wide the doors to growth. The ultimate justification of freedom is that it provides the space wherein the expansion of knowledge, skills, and creative expression can take place. Let the venturesome ones run as far out, as far ahead, as they can. Growth partakes of variety, choice, comparison. Only where there are no oppressive dogmas, where ideas range freely in competition and contrast, can the new insights arise, the creative adjustments and explorations be made. Men create their own purposes and ideals, and it is in the stimulating conflict of beliefs and ways of life that moral insights break open to our usually conventional and sluggish imaginations.

Basic to our self-definition must be the espousal of the free-mind principle. It has not yet been clearly affirmed and practiced. The free mind is not without direction or method, for the result would be not liberty but libertinism. It accepts Curtis Reese's principle of "devotion to objective inquiry, involving respect for facts and integrity in dealing with them." The free mind is free to consider the evidence and to make judgments upon it, but it is not free to ignore evidence, to believe whatever it chooses.

By its very nature it is committed to the scientific method and attitude just as far as these can carry it. Where the range of objective study and analysis fails, it cannot believe whatever it chooses and become dogmatic. The free mind is not privileged to worship ignorance by altering its name to "faith," or to elevate sentimentalities into divine revelation in every crevice still unillumined by man's investigative intelligence. The free mind has modesty, integrity, and conscience. Its ready reply when facts are wanting is "I do not know." It is courageous enough to live with its own ignorance and dares to postpone the answering of questions that are as yet unanswerable. Dogma is composed of facile answers to unanswerable questions.

Conversely, the free mind must be ready to abide by the weight of evidence and to modify its opinion and practice in the light of available knowledge. It is ready to be transformed by the incursion of new evidence and experience. It willingly comes to terms with new knowledge and takes the consequences. These consequences are the discarding of invalidated opinions and the submission to growth and change under radically altered points of view.

Ministers say that they must begin with the people where they are. This is poor policy. It is better to start with the people where the facts are, for anything less is condescension and dishonesty. In the free-mind *fellowship* the mind of the minister assumes no privilege over the mind of the parishioner. He shares whatever knowledge and opinions he has and invites others to make of them what they can. All issues are discussed freely, just as he expected his professors in graduate school to treat him as an equal and as an adult. If this is not where the people are, the minister insists on importing the facts into their discourse, to see that it is where they arrive.

Out of this process the recognizable face of liberal religion will develop. The known facts about the universe and the human situation are not wholly equivocal. The nature and working of things are knowable, and they do not admit of every possible interpretation. By the admission of the facts, agreement of opinion about the facts will be indicated. If this were not so, the enterprise of science would be chaos.

We can trace where this procedure will take us by following some of the implications of the arguments in the first chapter of this book, the claims that this is one world and we are one humanity. Religion with its vaunted ideals of the brotherhood of man resists actual brotherhood as do no other cultural forces. Here our face can take on an original and valid cast. We can accept the evidence of one race and one culture and act according to its implications.

A face is known by the company it keeps. Some married couples come to look like each other. The face we develop will gain proportions and miens through our associations. Paradoxically, one is prevented from being some things by becoming inclusive. One cannot belong to a white citizens' committee if he desires equality for all people. If liberal religion is inclusive, it cannot identify with exclusive movements. We need not discard what we find of value in exclusive movements, but we cannot unite with them. We must seek a wider base for our associations.

Many of us were born Christians but have discarded some of Christianity's beliefs. We can retain, however, all that continues to be valid for us in Christian teachings and traditions. We could have continued to call ourselves Christian and belonged to Christian churches if the only problem had been the amending of old beliefs, for there is much still available to us in Christianity.

It is not our disbeliefs but our liberal beliefs that make it impossible for us to be Christians. We have added so much to our family of beliefs and appreciations that cannot be contained in Christianity, that it has become inadequate to house our religious experience. In thus widening our scope of appreciation we have not been converted to another tradition, to Judaism, Islam, or Hinduism. We can accept their offerings without their names, which have the same limitations as does Christianity.

To talk about a liberal Christian, a liberal Moslem, a liberal Buddhist carries an inherent contradiction, for one cannot follow out the full demands of the liberal viewpoint and remain conclusively identified with a religious movement that identifies with only a portion of the race and of human culture. Liberalism is the corrective agent for all regionalisms.

This is not to say that many Christians, Moslems, and Buddhists are not liberal in many ways, often more liberal than those who call themselves liberals. But they are liberal in spite of, not because of, their sentimental attachment to a parochial religion. Many are illiberal just in those areas where they insist on identifying themselves with a regional or ethnic religion. Most prejudices are not so much pre-judgments as they are pre-loves and pre-belongings.

Hidden within provincial religions, lurking beneath high-flown idealism, is a barbaric need to be superior and unique, to be God's chosen people, to be the privileged possessors of the truth.

Unforeseen results occur when we give up a family affiliation with a provincial religion to join the wider fellowship. Ancient emotions and attachments cool and adjust. Childish rebellions and resentments are outgrown. In time one can return to contemplate his first religion in the same spirit as he would the religion of the African tribes, the Aztecs and Incas, the Manus Islanders, or the Hindus. I have discovered Christianity anew as a charming folk religion, belonging among the other folk religions quite fittingly.

It is the task of the free church to be contemporary. The church cannot set itself up in a world apart and claim that the laws of research in the material world do not apply to its "spiritual" realm. Not unless it wishes to be the captive of traditional illusions, fears, and monstrosities. If anything is clear, it is that religions are natural and human accumulations, and they can no more profitably exempt themselves from the criticisms of new knowledge than can medicine or psychiatry.

The free church can provide the refreshing variety of a religious institution without a special ecclesiastical lingo, without a special order of myths, an atmosphere continuous with that of the practical world and the classroom and laboratory, where with ordinary intelligence and insight men approach their common problems. Here is a clean, fresh wind blowing through the dusty aisles of the cathedrals. In the free church that wind can be stronger, more ruthless, more invigorating than anywhere else.

The free church should be the most civilized of all institutions, the most urbane, moderate, candid, and realistic of societies. It need no longer be involved in the barbarisms and sentimentalities of the orthodox. It can go beyond other institutions because it is not involved in the practical compromises of the nation-wide and community-wide institutions.

For a time I looked with envy upon the life of a university professor. I would no longer care to trade places, for long association has caused me to decide that I am freer in the pulpit than I would be in the classroom. I have watched professors tread with discretion when issues of religious dogma came up. Criticism of religious denominations was tacitly taboo. The pressure of political conformity weighs upon the state universities. The public servant is answerable to the entire public, and he is trapped in the mesh of prejudices, dogmas, and rivalries of the public he serves. The politician must court the votes of all groups and all faiths. He cannot afford to criticize the taboos and stupidities of the tribe.

I am convinced that the free church is unique in this, for it can be a completely critical and civilized society if its people are sufficiently liberated and informed to establish it. Here all scientific innovations and theories can find a ready reception, a place to be scrutinized and tried. New interpretations of the universe and of human destiny can be welcomed and explored. New philosophies can be welcomed and tried on for size. Ideally none of the restrictions and inhibitions of other institutions should apply to the liberal church.

The free church is avowedly an idealistic society, in contrast to the world where idealism is falling into disrepute. This is an era of *Realpolitik,* of compromise, practicality, of public opinion polls, sales technique, and box office strategy. Surely the conventional church does not realize how thoroughly it has been debauched by the bitch goddess commercial success. All the impracticality of the idealistic artist, poet, and dreamer should characterize the free church, for this should be the institution bent on visions and prophecy.

In the so-called "practical" world we are willing to sacrifice the lives of our youth in the indescribable insanity of war. Industry has traditionally held the lives of the workers as a cheaper commodity than the goods being manufactured. But the free church asks, in its starry-eyed idealism whether the life and welfare of the people are not the only and final good.

225

Some institution must insist on rubbing the nose of the race in its own nasty brutalities. Never to relent in its struggle against racial discrimination, human slavery, inequality of opportunity and recompense for labor, discrimination against women and all minorities, our medieval horrors in law and punishment, culminating in capital punishment, the shame of murder by the state — it is a sensitive and imaginative conscience that the free church must have. It must be able to penetrate beneath the crust of habit and custom and law to the human misery and poverty, the ignorance and violence and degradation to be found in every community. We must accuse. We must cry shame. We must never be weary, never be satisfied.

For the practical people religion can become the clothespin on the nose to keep them from smelling the decay and putre-faction of the cities in which they live. Their sanctuaries, where they come in their best clothing, freshly washed and perfumed — what relation do these boudoirs of narcissism have to the winos in the gutters of the skid rows and the stinking hallways and alleys of the slums? Behind this pose of sancti-mony the liberal religionist must go, or he is only another snob from another moralistic social clique with a slightly different brand of perfumery.

There is something repugnant about a halfhearted religion. Religious experience and faith should plow up the outreaches and excesses of our beings, just as a symphony exploits the final reaches of emotional power. The liberal church should be a living prophecy of a new world to come. To the final measure of our prophetic insight and wit, we should build into it our visions of the ideal society of the future evolution of the race.

The highest function of the liberal church is to be just that, a foretaste of a world that is in process of self-creation. It should be a community of universal peace and brotherhood, the beloved community. Open to men of all races, nationali-ties, and creeds, it must echo the known unity of the human race and the cultural history of man. It is for this reason that we are attempting to create the equipment and furniture for such a universal community, gathering the symbols, music,

226

literature, idealism, and art of all times and places into one assembly and projection. We feel the same necessity that is felt in the libraries and museums and universities. The whole panorama of mankind must be brought into focus.

Clearly a unified world is being born. Nationalism is in its death throes. The languages and lores are melting into a common pool of human history. And out of the accumulation and crossbreeding of all the local arts and cultures something new is being born, a single, homogeneous culture of humanity. The liberal church must not only see this but foresee it, and move up front to make the first trials and tests of this new era.

It has become a cliché in architecture and industrial design that "form follows function." The use of the building or the machine should define the shape it is to assume. This principle is violated with fake façades that dress up the true structure of buildings, and metal skins draped over automobiles to give them a different form from that dictated by the machine beneath. The form given to a structure by one material and its limitations will be imitated long after the materials have changed. What was true to one material becomes false to that which follows it. Egyptian stone pillars are made in imitation of earlier pillars made from bundles of reeds, and early Greek pillars and temples made of wood are imitated in later temples made of stone. Then we further imitate a stone temple, which is already an imitation of a wooden temple, in buildings made of steel and concrete.

What applies to architecture also apples to customs and institutions. Our particular concern is the form and function of an institution of religion. Like bad architects, we try to keep the old structure of the religious organizations of the past, long after the purpose, use and philosophy of the institutions have radically altered. Retention of the outmoded structure creates the same sense of falsity, even deformity, that distresses us in buildings and machines. Conversely, it prevents us from developing our own true form, which would give grace and attractiveness to us as an organization, as well as immensely improve the effectiveness of our operation.

The true form of a new type of machine, such as the airplane, has been achieved only after long experimentation and development. The same may be said of the best of architecture built to the employment of the new materials and for the new dimensions of living in the twentieth century. Even so, the liberal churches are slowly coming to an awareness of what the form and structure of their institutions and operations must be. We have been personally involved in this at the Charles Street Meeting House to an exaggerated degree, for we have organized ourselves as an experimental laboratory in order to discover what the new forms and functions of liberal religion might possibly be. We have not assumed that we will come to any definitive or dogmatic conclusions, but only that we may perhaps vaguely perceive certain effective lines of development.

Beneath the surface intricacies of theory and philosophy there is always some simple, basic principle at work, in institutions as in all other things. If this principle can be discerned, and its implications apprehended, then the nature of the function involved, and of the form necessary to that function, becomes self-evident. The clue for the new structure for the liberal church is not hidden. Its essential nature was announced in a book title by Julian Huxley, *Religion without Revelation*. It is the difference between an institution that conceives of itself as *having* the truth and an institution that conceives of itself as *seeking* the truth. The difference in the behavior of the people is the difference between *believers* and *seekers*, between dogmatists and liberals. Beneath these differences is the yet more fundamental difference in belief as to the nature of truth or evidence. One believes in revelation and authoritative scriptures, the other in the gradual discovery of knowledge through human effort, with the constant necessity for further search and correction of knowledge.

How will such a difference be reflected in the form and function of an institution? The answer is simple. An institution designed to propagate *the* faith, to hand down dogma, to propagandize a complete and perfect revelation will be set up and will operate in a prescribable way to that end. But an institution designed to search for and discover new and tentative convictions for mankind will be set up in quite a different manner, with radical changes in its program, its approaches, and its methods.

The failure of liberal religion so far is just this: it has not seen how its structure and methods must of necessity change in order to be true to its new philosophy, theory of knowledge, and world view. It has thought it could put its new wine in an old bottle. The liberal church, in its program and methods, its schedule and type of events, even to time and place and manner of its meetings, is almost the same as the orthodox church. Its expectancy of its ministry and other leaders, the manner of their training, and the character of their function have hardly changed at all. Thus the truly radical departure in point of view is hidden behind this failure to create new methods and structure of institutional life and approach. We *look* and *behave* just like all other religious groups.

The fact is that we continue to operate as if we were a dispensing agency for a divine revelation, even though we profess to be seekers after truth. Practically all our operations are set up to promote and peddle opinions already consolidated. A brief run-through of our typical program will illustrate this point.

The service of worship still features the sermon, which has served traditionally to hand down dogma through the agency of an elected intermediary of divine wisdom, an apostle, a reverend, a "man of God." The sermon is wrapped around with readings, hymns, anthems, and rituals from the hymnal, the bound and stabilized font of authoritative worship materials. With rare exceptions, there is not even a place for a reaction of the congregation to the edicts of authority, much less the democratic procedure of a discussion period. The meek pew-sitter has no part in the making of the service, no opportunity for rebuttal.

Many liberal ministers and church attendants will rightly protest that this does not mean that the sermon or the materials of the service are dogmatic in tone or content. More than often they are not, but the service that embodies them is not designed to handle liberal and non-dogmatic materials, but their opposite. The average liberal service frustrates and deforms

229

the liberal principles underlying the viewpoint of the people involved. This is the basis for the discontent we have with our worship experiences in the liberal church.

In general the same criticism can be leveled against the liberal church school. Here progressive methods and project-style learning situations have been adopted. But the whole setting of the classes is that of traditional education, where the student came to receive a quota of classical knowledge and basic skills. The same indictment can be made against the public school. It too is primarily designed to aid the student in *receiving* knowledge rather than in *seeking* knowledge. How can a serious search for new truth and experience be carried out on Sunday morning, with the students attired in their Sunday best, herded together for one or two hours in crowded rooms? The public schools, poor as their performance may be, do have a more realistic setting and time schedule. Although they may use their laboratories to repeat experiments already made, rather than to make new ones, they do have laboratories. Liberal religious education has not begun to consider the revolution in setting, approach, and performance that will ensue when the student, rather than being taught, is accompanied in his search for understanding.

The other youth and adult programs fall into two categories, entertainment and learning, or a strange mishmash of both. The entertainment is usually traditional and stereotyped, with little or nothing "liberal" about it. The study groups generally rely on bringing in a substitute for the preacher or teacher, an "expert" or a "resource person," to whom the gathering listens, with a discussion period following. Occasionally there are courses of study, but here a book or a discussion manual is likely to replace the authoritative person. Again, the method is that of receiving, not that of seeking.

When it comes to the "liberal" function of church fairs, dinners for moneymaking, other commercial ventures, card parties, etc., the less said the better. There is real question whether they have anything to do with any kind of religion, orthodox or liberal.

The attitude of the people toward the liberal church is similar to that of the orthodox. They look upon it as one of their leisure-time activities. They come to be interested, occasionally amused, or inspired, and they hire someone they hope can make them so. They do not look upon the church as a place where one does serious labors. These are part of their own jobs or carried on in their homes. They hire professionals to carry the load of study, labor, and performance in the church, except for the few "workers" to be found in each congregation. Only a few will be stimulated even to some serious reading in liberal religion, as receptive an activity as this is.

Assuming that this is a fair analysis, what should be done to make the structure of the liberal religious institutions embody the principles of liberalism? We get an analogy from education. We repeat the same comparison considered in the chapter "Fellowship in Creation." Formal education is at its best in kindergarten and in graduate school, and what lies in between is sad. We do not intend, as adults, to return to kindergarten, although we might look at it for an answer to our church schools. As adults we might look at the graduate seminars of our universities. By the time the student has reached this status, the distance between him and the teacher has all but disappeared. The frontiers of knowledge have been reached. The problem facing both student and teacher is not the propagation of knowledge already won but the penetration of areas of ignorance where no one has gone. As they face the unknown and the unexplored, all, students and teachers alike, are seekers and workers. They are equals at last.

There is a real satisfaction in attaining the status of graduate student, wherein one's questions and theories find respect and appreciation in the eyes of the professors. To be able to try the mind and skills on new problems, rather than surveying the burned-over fields of scholarship, gives education a new vigor and glamour. The school becomes a workshop, not a lecture hall. The need for the ritual of the scheduled class session and lecture, a ritual just as compulsive and as orthodox as that of the weekly worship service, disappears. The seminar group meets functionally and informally, to share and criticize and correlate the findings of the searchers in their related projects. They are concerned with improving techniques and concepts, as well as with cross-checking results. This is a democracy and a shared questing of those who seek for new and more dependable, more enlightening knowledge of their world.

To carry the analogy of education one step farther: Universities are faced with defining the nature of their primary concern. Are they to merely pass on information and skills already in hand to the students, or are they to be laboratories and research centers for the creation of new understanding? Some schools hew strictly to their teaching roles. Others specialize in graduate studies, even to the degree of the School of Advance Studies at Princeton. Many combine both functions, feeling that basic research will invigorate the teaching program, and vice versa.

What is wrong with the liberal church structurally? It follows the attitude of the college, which says that its function is simply to teach, not to seek new knowledge. And even for this purpose, its methods of propagating knowledge are outdated. The liberal church should become, in structure, an institute of experimentation, study, and promotion. This conviction grows out of years of working in a church set up as a "pilot project." It was set up as a church to engage in pilot projects, but it more logically follows that a liberal church should be set up as a pilot project that also functions as a church. This may seem like a minor difference, but it is more in the nature of a revolution in viewpoint.

The truly liberal and universal church does not yet exist. As a philosophy and as an institution, liberal and universal religion is still being born. It is still seeking to find its true nature and function. Therefore it must set itself up in its organizations for this purpose. Furthermore, since it believes that truth-seeking will be an everlasting process, this will be not a temporary modification of structure and method but a permanent one.

Some may suggest that what we are considering should be done in denominational headquarters, by the curriculum committees of the educational departments, and in the graduate schools of theological education. Yes, it should be done there

232

as far as possible, and much more than at present. But these agencies never will be able to substitute for the necessary creative, experimental, and research functions of the local churches in the liberal fellowship. For one thing, the methods of fellowship, shared seeking, and development of suitable types of assemblies and celebrations can be created effectively only by the congregations themselves. The congregations become living laboratories, trying their ideas and experiments and new knowledge upon themselves. Any valid innovation in experience as profound and interior as the experience of worship or celebration will have to evolve slowly within the creative matrix of the religious fellowship itself. It cannot be delegated to headquarter agencies or theological seminars. The church itself must become a self-creative organism.

This approach will demand shifts in attitude and expectancy that may well prove to be traumatic for established congregations. Several come immediately to mind. First, the expectancy of the church, in all its operations and services, turns to novelty and change, rather than continuity and tradition. Since religion has been inherently traditional and conformist, with only very slow and gradual change in ritual and content of services, where this is possible at all, to turn a church to the exact opposite will be a difficult matter. It is for this reason that ministers who have sought reformations in worship services and other programs in so-called liberal churches have had such rough times. But if we are to function as creators and seekers the change must be effected; otherwise we had better give up our pretensions and succumb into dogma.

Secondly, the prevailing emphasis on regularity of services and functions will be altered. Now it is our habit to meet, with all other faiths, on the "holy day" of the orthodox, and to have our school sessions, study groups, and programs on a weekly or monthly basis. This is the pattern of receptivity, not creativity. I can see a day when a liberal congregation will have a service of celebration *when they have one created*, not at eleven o'clock each Sabbath morning. My feeling about this hour, because of its deadly habitude, is that of remembered games of hide and seek, "Here I come, ready or not."

Perhaps it might be better to have a half-dozen services a

233

year, with full preparation, creation, and participation on the part of an involved group or people, rather than forty or fifty stereotyped and thrown-together services such as we now have. There would be time then to create dances, drama, choric readings, new literary materials, new uses of art and symbolism, to say nothing of addresses given ample time in their preparation. The church would then, in its celebrations, resemble a theater group, putting on its celebration only when it was ready. Perhaps then we would create arts of worship worthy of the name.

As for the preaching, this would, let us say, take the form of reports from study, research, and experimental groups, as well as pronouncements from individuals who believed they had ideas and convictions ready to share with the larger group. The preaching function would be widely shared in a congregation where everyone considered himself to be a full and orginal creative source of the message and means of liberalism.

The architectural "tools" of the average liberal church today are auditoriums and classrooms, dining rooms and parlors — places for various kinds of "feeding." Can you envision a church made up of studios for dance groups, theatrical groups, musical and speech groups, as well as studios for painters and sculptors, and libraries for historical, philosophical, and inter-cultural research? There would be more mundane workrooms for carpentry, furniture making, printing, and facilities for those involved in social and political action, in communication with other groups, speakers' bureaus, and publicity and information bureaus.

If you think this is quite impractical, because of the limited time of the members, who would be employed in other operations and professions, then listen to the worries of the social scientists as to what men and women will do with increased leisure time now that automation is upon us. How better employ free time than in the creative enterprises of liberal religion? But if our people are going to be employed, our churches must change their structure into that of operations, with full and creative use of the persons involved.

These considerations are not the fabrication of an overheated imagination. Nor are they entirely theoretical. They are the product of fifteen years spent in a liberal church that has been slowly evolving into the kind of institution described. We have gone only partway toward this goal, but the direction of our movement has been unmistakable. In the experience of developing from one form of structure to another, we have become convinced logically, emotionally, and aesthetically of its justification. Many of our efforts have been failures, but in each failure we have been persuaded that we would not have failed had there been sufficient participation and support. The feeling of the effort was good and right, even if it fell short of its goal. Other of our efforts have succeeded far beyond our anticipation.

Much more important than any single project in which we have been engaged is the new structure and function that we have assumed as an institution. Incomplete as yet, it is validly predictive of the future. This new form has been discovered by getting into the midst of it and living it. It has been not a theoretical conclusion as much as the slow accumulation of a lived experience. Liberal religion is everybody's business. Regardless of his profesional involvement or area of interest, the member has a peculiar contribution to make in the development of liberal religion itself. He is not in a liberal church to get or to receive a religion, but to create, to seek, and to discover a religion.

His search is for a religious viewpoint and behavior intellectually and emotionally satisfying to himself. But he is also concerned to make a contribution to a broader pattern and content of a liberal tradition which will satisfy the religious needs of the race. He is helping not only to create a local congregation, its activities and preachments, but to add new dimensions of insight, understanding, sympathy, art, and brotherhood to the human race as a whole.

Religion is that human preoccupation which tries to make sense and goodness of the whole of life. Engaged with the religious task before humanity, it is time for the liberal church to cease being a group of neighborhood dispensaries and filling stations, operated for the amusement and dilettante dabbling of discontented intellectuals, and to become creative workshops wherein the problems of humanity can be investigated and alleviated. These problems, in their depths and heights, are religious. The liberal churches, in theory and pretension, have dared to claim them as their own. Now they had better make themselves into living instruments whereby this new religion, this new way of life, may grow and flourish amid the family of man.

If an institution intends to assume a prophetic and remedial role in society, there is one place where it must declare and evidence this conviction: in the training of its leaders who are being prepared to institute policy and to be the spokesmen of the institution in the next generation. The schools which liberals have established for the training of their ministry should be preparing men, not primarily for what the movement is now or has been, but for what we are convinced is the future into which the liberal movement is developing. The time has come for a fresh view of ministerial education.

To an even larger extent than our churches, our theological schools have maintained their identity with Protestant Christianity. In some cases they share the faculty of nearby Protestant seminaries, or else the liberal students are a minority group within a larger group of Protestant theologs, and are subjected to a curriculum designed almost entirely for Christian ministers. Even where our schools are quite independent of such associations, their areas of study and manner of approach are typical of the Protestant schools.

Only a self-sufficient institution can establish its own self-worth in terms of internally held standards, and ignore the rejection of others. Our theological schools have desired to be acceptable to and to be graded by the accrediting bureaus of Protestant theological education. One might ask, why not seek the authorization of Jewish or Catholic or Moslem accrediting agencies? The answer is that we have evolved from Protestantism mainly, and we still look to it for a sense of belonging and status. This is denominational infantilism. We should, after a century and a half, be ready to establish our own schools and our own standards of study and attainment, apart from the educational policy of any other religious movement. Our behavior is as sensible as would be that of Lutherans who still sought authorization from the Pope.

The game is half won if you can get your opponents to play your style rather than their own. Our chances of attaining distinctive personality and power are slender as long as we play according to the rules and style of Protestantism. This we do out of lethargy, dullness, and fear of isolation, not only in educating our ministers but in setting up our institutional structures, organizations, and activities. We are so concerned with being like unto and acceptable by the other churches that we cannot attain the character and distinctiveness that is indigenous to a religion for one world.

This matter may be settled for us by the Protestants themselves. When the Universalist denomination requested admission to the National Council of Churches some years ago, it was denied, since the Universalists did not meet the creedal qualifications of Christians. Now the Protestant churches are refusing to allow their students to enter our independent theological schools, even when our schools would welcome them. And there are rumors that we will be asked to leave the two state councils of churches to which we are still permitted to belong. The Protestants know that we are not Christians even if we do not.

The areas of study in Protestant seminaries are logical for them, but not for us. They consist of Old and New Testament studies, Greek and Hebrew, Christian Church history, Christian theology, religious education from a biblical viewpoint, and preaching and parish administration relating to typical Protestant practices. Our failure to break with this pattern has been a constant handicap to the creative growth of our own movement. We are continually returning to the forms and limitations of our past associations, rather than developing the forms and substance inherently called for by our new principles and ideals.

Underlying these areas of study for Protestant Christians is the world view and historical background of Christendom. They can be justified by nothing else. When we profess to have taken upon ourselves another world view and to associate ourselves with the historical background of libertarianism, science, democracy, freedom of thought, and a religion for one world, we can no longer justify such a formulation and outline of studies. It becomes abortive and illogical.

Let us take the study of the Bible as an instance. Most Protestant theological schools are munificent with courses in the Old and New Testament, going into every phase and specialization of textual criticism, historical research, interpretation, and appreciation. One would think that the only significant era of world history was that of the Hebrew nation and peoples for some two thousand years preceding and immediately following the time of Jesus. This peculiar bias can be justified only in the belief that the Jews produced a unique and indispensable revelation of the mind and will of God, and profoundly incorporated it into their writings. Such disproportionate study of the Bible is bibliolatry and can be condoned only if the Bible is something divine, to be worshiped over and above any other document of man.

Most liberals have been saying that they do not believe this is the case, yet we go ahead using the study of the Bible as if we thought it still were. To most of us the Bible is a literary and historical anthology of the writings of a small but great culture. It is a treasure of anthropological, literary, and religious source materials for the student of the human race. Even so, it tells us only about one very small segment of the entire human drama. Great as it is, it is not indispensable. Religious traditions of profound wisdom and moral sensitivity were developed in India and China, growing out of their own voluminous writings. An increasing number of people brought up in the Christian nations are finding these other Asiatic traditions at least as satisfying as the lore of Israel.

A further consideration has been accumulating for the past century. This is embodied in the findings of archaeology and anthropology and biology, which have been gathering the artifacts and writings from the many ancient cultures and the most primitive tracings of human occupation of the planet. The time has come for the human venture to be viewed as a vast panorama of interlocking and interdependent events. The religious quest and development of the human family cannot be subsumed within the history of the twelve tribes of Israel; to persist in this point of view is to revert to superstition, tribalism, and mythology. And the return to "biblical theology" on the part of the so-called liberal Protestants in this neo-orthodox age is just that, no matter how sophisticated and urbane they may consider themselves to be. Intricate and superficially profound theologies are often founded on rudimentary but basic fallacies. All follows if their basic assumptions can be allowed; but of course the basic assumptions are just what cannot be allowed. This is why so many seemingly intelligent and well-educated persons can in the end be so mistaken and so ill informed. They were wise enough to delve only to the secondary, not to the primary, level of the issues at hand. But when they are vestured with all the trappings and degrees of academic prestige, they can seem impressive enough so that even the liberals yearn for some of this royal purple to rub off on them.

In place of the study of the Bible the liberal will develop a course of study that incorporates a unitary view of the human enterprise. It will be at once a study of history and a study of religious arts and literature. The time and courses now devoted to Bible study will be incorporated into an over-all survey of the history, institutions, philosophy, and literature of all religions, beginning with primitive man. This may seem like a tremendous task, and it is. It will be assumed that the completion of this task will occupy the study of the religious leader for the balance of his life. But it will be the purpose of the few years in school to give him a thorough introduction to the basic materials and world view involved. The Judaeo-Christian history and traditions would be included within this study as an integral part of the whole, but in no way set aside as unique or of transcendent significance.

Ambitious as such a course of study might seem, it is not at all impossible to outline and to fill in. True, new texts would have to be written. But there are at hand an amazing number of books that would fill out the reading list of such a course. It would be possible to bring in archaeologists, anthropologists, historians, persons in the arts and literature, even as such experts are now brought into the general humanities courses that are used in the first two years at some colleges. In fact, if a course of study in undergraduate work were prescribed, a considerable groundwork in world history, world literature, art, and philosophy could provide a background already in hand for the student coming into his graduate studies. The parochialism of our universities in their bias toward Western culture would have to be overcome to permit the college student to acquire such a preparation.

Since we see no peculiarly sacred and secular division of knowledge and experience, the outreach of our kind of study should be made that much easier. Rather than a study of theology, which in root meaning stands for the study of the revelation of God, we would choose the study of philosophy, especially that relating to wisdom and ethics. What could be more valuable to the training of a preacher and a counselor of people, to the leader of a religious community and fellowship, than to have been trained to understand the best wisdom and thinking of all the traditions of humanity? The task is not as difficult as it might seem at first glance. The same basic ethical and philosophical problems pervade all the great religions. As the student went from culture to culture, he would come up against these enduring questions and problems over and over, learning both the similarity and the peculiar differences of viewpoint and emphasis. Could there be a better method of helping such a leader discover what his own convictions are than to have him come to terms with the best thought and criticism of the race?

This is already done to some extent in our schools, but the predominant emphasis on Christian theology, with the tendency to hold it as superior and normative over all other religions, holds back the liberal from the breadth and open-mindedness that he boasts characterize his thinking.

The study of the history of the Christian Church is of central importance only to those who consider themselves to be a continuing part of Christendom. The training of our leaders will shift from a study of the Christian Church to a study of the nature and history of human communities and associations. What is the nature and function of the democratic community? How have men gathered, organized, and cooperated in the past? What is the nature of the radical and critical minority? What endangers its continued and effective liberalism? What are the principles and arts of communication and group sharing and cooperation?

This can be given background in the study of human groups, religious and otherwise, both from the historical point of view and from a study of the various kinds of present-day organizations. The minister is expected to organize and lead a community of religious liberals. We have a record of ineffectiveness on the part of young men just out of school, which seems to indicate that little is done to help them understand people and how to work with them creatively. Save us from becoming public relations experts, but we need to know something. Too often the minister learns whatever skill he has in this matter at the expense of the first two or three congregations he serves.

Not only does the liberal minister need a global background and an appreciation of all points of view, he also should be an expert in his own distinctive philosophy of life. And this is not Christianity in any recognizable version. His philosophy is that of democratic liberalism, of open-minded and tentative truth seeking. We do not have a "divine theology" with its dogmas and prescribed catechism of beliefs which the minister can learn by rote and parrot to his congregations. The free-mind principle as it operates in his religious community places quite a different function and responsibility upon him as preacher, teacher, and adviser than are those of the Christian minister, who is a keeper of the faith. It is not enough that he know what to believe; he must know how to think. He must know how to lead a group process of free and experimental thinking, in which his own opinion is not authority and dogma but merely the voice of another participating individual.

The liberal philosophy has a history, a lore, a tradition of its own, which must be as well known and as close to the liberal as the Christian tradition is to the Christian, and the Jewish tradition is to the Jew. But by its very nature it cannot be found in any one culture or period of time. Liberals have arisen in all the great cultures, and liberal traditions have been established. How could Laotzu, Chuangtze, and Gautama Buddha be omitted? If Erasmus is included, then surely Maimonides and Spinoza belong, and the long line of scientists, artists, philosophers, and statesmen of the West, as well as

241

of the East. There are radically liberal philosophies in the great panorama of Hindu thought, and Chinese philosophy and political and social life have a variety and universalism that we in the West are only beginning to appreciate. The study of so-called primitive societies, with their different forms of organization, association, and intercourse, would be rewarding.

We can only mention in passing that religious education as conceived by the liberal will be something different from the stereotypes of Sunday School methods, primarily designed to indoctrinate the child into the true faith. This is the greatest adventure facing the liberal church: the rethinking of the nature of the religious experience, and the devising of materials and techniques whereby the growing child can be introduced to his role and responsibility in human society and the universe.

A quite experimental and creative approach must be taken to the whole problem of what the traditional call *worship* and we would call *the celebration of life*. The relation of religious experience and expression to all the arts is profound. So far the study of religious arts is a grievously misconceived area in our theological schools, since religious arts are assumed to be the arts as practiced by religious institutions. The arts in the churches are notoriously truncated, parochial, and abased. The world of art has moved out of the church and left it mainly in the ruck. Not until we have broken down the separation of the so-called sacred and secular arts, not until we realize that all art of any worth is indigenously and profoundly religious, will this field of study be given the attention and interpretation it merits. We will never achieve great celebrations until they are developed in and through the finest music, architecture, poetry, drama, painting, sculpture, and speech. The efflorescence of any religious tradition has been at the same time a renascence of religious art. All religious expression is in and through one of the arts; it cannot be otherwise. It is no accident that the prophets speak in poetry, and that religious convictions and aspirations demand their songs. When the schools for the ministry become occupied again with the arts, we will begin once more to attract persons of artistic interests and abilities into the ministry.

I am convinced that the definitive act of maturity on the part

242

of the liberal churches will occur at that time when they cut the education of their ministry free from the apron strings of the Protestant churches and declare themselves independent and self-sufficient and distinct. It will be analogous to the act of maturity on the part of the young man and woman, when they move out of the parental abode, marry, and set up house for themselves. Then they are ready to have their own children and raise them with whatever store of wisdom they possess.

Up to now, we have been like those birds who do not build nests of their own but either steal the nests that other birds have built or take over discarded ones. We are like the sea animal that houses himself in the discarded shell of some other creature. The schools we occupy are not made for our needs. They are designed to serve the purposes of another species of religion.

CHAPTER 13

Caught out

SUCCESS IS FAILURE

Inherent in the method of any operation such as an experimental and prophetic religious movement are the assumptions as to what will constitute the success of the venture. If we make a trial run in constructing a religion for one world, how shall we judge whether or not the experiment is successful? This question has been posed to me over and over by persons outside the project. They will say, "How is the Meeting House doing?" They are asking whether or not the venture is successful. What can I answer? According to the common standards of success in religious institutions, it is definitely not a success. If we were to judge what we do by conventional standards of achievement, we would be doing poorly. But whatever it is we are trying to do, it is not to attain a "standard and conventional success." Therefore we must find some standard of success that is generically related to what we are doing, whereby we can evaluate its progress and achievement.

What is the nature of success? Is success a personal accomplishment, something taking place in the personality and life of the individual, or is it social? Is the success of a venture to be measured by its acceptance and popularity, or in terms of its possible potency in long-range influence?

Such questions are important to individuals and institutions in our status-seeking age. Often enough to be tantalizing, the man who was a social failure during his life turns out to be successful in his influence in future generations.

The art world of the immediate past has provided us with four examples of this generalization in the painters Van Gogh, Gaugin, Modigliani, and Cézanne. Initial rejection is so often the fate of creative and innovating artists in every field that one who is successful in both his own and succeeding generations seems to be the exception. William Blake, Keats, Whitman, Emily Dickinson can be added to the list from poetry. In religion almost every innovator has suffered opposition, if not martyrdom, in his own day. The Old Testament prophets were scorned and persecuted. Jesus was martyred. Buddha and his arhats met scorn and charges of heresy. Confucius was ironically humorous about his failure to influence the governments of the Chou Dynasty. Mohammed was bitterly opposed. In science Galileo, Pasteur, and Bruno met the wrath of the church and their colleagues, while Copernicus escaped retaliation by having his writings published after his death. Frank Lloyd Wright finally won the praise he deserved as an architect only because he lived to be eighty-nine, surviving years of neglect before he won acceptance. But long years are no guarantee. John Dewey, who lived into his nineties, survived to see rejection of his ideas in pragmatism and progressive education.

A definition of "success" must be laid down for the purpose of discussion, and although the following definition may be judged arbitrary, we believe it can be upheld. Success in living is both personal and social; the two viewpoints are only two ways of looking at the same life. A man is successful in himself if he realizes his own potentiality in growth, creativity, and productiveness. He is a failure insofar as he does not become the person he had the potentiality to become. Social success stems from the individual's making the largest and most significant contribution he has within him to make to the shared life of humanity. Success or failure is relative to the potentiality for influence that he has. Even if he makes a substantial contribution to the human good, he is a failure if he was capable of making more of a contribution and did not meet the issues and opportunities of his engagement with life.

This definition of success derives from a theory of human nature. Man is conceived to be an organism that is growing and that is potentially creative. Man is not a creature but a creator. It is not sufficient for him to receive and to conserve the creations of others; he must himself participate in the creative development of his species and its culture. If he fails in this, he fails to develop the finest attributes of his own nature. He has not become himself, since he has not developed into the person that he might have been. Man is not something that is born complete. At birth he is undeveloped. The success of his life depends upon the fullness of his development and the satisfactions coming from growth, training, self-expression, and productivity. Life is a process, an evolution within indivduals as well as in the species.

From this point of view, the marks of success current in our world are actually the earmarks of failure. This judgment cannot be made universal, but contemporary success will most often indicate the likelihood of long-range failure. If what a person does finds quick and widespread acceptance and reward in his own time, it is something to which his generation is accustomed and which it is prepared to accept. People honor what they understand, what is agreeable to them. They prefer that which resembles their past experience. Music that has been already heard and enjoyed finds a ready path of acceptance and recognition in the listener. But music that represents problems to the hearer, that surprises and shocks his ears and his sensibilities, will ordinarily be rejected and even ridiculed.

Both aspects of this kind of social behavior were illustrated in the career of Charles Chaplin. He is acclaimed a genius as an actor, an inventor of characters, as a writer and producer. In his early career Chaplin received a universality of success that was phenomenal. His films struck a responsive chord in people in all parts of the world, whatever their stage of civilization or their cultural background. His stories were simple, dealing with universal situations and emotions.

We cannot say that Chaplin lacked creativity or productivity, or that he failed to contribute to human happiness and culture. He made a great contribution. But as he developed in artistry he became more difficult, more critical, more controversial. He was not content to be a great clown. In *City Lights* and *The Great Dictator* he satirized the evils of technology and government. His later films were even more pentrating and disturbing. He was persecuted in this country; his films were neglected or banned from distribution. He left the United States for Europe.

Chaplin's early films were based on stock characterizations from the British music halls. He made the wistful little clown indubitably his own creation, as does every genius. But his own creativity was spent in an elaboration of the past, not a break with the past or a criticism of traditional ways. We cannot say that his early years and their success marked him as a failure. They did indicate how Chaplin might have failed.

Some artists develop an attractive style when they are young, one which is commercially successful. They decide that since they have a marketable product, they can spend the rest of their lives imitating themselves. A comprehensive showing of an artist's work after his death often demonstrates that once his style was established early in his career, he painted in much the same way ever after. With great artists this is never true. Their work continues to develop, becomes more profound, more experimental. The later plays of Shakespeare, the late string quartets of Beethoven, the late water colors of Cézanne are definitive examples.

If Chaplin had wished to emulate the comic style of his early films, to stay out of controversial artistic, political, and social issues, he would have maintained his acceptance by the people and by those in high places. If he had done so, his continued success would have then marked him as a failure, for he would have failed to become the profound and disturbing artist of his later years. He would have sacrificed the artist into which he has developed, to become the empty imitator of the artist that he had already become.

Regardless of the success attained at one stage of development, a man is a failure if he does not continue to grow and to enter new realms of endeavor. Growth and creativity are not the attributes of but one stage of development but should

247

continue all during life. Growth and creativity are the signs of the healthy, developing personality. Success in being a human being depends upon continuously becoming more than one has been. As soon as human beings cease to develop, they begin to shrink, to become less than they have been. The artist who is imitating the paintings he made last year is less than the artist he was last year. One breath must be followed by another or we die. One phase of growth must be followed by another, or the creativity of the personality deteriorates.

Each man's creativity must be his own. Ultimately he must be his own judge as to what is seminal, valid, and meaningful in his own work. If his own judgment runs counter to that of others, he should examine his own motives, ideals, and standards and be as objective as he can. But if, when he has done so, he still believes that he is justified in his departures, he must follow them whether he is accepted or rejected by society.

If he fails in this course, he will allow the opinions of others to overwhelm his own confidence and judgment. He then resigns from his own opinions and his own self-elected destiny; he will have resigned from being himself. Once he has lost confidence in his own reason, sensitivity, intuition, and conviction, others will move in and take him over. He will become servant to the goals, decisions, and views of other men. He will be an extension of their movement, having no direction and movement of his own. He can then no longer have any success in and of his own person, because in the ways of growth and creativity he will have ceased to be a person. He will be someone else's tool, used as someone else directs.

Many are counted successes who have taken this road. Many have never had a job of their own. In school they have submitted to a program of education set up for them. Upon graduation they have sold themselves to the highest bidder, to the use of some employer, to make what he asks them to make, in the way that he asks them to make it. This subservience to the will of the employer is the mark of the successful employee, the good team man. Some employees never make a basic decision or innovation in their entire professional life and, what is more tragic, never expect this function of themselves.

Idea men are set aside to have ideas. Managers are set aside to manage. Owners are set aside to own. The worker does the work to which he is assigned. Workers are successful, as we define success, as substitutes for another's hands. There is no success in *their* hands. Therefore, after eight hours of working at someone else's job, they go home to their own workshop to work at a job of their own choosing. The tragedy is that they can be their own workmen only as a leisure-time activity, and not as their main issue and occupation.

If we accept the evolutionary nature of the processes of life and society, everything is in process of development. The direction that human development will take depends on the imagination, inventiveness, and creativity of people. There is no special privilege of class or birth, of race or position. There are no authorities for the next step in growth. The future is unproved and unpredictable. Evolution is emergent, and we cannot tell from what has already developed what the next stage of development will be.

Every individual who elects to participate in this evolution becomes his own authority. He moves out into new ranges of experience. No one will have gone before him to answer the questions that his new trials will raise. The creator must raise his own questions and make his own answers. He will confer with others, ask their judgments, and consider them well, but the final decision must be his own. His judgment may be wrong, but even this failure is a kind of success. The root failure of all is to fail in the responsibility to make one's own judgment, to fail as judge, whether the judgment is right or wrong. If one does not dare to risk his own mistakes, he will not dare to make his own success.

As patient, as considerate, as teachable as the creative person may be in his relations with others, there comes a point where he is quite stubborn and intractable. When he has decided on the way he must go, he will go that way despite the opinion of anyone else. We are talking in a certain context: we are assuming this person is well intentioned, idealistic, and creative. When the conscientious objector cannot enlist for military service, he will go to jail as if he were a criminal before he will compromise his principles. He believes this to be the only way to be true to himself, and to be the only way peace can come. He is making his judgment not only for himself but for humanity, inasmuch as his decisions will shape what humanity will become. But the free man must at last refer to his own standards of the good as his final guide. He may have to go alone, or with whatever few will go with him. It is here that his failure becomes the mark of his success. His failure announces that he has been successful in following his own principles and ideals. He has been true to himself, and thereby he has been true to his vision of the good for all men.

This is a matter of decisions, and in these crucial decisions the trend of an entire life is sometimes determined. The chain of decisions is endless for the growing person. There is another issue that is even harder to resolve. It is one thing to meet the urgency of a crisis, to marshal one's energies for basic judgments. This is an issue of excitement, of momentousness. One is then the object of attention and of inducements from those who wish to influence the decision. Many persons have been victors over temptation and coercion at this point.

These same persons may succumb when wearied by long years of neglect and disregard which have followed. The real success is the product of patient years of building that prove out the way one has chosen to go. It is one thing to take a fork in the road, to choose to walk the untrodden way or to break a new trail in the brush. It is another thing to walk on mile after mile, year after year down that road, alone or with few companions.

The farther one goes down the chosen road, the farther he is from where he started, the farther he is from his own familiar past and surroundings, and the farther he is from the appreciation and understanding of others. But he can do nothing else, if the longer he travels this road, the more certain he is that this is the way for him to go, and the more certain he is that the best service he can do for others is to beat this new trail. He must keep on, until others mark his trail and begin following it, or he begins to meet those who are beating trails toward his. He is seldom fated to be entirely alone, but he must accept even this if it is required.

The distance from others is not a matter of geography, but a social distance. This is called failure. When a person is unaccepted, when his product finds no market, he is a failure. When Modigliani had to trade his drawings for food because no one would buy them, he was a failure. He had gone down his road of painting farther than the eyes of those who bought paintings could follow him. He went down that road inexorably, until his last paintings are perfectly conceived and executed. Now a room of his paintings is worth half a million dollars. This is a considerable "success," just forty years after his death. The stubbornness and integrity of his failure while he lived is the measure of his ultimate success.

This is religion: the courage and the patience of the idealist. The religious man is he who elects for himself the best way that he knows, and who goes that way whether or not others go with him. We honor the social necessity for this individualism in the separation of church and state. The law indicates our judgment that the country is benefited if it puts no ceiling or restraint on the moral strivings of its citizens. A man is permitted to hold his religious ideals as a higher loyalty than his commitment to his country's policies.

Freedom of religion is of little use if people voluntarily absolve themselves from it, or if the religions they espouse are so timid and conventional that they only serve to habituate their believers the more solidly in the trite and careless moralities of society. Unless a religious conviction somewhat stirs a man to become more than he would be otherwise, it is of little merit.

The success of a religion can be measured by its failure in its own time. If it declares practices and ideals sufficiently different from popular conceptions, it is bound to be unpopular. If it is leaven it will not be taken for cake. There is only one sufficient measurement whereby we can test a religion for one world. Are we completely honest and clear

251

in the goals and ideals we propose? Are the methods of our group life in accord with these principles? Have we created in our temples a miniature of what we propose for humanity? Do our symbols, arts, rituals demonstrate the kind of fellowship that we hope will one day prevail among the quarrelsome branches of the human family?

If we can say that we have accomplished our aims as fully as we are able, then no matter how we may have failed by the ordinary counters of success, in numbers, funds, popularity, we will have succeeded.

CAUGHT OUT

These considerations on being "caught out" are an attempt to formulate a psychology of behavior for liberal religion, and, in similar application, for all individualistic come-outers and members of small minority groups. The central emotional problem for many liberals is a sense of isolation, of being different, of standing alone and apart from the majority of people who hold to conventional and accepted views. To find self-sufficiency against the majority is not easy. To continue to be oneself, honestly, without fear or favor, and without resentment, is not easy, for the prejudices against the minority opinions and attitudes are deep seated and persistent.

The experience of some lone religious liberals upon discovering a Unitarian or Universalist society, and others of their kind, is similar to the experience of Elijah. Elijah had earned the displeasure of Ahab and Jezebel by overthrowing the prophets of Baal, and he fled for his life in the wilderness. Poor Elijah was caught out as few liberals are today. His sense of isolation, of aloneness had reached a pitch of ultimacy. He was hiding in a cave, and a voice spoke to him asking what he was doing there. Elijah answered, "I have been very jealous for the Lord God of hosts: because the children of Israel have forsaken thy covenant, thrown down thine altars, and slain thy prophets with the sword; and I, even I only, am left; and they seek my life, to take it away."

The voice gave Elijah some practical advice about overthrowing Ahab and then assured Elijah that he wasn't as alone as he thought, that indeed there were seven thousand of the faithful in Israel. Whatever comfort that gave to Elijah, it cannot have been too much greater than the sense of acceptance and security that has come to many religious liberals who feared they were alone and then discovered a religious fellowship of their partisans. Our numbers are still not too many more than "seven thousand," but they are enough to establish our fellowship, our belonging in the human community.

If one is a compulsive reader, there is very little of all the bales and bales of printed paper he consumes that bears a second reading. And still fewer are those books, essays, and poems that one delights to return to year after year. A few, like good wine and cheese, improve gradually and subtly with age. Most writing becomes banal with repeated contact, but a few pieces take on a luster from one's own increase of experience, and gain in depth and overtones and fullness of meaning with each rereading.

Such is Emerson's essay "Self Reliance." I can remember that I was somewhat fearful upon reading it in high school that it might be an overstatement of the case, and even more troubled by the suspicion that I liked it because I was an adolescent, and might think it quite high blown when older. Now I am convinced that it contains an essentiality of wisdom that can be fully known only by a very old man. And the seemingly absolute dicta rendered are but the necessary strength of statement for a very fundamental and unalterable necessity.

This is a preachment that unabashedly advises you to go ahead and get "caught out." "Whoso would be a man, must be a nonconformist." Depart from society, says Emerson, if that is demanded by the true statement and the living of what truth you know. I can imagine that if the voice that spoke to Elijah in the cave had been that of Emerson and not of Jehovah, and under the theory of the oversoul this might not be as weird a conjecture as it first appears, Emerson might have been a little less compassionate than was God. Emerson might not have assured Elijah that there were seven thousand other faithful. He might have said, "So you are alone in a cave in the wilderness, hiding from Ahab and Jezebel. Isn't that where you should be? Be self-reliant, man. Nothing is at last sacred but the integrity of your own mind."

Surely it would be difficult to imagine Jehovah making that last remark, since Jehovah seemed to be of the opinion that nothing is at last sacred but Jehovah. Indeed, Emerson puts the stamp of sacredness within the character and integrity of the individual, and not in some deity without. We might ask whether man is justified in giving such honor to his own opinion and judgment, that he would make it the final abode of the sacred. But it is such seemingly absolute statements as this which, surprisingly, stand up with many re-examinations, and become more rather than less convincing, the longer they are pondered.

For if a man deserts his own honesty and his own judgment, where then will he go for authority and guide for choices and actions? If he is not his own authority, he must accept someone else, or some institutionalized body of others, as his authority. But if he thinks they are only men like himself, as fallible as himself, he has not discovered an authority superior to or more dependable than his own. He is merely derelict in his own self-reliance. He is, as Emerson bluntly puts it, a coward.

This statement continues to ring true because it has many implications beyond its seemingly simple meaning. That which is sacred is the integrity of one's own mind. "Integrity" is a term laden with emotion, for it is the very root of personality and character. Before the psychologists attacked the term, we used to call it "will power." It has nothing to do with narrow-mindedness or fanaticism, for if the mind is free and open, its integrity will entail the questioning of the finality of any of the views the mind may hold.

Furthermore, if one does not hold the integrity of his mind sacred, if he is not committed to his own honesty and does not refrain from self-corruption, he is unlikely to hold the integrity of the mind of other persons any more sacred than his own. We do not give others any more honor than we give ourselves. There is a nasty and inherent contradiction in both the mind and the character of any man who insists on freedom of thought for himself and denies it to others. In fact, a person thus sick emotionally in his relations with others is surely also sick within his own mind and person, and his vaunted freedom of mind is a delusion.

There is a social extremity to Emerson's statement. Religious liberals might well be given pause that Emerson found it impossible to maintain the integrity of his own mind and remain in the Unitarian ministry, since the Second Unitarian Church of Boston insisted on the sacrament of Communion, in which the integrity of his own mind would not allow him to participate. "Society *everywhere* is in conspiracy against the manhood of every one of its members." One wonders if the inclusiveness of "everywhere" was not itself an echo of his own experience with the limitations of the social institution of liberal religion, in spite of its verbal dedication to the free mind.

Thus the sacredness of the integrity of our mind is placed even above that of religious institutions. How can we justify this statement emotionally and socially?

First, we must assume that the assertion and stubbornness of our integrity will in no sense derive from antagonism to others or be an agent of attack upon others' right to the same integrity. The assumption is well illustrated in the American institution of the separation of church and state, and the freedom of every man and group to hold and propagate his own religious beliefs. We must respect the other man's rights to his beliefs, even when we have little respect for their intellectual and factual validity. We can attack what we hold to be superstitions, but we must not attack the privilege of others to be superstitious, or rather what we deem to be superstitious. Thus a basic respect for persons is here involved.

How can we behave, then, to maintain the integrity of our own mind, and to give no offense? Here I believe there is a clear distinction between giving offense in the way one holds and presents his view, and *taking* offense at the view someone else holds. Some people, some religious liberals included, are offensive in the way they hold, present, and practice their convictions. They act as if it were an insult for anyone to have views in conflict with their own. They will use unethical means to put their opinions into power. They harangue, argue, and browbeat their opponents in an argument. We must still fight for the privilege of such persons to have the freedom of their opinions, but they make it as difficult as possible for us to defend them. If they are caught out, are rejected socially, we can't help feeling that they did much to deserve their social isolation.

It is such persons who often take offense at the views of others, even though there was nothing offensive in the manner or behavior of those who differed from them. For some people feel that certain convictions are inherently offensive; they would take offense even if these views were expressed by the Virgin Mary. The liberal in religion is likely to possess a considerable stock of these inherently offensive opinions, in the social realm as well as the intellectual. What should be his psychology of behavior in his relations with his fellow creatures?

He should do everything to avoid giving offense, but he should do nothing to prevent others from "taking offense" if that is what they wish to do. In his everyday social intercourse, he should feel free to express his convictions on matters of religious beliefs, of ethical behavior, of human relations in all situations. Regardless of the "extenuating circumstances" which for political and other considerations might counsel him to refrain from stating views that he knows others will not appreciate, he should give them nevertheless — quietly, lucidly, and unhesitatingly.

There is one example that is of common occurrence. Racial, ethnic, and religious prejudice is everywhere, and it is impossible to avoid running into its expression. Some persons, averse to "giving offense," will let bigots rant in their presence and say nothing. But by their silence they are giving a tacit consent to these prejudices and are helping to increase their social weight and power. It takes courage to state your own contrary views in such cases, since the racist often is very emotional in presenting his opinions, even violent in their expression. But we violate the integrity of our own minds if we remain silent. We should quietly counterpose facts and contrary convictions to his arguments. That done, it is futile to carry the matter further, for the result would be mere dispute. Let others take it on if they wish.

The religious liberal often finds himself in similar positions in regard to religious views, since his own ideas are deemed heretical and often are inconceivable to others as religious. Sometimes, after hearing what the liberal thinks, the orthodox may say, "Well I guess you can believe that if you want to. It's a free country. But I can't see why you call it religion." Religious arguments are futility of all futilities, but the quiet statement of your own opinions when they are called for is a just and necessary exercise of freedom of expression, and the avoidance of personal cowardice. Often the quieter and more moderate the statement, the more effective it will be. If anyone is then offended, he will have *taken* offense. You will not have *given* it.

What applies in discourse also applies to actions. The integrity of our minds is not proved until it is necessary to put our convictions into behavior, to take a stand on them. This can be costly. Some years ago the editor of a Boston newspaper printed an editorial stating his convictions on an important issue during a political campaign. He knew that it was in opposition to the views of the publisher, and that the publisher required his reporters to serve his views not their own. The editor was immediately fired and I believe had to leave the profession of journalism. But he had no choice if he was to be faithful to the integrity of his own mind. During the McCarthy trials, many people were placed in this position, since politic lies and recanting of unorthodox views were highly regarded by the investigating committees, but stubborn integrity was brutally punished. Numerous persons, however, took personal loss, even ruin, as a necessary price of integrity.

This is the issue of being caught out. It isn't comfortable to be fleeing for your life, hiding out in a cave in the wilderness, because you have shown up the priests of Baal. (Granted, since Elijah had all the opposing priests slaughtered, he *gave* offense even as Ahab *took* it.) Many have second thoughts when they consider the penalties exacted for the exercise of integrity of mind. How much can one afford to pay for it?

257

Should one risk being caught out just to hold to opinions?

It is here that the finality of Emerson's statement comes home: "Nothing is at last sacred but the integrity of your own mind." If you violate that, you violate the very seed and essence of your own dignity and self-respect. You violate the very source of your own convictions and thought, which lies in the free and fearless working of your own mental processes, your powers of weighing evidence, of concluding what is valid. If man is not a thinking animal, then he is just an animal. If he violates the integrity of his thought processes, he violates the source and sustenance of his human nature, his power to reason and to act on the results of his reason.

Rather than do this, which in liberal context might be called "the unpardonable sin," one should be willing to suffer any consequence. Social difficulties, rejection, misinterpretation, isolation — if all that is the price to pay for integrity, then let it be paid.

But how bad is the situation of being caught out? What are you caught out from? Is it not merely the acceptance of a portion of human society? It is not all of society, for as Elijah discovered, no matter how liberal and heretical you may be, there will be "seven thousand" others in a like situation, and they will give you comfort if you can find them. There are quite a few such groups in our society, pacifist organizations, sects of occult and strange beliefs, single-tax societies, funny-money clubs — no matter what the oddity, the heresy is shared by others. And often the companionship found in reaction from the general isolation from society, is warmer than any outside a minority group.

Robert Frost gives us another assurance in his poem "A Lone Striker." He pictures a man who was late getting to the mill in the morning. If he was not there at starting time, the mill gate closed, and he could not get in for half an hour, and he would be docked for half an hour. He was caught out. What should he do? I have worked in factories where some such rule was in force. Some men would stand and fret for half an hour until the gate reopened, counting the money they were losing.

But Frost's worker is of another stripe. What is he caught

out from? Just a dusty, noisy mill. There is the whole world of nature, and since he can't get into the mill, why not spend the day outdoors? Who is really caught out? Or rather, if he is caught out, are not the workers in the mill "caught in," and who is to say which is better, to be caught in or to be caught out?

Those who are joiners, the organization men, the togetherness boys, pay the price of their acceptance, their popularity. And the price is to be on the inside and to conform to its ways. If that is your nature in any case, and your mind is a conforming mind, then nothing is lost. But if it is not, then perhaps, as a price for not being caught out, everything is lost. Says Emerson: "A man is relieved and gay when he has put his heart into his work and done his best; but what he has said or done otherwise shall give him no peace."

This is the final issue. Can a man have any peace or satisfaction unless he is true to his own mind, true to his own self? Can he keep himself from knowing that he is unfaithful to it? Can he hide his own fear and equivocation from himself, even though he may be able to hide it from others?

To Frost, to be caught out meant to escape slavery in the factory into the freedom of a man's own being and his own world. In his quiet way as a poet, he puts the case without giving any offense. Yet a profound indictment of the world of social and industrial conformity is implicit in his words.

It is all in the point of view. The man was not caught out from the mill. The mill was caught out from him. His was the act of freedom. If the mill wanted him, it would have to come after him. What is implied is that then it would have to take him on his terms, not the mill's. If he had stayed at the gate, fretting to get in, he would have shown that he needed the mill and its wages, and that he would do whatever was required, even submit to its disciplines, to get it. He would have lost a portion of his human dignity. He would have lost his bargaining position.

But as a free man, who had gone his own way, only if he had something essential to give to its operation would the mill come after him. If it needed merely replaceable human parts in a machine, it could find them. But if it needed a free man, and if industry was about to die because he had deserted it, then he would be available.

The beauty of this poem lies in the fact that Frost neatly turns the tables on society. Originally the man is caught out, but he turns this situation into an act of declaring his freedom, and in the end it is society that is deprived of him, and must come seeking him. This is the insouciance of the free man. He forces society to take him on his own terms or not at all. His own self-sufficiency, the fact that he has no compulsive need for society, especially if it demands that he violate his own integrity, puts him in the position of power. The only power society has over him, he gives to it by his need of what it has to offer and his fear of being deprived of its comforts and security.

But the nub of the whole matter is that a free man cannot give to society that contribution he has to offer, his own unique offering, if he is caught within the meshes of society as it is, and has not the privilege to be original. If he violates the integrity of his own mind, if he will not risk being caught out, he will deprive the world of what he, and he alone, has to give it.

Let us conclude with Emerson: "There is a time in every man's education when he arrives at the conviction that envy is ignorance; that imitation is suicide; that he must take himself for better for worse as his portion; that though the wide universe is full of good, no kernel of nourishing corn can come to him but through his toil bestowed on that plot of ground which is given him to till. The power which resides in him is new in nature, and none but he knows what that is which he can do, nor does he know until he has tried."

HOLDING ACTION

The process of an experiment has two parallel involvements. The experiment is trying and testing an idea and materials and methods to formulate the ideal. That is the first involvement. But the experiment is also testing the means and method of the experiment itself. For example, the scientist is not only testing a hypothesis in his laboratory, he is also testing the scientific method at the same time. This is why it is called the "self-

260

correcting" method of science. The testing of the experimentation is an intriguing by-product of the experiment. You start out seeking an answer in a particular field and sometimes you discover that you have learned more about the art of experimentation than you have learned about the subject under scrutiny.

This has been borne in upon us many times as we have worked with the "pilot project" at the Charles Street Meeting House. We have elsewhere commented that probably the most important thing we have learned is that the experimental approach in itself is the true medium and mood of the liberal religious fellowship. In trying to create a different kind of religious symbolism we have discovered a new way of being a religious group. Experimentation teaches its own lessons, regardless of the aims and intentions of those engaged in it.

Here we would like to talk about one aspect of the experimental religious method, that part of a project or an experimentation that can best be described as a "holding action." The first reaction may be that "holding action" is more applicable to orthodoxy than to liberalism. It sounds like conservatism and stand-patism, rather than growth and trial. Yet it is a basic ingredient of any long-run testing of a basic idea. If an idea can be adequately tested only by a long-term trial run, then a good deal of the period involved can well be called a "holding action."

The reason why a holding action succeeds each part of the experiment rises out of the nature of a religious experiment. A religious fellowship and its set of practices is something within itself, a group life, a temple, a community of people. It has its own "private" life apart from the world, and in some sects this is very much apart from the world. The religious fellowship attempts to establish its ideals of thought and living and relationships in miniature within its own institutions.

Either explicit or inferred is the assumption that the purpose of the religious fellowship is to reform the whole of the human community in the direction of its ideals. Christianity conceives itself as the leaven in the lump of the world. Buddhism and Islam have been missionary in character. Religions like Judaism that have denied missionary intentions are con-

261

cerned that their concepts of righteousness and piety spread through all society.

Before the day when you could buy yeast in any store, there was a kind of holding action in leaven. After the bread had risen, was kneaded, and was ready to bake, some of the dough impregnated with the yeast was always held over, to provide the yeast that would spread through the next batch of dough. Even so the religious community must keep itself as a continuously working and ready bit of leaven.

One example in relation to the liberal religious society is in the leaven of freedom of assembly, speech, and belief. Although freedom of ideas is a part of our democratic society, abuses and suppressions continually arise. There will be persons who are refused a platform for their ideas, groups that cannot find a place to meet, ideas that are considered heretical. Then it is time for the leaven of freedom within the liberal religious society to work, making its building available to the denied group, by inviting the suppressed persons to speak their opinions. It may be that such a crisis does not arise for months or years, but whenever abuses of freedom appear, then free religion must be ready for its engagement. Our basic concepts of freedom may themselves not change much over the years, although they work to enlighten many kinds of problems. Keeping freedom alive within the society, and ready to work outside it, is the holding action of which we speak.

The problem is how to engineer an effective advance in the presentation and performance of an ideal, in the face of society's reluctance to make changes with any speed and thoroughness.

There are two general phases to any experiment. First there is the experiment itself, the basic design, and the period when it is constructed and elaborated. In the Meeting House this was the period when the basic idea was formed and the various phases of the project were set in motion. This phase lasts until the project has been as fully realized as it can be in its initial stages. We have come to the end of this phase, as nearly as one can actually draw a line between the first phase and the second; there is a considerable overlap. More can be done in all of the various aspects of the

262

project, but each aspect has been sufficiently rounded out so that the full scope of the experiment is now in view.

The second phase is what we are calling the "holding action." This means keeping the experiment intact and in operation as a unit. It involves the study of the project and a reporting of the findings, of which this book is the major implement. The holding action is not a static phase, since the building of the project is never complete. New elements are continuously being added to the structure, and in the development of festival services the project itself attains an increasingly adequate exercise, proving, and correction. For as we discover how to use the setting, we will learn more and more what the setting is and what it is not. Out of this knowledge should come the initiation of future projects.

The holding action has two factors. One is solid, enduring, in that it continues without being constantly exercised. This is the efficacy of the temple structure, which maintains and perpetuates its influence in its very endurance. It preaches its own sermons, makes its own testimonials, since these have been built into it during the previous building program. This program is sufficiently demanding in itself, since it involves continuous upkeep of the temple, repairs, custodial service, heating, along with insurance and all the expenses that harass the most orthodox church. For once it has reached the holding action stage, the project demands the same upkeep as all other institutions.

The bulk of the temples in our world represent the traditional and prevailing mythos. They are fully accepted and respectable in the society, since they preach the prevailing morality and mythology. They are no longer, to any striking degree, the leaven in the lump, since they are mainly the lump itself.

There are other temples, a very few, that represent a controversial ideal. They do not congratulate the folkways around them but set up a criticism, since they point to what society should be, rather than what it is. There are two kinds of ideals at work in the world. There are the ideals that society has accepted as rightful. Whether or not they are universally practiced, there is no longer any argument that they should be

263

practiced. Ideals relating to murder, theft, and honesty are obvious examples. There are other ideals that society has not yet accepted as its own, and that it practices hardly at all. The laws, as well as the standards of respectability, may be counter to these ideals. The ideal which we are herein espousing, a religion for one world, is such an ideal. The tribal ethics that prevail around us contain notable ideals, but since they emphasize the cohesiveness, if not the exclusiveness, of the tribe, they carry an inherent denial of universal religion. Our society does practice the ideal of religious tolerance, but this is tacitly based on the various religions keeping their separate identities, in order that they can behave decently to one another. The ideal of bringing them all together in an expression of unity cutting across their several boundaries runs counter to tribal and sectarian concepts as such.

The simple endurance of the first kind of temple is of no great moment in itself, since thousands of other temples carry the same principles. Many individual temples come and go in the large, traditional denominations, and the denominations themselves go on as before. The particular temples are replaceable parts, since they have no sufficient individuality or uniqueness.

But if a temple carries a novel and controversial ideal, projected nowhere else in the same way, the perpetuation of this temple can also amount to the perpetuation of its ideal, at least in the form and character of its presentation. The ideal of a religion for one world rises above and includes the ideals that have preceded it. It does not deny the principles of the less universal religions, but rather incorporates them in a new and inclusive setting. If this is a valid improvement in religious conceptions and idealism, then to hold this temple in existence is to perpetuate the embodiment and activity of a revolutionary viewpoint within the social structure. The yeast is being kept in the dough.

The second factor in the holding action is its constant renewal. A creative and experimental project must never lose this character. It must always be testing itself, trying itself, and making improvements in its conception and elaboration. If the existence of what has already been accomplished begins to inhibit the emergence of further creative advance, it is time for the project to be reviewed, altered, and improved. It must then somehow be opened up so that new growth can occur.

There is a continual experiment on oneself in living with a new form of religion. What does it do to you? How does it affect the children who grow up within it? The validity of a new world view such as this can never be conclusively known until children have been born into its fellowship, have grown up within it, and in their maturity can look back and judge whether or not it effectively and meaningfully introduced them to the world and the human enterprise. Only the generations can run the tests on a new religion; time alone will tell.

The Meeting House as a new kind of temple may become "old" to some of us who have labored in it for years and are familiar with its design and meanings. But it will be continuously new to those who come into it for the first time. The holding action keeps it "there" in the world, keeps it ready for people to discover it. The world in time will become accustomed to living with this new idea, with a different expression of religious idealism. People come in and say, "I didn't know there was this kind of religion." Now they know that there is. Their experience of acquaintanceship may not have converted them to it, but their range of religious alternatives and varieties has been broadened. This new alternative choice may work in some future occasion when they must select the direction in which their ideas and loyalties will go. And again, they may tell someone else about it simply as a curiosity, and it will prove to be what the other person has been seeking.

As a new form of temple, it enters the list of available "temple ideas" that will present themselves to liberal and other groups when they are faced with building a temple for their group. Already six other temples "in the round" have been built or are being built in several parts of the country, since the Meeting House changed into this shape of assembly some nine years ago. It does not need to sell itself in any other sense than simply to exist as an alternative choice, for it to work this kind of influence.

A holding action may also take the form of establishing a standard of excellence and then maintaining it. If we could, for example, obtain the finest representations of Chinese religious art that could be found, there would be no way of improving on the artistic and symbolic excellence. We would have reached the acme. Then we could only hold it. This is what museums do — act as holding companies for great art. They consider themselves treasuries of beauty and excellence. New acquisitions are part of their program, but the exhibition of their collection is their main function. We have achieved this status in some of our primitive art, and in the collection of the Kaethe Kollwitz etchings. In this case it is progress to stand still; survival is progress. For the excellence of what one has is itself an ideal in contrast to the shabbier standards that prevail at large. It is progress to demonstrate that religion can again be concerned with using great art in its symbols and demonstrations, as was habitual in the past. If men can today return to building temples and creating religious art as great as that of their forefathers, this will constitute progress, for we have slipped badly behind the achievements of our ancestors in this area.

Since a creative project utilizes ideals of growth and creativity, as long as it can continue to practice those ideals within its continuing growth it constitutes a holding action of the ideals themselves. The ideals of freedom, creativity, experimentation, and growth need to find treasuries in which they can be protected. We must keep the scientific attitude alive. But these are not art works that can be filed in a case; they can be kept alive only by employing them. The scientific method and attitude is kept alive only as the work of pure and applied scientific research continues. And the experimental approach to religion survives only as long as religious groups continue to experiment.

The Meeting House is a setting that invites new things to happen. What will such an environment call forth in succeeding generations? This we cannot predict, but we can keep an open and creative society in operation to which our children will be free to bring their innovations.

The creative project is "open ended." Further potential realms of development can be discovered only as we live out what we have already created. If we live with it and use it, we will discover the potentialities latent in its forms and structures. We will gradually perceive the suggestions and intimations at present indiscernible. All that has been done is a means to what will be done, not a wall but a doorway. When we have lived in the room long enough to know all that it means, only then will doors be perceived opening into the further rooms that this room implies.

This knowledge necessitates living in depth, staying with the thing until it becomes part of yourself, enters the deeper regions of your memory and associations, and prompts new insights. When it has become part of you, it can generate its conclusions beneath the level of surface rationality. Its further necessities will grow naturally out of living experience. This kind of growth cannot be forced by artificial means. Here the holding action is to live the thing out.

The experiment as such is not over when the first construction has been accomplished. It is complete, if it is ever complete, only when the long holding action has proved or disproved it. Automobiles undergo extensive testing before they are put on the market, but even so "bugs" show up after the cars are on the road. Recently a commercial airliner was called back to the plant for drastic modification; it had proved faulty in use. Practical use is the only valid testing in the experimental process. The finding is proved only when it works. And this process is endless, since no product is ever finished to the point that no further improvements are conceivable.

The first building stage of a creative project has immediate rewards and enticements. But there is a longer excitement in the holding action, in waiting to see what evolves generically within the project after the first splurge of ideas and the forced growth. When an idea emerges, it demands an initial run-through, a preliminary projection. Following this comes the need for patience and dedication. The people will then continue to have such an experiment, and its future findings, only if they deserve it. The only way they can deserve it is to live with it during the long hard period of the holding action.

Experimental organizations are generally short-lived. The people who will engage in the first enthusiasm of a new idea and its elaboration are often not those who will stay with it during a long and trying period of testing. Often such an agency flares up for a day and as quickly dies away. Because its ideas are new and bizarre, society penalizes it rather than providing support. The demands made on the initiators in the slow period of sustenance and endurance usually exceed their capacity. There may have been a flighty and extremist motivation in the willingness to make the first experiment that is the opposite of the patient, tenacious temperament required during the holding action.

The holding action consumes centuries and millennia. The Jews have been in a holding action relative to certain basic beliefs and attitudes for three thousand years, the Buddhists for twenty-seven hundred years, Christianity for two thousand years, and Islam for thirteen hundred years. Has religious liberalism, universalism, the motivation toward a religion for one world, a comparable patience? It may need an even longer capacity to endure, for no one can predict how long it will take mankind to conquer its ancient tribal antipathies and to come together into one human fellowship. We will prove the measure of our religion, and the measure of man's capacity to respond to its principles and ideals, in the holding action.

PART III.

THE PROJECT

CHAPTER 14

The Project

THE MEETING HOUSE PROJECT

The basic theme of the Meeting House Project is a simple one: the premise of unity. It can be variously expressed as follows: There is one natural world, made of one matter, following one natural law. We live on one planet, the earth, and it is the common home of all the children of men. There is one life process, in which all creatures are united in interdependence in one fellowship of life. Man is one animal species, and the biological unity of the human race is the basic determinant of human brotherhood. There is one human culture, for all the basic cultural inventions are shared by all the branches of the human family. There is one human religion, in which a common shared quest for the good life is sought by many various means. We now live in one world, in which all tribal barriers have been broken down, and we are entering an era where only international cooperation, understanding, sharing, and brotherhood can afford the means of peace and survival for the family of man.

Coeval with the premise of unity is the premise of individuality and difference. It can be variously expressed as follows: Although nature is one, it proliferates into myriad forms and creatures, all significantly different from one another. The one planet has many varied landscapes, and each island, zone, and continent has its own loveliness. The one life process contains

271

myriad species, each unique and individual in form and personality. Although man is one species, every human creature is unique and possesses his own dignity, individuality, and significance. Within this one human culture there is a dazzling diversity of cultural forms and expressions. The one human religion contains many tribal differences, each with its lessons of viewpoint and mystery and aspiration. In this one world of human society in which we now live we must keep one peace within the human family, but we must also prize and cherish the freedom, dignity, and unique value of each person.

There is a fundamental experience relating to this diversity within unity that we have tried to make manifest in the Meeting House Project. It can be illustrated by looking at music as an art that is practiced in the various human cultures. One who has been brought up to accept the rhythms and harmonies and modes of Western music as normative, may find his introduction to Hindu or African music a disturbing experience. Much of it will sound like cacophony, yet there will be recognizable structures and patterns and strange harmonies that insist on being recognized in spite of his prejudices against them.

The first few experiences with ethnic music will leave him impressed with the vast differences between the various musical cultures. But if he goes on to study many more types of music, and extends his appreciation and acceptance of other forms by long listening to them, a time will come when the differences fall into place as against the basic likenesses that are common to all music. In the end he is likely to be more impressed with the similarities of all the varieties of music than with their differences. And the one fact that will insist on its proper emphasis will be that *all the tribes of man have music.* The fact that their music varies will seem much less momentous than the fact that they all have music of some kind, based on the common principles of rhythm, melody, harmony, and played on percussion instruments, bowed instruments, plucked instruments, and wind instruments. When he sees the picture whole, there will be one vast panorama of music-making, with many charming variations, but with the family characteristics predominant.

This same experience will occur in every field of human endeavor as a person moves in his identification from a tribal to a world-wide reference. The confusion of tongues merges into the loom of language. In religion such terms as "heathen," "pagan," "heretic" become as offensive as "nigger" and "chink" and "kike" in racial and ethnic prejudice. On the other side of the offense of difference lies the empathy of identification and belonging, which can be discovered by exploratory experience in a hundred fields: in the arts, in philosophy, in biology, in history, anthropology and archaeology, in face-to-face living with people, in business, trade, medicine, science, and above all in religions. All the seeming contradictions in any field of human occupation resolve themselves into mere variations within a common pattern and unity. This does not mean that all the variations are taken as having equal validity and justification in practice, but they belong to the same complex, and the basis of choice between them is relative and not absolute.

In the Meeting House Project it has been assumed that the main function of religion is symbolic. It is the function of religion to create the concepts, symbols, and presentations whereby the basic realities of the human situation can be confronted, and to make orderly and meaningful arrangements of these concepts and symbols, in order to show their existing interdependence and relatedness, and to afford paths and methods whereby creative interchange can result in ever more adequate concepts and symbols. From this point of view, the function of religion lies more in the realm of the expressive arts than in the realm of practical commerce.

The Meeting House Project, then, has been mainly concerned with art, symbolism, poetry, music, ritual, architecture — with the problems of conceptualization and communication. The essential problem is to provide the concepts and symbols and ritual acts whereby mankind can acknowledge, in its full emotional and intellectual force, the fact that we live in one world. What mankind has produced up to now is mainly a magnificent panorama of local and tribal arts and ceremonies elaborating the differences between men, rather than the shared themes and behaviors that unite them into one family of life and culture.

As the project has developed, we have discovered that our task is one mainly of assorting, relating, and composing what is already given on the natural and human scene, in order that the existing unity will make itself manifest. We did not have to create any new symbols. As far as I know there is not one symbol in the entire collection which we can call our own invention. The symbols needed simply to be gathered together and arranged in order to display the generic oneness of man's symbol-making activity and to make clear the interdependence of the many symbols in one network of proliferating forms and meanings. For we are convinced that when all the many symbols of human culture are brought together we will discover that man has created one great vocabulary of symbols, a universal language belonging to all men, regardless of their extraction.

We talk about "foreign languages," and perhaps the above consideration will give a clue as to why the study of foreign languages is so appealing to people. But these are not "foreign" languages; they are all human dialects, part of one great loom of language invented and used by man. We demonstrate this continuously by borrowing words and phrases and rhetorical ideas from "other" languages and making them part of our "own" language. From the widest viewpoint, nothing on the human scene is or can be foreign to us.

In the Meeting House Project we have tried to select the various component elements of the human situation and compose them in a symbolical arrangement demonstrating the predominant reality within them. That is, our purpose was appreciative rather than critical. We found that what humanity ought to be, in terms of society, brotherhood, and cooperation, was inherent in what humanity already was in reality, that which lay unrecognized and unacknowledged as the groundwork of the development and existence of the race. If we could become more fully aware of and respond to what we were already, we would be well on our way to healing our enmities and conflicts and misunderstandings. Our pride and meanness of spirit was an inheritance from ignorance. We sought to symbolize a factuality rather than a prophetic fancy.

To give again the rude list, this was one universe, composed of one matter and energy. We were members of one life process, living on one planet, members of one animal species, with one human history, one human culture, one human commerce, and one religion. Some of these assertions will strike the partisans and patriots as fantastic. We can only assert that whoever goes through the educative and appreciative process such as was outlined in relation to music above will see the adequacy of these judgments of unity demonstrated.

The problem, then, was to find a basic symbol in which all the particular symbols could be composed, in order to make clear that they were all part of one living organism, even as the many cells of the body are but elements of one organism. The best symbols are analogues of reality, simplifications and abstractions from reality. We chose such an analogue as our basic symbol: the circle. The horizon of the earth is a great circle around us, wherever we stand. The earth itself is circular, a globe, as are the sun and the moon. If we travel over the globe we move in a circle. The galaxies in which billions of these globular stars and planets gather are circular, with great arms spiraling out from the center. The moon circles about the earth, and the earth circles about the sun, and the galaxy slowly turns like a great wheel. A circle is perfect, self-enclosed and whole. It returns upon itself. Thus when the seasons come back and begin their cycle again, the circle is their fitting symbol. The circle appears again and again in nature — in the ripples that spread out from a stone dropped into a pond, in the shape of many flowers — and men and women sit in a circle around their campfires and in their councils and many of their dances are circular.

The beginnings of the use of the circle as a symbol are far back in the Old Stone Age. It had come to symbolize the sun, the moon, the earth, the universe, unity, perfection, infinity, and holiness. In the form of the dome it gave the shape of the heavens to temple and mosque, and roofed the observatory and planetarium. The circle presented itself as given to serve as the basic symbol for a religion for one world. There was no arguing with it. The experimenter in religious forms listens for the intuition of rightness, then accedes to it.

The project seemed almost to make itself. We copied the axis

of the earth in order to bring a line of tension to cut across the
serenity of the circle. The many varieties of man's religions
seemed to compose themselves rightly within the circular enclosure. The principle was the same as in drawing. If the
outline of the figure is well drawn, the features and the model-
ing will compose themselves rightly within it. But if the outline
is wrong, all the accuracy attainable in drawing the separate
features will not save it from being a bad drawing.

The aspects of the natural world and the common elements
of man's religious expression dictated what should find its place
inside the circle. Mankind itself had selected the elements by
its religious development and expression. These elements were
literature, in the form of poetry, myth, legend, history, philosophy, and moral teachings; symbolism of various kinds, in
abstract and pictorial forms, and in the symbolic significance
of plants and animals and natural forms; instrumental and vocal
music; painting, sculpture, weaving, and pottery; ritual vessels
and implements; rituals and festivals; temple lamps and various
uses of fire and light; dancing and drama, often combined in
dance drama; temple architecture; symbols and representations
of the natural world; and the intangible but no less real arts of
human relationship, and man himself.

The arts, which are the inevitable vehicles of religious vision
and expression, divided into two types and presented us with
two different but related problems; these are the plastic arts
and the performing arts. The plastic arts presented an inherently simple problem — that is, the problem was simple in
theory, although often exceedingly difficult to solve. By their
nature the plastic arts are capable of making a continuous
presentation. Once the temple is built, it manifests its meanings
to whoever regards it with comprehension. The same applies
to the symbols, paintings, hangings, sculpture, ritual objects,
books, and vestments that constitute the temple furnishings.
We decided to approach this aspect of the project in depth and
full extent, to make a world-wide collection of such objects from
as many of the world religions as possible, limiting the wealth
and diversity of material only by what could be gracefully
housed in our temple area.

The theory put to an experimental test was this: If these

objects from all the world religions can be seen together, significantly arranged, the basic unity that underlies their diversity will make itself clear. Thus in one room there is now the full scope of man's religious arts and symbolism gathered together. It may be that there is not another room anywhere in which such a comprehensive collection of art and symbols is on view. Many museums, of course, have collections that would dwarf ours, but these are ordinarily housed in many separate rooms, so that only the art of one culture can be seen at a time. This method has its own justification, and we have followed it in the display cases in other parts of the building, where, for example, the art of Mexico can be seen as a unit.

The arrangement of the plastic arts creates an evocative setting for the performing arts. Modern recording technology has helped us to assemble the arts of religious performance. Through tape recordings, records, slides, and films we can bring reproductions of the performances of other peoples and places into our gatherings. This has limited validity, to be sure, and cannot be compared to a living performance. The ideal would be to have a Hindu dancer perform the Shiva dance in one of our festivals, or to have an orchestra of Hindu musicians, with Hindu singers, take part. But this ideal is extremely difficult to realize. The fact that films and sound recording have become fine arts, and that we are adjusted to accepting them as substitutes for live perfomances, makes such use feasible in religious services. Thus a sound system and projectors become part of the temple equipment. The books in the bookcases not only serve as symbols of the world bibles but are instruments for readings, which become part of the performance of the celebration.

The performing arts are made feasible by the musical instruments, the piano and pipe organ, by the floor areas and arrangements designed for dance and theater, by the lighting facilities, and by the continuous experimental nature of the various weekly and festival services in the Meeting House. The projects in hymns, anthems, and readings make the literature and teachings, the ritual and ceremonies of the world religions functioning elements in a religion for one world.

The total project can best be described as a many-layered

presentation of a complex and yet unified reality. The theory is that if the presence of the family of man, our fathers of the past, our brothers now living, and our children some day to be born, is brought into one symbolic and artistic assembly, the emotional and intellectual power and attractiveness of a religion for one world will convince us in the terms of religious experience. The thesis is no different from that practiced in the temple building and religious performances of all time. The only new thing is the attempt to create a temple and celebrations for a religion for one world rather than for one tribe or ethnic group. The experiment uses ancient means to accomplish a new end, an end that we have not invented, but that has been thrust upon us by the evolution of the human situation.

The project to be described in succeeding chapters is still in progress and will probably be in progress in the Meeting House and elsewhere for many centuries. It will endure as the next step in man's religious development until some as yet unforeseen evolution in the human situation makes another reorientation and redirection necessary. In some fifteen years we have but made the first rough run-through of the possibilities and difficulties and imponderables involved. What we have accomplished, like all beginnings, is necessarily inept and fumbling. This book is being published in the hope that others will be encouraged (that is, given the courage) to grope with us to a religious answer that may help to avert the possible tragedy that hovers over the human family.

The publication of the project is being made at this time because we seem to have moved in basic forms and structures as far as our limited comprehension and imagination can take us. It seems to us that certain symbolic necessities are dictated by the growth of culture and religion up to this present turning point and crisis. We present the findings of the project, not as something that we have created, but as something that already existed, which we have performed the humble function of gathering together and arranging in a meaningful order. It carries with it no dogmas of interpretation, philosophy, or theology. It does not attempt to prophesy what the future development of man's religious belief and practice will be in a religion for one world. We have certain opinions in this matter,

278

but we hold them simply as our opinions. We have attempted to make a presentation drawn from all of the human scene and from nature itself, our intention being to be fully universal, in that we believe that any person from any corner of the globe and any culture, should be able to be as much at home in this temple setting as any other person.

We know that some people will feel more at home in this setting than others, but we believe it is not because they "belong" there more than anyone else but because they have learned how to identify with all the ways of mankind, and not just with those of their own sect and land. None has been left out. If he feels alien, his alienation from his brothers must stem from himself.

INITIATING THE PROJECT

Ecclesiastes notwithstanding, there are new things under the sun. As far as we know, the Meeting House Project is one of them. We do not know of another instance where a religious society was set up on a distinctly experimental basis, in order to produce inventions in religious form and practice. The experimental laboratory has been applied to the field of religion.

It was but a generation or so ago that Edward Scribner Ames, at the University of Chicago, pioneered in the concept and attitude of a science of religion. Religion has been by nature traditional, authoritarian, deriving its scriptures and practices from sources claimed to be divine and revealed. Where God is the inventor, mere human inventors must necessarily fear to tread. But the field of religion has been opened to science, even though Descartes had set it aside as a special province. It wasn't until religion and such matters as rituals, symbols, art, and the organizational structure of the religious community were regarded as human and natural affairs that an experimental and laboratory operation could be applied in the areas of religious concern.

Although experiments have been carried on in other religious societies (sometimes openly acknowledged as such, more often not), the Meeting House took upon itself the charge to be a "pilot project" society, to make experimentation its major concern, within the context of a general parish program. Perhaps of necessity, the initiation of such a religious oddity would have to come about partly by accident. Those who brought the Meeting House Project into existence had little or no idea what it was going to do or in what direction it would move, for the person in charge — namely, myself — had only the most general idea of where the project was headed.

A bit of history will be instructive at this point. Boston had been the center of early and later developments in liberal religion, for both the Unitarian and the Universalist movements. But the tides of migration and urban sociology had had a severe effect on the Universalist churches in the City of Boston. Twenty-two had grown and died. Boston was left without a Universalist church, and the churches were withering fast in the surrounding suburbs. It seemed intolerable to the Universalists not to have a Universalist church in Boston, the home of the national headquarters.

The Massachusetts Universalist Convention decided to remedy the situation by establishing a new church in the city. The Convention was then in a liberal phase, and it reasoned that since the twenty-two churches that had died had been traditional in form and practice, there was no hope for a conventional Universalist society in the city. It decided, therefore, to set up a society for the express purpose of being innovational, purchased the old Charles Street Meeting House as its home, and began looking for someone to lead it.

Since experimentalism is rare even in the liberal movement, there wasn't much to choose from in the way of leadership. Whatever had been done of this sort had been sporadic and episodic. I had done a few things in worship in summer conferences and at Madison, Wisconsin, had done some writing and work in hymns and readings, and worked in the planning of the experimental Frank Lloyd Wright building, then about to be built in Madison. This latter embodied a radical concept in the use of a religious building, namely, that the auditorium should be multi-functional. It was designed as a "parish living room," to serve for worship, forums, concerts, dancing, parish dinners — for whatever were the large-group activities of the society. The rest of the building was designed as an educational wing, to serve during the week as a nursery school.

Such was the quite inadequate background in experimentation that I brought with me to the Meeting House. All who were involved began from scratch in a totally new kind of venture. Misunderstandings were inevitable. Not only were the projects which were engaged in at the Meeting House experimental, but the Meeting House itself, as an institution, was an experiment, one that is still going on, for we have not yet shown that such an institution can survive and become a self-sufficient social organism.

It turned out that the major perils to the Meeting House came from the very Massachusetts Universalist Convention that had brought it into being. For five years our project was the major controversy in the State Convention, with its survival in jeopardy from one annual meeting to the next. Its opponents acquired the power to liquidate it less than a year and a half after its inception but postponed the action for a year, hoping to increase their power and get a clearer mandate for the step; then they lost their control of the Convention in the next annual meeting. The survival of a project can hardly be more precarious than that.

The major point to make here is that a considerable number of the Universalist churches in Massachusetts were exceedingly reluctant supporters of the project they had initiated. The project did have very strong support from the rest, sufficient to keep it going. But there were other problems. Although the Meeting House had been charged to be a pilot project, no one knew what this meant in terms of support and enablement. The Meeting House was supported just as any conventional church extension project might be supported. No financial assistance was forthcoming for the operation of the experimental side. There is no clear division of cause and effect here, of course, since the aid given the Meeting House supported all the activities in which it engaged, by providing housing, upkeep, ministerial salary, etc., on a gradually diminishing scale over a ten-year period. But appeals for specific aid for experiments as such met with no response from the State Convention. Some collaboration did come later from the Universalist Historical Society, under the leadership of Melvin Van der Workeen, but that is another matter.

The conclusion to be drawn here, in order to give a realistic appraisal of the experimental operation in a religious context, is that even when experimentation is engendered by a headquarters or denominational agency, little support is likely to be forthcoming. Experimentalism is, perhaps inevitably, the province and responsibility of the few stubborn persons motivated to do the experimenting. It will be done by individuals, by minorities within local congregations, and in rare instances (as in the Meeting House) by local congregations acting as a whole. Even here, a cautionary estimation is necessary, since many of the members of the Meeting House over the years have not been favorable to an experimental approach, or else they have supported some of the projects and not others. But the main weight of our parish operation has been in this direction.

Nevertheless we are unendingly grateful to the Massachusetts Universalist Convention for bringing us into being, and for their continuous backing albeit at times without universal enthusiasm. And certainly the gesture of the Convention, in one of its last meetings, in providing a subsidy whereby this book, the report of the project, might be accomplished makes up for much of the insecurity suffered during the intervening years.

The experimenter must be endlessly opportunistic. Society is always reluctant to open its door to innovation. Growth is an awkward camel, always getting its nose in the tent, but always considered an obnoxious interloper within the tent. Whitman made the conclusive statement in his poem "Beginners."

> How they are provided for upon the earth, (appearing at intervals,)
> How dear and dreadful they are to the earth,
> How they inure to themselves as much as to any — what a paradox appears their age,
> How people respond to them, yet know them not,
> How there is something relentless in their fate at all times,
> How all times mischoose the objects of their adulation and reward,
> And how the same inexorable price must still be paid for the same great purchase.

The issue is that the beginner can never expect someone else, or some institution, to pay the purchase price for him. If you want to experiment, especially in something as traditional and averse to change as religion, expect and prepare to pay your own way. Part of the reason why I came to the Meeting House to head up a "pilot project" was curiosity. It seemed too good to be true. It was. But it did let the camel get his nose in the tent. For a camel to be established in an old Meeting House in the center of Boston is certainly one of the oddest spectacles in human history.

The innovator has a certain strategy for survival. Since he is moving forward, he has the weight inherent in the momentum of his movement as his advantage over the conservative who is standing still, and who is mainly concerned in blocking his advance. The immediate opposition that the Meeting House Project faced operated to accelerate the program of experimentation. The project had been engaged with a feeling of comparative gentleness; we proposed to make the innovations slowly and let their impact accumulate over many years. But when we were forced immediately to fight for survival, there was no time for the patient approach, and we initiated one experiment after another, telescoping into a few years what we had hoped to accomplish in many.

We have kept this strategy at work all during our brief life. We never put off until tomorrow what we could do today, for tomorrow was a rug that was jerked out from under us at the very beginning. The descriptions of the various projects that follow must be seen in this context, or the whole human point of this report will be missed.

For this has been a completely homely, earthy, laborious project. It is best described as a family work project. Only because we have been willing to be our own janitors, plumbers, cooks, secretaries, carpenters, painters, printers, binders, electricians, organ builders, decorators, photographers, brokers, collectors, librarians — only because we have been willing to assume all the menial functions of our operation — have we become privileged to be the experimenters, the creators of a new artistic, symbolic, and operational approach to religion.

The only just comparison that comes to mind is this: Maillol and Picasso have the physiques of peasants. They are laborers, for sculpture is heavy labor, and draftmanship and painting are the most demanding work that man knows. There is a blunt and, as far as I know, a new adage that applies in all such cases: Either be willing to work damned hard or be damned.

THE OPEN HYMNAL

The Meeting House Project is an integrated and over-all project which is composed of many smaller projects. There was not in all cases any logic involved in the order in which the various projects were undertaken. Several projects had not yet been conceived at the beginning, for there has been a generic growth within the project as a whole. Many aspects of the total project have emerged out of necessities and suggestions that have appeared as it unfolded.

In the very beginning there was little more than a sense of urgency that something needed to be done, and a few vague ideas as to what this might be, slowly taking shape as out of a mist. I can remember that it was while I was shaving one morning, about six months from the time we started, that the general outline of the project took form in a series of images, rising out of the confusion of ideas and problems with which we began. Although it has been expanded, modified, and elaborated, that basic design has inhered in the project ever since.

The first project was one that I had brought with me from my earlier experience and had been toying with for some time. Those who take a naturalistic and humanistic approach to religion had found the traditional worship materials, and the hymnbooks that carried them, unusable. It was not so much that they were against theistic hymns and readings, but that these materials simply did not convey the emotions, insights, and aspirations that the humanists sought to express in their services. Several individual ministers and a few conferences had brought out collections of readings and hymns, but none of these was an adequate substitute for a hymnbook, nor did all of them together provide the quality and variety of materials sought.

The answer that had met almost universal usage was a printed or mimeographed order of service for each Sunday, including new readings and hymns. But this was an unsatisfactory solution, for a good deal of work was entailed in producing the order of service each week. Since it was almost impossible to print the music along with the words to the hymn, the already poor congregational singing was further hampered. If a good reading or hymn came into usage, it would have to be reprinted a dozen times over a few years, a very inefficient method. A solution had occurred to me, which I had not found an opportunity to put into effect. It became the first project at the Meeting House.

The "open hymnal" was the idea of unbinding the hymnbook. We acquired black spring-steel-backed notebook covers, with the name of the Meeting House stamped on them. They were chosen because the pages could be put in and removed very easily, without being punched. Our service materials were then prepared on single sheets, which were assembled in order for each occasion. In effect, the result was a new hymnbook for each service, specifically prepared for that service alone. There were several advantages.

The open hymnal eliminates leafing through a large hymnbook to find the various hymns and readings. It also eliminates the awkward bulk of a large book, often of some six hundred pages, only four or five of which are utilized at any one time. I can remember how my hand tired from holding the book in front of me during a long hymn. The open hymnal offers a slim collection of material, all in the order in which it is to be used.

Since the materials themselves are presented in the order used, there is no need for an order of service, which is awkward if pasted in front of the hymnal, where one must keep looking for it, or if printed on a separate card. This method limits the orders of service to one or a few which are printed for stock use, or else a new service must be printed for each Sunday, with the disadvantages noted above. The open hymnal enables the participant to simply read through the service in the order given.

These operational advantages are secondary to the primary advantages. This method opens the services to a fully experimental and creative process. The society is no longer limited to whatever happens to be in the hymnbook it may own, nor to the type of material this presents. Each society can create and collect those hymns, readings, and other elements adapted to its peculiar disposition. There is no need to buy ten hymns it does not want in order to get one the people can sing. The new procedure is truly open, for new pages can be printed or mimeographed whenever they are desired, and once published they are on file for any future use.

The open hymnal is a practical invitation to experiment. New material can be added with ease. If old material becomes outworn, it can be dropped from usage by simply removing those pages from the file. If a special service is planned, complete flexibility is at hand. Liberal religion should have its major celebrations, structurally complex services in which there are many more service elements than in the ordinary Sunday morning order. The open hymnal enables any assortment of materials to be assembled in order. In the Jewish and Episcopalian religions the materials for long and ritualistic services are provided in books of common worship. These operate with fair efficiency if the participants are fully familiar with the worship manuals and the ritual procedures. It was my experience as a stranger that after five minutes of trying to follow the service I was hopelessly lost, since the leader seemed to be skipping back and forth through the book. By allowing the material to be arranged in sequence, with full notations and explanations appended, the open hymnal facilitates the production of the most ambitious worship experiments with the minimum of confusion to all participating.

Long use of the open hymnal has provided an insight relating to festival services, experimentation, and books of common worship. The open hymnal made it possible for us to create a good deal of new material, for use both in regular services and on festival occasions. We discovered that material created for a particular festival service, or selections from it, was also usable in the regular services. And often in planning a new festival service we found that materials created for our regular services needed but to be selected and assembled to give us ready-made a considerable proportion of the festival service. Through this insight we came to a new understanding of the Jewish Prayer Book in particular, and how it had accumulated over many centuries from the various usages in the temple, both in regular Sabbath services and in the traditional festivals. Through the open hymnal we were in process of composing our own liberal "book of common worship" without ever having planned to do so. The open hymnal had provided us with the same kind of flexibility and freedom of creative accumulation of religious literature that had prevailed in less formal and more spontaneous societies. Worship materials are a folk literature, developed for use in assemblies of the folk, and the open hymnal was supplying an institutional memory system similar to that of the ancient bards and the memory of the folk for songs and traditions before formal education and printing came on the scene.

The more ritualistic religions move within a large corpus of worship materials in contrast to most Protestant groups, which seldom use more than a few hymns and readings. The Jewish materials have been accumulating for over three thousand years, and the wealth of this religious literature and ritual provides one of the strongest bonds of the Jewish community and culture. Our own literature and songs and rites are pitifully thin in comparison. The only way we can overcome our poverty is through our own creative efforts, and to this end we need instruments to implement our creativity, and to collect and store the results in a living corpus, such as the Jewish Bible and other oral and written compendiums.

The traditional Protestant hymnal is a poor device for this purpose, nor are we recommending a liberal book of common worship, for this comes at the end of a long and accumulative process rather than at the beginning. Liberalism must develop its own instruments for its own growth; a new kind of religious tradition cannot make do with devices suited to other species of religious development.

The old hymnbook was developed for orthodox religion. In the fixity of its contents it makes the operational assumption that there is a standard, divinely inspired body of materials, if not "once and for all delivered to the saints," at least constant enough to need only gradual modification. The average hymnbook is expected not to need revision for twenty-five years, and then it is expected that the revisions will be minor, and that the large body of traditional material will be carried over intact. Orthodoxy places much the same assumptions upon the hymn-book that it does upon its bibles; they are supposed to endure for eternity.

Liberal religion has been uncritical, unimaginative, and unenterprising in adopting the hymnbook of orthodox religions. The hymnbook is an anachronism in the free church, typifying too much of the worship of liberal religion which is only a dead borrowing from a dying past.

In terms of simple mechanics and economy the open hymnal is practical. It takes a minimum of labor to reassemble the books for the new services, much less than the labor necessary to gather and print an order of service, to say nothing of the saving entailed in not having to reprint a new hymn or reading every time it is used. The notebook covers are more costly than they should be, but they are durable. The entire operation is much less expensive than the expenditure for hymnbooks plus that of printed orders of services and all the work entailed in the makeshift of present practices.

Since the open hymnal was the first project instituted, we have had some fifteen years of its operation to test its validity. A basic intention of the pilot project idea was that the Meeting House should pioneer in various areas, then make its findings available for other societies, just as a laboratory in science and industry makes findings and evolves solutions to problems which are then adopted by agencies primarily engaged in man-ufacture and production. The open hymnal has been able to make a full cycle in this process.

The distribution of the materials accumulated in the open hymnal began with a series of mimeographed pamphlets con-taining responsive readings and festival services, and a loose-leaf collection of hymns called "Hymns of Humanity." These were called "works in progress" and were designed to convey our materials to other societies for their use, even though they were incomplete. Some of the material was of a confessedly experimental nature, in that we had doubts that it would be of ultimate utility. We hoped that other societies would partici-pate in the winnowing process, whereby the best might be fi-nally selected, and used temporary mimeographed editions to this end.

The practicality of the open hymnal technique was demonstrated here, for when we printed or mimeographed materials for our own services we made copies for the pamphlets, and "Hymns of Humanity" was in fact a collection of single sheets of the hymnal file from which we made selections for our own services. Thus one mimeographing or printing sufficed both for our own use and for distribution to other groups.

Later, after we had instituted Meeting House Press and had our own printing equipment, this process was reversed. When we printed books of worship materials for distribution, we used the same type to put the pages of our own open hymnal into printed form. The production of the book of services and responsive readings, *Readings for the Celebration of Life,* made it possible to process a large amount of material for both uses at the same time. That is, the coalescing of the publishing and the open hymnal made it feasible to spend more time in the production of new worship materials than would have been possible if these ventures had been pursued separately. In actuality they became one venture with both local and denominational usage.

After the open hymnal had been in operation for some ten years, the Universalist and Unitarian fellowships established a joint hymnbook commission to create a new hymnbook for the now merged Unitarian Universalist Association. My work on our local projects had given me sufficient background so that I was made a member of the commission. This circumstance in itself is instructive. Experimentation in the local societies will train persons in various areas, who will then be equipped to be useful in denomination-wide projects.

The hymnbook commission set out to accumulate everything it could find that had been created in the twenty-five years since the former hymnal had been published, in order to sift it for possible new hymns and readings. The considerable accumulation of several hundred hymns and readings from the open hymnal project was then contributed to the "hopper" of new materials under consideration. Also, with the double motivation and justification of both the hymnal commission and our own project, we engaged in research for new materials on a scale much more extensive than before and produced several hundred more possible hymn verses for consideration. Thus our local project worked as a part of a denominational agency during the labors of the commission.

As we have mentioned above, several men had worked in this field and had published their products in one way or another. There were, however, only two situations where sustained efforts and experiments had been made, at the Meeting House and through the efforts of Vincent Silliman in his several parishes. Through a workshop approach, and using another type of loose-leaf technique, Silliman had developed a great many hymnal materials, mainly for children's worship, which had been published in *We Sing of Life* and *We Speak of Life*. A considerable proportion of his efforts was suitable for adult usage, and this too went into the hopper of the commission. What was significant was the disproportionate amount of material that had come from these two experimental projects, in contrast to the hundreds of other parishes where no such organized research and development had occurred. The amount of material from these two sources that weathered the evaluation of the commission and found its way into the new hymnal is a practical and unarguable justification for the experimental, laboratory, or pilot project organization of the local society. It is demonstrably much more creative and productive of materials for the entire movement than are societies of a more traditional organization.

Is the open hymnal method advisable for most groups? This question remains unanswered. When instituting it we had tried to involve other societies in similar efforts, hoping to receive new materials from them and, through joint publications, to cut the cost of printing new pages of hymns and readings. When we published *Readings for the Celebration of Life,* we printed a stock of single sheets, offering to make them available to societies wishing to set up their own open hymnal. This material has found no market, and we have ceased trying to push it. A few ministers have tried to set up a version of the open hymnal in other societies, but the efforts have proved transient and ineffectual. Thus the open hymnal remains a system in which the Meeting House is convinced that it has found a new operational technique of real significance to the liberal movement, but we have been unable to promote the spread of the idea.

A second effort was made in this direction. During the first years of the hymnal commission meetings, I worked for the consideration of a dual publication, in the form of a bound hymnal and on single sheets as an open hymnal. But my efforts came to naught, which means that any such effort on a denominational level will probably have to wait another twenty-five years, if it ever develops. I have experienced a fundamental disillusionment on this score, for the other members of the commission had worked through the materials produced by the open hymnal method and still were not convinced that the method should be encouraged for any wide application.

My present judgment is that there is insufficient creative motivation in most societies to make the open hymnal attractive to them as a laboratory instrument. They just are not laboratories and do not desire to be. In the absence of this motivation, the utility of this system as a method of presenting worship materials for a service does not seem sufficient to move them to break the habit of using hymnbooks and printed orders of service.

As we have seen demonstrated in almost every aspect of the project, the most difficult reform of all to institute is that of form. There is opposition enough when you try to insert new elements into an old form, but this can be done — indeed, is being done continuously. It is possibly the most effective working of evolution for new materials and meanings to infiltrate the old formal patterns of behavior. The populace then has a sense of continuity and security in the formal stability and is able to allow some alteration in the materials assembled within the forms. An intriguing example is the monarchical and aristocratic forms that still endure in Britain, even though the practice of the country has become radically democratic. Even so, the liberal church treasures the old forms of orthodoxy even as it radically changes the content and meaning of its religious life and practice.

The tragedy is that only a limited amount of evolution and progress can take place by putting new wine in old bottles. Form follows function, and function also follows form. There are many kinds of worship elements available to a religion for one world that we will never recognize as belonging in our celebration, and never be able to utilize, until we have undergone a formal reconstruction. The reconstruction of content can go only so far unless the formal restructuring demanded also occurs. Perhaps what most often happens in cultural evolution is that formal evolution takes place in any vital way only by an imperceptible series of alterations due to the gradual changing of the content. Using a biological analogy, perhaps the slow accumulation of changes in content are the mutations which in time will accumulate until a new creature and new species will have developed — so slowly and gradually that no one will have been aware of the process.

Cultural evolution, however, does not seem necessarily to follow the same patterns as biological evolution. It may be that the local inception of formal revolutions, such as that of the open hymnal and other experiments at the Meeting House, have a potentiality of influence and change far greater than evidence now in hand would indicate. In any case, the experimental wisdom would seem to justify our going ahead with our open hymnal practice, despite its seeming inability to win a following, just to see what the long-range evolutionary efficacy of such a formal break might be.

This is our intention, even though a paradoxical situation now confronts us. The new hymnal has been so considerably changed from the previous hymnal, by the efforts of our own project and the efforts of Silliman and others, that we could probably use the new hymnal at the Meeting House and find a fair selection of material of our conviction and temper within it. The efforts that have brought us this far have been expensive and arduous. Why not rest on our laurels, scrap the open hymnal project, and sing the hymns and use the readings that the new book provides? Why not bend our efforts to promoting the new hymnal, which includes many innovations not in current use, rather than charging out after still other innovations? Margaret Mitchell, after she had finished *Gone with the Wind,* never wrote another novel. She was content to live off the one she had written.

But the answer to this temptation is inherent in the experimental temperament and experience. Many of the pieces proposed for the new hymnal were not able to weather the selective process of the commission. There are too many new things already in existence to make us fully satisfied with that substantial body of material that did make its way through the commission's sieve. The make-up of the commission was strikingly liberal, even for the liberal movement, but even so it carried a heavy weight of traditionalism and conservatism within it. Many pieces that could have received a considerable acceptance by a significant minority of liberal societies were excluded because of the inherent reactionary make-up of all official commissions. It is intolerable that hymns that many of us are ready to sing now must be deferred for another quarter of a century because they failed to survive this particular commission and find their way into the new book.

What we propose to do is to keep the open hymnal in operation. In it we will use, not only the material in the new book, but also the things the new book could not digest. We are issuing a new "Hymns of Humanity" immediately, which will be composed of the new material that is not as yet available in any official publication. This is necessitated not only by the considerations above but by the fact that several new elements have appeared in that year or so between the closing of the commission's consideration and its actual publication. These should have been considered by the commission and deserve to be in the new book. Thus, solely in view of quite new items, the new hymnal will be out of date even before its publication. Creativity and innovation are a continual process, and the bound hymnal is an awkward creature that bestrides this flowing stream; it does not swim with it. The open hymnal, on the other hand, is native to the stream. It has no publishing date. It does not have to wait for a generation to consider new materials. But it will face a more difficult social situation now than it did fifteen years ago, and partially because of its own success during that period. Most of the societies are going to be too busy in the next several years bringing the new materials in the new hymnal into usage to be much concerned about even more new material that didn't get into the book, or that is being produced after it closed its canons.

Thus, as soon as we have won acceptance for some of our creations, we must launch out with others even more unpopular. But there is no relief from this necessity unless the creative chain is to be broken.

The answer of morale and motivation is inherent in the process itself. Those hymns and readings now in the official hymnal lend the example of their ultimate acceptance to the newer experiments that still await such official acknowledgment. Should one's regard be for the eggs already laid or for the goose that laid them, and will lay more, given sustenance?

Another consideration grows out of the fact that moving into unexplored areas not only uncovers new territory but reveals to the explorer wide areas still farther on where he has not traveled. In working on the open hymnal thus far, we have discovered that many writers have been creating materials for us, poems and meditations, without intention or awareness. The reorientation of a natural and human and one-world religious view brings many writings and other works of art into the scope of our consideration and adoption that most writers and artists would not consider religious. In order to find what is already available to our use, we would have to make an exhaustive survey of world literature and art.

Just a few months of such research that have been squeezed into the summer recesses have turned up a volume of possible material that fully justifies a long-range investigation. It would take five years of full-time probing to make an adequate survey of the field, and its result, we are convinced, would be a wealth of literary resources that would be almost overwhelming. We might discover that we already have a tradition, unlocated and unacknowledged, of a richness and depth comparable to that of Jewish religion.

There is little hope of finding a subsidy for this project. The movement has just finished investing in one hymnal, and it will have no immediate motivation to engage its funds in such a venture. Another problem is the fact that such material is not readily recognized, except by someone thoroughly grounded in the most esoteric areas of the philosophy of liberalism and the present literature of the movement — and sensitive to what things make suitable worship elements in terms of poetical and other qualities. Such a search must be undertaken by a member

294

of the group. It cannot be farmed out to some literary scholar on the outside, who might know where the sources were but who would not be able to recognize what we were seeking even when he had found it. One's feelings in this matter are somewhat like those of a prospector who has uncovered a rich vein of ore and cannot find anyone to invest in its mining.

Our only alternative is to proceed as painfully and inadequately as we are able, sandwiching in among many other projects and obligations an opportunity that merits a full-time effort. It will be evident that this condition and its accompanying frustration apply to practically all of the several projects that the Meeting House has undertaken.

The emergence of a new hymnody out of an old, involving a definite break with tradition, presents several other problems. The innovators are inexpert and fumbling. At first they know what they do not want a good deal better than they know what they do want, and they may appear to be iconoclastic. Conversely, the new ways grow out of the old ways, and in terms of the consistency of the new philosophy they are not as iconoclastic as they should be for the sake of their own integrity of position and expression. A new liturgy and literature cannot be created out of hand. The methods of procedure have been several. First of all there was an attempt to salvage something from the great store of Christian hymnody. This was no problem for the liberals who still identified with the Christian tradition, for much of the Christian worship materials still spoke to their condition. But the theistic and supernatural elements, expressions of faith in immortality and the predominant Christian idiom, make these hymns foreign to the natural expression of those humanistically oriented, who are moved to an expression directed to the world community rather than to one tradition within it.

One device issued mainly from poverty. Some hymns were truncated, with the acceptable verses retained and those that "took off for heaven" omitted. The number of such finds was small, and most of them were left with an unfinished, lopped-off literary quality. Another expedient was to rewrite objectionable lines, or to go through, changing the word "God" to "good." The results of such tinkering were awkward, even em-

295

barrassing. The whole attempt was a scavenger operation at best, and a clear admission of literary sterility on the part of the humanists and universalists. The more virile course would have been to launch out on the writing of new hymns of their own.

A more pervasive problem stems from a carry-over of expectancy from a traditional past into the whole area of hymnody. Christian hymns carry assumptions about humanity, life, and the universe, and these gather into certain general classifications. Hymns are a specialized musical and literary field. Naturalists and universalists unwittingly adopted the thematic limitations of traditional hymns. There are certain subjects with which hymns do not deal, and even when alterations in content were accomplished, the restrictions relating to general attitudes and themes were seldom eliminated. Many of the most exciting and vital values in natural religion have not yet been touched upon, much less exploited, by new hymns.

The traditional classification of hymns is patent in the indexes of the hymnals. The headings in a Methodist hymnal are Worship, God, Jesus Christ, The Holy Spirit, The Gospel, The Christian Life, The Living Church, The Christian Home and Family, Hymns for Children, The Kingdom of God, The Eternal Life, Special Seasons and Services, The Holy Communion, Responses and Canticles. A Universalist hymnal of 1917 presents this classification: Morning Service, Evening Service, Close of Worship, Processionals and Recessionals, God, Christ, The Holy Scriptures, The House of Worship, The Ministry, The Church, Evangelism, Social Service, Patriotic and Memorial, The Spiritual Life, The Christian Year, Life Everlasting, Chants.

Many of these classifications were carried into *Hymns of the Spirit*, the latest liberal hymnal before the one now in publication. But this was the first hymnal in which humanists had a considerable voice, and new areas of preoccupation emerged. In none of the new areas were there *enough* hymns of sufficient quality or variety of subject matter, but it was a significant accomplishment that they were for the first time given consideration.

Some of the new areas are: Man in the World of Nature and

Society, with subheadings (1) His Relation to the Universe, (2) His Relation to Human Society; Times and Seasons; Human Relations, with subheadings (1) Family and Friends, (2) Brotherhood, (3) The World of Labor, (4) Times of Adversity, Doubt or Oppression, (5) Social Justice, (6) The Coming Day, (7) The Heritage of Man, and Peace Among Men.

Even so, the general tone of the humanist hymns still echoes the attitudes of traditional hymnody: an uplift, an onward-and-upward-forever utopianism, a sweetness-and-light optimism. If humanists no longer believe in a heaven beyond death, they sing as if they yearned for heaven on earth. Although we want to improve the conditions of life as much as possible, there is an essential tragedy to human experience, transiency, parting, loss, sorrow and death, and frustrations that surround the most salutary accomplishments. We celebrate motherhood, but with the sentimentalities of Mother's Day. Samuel Johnson wrote dignified and literary prayers, but they fail to have the bite and zest of his *ex cathedra* statements, such as one about the desirability of marriage: "Marriage has many pains; celibacy few pleasures." One cannot imagine the appearance of this realism in a prayer or hymn dealing with the "Christian Home," or even under the humanist heading of "Family and Friends."

Why should we lose all sense of humor, irony, wit, as well as our sense of tragedy and darkness and the proper proportion between darkness and light in human experience, as soon as we begin to "worship"? The ancient conviction of salvation and eternal life, the final conquering of all evil by divine love, still permeates the moods of humanist celebrations, in the form of a bland optimism. The observation that Universalists believe that God is too good to damn man, and the Unitarians are convinced that man is too good for God to damn, carries on into the reformist simplicities and brightly smiling attitude of the humanists.

The Jewish Bible is the literary anthology of the Jewish people, as well as their holy book. Its strength and appeal lie in the richness and diversity of its contents, in which the evil and virtue of humanity, the tragedy and happiness of human experience are projected. Our hymnals are thin and pretty documents in comparison. Where is the invective of Amos, the world-weary wisdom of Ecclesiastes, the paradoxical mixture of strength and weakness in David, and the love poems of the Song of Songs? An attempt to get a responsive reading from Job into the new hymnal failed. His despair is uncongenial to our hopeful age. It is a threat to social security.

The literature of the race has been equally lush and diversified in succeeding centuries, but the church has impoverished itself by dividing it into the sacred and the secular. The sacred literature has had the worst of it in this division of the sheep from the goats, for the goats have been the more vigorous breed. Most of the great names of literature appear nowhere as authors of hymn verses and readings, whereas the list of contributors is rife with third-rate poetasters. The writing of the masters has been too good, too alive, too naturalistic, too human, too vigorous, too full of the torture and ecstasy of living, and too realistically marked with the evil and spoilage and grief of man's tragic state. These characteristics did not keep the literature of Israel out of the Bible, but it has kept the lusty richness of subsequent literature out of the sacred canons of Christendom and liberal religion. The puritanical nastiness, the life-loathing and flesh-hating of the church have locked the poets, novelists, and song-writers out of religion. The true literary prophets of liberal religion and of a religion for one world have been laboring outside the church for centuries, even as they do today. They have been composing a bible of humanity, free from the excluding canonizations of the priests. Not even the Index has been able to restrain them. The church has not prevented the poets from making songs out of the fullness of the stuff of life.

It has been the avowed intent of our open hymnal project to bring the poets into the hymnbook, and we have succeeded in a significant degree. Many of the poets will be in the new hymnbook for the first time. Others are in "Hymns of Humanity," and thence they too may one day make their way into the official publications. New categories have been introduced. Hymns on beauty and the arts, on nature mysticism, on the delights of the senses, on the splendor of the earth and the universe, on world brotherhood and a religion for one world are making their appearance. Some hymns deal with the evolution of life and culture; a few are paraphrases from the writings of the world religions. Most of this latter material is found in the reading section. A few hymns even look calmly at death without the wishfulness of immortality, and others sing a pagan celebration of this life.

One area where it is very hard to break through relates to poems about love of men and women, which assuredly has many dimensions worthy to be named religious. Literature has many love songs of a delicacy and dignity worthy a place in religious celebration.

When we have learned how to sing our faith in man and nature and the fellowship of one world, then our religious expression will have worked its way down into the roots of our feeling. Too long liberal religion has been largely an intellectual conviction without the penetration of the emotions necessary before the whole person is involved in a way of life. This lack bespeaks our need for music and literature and the other arts.

Closely related to the hymnal project is an anthem project, which has proceeded on three levels. First is the research to discover what choral works already in existence, which have been considered secular music rather than sacred, have human and universal sentiments that suit them for celebrations of a religion for one world. We have done a small amount of such research, being handicapped by the fact that choral music is very poorly catalogued, and there is hardly any approach other than that of a random hunt through the files at music stores.

A considerable amount of such material has been turned up. One point of frustration lies in its performance, since it is often too difficult for the small and often amateur choral group to perform. Such magnificent items as the cantata composed by Hindemith for Walt Whitman's *When Lilacs Last in the Dooryard Bloom'd*, which are so apt that they could not have been improved upon if they had been commissioned by us for our use, have already been produced, but this particular work would require a symphony orchestra, a fine choral group, and several top soloists to perform. What liberal churches there are that might attempt it seem more interested in putting on another of the interminable performances of Handel's *Messiah*.

The liberal movement would be well advised to finance an

exhaustive research into existing choral music and to create a catalogue of suitable works for liberal societies. The project should be kept up to date by a continuous review of all new choral music being published. But our movement is as yet far from being sufficiently mature culturally to see the advantages of such a service, and it is too large for any single society to attempt. What the Meeting House has done in this area has only served to tantalize us with the possibilities.

A second project would be to commission new choral music for suitable texts which we have at hand. A great many such texts exist, for the utility of poetry for the texts of choral music greatly exceeds that of hymns. Choral music is far more flexible and adaptable to the idiosyncracies of the texts than are hymn verses, and since choral groups are more proficient musically than congregations, more difficult treatments are acceptable. The Meeting House has only touched on this field, but we are developing contacts with composers, and several have done such composition voluntarily. The work of the Hymnal Commission turned up many texts unsuitable for hymns for one reason or another that are eminently usable for anthems.

The third project is to take already existing choral music of fine quality and to adapt liberal texts to it. This is where the Meeting House has been most busy. We have produced about fifty anthems of this variety, some fairly acceptable. In certain cases adaptations for choral purposes have proved to be equally usable as hymns and have found their way into the new hymnal. Music is not in itself theological. It presents a certain mood and spirit but no logical content of a verbal nature. If a liberal and universal text suitable in mood can be found for music by Bach or Praetorius, these great composers can serve our celebrations as well as those of Christendom.

The use of music for variant texts is an old story, in anthems as well as in hymns. Often the translations of German texts, for example, vary widely from the originals, and some musical scores have been used for a great many different texts. Care must be taken to marry the text to the music. In some cases the music of the composer is so subtly suited to his original text that it can hardly be used for any other purpose. Here is a challenge to the poet to create a text for such music as beautifully adapted to the music as the composer adapted the music to his text. Whether this can be done only many attempts will demonstrate.

What is clear is that the musical and poetic resources of humanity are available for the enrichment of our artistic and devotional life. We must have the wit and diligence, the artistry and the dedication, to use them. The greatest challenge now confronting a religion for one world is to make the art, music, poetry, and teachings of all cultures and religions into one great resource for the expression and embodiment of a religious viewpoint capable of including all the human family in its inclusive scope.

The experimentation with choral music has lain not only in the production of new materials but in its usage in celebrations. The bane of Protestant and liberal services, from one point of view, is the spot solo or anthem that is an isolated performance, generally having no inherent structural relationship to the theme and development of the service as a whole. Our celebrations need the kind of integrity and development, the organic interrelation of elements, found in the Catholic Mass.

Our anthem project has made a gesture in this direction by adapting the texts of a service to a series of anthems, whereby the reading of the service can be echoed by choral responses paraphrasing the spoken word. We have also adapted such material for solo voice; thus an individual singer can act as a sort of cantor in liberal services. But what we have done is quite experimental in nature, hardly more than an initial dabbling, and its only value is to suggest what might be done with sufficient interest and investment of talent.

THE DISCUSSION PERIOD

Symbols are behavioral, as well as matters of brass and wood, painting and sculpture, dance and architecture. One behavioral symbol, which we introduced into the Meeting House Project at the beginning, was the discussion period. The generative idea of the discussion period is that at any service there is not just one legitimate point of view and statement thereof, that of the preacher, but that every member of the group assembled has

301

the privilege of his own point of view, and that an honest service would give him an opportunity to express it. The presumption of a diversity of viewpoints in the congregation is of a piece with the assumption that there is but one human religion, with many variations within it. This concept is most congenial to Hinduism, in which orthodoxy of belief has never been considered important. There are hundreds of different schools and philosophies in Hinduism, yet any one is considered as rightfully Hindu as any other. Hinduism is an ethnic inclusion, not a doctrinaire exclusion.

The idea of a discussion period as a follow-up to the address had appeared elsewhere before its inclusion in the Meeting House Project. Various techniques had been tried. In some cases the formal service was shortened and part of the usual hour given over to questions and answers or open discussion. In other cases the discussion of the sermon would occur at another meeting, say on the Monday evening following, or during the hour preceding the service on the next Sunday. The faults of these devices were several. In the first instance the formal service suffered in being truncated, or in having formally uncongenial elements included. Where the discussion was held at a later date, the reaction to the address had cooled off, or the group was different from the one that had heard the address.

At Madison, Wisconsin, this practice had been introduced for special and controversial topics and during a summer series, but it had not become a regular tradition. Its innovation had stemmed from psychological as well as from social justifications. When the minister resigned from his position of eminence to sit down with the people, a change in attitude and orientation came over the assembly. Everyone was then privileged to speak out individually, for this was then an accepted behavior in the service. If someone had spoken out during the formal service, to interrupt the sequence of readings, hymns, meditation, and sermon, he would have felt very conspicuous. It would not have been the thing to do in that arrangement.

During the discussion the people began to look at one another and to address one another. Conversations sprang up. Whereas before all faces and ears were directed to the front and bent upon one man, the minister, now the points of attention developed wherever someone was entering the discussion. People became acquainted with one another through the sharing of reactions and comments. Laughter and informality came easily.

Something was happening to the preacher also. He had often ended the service with his stomach tied in knots. The main burden had been upon him alone, to construct the service, to do most of the readings, to deliver the whole message. Often he would go home without any appetite for Sunday dinner; it might be the middle of the afternoon before his appetite returned. But when he could descend to sit with the congregation and let them take over, the heat was off him, and he could feel himself loosen and relax. What had been tension became enjoyment. He was then just one of the people, listening to others, sharing the office of enlightenment and wisdom. This was real and honest. He no longer pretended to be an agent of unique authority and election. The nature of the assembly did not set him aside as such. By the time the discussion was finished he had returned to a normal gastric condition and was ready to go home and enjoy his dinner. Perhaps the members of the society who had lost some of their appetite in taking umbrage over a remark of the minister were also better prepared for dinner, since they had been able to vent their disagreement, and no longer felt they had been but unwilling receivers of the minister's bias.

The arrangement of the discussion period is such that it retains generic connection with the formal service preceding it, yet does not intrude upon the design and integrity of the formal service. It demands a group of people who are willing to let the service last two hours rather than one. The formal service concludes with a benediction, following which there is a break, so that those who wish to avoid the discussion period may escape, as they would after a traditional service. Those who so desire go to another part of the building for coffee, which provides refreshment and a period of sociability. It has been discovered that the coffee period acts as an effective lubricator of the discussion session.

Following the coffee hour the discussion period takes place in an entirely unplanned and spontaneous manner. It can be presided over either by the minister or by a member of the adult education committee. The important thing is to facilitate a continuous conversation among the minister and the members of the group, that goes on from meeting to meeting, and from year to year. From the point of view of the minister, I now consider this to be indispensable. My future preaching grows generically out of these conversations. They enable me to confront and participate in the reactions to my previous thinking as it has been received by the society.

A formal revolution will in time institute a revolution in content also. I have discovered that my attitude to preaching has changed with this alteration of the setting of the sermon due to the discussion period that follows. Previously the address needed to be an entity in itself. It demanded a conclusion, even though its theme might have left the speaker logically and honestly in a quandary rather than readying him for a pronouncement of divine wisdom. But with the new form it was logical and fitting to let the address serve a provocative function, to stimulate a discussion rather than to be an end in itself. A sermon in this setting could be the exploration of a common problem, to which no solution seemed to be forthcoming, and those present could then be invited to sit down and talk it over.

Max C. Otto at the University of Wisconsin would occasionally tell his philosophy classes that his one intent of the hour was to give them "a pain in the head." In like manner, the minister in this open setting can function to expose issues, to disturb, to excite, and the discussion period serves to round out the presentation through the group's seeking possible answers together.

A religion for one world cannot develop except in the fellowship of the free mind, for only there can the fertile differences of the various faiths live together peacefully and invigorate one another through the interplay of their contradictions and variations. Some such instrument as that of the open discussion group must evolve to facilitate an exchange of opinion and a matrix of understanding and intellectual sharing.

The best example of how the discussion period might function occurred in a service at the Meeting House in which I was preaching on naturalism and Chinese poetry. Edward Chin

Park, a Chinese-American architect, was in the congregation, and, without any pre-planning, I suggested that he might like to lead the discussion period. It took quite a different turn that morning, for Mr. Park proceeded to give an appreciation of Chinese poetry as a Chinese that perfectly supplemented my efforts to appreciate it as an Occidental.

By coincidence, a poem that I had read in translation was one Mr. Park had known as a child. He recited it to us in Chinese from memory, along with other poems, and gave us English renderings of them. Since he had actually lived in both cultures, that of China as well as that of the United States, and since he was a member of our liberal fellowship, he acted as a perfect bridge that morning between the East and the West. We felt at the end that we had experienced an entirely satisfactory and convincing demonstration of the fellowship and reality of a religion for one world.

THE BOOKCASE

New symbols evolve out of old symbols by a process of emendation and elaboration. This truth is nowhere more evident than in the bookcase, which has become one of the central symbols of a religion for one world developed at the Meeting House. We claim no originality for it; it grew out of the past.

Holy books are as old as human writing, and, as the oral traditions of the bards, they existed as memorized materials long before the invention of writing. The Navahos, for example, developed long ceremonials that went on for many days, with hundreds of songs and chants, rituals and sand-painting designs, all perfectly committed to memory by the shamans. These are their bible, which is now in the process of being recorded and put into printed form. All of the major cultural religions have their holy books.

The tradition from which we have stemmed has been aptly termed by Islam "the people of the Book." The Ark containing the Torah has a central place in the synagogue and in Jewish worship. The Koran is the indispensable holy book of Islam. Protestant Christianity, even more than Catholicism, makes the Bible an ascendant authority.

Those of us who came from a Protestant tradition remember the pulpit set in the center of the platform in the auditorium; always on it was the large pulpit Bible. Thus it held a position as central in Protestant worship as did the Ark of the Torah in Judaism, and readings from the holy book were part of the ritual in both faiths.

One of the early gestures toward a religion for one world occurred in the Unitarian Church in Evanston, Illinois. Instead of one pulpit Bible, a bookshelf was constructed on the wall behind the pulpit, and on it was a selection of the major holy books of the world religions. This had always impressed me as a very apt symbol of a new religious viewpoint, growing out of a traditional symbol, having thus good roots in the past as well as a bold thrust into the future needs of world religion.

Thus one of the first projects visualized at the Meeting House was a simple expansion of the bookshelf into a bookcase, to contain the major books of the world religions. The bookcase was designed by Ralph LaBlanc and Arcangelo Cascieri, an architect and an architectural sculptor, and it was built by a master cabinetmaker, the father of Roland Stowe, one of our members, and presented to the Meeting House as a gift. No one involved made any charge for his services. This kind of generous participation has characterized all the projects in which we have engaged.

The bookcase is large, simple and modernistic in style, and the style of this our first piece of furniture has been carried over into all the pieces we have built since. The bookcase has a large compartment at one end for very large books, like pulpit Bibles and Korans for ceremonial reading. It is placed centrally on the platform at the front of the Meeting House auditorium.

In the beginning we considered a formal research project, in which we would seek out the best translations of the world scriptures, purchase them, install them formally in the bookcase, and in time publish a bibliography of the collection. This has not, however, been done. The main reason is our discovery that this process was occurring spontaneously, as new translations were published, usually by non-denominational publishing houses. A great deal of translation and publication in this area has taken place since the bookcase was built. We were like the country doctor who styled his part of the birth process in the following doggerel: "Here I sit and twiddle my thumbs, and catch the baby when it comes."

Publishing a bibliography of these works would have the same disadvantage as publishing a hymnal — it would be out of date before it was off the press. We may do something of this sort in time, simply to suggest the scope and variety of materials now to be included in a "bible of humanity," but it could never have more than a suggestive significance. We have, instead, let the bookcase be "open" even as is the hymnal. The assortment of books within it is designed to cover the various cultures of the earth, but the selection has never been set; it is fluid and informal.

In the beginning we projected a ritualistic use of the bookcase. The person doing the reading for the service would go to the bookcase, choose the scripture from which the reading was to be taken, go to the reading desk and do the reading, and return the book to the bookcase afterward. If there were several readings taken from several scriptures, as sometimes happened, several trips to the bookcase might be entailed. Since the present arrangement of the auditorium has been changed, as will be described in the chapter "The Shape of the Assembly," this ritual is not in current use. It might be revived, however.

The Meeting House always has several details of the over-all project that have been discussed for some time but have not as yet been initiated. One of these is the designing and construction of four reading desks for the auditorium, to stand at the four sides of the central circle. There would be a reader at each desk, each responsible for a reading from a different book. It well might be that each reader would go to the bookcase, select his book, return to his lectern, make his reading, and then replace the book in the bookcase. This procedure would give movement to the service and would symbolize both the unity and the diversity of man's religious traditions — the unity, by the many books all in the one bookcase; the diversity, by the four readers at the four sides of the circle. This latter also echoes ancient traditions, since the idea of the four directions, the four quarters of the earth, each with its guardian figure, is an ancient and enduring symbolism in China and the Orient and has its counterpart in the West.

In any service of celebration the teachings, traditions, and rituals of the past are brought forth to be reconsidered and appreciated in the present. Our immediate problems and considerations are then viewed in their light, upon which we move to a reformulation of ideals, attitudes, and purposes for our own times and the future. Readings from the past do not serve as authorities, but as traditions, suggestions, and teachings. This use of ancient writings is more characteristic of Buddhism than of the Judaeo-Christian-Islamic tradition, which tends to see in the books a perfect revelation, the Word of God, rather than the teachings of Buddha, who was only a wise master.

The bookcase is an operative symbol, since it indicates that we honor the wise teachings from all times and places and welcome them into our meditations and considerations. The presence of Buddhist sutras in the bookcase elucidates, symbolically, the presence of Buddhist teachings in our hymns and readings.

As we made our collection of the art of the world religions, to be described later, we discovered that a great deal of the religious art of the world has to do with the making of the holy books, the arts of book-making, of calligraphy, and of illumination. An expansion of the original bookcase into two bookcases was demanded by the exigencies of the project itself. The second bookcase, on the other side of the auditorium, would house the originals of the world bibles, while the first bookcase would house the translations. In time this new bookcase was built as a permanent fixture, and in it are now a Torah, a Megillah, a Koran, Christian psalters, pages of medieval manuscripts, Japanese Buddhist books, a palm-leaf sutra from Ceylon, as well as numerous appurtenances that accompany the books, such as the Torah shield, pointer, and crowns of Judaism. The collection is incomplete, as indeed it will always be, but it will be gradually made more nearly universal and inclusive as we make new finds and receive contributions, such as the Koran for use in a mosque, which was sent to us from Pakistan.

The purpose of such original books is symbolic, not utilitarian. Most of us must turn to the translations in the bookcase at the other end of the auditorium if we wish to read them. Whether the labor and expense of collection and display are justified or not, depends on the efficacy and influence of symbolism in our lives. Just how much evocative power do such items have? The answer will be different to every person. We have felt the justification was sufficient to expedite the project.

I can give a simple testimonial, for what it is worth, that I never appreciated the veneration of the Jew for the Torah and the Megillah until we had these scrolls in our possession. To receive the inner meaning of the long and exact labors whereby the Torah is hand-lettered by ancient law, and to respect the veneration of the Jews by the veneration of the scroll now in our custody, is to come to sympathy and understanding by an act of identity and participation. For the Meeting House, in the name of a religion for one world, is now the keeper of a Torah, even as is the Jewish synagogue.

We have a Megillah, made on what seems to be deerskin, which came from Yemen, where the traditions and folk styles had hardly changed from biblical times. This scroll gives us the feeling of a scroll from thousands of years in the past. Some might think such an item a mere "museum piece." But an object in a museum remains a cold and detached exhibit only to the viewer who fails in the act of understanding, imagination, and love whereby it is made alive in his appreciation. The bookcases and their contents are rich symbols, deep, profound, resonant. But we must be as established in lore and wonder within ourselves as these books are in themselves, if they are to become evocative symbols of celebration and brotherhood for us. A young man stood before the bookcase with the original scrolls and other ritual items the other day. His reaction was, "This is beautiful." It is indeed — beautiful with the longing, aspiration, faith, and suffering of all humanity, echoed in the epics, the myths, the moral teachings, the philosophical arguments, that compose the immense, yet single, bible of man. The beauty is there for you, if you have the sense of this beauty within yourself.

THE SOUND SYSTEM

The use of music in developing celebrations for a religion for one world presents problems. It is a simple matter to provide the art, symbols, books, and translations of the writings of other religions, but to find people who can perform the music of other cultures is rarely possible. We cannot sing the group songs of other peoples because of the peculiarities of their harmonies and idiom. The performance of music presents the same kind of difficulties across cultural lines as does the speaking of language.

But when it comes to listening to and appreciating the music of other peoples, the problem is quite different from listening to their speech. With a little study and application, we can substantially appreciate a musical tradition other than our own. For this reason recorded music offers an apt facility for appreciation and communication in a religion for one world.

The use of recorded music in services of worship or celebration has become increasingly common in recent years. At the time the Meeting House installed its sound system it was comparatively rare, and no other society made as extensive and varied use of it as we did in our project. Many churches still shrink from using "canned music" in a worship service, and we make no pretense that it can compare with live music.

Church music is a continuous problem that haunts any minister and congregation of aesthetic discrimination. Good music requires one of two conditions. There must be accomplished musicians within the society who will volunteer their services and create excellent musical expression by the members of the society itself. This is the ideal condition, but one which is seldom attained. The only places where it pertains seem to be in monasteries, where the monks can devote their lives to religious music and the worship arts.

The other alternative is for the society to have sufficient wealth to hire professional musicians. A few churches and synagogues are able to provide a music budget several times as large as the total budget of more modest parishes. But this solution seems unsatisfactory, because religious expression should be the outward manifestation of religious convictions held with fervor. The Psalmist wrote, "I will make a joyful noise unto the Lord." He did not say, "I will hire an unbeliever to make an imitation of a joyful noise unto the Lord in my place." Religious song should be self-expression. For the professional musician it is a performance, a professional simulation of religious piety. Although such a performance might have artistic integrity, it is difficult to see how it can have a religious integrity, when the singers and players may hold religious convictions far removed from those expressed in the music.

There are Jewish synagogues in which the choir is made up entirely of Catholics and Protestants. I knew one young Catholic, a tenor, who sang regularly in a Congregational church, a procedure strictly against the regulations of his religion. His priest chided him about it and asked why he didn't sing in a Catholic church. He replied that when a Catholic church would pay him as much each Sunday to sing as he could get from a Congregational church, he would be glad to do so.

Every religious society should develop its own musical potentiality to the utmost. But it takes a large city, combining public subscriptions and gifts from wealthy patrons, to maintain a symphony orchestra, an opera, or even a chamber music group of first rank. Is the religious society then to resign itself to mediocrity or worse in its music? That is no longer necessary if it can bring itself to accept recorded music as a *supplement*, not a replacement, of its own musical efforts.

Having experimented with the use of recorded music in summer conferences, I had wondered what could be done with such an implement under ideal circumstances. At the Meeting House we were faced with the building of a new congregation. We began with little money and few musicians. The organ was an inadequate and unreliable antique. The organist, a paid musician, did not understand the experimental nature of what we were attempting to accomplish, and his selections kept dragging the services back into the ruts of habitual church custom. Since we were newly instituted, and without any prejudices of congregational tradition, I was able to convince the society that we should try recorded music.

Knowing the possible reactions against the venture, we determined to establish every possible factor upon our side. We displaced the budget items for organist and janitor and used this money for monthly payments on the equipment. With generous contributions from some of the members, we managed to acquire the best sound equipment available. Even so, in contrast to what many parishes are willing to pay for a pipe organ, the total expenditure was modest.

We invented a new kind of "pulpit" to house the equipment, consisting of a reading desk with a large speaker, amplifier, turntable, FM tuner, and tape recorder enclosed within it, all integrated into one system. It was so arranged that the one responsible for the service could operate it with a minimum of difficulty. With experience and planning, complicated musical additions could be incorporated into the service unobtrusively. Manual operation was at a minimum and was hidden from the congregation.

Following up our conviction of the unity of art and religion, as expressed in previous chapters, we use the sound system to bring the whole culture of music into our celebrations. A service is often built upon one long major work, a symphony, a string quartet, or a choral work. The first movement is used as a prelude before the service, and the Andante becomes an accompaniment for the meditation. This allows the meditation to be separated into passages, with periods of music interspersing the spoken sections, where the music is softened. A rehearsal of the relation of the music with the reading will enable the reader to allow the music to take over during periods of crescendo and climax and to underlie the reading in the pianissimo passages. When the reading is finished the music continues, and the remainder of the movement becomes a musical interlude in the service, suited to meditation. The congregation has time to meditate, such as is often provided by a period of silence, but without the sense of embarrassment sometimes felt when silence is extended for several minutes.

The use of recorded music as background to readings is merely an extension of the common practice of the use of organ music and choral responses in introits. Background music has become an essential and integral element of movies and radio and television productions. If it identifies with and supports the readings in mood and expression, the emotional and expressive power of the readings is heightened. Very similar is the practice in the Near East in Islamic and Orthodox and Jewish services of chanting the readings from the scriptures. In music a correlative means of expression, at a level deeper than that of verbal expression, is united with the meanings of the spoken word.

At times the entire service has consisted of a long reading "married" to a major musical work. On one occasion a symphony of Tschaikowsky was joined to a series of readings from Thomas Wolfe. Similar treatment was given to selections from Whitman. The result was something like a cantata, except that the words were read, rather than sung. In some contemporary compositions by Hindemith and others a reader is used in conjunction with a chorus and orchestra.

The major significance in the sound system for a religion for one world is that it enables us to cross cultural boundaries in the use and appreciation of the music of other peoples. An increasing library of ethnic music is available on recordings, from the Ethnic Folkways Library and Columbia Records, and UNESCO is now publishing a series. There are many other sources, and any LP catalogue will list what is currently available. In many cases this is a recording of actual religious music from Buddhist, Hindu, and other services. A considerable library of Jewish Cantorials has been recorded.

If the service deals with Hindu thought, for example, all of the recorded music used will be from India, and Hindu music will serve as a background for the reading of translations from Hinduism. We have discovered that this helps to give the English translation the flavor of the Hindu original. If we cannot actually read and understand Pali, Bengali, or Hindustani, we can surround the translation with the authentic music of India. To use Jewish Cantorials as background for readings from the Old Testament restores the implications of the readings to their real Jewish sources. It gives the Old Testament back to the Jews, rather than implying that it belongs to Christianity, which has adopted it. In some cases we have found archaic music for archaic readings, which then gives the literature the setting of its own times and provokes the imagination to comprehend it as an expression of our ancestors, rather than as a contemporary statement. A recording of Chinese Classical music can accompany readings from the Analects and the Tao Te Ching.

Often we will have readings from several different cultures in a single service. Then we can make a transcription from Is-

313

lamic, Jewish, Hindu, and Chinese music on tape as background for selected readings from the wisdom of these cultures. In this case the ordinary selected readings are converted into a semi-ritualistic and richer element of the celebration.

The richest use of recorded music is made in the festival services, which will be given more attention in a later section. Sometimes the basic theme of the festival is to move around the whole circle of the temple, going from center to center, bringing the poems, myths, art, symbols and music, and on occasion the dances, of the various cultures together in one world-wide appreciation. This we have done in our Mid-Winter and Spring Festivals. Then the recorded music of all these many cultures is the shifting musical background as we complete the circle of humanity.

Thus a major use of the sound system is to bring all the variety and richness of man's musical heritage into conjunction with the art, symbols, literature, and idealism of the world religions. When the peoples of the world sing and play in our celebrations, if only on recordings, the echoes and overtones of one world and one humanity invade our imagination and dispel some of our isolation and provincialism. When persons from these other parts of the world have been in the services, the use of their music has helped to add dimensions of universalism for them. On one occasion a piece of Chinese music was played which happened to be the favorite melody of the mother of a Chinese-American woman in the congregation. She was deeply affected. This incident recalls something that occurred in relation to the paintings. I happened to mention that whenever I looked across the room to a painting of Laotzu on his water buffalo I felt a warm sense of truly belonging to the thought and world of China. Upon which Edward Chin Park rejoined that he had the same feeling when looking at a reproduction of a painting by Fra Angelico of St. Francis giving his cloak to a beggar.

THE MURAL OF THE GREAT NEBULA OF ANDROMEDA

A religion for one world must have a symbol for the world itself, or, in its exclusive sense, a symbol for the universe. This could be either a symbol of the infinitely small or the infinitely great, and since these two poles were not mutually exclusive, but rather mutually essential, we included them both.

At one end of the Charles Street Meeting House auditorium there is an arch some twenty-five feet tall and fifteen feet wide. When we came to the building it was completely empty. What should we put in it? Surely this was the place for a major symbol. There was a committee at work on this sort of thing, and they made several suggestions, but none of them seemed to have the inevitability we were seeking.

After some deliberation we settled on a substitute, to fill the space until the answer came to us. We hung a dark-blue velvet drape in the arch, and over it a large golden circle, for the circle seemed to us then, as now, the inevitable symbol of one world. In the meantime we looked and waited for the symbol that belonged there.

The suggestion came from several sources. We had seen a number of large photographic murals in railway terminals and other places, and it occurred to us that if we could have such a mural made from the negative of an astronomical photograph, we would have a symbol of the universe in a depiction of the universe itself. But when we began to inquire we learned that large photographic murals were very costly, and so we sought another solution to the problem.

What cosmic scene would be the most symbolic of the universe itself? We investigated sources of astronomical photographs and learned that the California Institute of Technology and the University of Chicago Book Store, connected with Yerkes Observatory, were the best agencies. We wrote for their catalogues and finally decided that the Great Nebula in Andromeda was the scene we were looking for.

Our reasons for this choice were several. This nebula is the only extra-galactic object in the sky visible to the naked eye. It is the next-door neighbor of our own Milky Way nebula and, according to the astronomers, almost a twin of our own galactic system, even to the point that both have two large star clusters adjacent to them. The photographs of Andromeda, of necessity, include those stars in the Milky Way nebula that lie around it

315

as we look from the earth to our neighboring galaxy.

Our choice was wise, because since we made it the astronomers have been saying that our universe is galactic centered — that is, it is characterized by the existence of these giant star colonies, hundreds of millions of them, with vast tracts of nearly empty space lying between them. Thus we chose an astronomical object that best typified the nature of the universe itself, and our place in the universe.

We have called the arch that encloses the mural "a window into the universe," through which we look through a screen of stars in our own galactic system out across the heavens to our nearest neighboring star system. We have called it a "symbol of the fact," since it is simply the enlargement of a photograph, with no attempt whatever to interpret it for the viewer. We have said that the onlooker might say, "The heavens declare the glory of God," or "The heavens declare the glory," or simply, "My heavens!" The choice is up to him.

The manner in which the project was effected was quite simple. We sent for a series of photographic enlargements of the nebula and the surrounding area. Then we invented a way of painting and installing the mural that would avoid exorbitant expense and tying up the auditorium with a lot of unsightly and expensive scaffolding. Through the kind cooperation of a neighboring minister who had the owner of a paper mill in his congregation we received the gift of a carton of poster board panels. We then "squared off" the photographs in accordance with the dimension of the panels, set up large easels in the assembly room downstairs, and painted the mural in sections on the panels. When the mural was finished, it was attached with a strong adhesive to the wall of the arch.

We wondered if there were any way to create a simulation of the night sky, and to make the mural glow as if it were emitting its own light. Here my "misspent youth" as a sign painter came into play, and we adapted the "black-light" technique used in lighting road signs to the mural. We went over the white paint of the stars with fluorescent paint and acquired a black ultraviolet light. When the auditorium is dark, the nebula appears strikingly as it does in the sky when viewed through a telescope.

Our mural was finished in December, and we were interested to learn later that the following summer Andromeda and other celestial scenes were being painted with the same black-light technique in the planetarium in Chicago, and a year later in New York. Whether those responsible got the idea from us we do not know, but we had been in correspondence with people in Chicago about our project and had secured our astronomical photographs from there. In any case, the astronomers themselves now use the same method to demonstrate astronomical scenery in their planetariums that we initiated for religious symbolism at the Meeting House. For once a religious institution was ahead of the scientists in their own field.

The painting of the mural was a family workshop project, and many people participated in painting in the myriad stars. One person had a kind of proprietary interest in one portion of the heavens which was her handiwork. From a practical point of view (that is, can such projects be "afforded" by religious societies?), the total cost of photographs, materials, and equipment for the mural was under fifty dollars. Our own labor had made possible what we could never have afforded to buy.

As to the effectiveness of the use of such astronomical scenery as a symbol of a religion for one world, we can affirm after many years of living with it that it is entirely successful. This symbol of the fact does not wear out, in terms of interest and response, any more than flowers and children and life itself ever pale in inherent meaning and beauty. It is endlessly provocative.

For example, we are told that if we want to get a sense of our own situation in space, we had best look at the Andromeda nebula and imagine that our solar system is one of the infinitesimal points of light in one of the outer arms of the spiral. Then we might get the sense of our own location as if we were in the nebula looking out toward the Milky Way and the earth and its sun that were part of the vast island universe.

The astronomers are convinced that there are many millions of stars with satellites such as our earth on which life systems similar to our own may exist. If this is the case, then this nebula is not merely a lifeless chaos of suns and planets but the home of many colonies of living creatures. This conception gives the nebula a vast *living* significance and makes it a symbol not only

317

of the grandeur of the universe but of the vast fellowship of life, which one day we may explore if we go traveling about the universe, seeking out other living creatures on planets similar to our own. One day the concept of one world will be inadequate to insure the scope of brotherhood and peace, and men will begin to talk of one universe. Our mural is a symbol of an as yet far-off, but eventually necessary, religious idealism.

THE CONSTRUCTION OF THE ATOM

At the other side of the auditorium, opposite the mural of the Great Nebula in Andromeda, we wanted a symbol of the atom. The planet earth and the creature man exist midway between the opposite poles of the macrocosm and the microcosm. Man is as large in comparison to the electron as he is tiny in comparison to the universe. It has been conjectured that there are as many possible connections between the neurones of the human brain as there are atoms in the universe. The fields of biochemistry and biophysics are beginning to give us a realistic estimation of the proportionality of the human creature in relation to the cosmos. There is no longer any reason either to feel proud or to feel insignificant. If the congregation could sit with a symbol of the atom on one side of them and a symbol of the universe on the other, they would become their own symbols of man.

The relation of the Meeting House Project to the artists around it has been a problem. We have been very poor, and thus have been unable to go out and commission music and art to be produced for us. Furthermore, we have been dubious that we could find artists and others who would be sufficiently comprehending of what we were trying to do so that they could speak for us. Also, many artists are suspicious of and even antagonistic to institutionalized religion and simply do not make themselves available by joining and participating.

One young artist did join our group. He was identified with the constructivist school of sculpture, and he offered to attempt to create a symbolic representation of the atom. The piece now hanging in the auditorium is the second of two attempts. The first was used for several years, and when he said he wanted to

318

take another trial at it, we told him to go ahead. All of this was done at his own expense, and the products were donated to the Meeting House. We do not recommend this procedure, for the artist is worthy of his hire, but it is possible that there are people in the arts who are unable to make any substantial financial contribution to the support of a religious organization, but who would be happy to make a contribution in and through the arts themselves. It would certainly be a much more meaningful participation than the writing of a check and would bring back something of the social reality and participation in religious activities that existed in primitive and tribal societies. I doubt that the ceremonial sculptor or dancer in the Yoruba tribe of Nigeria ever sent a bill to the treasurer of the parish for his services.

Mr. Jack Burnham is now on the faculty of the College of Liberal Arts of Northwestern University. His own interpretation of his work follows:

At the instant of writing, I find it more than difficult to explain a work conceived and constructed five years ago. This because, while for me aesthetic goals do not change readily, the means for achieving them do. So, one is confronted with the situation of explaining a once ardently felt expression when complete conviction is no longer present.

My construction has for its theme the atom. Currently no subject reflects more scrupulously, by means of the models conceived, where men stand in relation to the universe they inhabit. During our century we have experienced a series of continually increasing refinements in atomic physics, to a point where technology and warfare have demonstrated their certitude — to a degree. This limit has been the position where mathematical reason and experimentation bog down at the dilemma of an atomic model of ever increasing complexity. Now, nearly each year, to satisfy computations, particles and anti-particles are anticipated and eventually detected. The new discoveries, in turn, demonstrate ever greater imperfections in recent particle theory. The result is that some scientists strongly suspect some fundamental errors in established atomic theory.

When the artist is given the task of representing the atom, he has good reason for not resorting to the standard convention of a spherical nucleus composed of neutrons and protons surrounded with a given number of smaller spheres orbiting in concentric electron shells. For this is a model which scientists frequently admit has no basis in physical fact.

The immediate aesthetic origin of my construction lies in the philosophy of the Russian-American artist, Naum Gabo. The essence of his credo is the opening up of mass so that space becomes as important as material in the expression of a three-dimensional work; the "construction" of a sculpture in modern materials with modern means of fabrication; and perhaps most important, not resorting to the traditional anthropomorphic images of art, but artistic equivalents of change in science and society or, in Gabo's words, "essences of a world that is being striven for. . . ."

What I attempt in this equivalent of the atom is an outward expression of energy, interdependence, complex symmetry, and severe order. The construction is not one but three, an exterior skeletal structure of sheet steel painted white, an intermediate structure of sheet plastic, and an internal form of blue neon tubing. Neon illuminated casts its own intense light and also acts as an internal source which defines the structure of the metal and plastic which house it. Transparency of the plexiglass allows the neon light to seem to hover within the space created by the steel framework.

What remains is not a religious symbol, for the result is devoid of moral content, but an object of thin, cold, aloof beauty — more feared than loved, more possessed than understood.

The only qualification that I would make to Mr. Burnham's statement relates to his implied judgment that a religious symbol must have moral content. There is also religious awe in contemplating the "thin, cold, aloof beauty" of the atom that his construction translates into plastic terms. It is for this reason that I prefer to talk about a "naturalistic" rather than a "humanistic" religious philosophy. Nature includes the whole cosmic scene, whereas man is but one creature within it. Nature mysticism includes all the profound emotional appreciations of human nature, but it also includes an intuitive response to and identity with all other forms and creatures in nature. Furthermore, Mr. Burnham's appreciation of "cold, thin, aloof beauty" is a human appreciation, and, from our point of view, a religious one.

A religion for one world must include not only the human scene, the many nations and cultures of the human family, but the cosmic scene as well, which brings the same awesome import to all branches of the human species, wherever they may live. We may seem to live far from one another on the surface of our planet, but we are very close together under the one sky, within the one universe, in which the paltry distances of the earth are shrunk until they exist not at all. The atom and the galaxy teach us a lesson about the insignificance of separations in time and space.

THE SHAPE OF THE ASSEMBLY

Dean Aylsworth was a pleasant and proper gentleman, serving as the Dean of Students in a small midwestern college. He had done his graduate studies at Yale Divinity School, and like most theological students, he had a week-end preaching station. Dr. Aylsworth was from the Midwest and unacquainted with the ways of New England. His pastorate was a small parish in a small town, and on his first Sunday morning there was only a handful of elderly people to hear him.

The pulpit was quite lofty, and he felt out of place perched high above the few attendants. When the opening service was over, he came down to the floor and stood before the pews to give his address on the same level with the people. This, he thought, was the gracious and modest thing to do. But as he was shaking her hand at the door at the end of the meeting, a stern-faced matron said to him, "Young man, we expect our minister to mount the pulpit." Henceforth, mount the pulpit he did.

The shape of the assembly plays an important if subtle part in the atmosphere and function of worship and celebration. Something is basically wrong with the structure of liberal religious services. Why should the minister be detached from the group and set off on a platform, with everyone facing him? He is not that important. The minister is supposed to be but another member of the group, with no special order of endowment or authority. Yet he assumes the same Sunday pose as the ministers of other churches, who believe they have been called by Almighty God to render to the people the Holy Word. He continues to mount the pulpit, however unhappily.

It is not only the position of the minister in relation to the people that is disturbing, but what this arrangement does to the people's relation to one another. A funereal hush descends over them once they are seated in the pews, an aura of holiness and sanctimony quite unjustified by a humanistic philosophy. Is this due to the fact that such an attitude seems consistent with the prevailing shape of the assembly? Shall we ever escape the attitude short of changing the shape, which has been designed to serve and elicit this attitude?

In one Unitarian church the people would gather before and after the service around the cheerful fireplace in the foyer. There was a free, informal spirit and interchange about the fire that was appropriate to liberal religion. Perhaps the service was of some use in order to provide an excuse for the gatherings around the fireplace.

The design and use of the temple area first became a matter of concern and speculation to me when the Madison (Wisconsin) Unitarian Society was planning to build a new church. We believed it was no longer efficient to set aside the major meeting area for just one purpose, the holding of a Sunday morning service. We began to think of the auditorium as a parish living room, with an adjacent kitchen, and a foyer with a fireplace, which served as a church parlor but could also be opened into the auditorium. The seats would be movable. This one area could then be used for worship, lectures, concerts, films, dinners, dances, social events — for whatever large-group purposes were desired.

Under the planning of the architect, Frank Lloyd Wright, this idea was realized. The building's usefulness since its erection has justified this departure in the shape and function of the room of assembly. Even so, the change was not radical enough.

The room is triangular, with the pulpit in a corner of the triangle. Thus the minister is somewhat set aside and up front. Since the seats face three ways, with seats in the center facing the pulpit, and seats on two sides of the triangle facing across the triangle, the people on the sides can look at the people in the center and across the room as well as at the minister. There is more intimacy, more of a sense of the group, than in the conventional arrangement.

Where did we get our shape of assembly? Why is it the shape that it is? How old is it? Excavations in Sumeria dating to 3000 B.C. indicate that the design of temples then was very similar to that of modern churches. There was an altar at one end, and the people faced it. The newspapers published the floor plan of a Mithraic temple that was excavated in the city of London during the rehabilitation following the Second World War. It had been built at the beginning of the Christian era. It was identical to the floor plan of the Charles Street Meeting House, three banks of pews facing toward the altar, where dwelt the miracle.

This plan was right for the use intended. People went to the temple of Mithra to see the holy rites performed. These were sacred and supernatural ceremonies, designed to bring the saving powers of the god Mithra to the people. The function was the same as that now performed by the holy Eucharist of Catholic and Protestant Christian churches. The people were primarily observers; the priests performed the rites and the people received them. All was directed toward the altar.

Since the Catholic Church adapted the salvation rites of the Mediterranean cults to Christian uses, it was functional for them to adopt the shape of the pagan assemblies also. The Protestant Reformation did not reform so profoundly as to alter this basic orientation of attitude and presence in the assemblies of the church; the Eucharist was still performed. The preacher and the holy book now needed to be front center.

When the liberal movement forsook most of the pretenses of divine election and special vision for their clergy, they maintained the folkways of orthodoxy. Although the people denied that when the preacher spoke he spoke the Word of God, they still placed him on the holy spot, and then dared him to be sufficiently convincing to make them accept his preachments. The liberal minister is put in the pulpit of authority even while the authority is denied to him.

On two occasions the experience I received in relation to a building was that which I would like to attain in a house of religion. One of the buildings was a planetarium, the other an observatory. In both instances the building seemed to symbolize with its dome the shape of the universe. In the planetarium this symbolism was heightened by the projection of the heavens upon the dome, and the panorama of the journey of the stars and planets through the changes of the year. In the observatory the great cleft with the telescope thrust into space projected one's imagination outward. Knowing that this powerful eye could gather the vision of outer space onto a piece of film held the observer in the presence of the whole universe while he was within its housing dome. Both times I felt, "This is what a temple should do to the people gathered in it. The building should itself be a symbol of the universe within which the earth and its creatures are rolling."

When religion moves from supernaturalism to naturalism, it must find a new symbolic shape for its temples, and a new symbolic shape for the assemblies of the people.

An observation that consolidated this conviction arose from the trends toward group participation in forums, seminars, and round-table discussions. When discussions are attempted in groups where the people sit all facing in one direction, as they necessarily do in most churches, it is sometimes impossible to get the talking started. It is difficult even to elicit a question from the audience. The setting is uncongenial. When the discussion does get going, the person who stands in the congregation to address his question or remarks to the platform is unheard by most of the people, for he is either talking away from those behind him or talking to the backs of the heads of those in front of him. Often the chairman of the meeting must repeat each question asked, so that the rest of the assembly will know what is being considered. It is almost impossible for extended remarks to be made by a member of the audience unless he comes to the front and faces the assembly.

For this reason the round-table form of gathering has become popular in seminars and discussion groups. Everyone is then facing everyone else and effective communication can take place. Group therapy was being attempted in a mental hospital, and the leader sat in front of the group in the arrangement often found in a classroom. He could elicit no effective interchange. But when he arranged the group in a circle and himself became but another member of the circle, the therapeutic conversation proceeded with enthusiasm. The freedom and democracy of seminar sessions (as against the deadliness of the lecture system in colleges) are due partly to the fact that the professor sits with the students in an informal group, rather than being set on a dais at the front of the room. The teacher can no more keep his role of sanctimonious authority than can the preacher when he descends from his lofty pulpit and becomes one of the folks.

A further suggestion comes from experiments with theater in the round. The old-style stage with the proscenium arch was set apart from the audience, the open wall of a strange room, wherein mysteries and illusions might be performed. But when the audience is seated on all sides of the stage, a sense of realism and intimacy replaces the separation of the conventional theater. It is as if one were watching events that might be taking place within one's own house.

If religious liberalism and a religion for one world are to be democratic, they must find the shape of assembly that expresses and expedites the processes of democratic sharing and equality. This can be found in what one might call "religion in the round." We can emphasize buildings in which the circle and the dome predominate, as is already common in Islamic and Romanesque architecture. Some Orthodox Jewish congregations have the altar and Torah in the middle of the room, probably owing to the democratic nature of worship in Orthodox Judaism and its often informal procedures.

In the liberal societies the circular assembly would express the symbolism of the democratic fellowship. The people are assembled to share the presence, ideas, and inspiration to be found in one another, rather than a supernatural sacrament or a divine revelation. The shape of the assembly should direct the people toward one another. In the old-style church they

325

can see only the minister and possibly the members of the choir, unless they turn to rudely stare about. Otherwise they see only the backs of others' heads.

At the Meeting House we could not build a new building. Scrapping the old pews and purchasing seats that might be set in a circular arrangement was beyond our means. We solved the problem by rearranging the pews for "religion in the round." Many different plans were drafted, until finally we had one that most perfectly adapted to the arrangements of the room and the possibilities of reconstruction in the pews. The labor of rebuilding and refinishing was our own, so that very little cost was involved. All that was needed, as is true in so many of these projects, was a willingness to experiment. The experiment lies in trying out upon ourselves in our own assemblies whether this new arrangement of our gatherings is more creative and permissive in terms of our aims, more indigenous to our kind of group process, than a shape of assembly that has endured for at least five thousand years.

Another consideration moved us to change to a circular arrangement. This will be described in full detail in a following section, but it needs to be considered briefly here. The circle is becoming for us the symbol of universalism, of a religion for one world. We felt the arrangement of the building, and, when possible, the shape of the building itself, should be the expression of the circle as a symbol. Thus the symbol is no longer an exterior construction of brass or wood to be viewed. The people themselves assume the symbolic shape in their gatherings; they are a circle of people. As the circle represents unity, the people assembled become a living symbol of one humanity, of world brotherhood, of one world.

The circular assembly was also necessary in order to make effective use of the collection of symbols and the collection of the art of the world's religions. The arrangement of the pews left a considerable area free in the center, to be used for dramatic, dance, and ritual performances. The arrangement also dispenses with aisles, leaving instead four large floor areas between the banks of pews, which can also be used for dance, theater, and whatever movement is desired. Thus the room no longer has any decisive focus of attention, so that one end would always be front, another rear, and the other two directions the sides. We can now "swing the circle" if we wish, and have the orientation of the service in any direction we choose. In our festival services the activity takes place in the full circle, and the center becomes the only point of orientation.

The air-age map of the earth has been laid in colored linoleum in the center of the floor, with a circle encompassing it. Thus the symbol of one world becomes the focus of the temple for a religion for one world. The land area is orange and the ocean area blue, with all national and man-made boundaries eliminated — one land, one sea, one world. This map provides us with a symbol in the center, and yet one which does not intrude itself between the people. It leaves the air space free and open. Some Catholic and Episcopalian churches have been built in the round, with the altar in the very center, but this puts the "miracle" in the center, and serves quite a different symbolic function from our use of the circular shape of assembly. The congregation relates to the altar and the priests and the mass, rather than to the people on the other side of the circle. The altar unifies them in one sense and acts as a barrier in another.

The map of the world is the hub and the key of the entire symbolic arrangement of the room. Around the outer walls of the room, between the windows, in the corners, and beside the doors, are the centers of the world religions. Each center features a temple lamp, a painting or wall hanging, and a mantel with statuary and ritual objects of one of the world religions. The symbol of this religion hangs on the facing of the balcony in front of the center. All of these religious centers radiate out from and are integrated with the map in the middle of the floor. Thus starting with the point at the North Pole, a line drawn out across the map will cross the country which is the home of the religion, pointing to the symbol and the center of that religion. The whole temple area is spatially a symbol of a religion for one world. It would be more effective if the room were itself circular, with a dome above. It is square, however, so we have drawn a circle within the square.

The arrangement of the room has a symbolic relationship to the world in another aspect: it has an axis, even as does the earth. The axis has several dimensions, running between and into the arches that originally designated the front and back of the room.

There is an axis made up of naturalistic symbols, with the mural of the Great Nebula in Andromeda at one end, the construction of the atom at the other end, and the polar projection map of the earth in the center. This axis runs thus from microcosm to macrocosm. The planet earth and man are dimensionally midway between the atom and the universe, and are so placed within the symbolic structure of the temple area. On either side of the mural of the galaxy is a panel of symbols, one relating to the activities and ideals of humanity, the other to the activities of nature.

There is also a musical axis, composed of the sound system and grand piano on one end and the pipe organ at the other, which is complemented by the choir when it is assembled in the pews in front of the piano. There is a third axis, that of the bible of humanity, with the bookcase containing the translations of the world bible at one end and the bookcase containing the original scrolls and books at the other. This is also complemented by the readers and speakers who ordinarily speak at the edge of the center circle on this axis line, although they can also stand on the other sides.

Several things ensue from the new shape of assembly. Whereas before there was a problem as to where to place the choir, the answer becomes ready and simple. The choir members sit in one of the four banks of pews, which all face toward the center. They are thus seated in the congregation and on the same level with everyone else. They are not put conspicuously up in front, nor seated out of view in the rear, singing to the backs of the congregation's ears and tempting the people to turn around to see the choir.

The minister is also seated with the congregation. He is thus symbolically but another member of the congregation and may therefore feel much more comfortable and honest. He speaks from within the circle rather than from the isolation of the platform. He is much closer to those to whom he is speaking, since they are sitting all around him. All distances are halved.

As for responsive readings, the minister need not assume

that his single voice is enough to counterbalance the whole assembly. Half of the congregation can read in response to the other half. It is a future plan to have reading desks at the four sides of the circle. Then there can be several readers in the service rather than one. This arrangement becomes practical, since the readers do not have to sit on the platform away from the rest of the congregation. They can merely rise from their pews, take a step or two to a reading desk, and be seated in the pews when the reading is finished. Readings with Eastern sources can be given from the reading desk on that side of the room, and readings from Western sources from the opposite side.

It is also planned to develop a "speaking choir" to balance the singing choir. Conversations between two or more people can take the place of sermons. With the circular arrangement, it is possible to let open discussion occur at any time in the service, or after the formal service, as it is desired. The arrangement is designed for this.

The room has already been used for theater in the round, and this proved to be very effective. Balconies overhang the center circle on both sides, and the free areas between the banks of pews allow the dramatic action to leave the center and move to any part of the room. The same facility and effectiveness have been proved with dance, which we have used in festival services.

It is in festival services, where action takes place at the various centers on the periphery, in the free areas, and in the center, that the arrangement in the round is most justified. For it enables the people present to virtually sit inside the performance and ritual of the service, which takes place behind, in front of, and to the sides of those present, wherever they sit in the room. This is quite the opposite of what happens in some large Catholic cathedrals, where the Mass is performed behind a screen in the apse, far removed and even out of sight of the worshipers in the nave. Some of the early churches, even into Renaissance times, were circular, and those celebrating the Mass were a part of the ceremony, like a family gathered about the table for a meal in a home. Some of this intimacy is returning in a few contemporary Catholic churches, as we have noted above.

On the occasion of naming services and weddings, the circular arrangement permits those assembled to surround the event. Thus the relation of the marriage and naming ceremonies to the human community is made manifest in the form of the gathering. The result is much happier than when the ritual takes place almost in isolation from those attending, at the front of a long auditorium.

Some consider such matters of form and design to be unimportant, but not if they are acquainted with the arts. The edict that style is everything prevails. Nothing can replace the necessity of composition, design, balance, and structure. If the basic design is bad, all the perfection of detail imaginable cannot save the total result from being bad art. Conversely, good basic design will compensate for a good deal of poor work in the details. Composition and form are the primary considerations and necessities.

Subtle influences of shape and design are pervasive in art, and in religion also. Until a religion for one world discovers its indigenous forms it will be handicapped. There is an undeniable awkwardness and inconsistency when liberal religion attempts to use manners and arrangements which are native to different religious and world views. The old forms persist for several reasons, and they are all bad.

The first is inertia, the inability to slough off the old, a conservative aversion to change. This has moved us to accept ludicrous inconsistencies and to persist in them for generations, weakening the entire structure and impact of liberal religion because of the injustice and inadequacy of its forms and ceremonials.

The second is insensibility, for often the deadness and falsity of form in relation to precept and concept, and the misshaping of content when forced into forms not its own, are unacknowledged by the participants. They wonder what is wrong with their operations, why they do not attract, and why they feel a vague unease, but they are unable to analyze their situation.

The third reason why the old forms hang on lies in a retreat from liberalism, a backsliding into the beliefs and practices of conservatism and orthodoxy, which, in fact, justifies the forms that should have been discarded, rendering them increasingly congenial and "right." This is partly due to the persistence of the forms. If we retain the trappings of orthodoxy they will work to cause us to revert to that orthodoxy to which they belong. Forms have their own logic, present their own symbolic arguments. They are powerful enough to bring the content of the service back into phase with the forms of the temple and its worship. If form does not follow function, function may be coerced to return to comply with form.

But if we find our own inherent and expressive shapes of assembly and celebration, then our expression and appeal will develop, even as the artist's picture flourishes when his composition and design are complete and justified. Then every detail belongs to the whole, contributing integrally to the accumulating and ordered beauty of the work.

Our celebrations of life should be the most significant events in the lives of the members of the religious community. These are the communal expressions of the relation of the people to one another and to the universe. They probe and project their highest ideals and aspirations. They seek and declare the pervasive and yet elusive meanings of existence. If our dreams of life are to be majestic, our celebrations must have majesty of proportion and be the symbols of our quests and our convictions of right and beauty.

THE SYMBOL PROJECT

A basic consideration in the Meeting House Project has been to find the inherent and adequate symbols for a religion for one world. This matter has already been introduced in the chapter on "Symbolism and Religion," presenting a philosophy of symbolism. Some repetition will be necessary in order to give a full survey of the project.

The problem in a religion for one world is to find a symbol, or a collection of symbols, that will possess an evocative power sufficient to suggest the inherent unity in nature and life and culture and at the same time do justice to the diversity of forms, creatures, and religions within that unity. One solution would have been emptiness, or a single powerful symbol such as the monolith in the meditation room at the United Nations, which is truly universal. The other solution, and the one we chose as the theme for our symbol project, was to find an over-all symbol which could enclose and unify all the symbols relating to the various human ideals and religions, and the diversity of nature itself.

These two approaches are not as different as they might seem to be. The monolith is a single symbol in which all the diversities are subsumed, since it presents a theme found everywhere in the world. Emptiness, the void, is a symbolic representation of the space that encloses all the forms of the universe. One reason why we chose the second theme for our project was that it presented more difficulties. The void and the monolith are quite simple to construct. Operationally, one's intuition will affirm their effectiveness even before they are tried. History too reveals their impact. They have one deficiency: The diversity is implied, not presented. Those capable of reading the implication will understand, but those not initiated will miss this meaning.

First we needed to find the master symbol, the symbol of unity, of oneness, of inclusion, of infinity. It was already at hand. Dr. Clarence Skinner and others among the Universalists had wisely chosen the circle as the symbol of Universalism. Dr. Skinner had experimented with ways in which some of the symbols of the world religions could be diagrammed within a circle. One group of Universalists had placed a Christian cross in the circle and to one side. This had come to be called the "off-center cross." The rationalization was that here was the universal symbol, and that the cross acknowledged the Christian derivation of Universalism, whereas putting it to one side made it no longer central. The other area of the circle invited the consideration of other religions than Christianity and their symbols.

Neither of these solutions appealed to us. To include several symbols within the circle created design problems, too much complexity, and confusion. The symbol was being forced to say too much. A great symbol has an essential singleness and unity. The off-center cross was unbalanced in its asymmetry. Even though the position of the cross indicated a willingness to have other symbols enter the circle, its inclusion also indicated a necessity to cling to Christian origins with a force implying something less than a full universality of sympathy and spirit. It still put Christianity front, if off-center. Its generosity was conditioned. It was an obvious attempt, symbolically, to have the cake of universality and to eat the cross of Christianity too.

We solved the problem by emptying the circle. The circle is used in several ways in the project. Ideally, it would have been the basic architectural form of the building, as in the planetarium. But since we were in a square building we created a circle within the square, and arranged the pews in circular order. The polar projection map in the center is circular and has a gold circle around it. A brass circle, larger than any of the other symbols, was installed in the middle of the sound-system and reading desk. There is another smaller circle among the others. Thus the circle is at once a master symbol over all the other symbols and also but one of them, a symbol of universalism as such. The Chinese Pi disc, the symbol of the heavens, is set upon the bookcase under the nebula. The large wooden circle that once was in the arch now containing the mural of the nebula has been moved downstairs. It surrounds a polar projection map of the world, on which the many symbols are shown at their point of origin. The large brass circle on the sound system is so arranged that one of the smaller symbols can be placed inside it. Thus on occasion we choose a symbol relating to the theme of the service and place it in the circle, presenting a symbolic motif.

Other master symbols are elsewhere described and need to be but listed here. There are the three nature symbols, the Great Nebula in Andromeda, the polar projection map of the earth, and the construction of the atom. The two bookcases and the books they contain are symbols of man and his religious idealism, expressed in his holy books. The sound system, the piano, and the pipe organ are practical musical instruments and also symbolize man's artistic expression. The three jade pieces on the bookcase, the cosmic disc, the Pi disc, and the t'sun, the earth symbol, provide three other master symbols of nature. A Chinese jade tree is used as a representation of the tree of life. On the center of the bookcase is the lamp, a symbol of the altar, of the hearth, of knowledge. In the very center of the room hangs a votive lamp, which echoes the meaning of the lamp on the bookcase. An astral globe, a symbol of the universe, which once was on the bookcase, has been displaced by the jades and is now used downstairs.

We have sought to find the most effective symbols of one world that were available in the world religions and to arrange them so that they would echo and re-echo one another, much as several related motifs are developed in a symphony. Whether or not such an assembly is successful will depend on whether they do reflect one another, and whether the whole arrangement is artistic, economical, and cumulative in power. Mere redundancy would weaken the total impact. Thus what is left out is just as important as what is put in, and there are no criteria other than taste and intuition for guides.

These master symbols provide the themes and the setting for the symbol project as such. Our concern was to find the most significant and evocative symbols of the world religions and of the basic human occupations and ideals. The project had four related phases, research and selection, design, fabrication, and arrangement. We proceeded without haste, since there was a great deal of ground to cover, and we had to educate ourselves in the field as we went along. The project lasted five years, a period that allowed us time to live with the symbols as we accumulated them. We had to depend on our own intuitions as to the valence of each symbol separately, how it related to the other symbols in the collection, and what size of collection would give full coverage of man's enterprises and his various religions. A multitude of symbols were available, and too many would cause confusion. On the other hand, too few would leave out essential cultural movements and preoccupations. The experiment was to find enough, but not too much.

The final collection ran to some sixty-five symbols and was completed about nine years ago. Since then a few symbols have come to our attention that might have been included, but we already have symbols as good or better in the same areas. As far as our judgment and intuition are any test, the selection has worn well and has increasingly justified itself.

The use and arrangement of the symbols has also evolved. In the beginning, before the pews were rearranged into the round, the symbols were placed one at a time within the large circle on the sound system. One symbol would be used as the theme of the service. If there were readings from several religions, the symbol of the appropriate religion would be put in the circle during the reading from its scripture. Thus several symbols were often used in a service, and the placement of the symbols became a simple ritual act.

As the collection grew, it seemed wasteful to use only a few symbols in a service. Many of the symbols were hardly ever on view. We rethought the use of the symbols and decided they should be on permanent display. Also, when the service was conducted from the circle rather than from the platform where the sound system was located, it was not possible to change the symbols easily with the readings. However, we may in the future combine these two approaches.

Our solution had to be adjusted to the building we occupied. If we had been constructing our own temple, we probably would have had the symbols carved as a frieze around the outer wall, above the centers of the religions. Thus they would have been an inherent part of the building. As it was, we adapted the facings of the balconies on the two sides of the room as panels and hung the symbols in front of the centers which they represented. Since the symbols are now a permanent installation, it is no longer necessary to put up the Yang and Yin when there is a Chinese reading; it is already there. Over the years the presence of the symbols has become an essential part of our religious setting. They have demonstrated that they belong together and that they have an inherent unity. A newcomer might find them a puzzling confusion at first, but they come to belong to the temple and its attendants over time.

The symbols that relate to the themes of nature's activity and man's occupations and ideals have been mounted on two panels and installed on either side of the nebula. The panel to the left contains the symbols of man, and the panel on the right those of nature. Most of the symbols are permanently displayed, but not all. On occasions such as the Midwinter Festival, when a group of the symbols are used ritually in the service, the other symbols replace those that have been removed from their ordinary setting. The other symbols are also used to indicate themes in the services. Thus, if anything, the sixty-five symbols are more than we need in our particular setting, but there are none that we would have omitted from the over-all selection.

The manner in which the project was effected may be of interest. The project was never a budget item in the operation of the Meeting House and cost the parish nothing. It was a voluntary contribution of three persons, myself, Ralph Edlund, and his sister Charlotte Edlund. The research on the symbols and their selection was mainly my task, since I was the person with a background in comparative religion, and the one with the time and concern to develop a library and do research in symbolism. Since I had been an artist before entering the ministry, the designing of the symbols fell to me. Miss Charlotte Edlund had experience in jewelry-making and metalwork, and she began working on the symbols. However, her brother Ralph became interested in them and took the job over. He had never done any work of this kind, and had no art training, but he taught himself and developed his skills as he went along. Charlotte continued to participate by buying the metals and materials needed, which were mainly sheet brass, copper, and silver. Her knowledge of metalwork she imparted to her brother. The symbols were donated to the Meeting House as they were finished. If we had hired professional researchers and designers and metal workers to do the task, it would have cost us thousands of dollars. In one year alone Ralph contributed five hundred man-hours to the project. This is quite typical of how many of the aspects of the Meeting House Project have been accomplished.

With the exception of the one large circle, the symbols are all of approximately the same size, indicating that all the religions of man are to be held in equal esteem. It might be objected that some religions are greater than others and should be given a position of superiority. But religions, like works of art, are qualitatively unique and incomparable. Each religion has its own distinctions and qualities. The more I study them, the more profoundly I appreciate them, the more I am convinced that the equality implied in the equivalence of size and position in the symbol project is justified. Just as people must be accorded an inalienable equality, so all of man's religions merit the same regard, respect, and appreciation. One need not take as much unto himself from any one as he does from another, but he is advised to bring to them all an equal willingness to understand and to appreciate, and, if he will, to adopt their insights.

THE ART COLLECTION

During the years in which the symbol project was maturing, we kept talking about one day making a collection of the art of the world religions that would supplement and reinforce the symbols. In a sense the research for the symbols laid the groundwork for the art collection. Since the symbols are themselves works of art from the various religions, they initiated the group into the extent and range which the art collection developed. What prejudices we had against a religion for one world were expended and digested during the symbol project, to free us for the labor and sacrifice involved in collecting art.

The theory behind the art collection is that the aura, precepts, and devotion of humanity are embodied and expressed in and through religious art. If we brought the art of all the world religions together, from all ages and all areas, it would create an authentic setting for a religion for one world. We would not have all the peoples of the world gathered together for common religious celebration, but we would have their emissaries in the art which these people had themselves created to make their religious convictions manifest.

Even as in the symbol collection, we had little idea where the project would take us when we began. Our assumptions were modest in the extreme. We had almost no money, and we had no idea what were the available resources of such art, or what it would cost. We anticipated that we might have to rely mainly on reproductions, for we had the amateur's misconception that "authentic" art pieces were fabulously expensive. Making a list of dealers from the "yellow pages," we began our quest.

What followed might be called a glorified scavenger hunt. It soon became evident that if one searched continuously, dug around in every odd corner and shop, attended the auctions, and played every chance and break that occurred, many originals of good quality from many parts of the world could be had at modest cost. The assumption that we would have to settle for reproductions was quickly discarded. Originals could be had. The reproductions in our collection now are very few, copies of such rare pieces that you will find the same kind of reproduction in the largest museums.

The pattern was the same as in the other projects. We taught ourselves the art and lore of collecting by doing it. It was soon obvious that an immense amount of study in art and culture would be necessary, and the educational process is still continuing. I know that personally I thought that I had a fair knowledge of world culture and religion, but I discovered that I had hardly touched the field. Approaching the cultures through their arts yields wholly unsuspected insights and panoramas. Where I had assumed there was "one" culture, I discovered a motley complex of many cultures and a rich diversity of art styles. This was especially the case with Mexico, and with Central and South America. My education was beginning all over again.

The purpose of the art collection was to find works of art from all of the world religions that most fully typified them in their viewpoint and religious spirit. These pieces would then be placed in the temple in order to bring the presence of these religions into our gatherings. We were assembling a group of "witnesses" from the religions of man.

As in the symbol collection, the problem in arrangement was to fit them into a room not designed for them. Again, if we had been privileged to build our own temple, it would have been designed with fitting niches, wall areas, mantels, etc., for the symbolic placement of these art works. What we did was to put mantels over the radiators between the windows, constructed also to act as heat deflectors, whereon we could place statuary and ritual objects. These, as we have related, were oriented to the polar projection map in the center. When the project was finished the persons assembled were ringed by centers of the world religions. We made various arrangements to find out just how many pieces could be used to best advantage. The average display has a painting or wall hanging, a temple lamp hanging before it, and three pieces of sculpture on the mantel.

The two sides of the room divided inevitably into the religions of the East facing the religions of the West. If the room had been circular rather than square, we could have somewhat avoided this division, but we do not believe the basic unity of our symbolism of a religion for one world has been prejudiced by it. The centers run as follows: Oceania, Japan, China, Tibet, India, Buddhism, Oriental Universalism, Egypt, Africa, Islam, Judaism, Christianity, Central America, Eskimo. In the balconies are centers of other religions, those of Polynesia, Java, Chinese Naturalism, Hinduism, Plains Indians, Roman Catholicism, Greece and Rome, and the Near East. In the four corners of the balcony are large wall hangings from the four major contemporary world religions, Buddhism, Hinduism, Islam, and Christianity. The symbolism is carried into the foyer at the entryway downstairs, with a Moslem prayer rug on one side and a portrait of a Chinese scholar on the other.

There is no orderly way to make such a collection, at least beginning without financial resources or connections as we did. We simply started to collect what we could find. Many of our early acquisitions have since been sold, traded, or given to theological schools. We purchased many reproductions of paintings, none now in use in the auditorium. The collection has been continually graded upward in the quality of the pieces and the adequacy with which they symbolize the religious aspirations of humanity.

As the collection grew, it overflowed into the rooms downstairs. This was our intention from the first, to have such art works in the Sunday School rooms and assembly rooms. But we found ourselves with substantial collections in several areas. The art of Buddhism can be taken as an example. In the centers in the auditorium there is Buddhist art from Japan, China, Tibet, and Siam, but the Buddhist collection grew beyond the capacity of the auditorium to utilize it in proportion to the space available and the other centers. Still these pieces had artistic, symbolic, and educational value. We solved the problem by making a display case in the assembly room for them. Here we have attempted to cover as widely as possible the variety within Buddhism. There are pieces from Java, Ceylon, Korea, Japan, China, Tibet, Cambodia, Siam, Burma, and Mongolia. Comparable display cases show the art of Mexico, Central and South America, China and Japan, North American Indians, Egypt, Africa, Greece and Rome, and India. Added to these are various paintings and prints on the walls.

We have met with considerable skepticism as to whether such a display of religious art can in any profound manner facilitate understanding, sympathy, and belonging among the branches of the family of man. The answer hinges upon the perceptiveness, responsiveness, and sensibility which a person brings to the appreciation of works of art. Those of us attuned to the arts can testify to receiving the deepest kinds of meanings from the art works of other peoples. They are a veritable pathway of communication whereby the longings and convictions of the people in one culture can be exchanged with those in another culture.

Some people think this interchange can come about only through living with other peoples, preferably in their own lands, and even so will take a long time to make effective. We would not deny the value of such personal association. But short of this we believe that truly magnificent exchanges of emotions, ideas, and attitudes can take place through the arts, which become a bridge over time and space. Indeed, when it comes to probing the cultures of the past, and the primitive cultures and tribal societies now disintegrating, the arts are the only means of communication left to us. The people and their societies have perished.

Those who are greatly involved in the arts need no convincing. Art is their language, the way they speak, and the way they receive messages. Interestingly, in many cases it has been the artists of the West who have led all others in discovering, collecting, and treasuring the art of other cultures, Oriental and primitive. The disconcerting thing about our experiment in collecting the art at the Meeting House is that, although those of us who can appreciate the arts may have accumulated an emotional and intellectual — a truly religious — reward in making the collection, studying it, living with it, and treasuring it, we are helpless to convince those without artistic sensibilities of

340

the potential value of this experience. They simply do not seem to have the eyes to see. The proof of the value of the project is in, but the proof is itself as incommunicable as is the experience itself. It is not something that can be put in a test tube in a laboratory or demonstrated by mathematical equations.

This project can be described from several angles. First let us take the viewpoint of those who collected the works. It has been an experience of measureless excitement, gratification, and sheer fun. Every piece added has been the result of a love affair, for each piece has possessed an innate appeal and beauty. If we had not answered its appeal but rejected it, it would have haunted us from then on. The excitement of watching the pieces fit together, watching the collection round out, has been an equal reward. We set a goal for ourselves far higher than that assumed by most museums of art, to find good and representative art works from every corner of the globe, and this we have accomplished. Often we have had to wait years for a piece to turn up; a few we are still waiting for. This lends an air of expectancy to the project.

A further gratification has derived from the fact that the making of such a collection was something in which we could become totally involved. We could believe in it, be dedicated to it, because of the spectrum of values represented. Religion for one world was itself being served and demonstrated by the collection. We felt that in a profound sense such a collection assembled in one room of religious devotion would "prove" the oneness of man's religious quest.

We were also closely identified with the ideals and values embraced by many of the objects collected. When we could not completely identify with what a particular fetish or ritual article designated, we had deep respect for it as an object of devotion and dedication of other members of the human family.

And there was the added value that each piece, as a work of art, had an inherent worth of beauty and style and integrity, apart from its religious or ethnic dimensions. I can testify that personally I have never participated in any project that contained as many and as profound realities and gratifications as did this labor.

One by-product was that it enabled us to share like enthu-

341

siasms with others. Some art dealers with whom we dealt — not all, I am sorry to say — had a true love of art and culture and identified with our project. Association with Dr. Samuel Eilenberg and Mr. and Mrs. J. Ray Shute, who made generous contributions from their collections to our project, was particularly happy. We met on the level of a shared devotion to an appreciation of other cultures and their arts.

The point being made is that the value of a collection of art lies not merely in what it adds to the aura and richness of the temple, but in the experience of the collecting itself. Religion is thus an act of building, of creating, and not just of appreciation. The act of acclamation and identification, repeated every time a new piece was discovered and added to the collection, was an act of worship or celebration. The collection project itself was a kind of free ritual in which we made manifest our belonging to a religion for one world.

The art project was financed almost entirely by free contributions outside the regular budget of the society. On a few occasions funds were appropriated from the general treasury, but in the main we depended on gifts from individual members, gifts of pieces and funds from interested persons outside the society and in other parts of the country, special discounts by dealers, donations through dealers of pieces left in their care to be used as gifts to worthy organizations, sales, and trades. By searching continuously and attending auctions, we added many fine pieces with modest expenditures.

A great deal of labor has been involved outside the collecting itself. There were mantels to build, display cases to construct, and the endless caretaking, research, labeling, and mending entailed in any large collection, plus the providing of insurance.

Since the purpose of the collection was not simply to add new dimensions to the celebrations of the Meeting House itself but to demonstrate a pilot project, continuous educational promotion has accompanied all of the experiments. This has been particularly extensive with the art project. One of the main avenues of sharing the ideas and experience of the art project has been the use of colored slides. Mr. Charles McCormick has taken as his special project the photographing of the art and symbol collection. Thousands of slides have been produced, and collections with scripts have been furnished to the visual aids department of the Department of Education of the Unitarian Universalist Association, for use in the liberal churches and fellowships of the denomination. Articles have been published, and thousands of leaflets and pamphlets printed and distributed by our own Meeting House Press. In addition, illustrated lectures using our own slide collection have been given at summer institutes and elsewhere in all parts of the continent. This present publication, for which most of the photography is also being done by Mr. McCormick, is but the climax of a continuing program of publicizing and making available the results and conclusions from our experiments.

A further service project growing out of the art collection has been the provision of traveling exhibits to liberal societies and to university groups across the country. The most popular items here have been three collections of the graphics of Kaethe Kollwitz, but other collections of prints and of sculpture have been made available too. On occasion reproductions from pieces in the collection have been used as illustrations for articles, covers, etc., by liberal publications.

A special project within the total art project has been the gathering of the prints of Kaethe Kollwitz. This German artist was the daughter and granddaughter of two of the leaders of the Free Congregation movement in Germany, a counterpart of liberal religion in America. Her works, dealing with the problems, tragedies, inhumanities, as well as the joys of the human scene, show her to be a truly universal artist. Although we have collected prints from several other artists, we decided to concentrate on Kollwitz, who peculiarly reflected our concern with mankind and with the alleviation of human ills. We have some eighty of her etchings, lithographs, and woodcuts, as well as reproductions of her drawings.

The significance of the Kollwitz collection is that the art of a religion for one world is not confined to the art of the great world religions. There are individual artists who attain universality with their works, who transcend the cultures of which they are products, and who belong to all peoples and all times. Such an artist is Kaethe Kollwitz. Others who come immediately to mind are Rembrandt, Van Gogh, Goya, Sesshu, and

Hokusai. There are many others. The art of a religion for one world will be drawn, not only from the world religions, but from the great artists whose works speak to the human condition.

THE LIBRARIES

Some of the projects have developed almost spontaneously, with little official initiation, planning, or sustenance. This is the case with the libraries of tape recordings, records, and books. An extensive library of tape recordings has been acquired, using the tape recorder in the sound system. These have been made from radio broadcasts and by transcribing records of ethnic music which we could not obtain in the original.

Because our tape recorder and player is not as high in fidelity as the performance we can get from records, we have used the tape library little in recent years. We do hope to be able to secure a finer unit, and to avail ourselves of the superior adaptability and facility of tapes over records.

Our collection of records has grown until we have music for almost any occasion that arises. It consists of two main categories, instrumental, symphonic, chamber, and choral music from the classical Western repertoire, and the folk, classical, and religious music of the world cultures. This library has been gathered by purchases of the society, but largely by the donations of one person, Mr. Roland Hueston, who has contributed generously from his own excellent record collection. Mr. Hueston has made the record collection one of his chief interests, sorting and cataloguing it, creating lists and reference files for its use, as well as giving records.

The record collection has been a utilitarian one. We have not attempted to make an exhaustive accumulation of all the records in our fields of interest, although this would have real value both to us and to other societies. The current record catalogues have handy references for ethnic and other records currently available, but there are many things out of publication and difficult to find. Enough is available, however, so that any society could develop a good working collection without difficulty. This is another area where the general cultural in-

344

terest and commercial activity, taking on a one-world orientation, are supplying impressive resources for the expression of a
religion for one world without any awareness that its materials
might be so used. We are rapidly developing a one-world culture whether a one-world religion emerges or not. UNESCO is
sponsoring many book publishing, recording, and art publication facilities that are eminently usable.

Our book library has simply grown like Topsy. There has
never been an official authorization for it, or support of it, on
a parish level. Mr. Hueston has taken this library under his
supervision also, has made many contributions to it, and has
catalogued it. It is available as a study library for the various
projects, and in many instances we have fine research facilities
within the project itself. Some of the art books have been purchased as part of the art collection and out of its special budget,
and books have been contributed by other members. There are
books on literature, liberal religion, world culture, anthropology, philosophy, science, symbolism, the world religions, and
a fine aggregation of books on world art.

The library serves as a resource for the adult discussion
group, providing correlative reading for almost any field that
the study group may consider. No research project in any of the
sciences could operate without library facilities. We have found
that the same thing applies to experiments in religion.

One example of the utility of such a library is demonstrated
by the problem of providing translations from the literature of
other cultures for the services. Most of the translations available do not have the rhythmical and poetic qualities demanded
in religious celebration. Often the original scriptures, such as
the Koran, are great literature in their own languages but exceedingly dry and tedious in English. The King James Version
of the Bible is a happy exception. We will not have suitable
translations of the other great religious writings until we create
them.

One project we have set out on is to take about ten translations of the Tao Te Ching and to see if we can adapt a para-
phrase from them in a style suitable for use in our celebrations.
We are still involved in this, and as yet have no idea how successful it may be. But if there is to be a religion for one world,

we shall have to dedicate ourselves to providing suitable translations of the many world bibles, in much the same spirit that Christendom has applied itself to the many translations of the Jewish and Christian scriptures. The library which we have accumulated has now grown to a point where it makes initial efforts to this end practical.

MEETING HOUSE PRESS

A project such as the one we are describing is likely to run into difficulties at any point where it is not self-sufficient. As soon as it must depend on outside support or on the collaboration of other agencies, its fortune is in escrow. Thus we have at every turn attempted to develop a cohesive and self-sustaining enterprise. This has meant operating as a workshop and utilizing many of the techniques of production that are more characteristic of frontier communities than of specialized industrial communities. When you have no money to hire outside experts to do your work you have to become an expert yourself. The Meeting House is a do-it-yourself project on a grand scale.

We soon learned that we could not depend on outside agencies to publicize our activities and to publish our findings. They were too off-beat for a conservative Boston press to give any appreciable coverage. The denominational publishing agencies had other concerns, and in some instances, because we were controversial and they were not sympathetic to our approach, we met real opposition. Another factor was that many of the kinds of publication that our project demanded were not commercially feasible. They would have to be done for their own worth, not for any profit. And some were "works in progress" and not well enough along for a final publication. A constellation of considerations made the development of our own press a necessity. We needed internal publication for our own open hymnal, and we needed a readily available facility to provide our results to others who were interested. The Meeting House Press was the answer. Freedom of the press, we found, in final terms means simply the freedom to own and operate our own press. We are not practically or wholly free if we must depend on the whim and the editorial policies of presses owned and operated by other agencies, even those of our own movement.

None of us knew anything about printing or publishing. We began with utter simplicity, with a mimeograph machine, a small hand-operated press, and a few fonts of type. Our original venture was a series of mimeographed pamphlets with printed covers, and a few leaflets. The pamphlets were in two series, "The Exploration of Life" being a sermon series on various themes of liberal religion, and "The Celebration of Life" a series dealing with the Meeting House Project. One of the pamphlets, "A New Bottle," was the first description of the project, of which the present book is the eventuation. We kept reissuing it until the stencils fell apart. Other pamphlets were on "Responsive Readings," "Hymns of Humanity," "Worship Elements," and "Worship Experiments." Much of the material in these publications was mimeographed from the same stencils that supplied the pages of the open hymnal used in our own services.

The pamphlets received considerable distribution within the liberal movement and have been out of print for a long time. They served to initiate our publishing project, but we needed more ambitious instruments. We had accumulated larger hand presses, a foot-pedal press, and much more type and other facilities, as well as gradually developing our printing skills to a more professional level. The next step would have to be a major advance. It came when the members of the board raised sufficient money from their own pockets to make the down payment on a power-driven letter press, a paper cutter, and other machinery sufficient to provide us with a good job press of our own. We then launched into the publishing of books, leaflets, pamphlets, and an abortive effort at magazine publication.

Meeting House Press, as we named it, not only has served to publish our own offerings but for many years did job printing for various denominational agencies and earned a considerable amount of the income that has kept the Meeting House solvent. There were many years when we would not have survived without the earnings of the press. The sale of the press publications has also provided an essential source of income. The press has attracted the interest and support of persons outside of Boston, especially the continuous and generous support of Mr. Corliss Lamont of New York City. The Universalist Historical Society entered into a cooperative arrangement with the press for the publication of three books, and we manufactured a fourth book for them. Now with the generous subsidy of the Massachusetts Universalist Association, this present book is being published.

Underneath any experimental laboratory is a great deal of labor that supports and makes possible the experiments but is not itself experimental. This might be called laboratory housekeeping. The same thing is true in art studios — indeed, in all kinds of creative enterprises. The Meeting House Press has been and continues to be a hard and laborious operation, but without it the other projects could not have been sustained and been given publication. Its publications have been kept as idealistic, as noncommercial, as is the Meeting House Project as a whole. Even the job printing was done only for related religious organizations. Resisting all temptations to commercialize our labors has resulted in a kind of integrity of effort in all our activities, from the most menial to the most creative. It has provided the same character to the institution that a similar selectiveness and idealism provide to the individual person.

The agency of Meeting House Press as an essential element of the Meeting House Project has been demonstrated in several ways. Without it the experiments we have carried on might very well end with our own small group. I have observed various experiments carried on in other societies, in some cases lasting for several years. But since these were not written up and published, they will have almost no influence on what is done elsewhere, and their memory and influence will die out even in the society in which they were developed. One church has done exciting things with instrumental music over a period of several years, largely because of the influence of the minister. He has now moved to another society, and his leadership has been removed from the activities. From my observation, it is very unlikely that the minister who follows him will have like interests and carry on these developments in music. None of the experiments has been described in detail, with accompanying philosophy, and made available to others. Much of the potential value of what has been done has, therefore, been lost. The publishing of findings is an inherent part of the experimental process.

Some years ago in London, Stanton Coit developed many innovations in worship as the leader of the London Ethical Society. From his work came several publications, a book of readings, *The Message of Man,* published in 1894, and the two large volumes of music and readings, *Social Worship,* published in 1913. These books are now collectors' items. Through them the labors of Stanton Coit and the London Ethical Society are still having their effect on liberal religion. Things were adopted from them for the new *Hymns for the Celebration of Life.* We use them at the Meeting House. However, as far as I know, whatever experiments in form and ritual accompanied the creation of this material in music and literature were not recorded. They may exist somewhere, but I have not heard of them. I have often wished that we could consult them for suggestions in developing our festival services.

The point being made is that publication is the agency of immortality and continued life, whereby what has been done in the past continues to live and work in the future. A corpus and a tradition cannot grow without it. The publication of experiments and findings is an indispensable part of the scientific method. It is how the members of the international community of scientists keep in touch with each other, how widely separated work can be correlated and cross-checked, and how the amassing of scientific knowledge and methods is effected. (Comparable efforts to develop a religion for one world will depend on similar publication.) This publication is instrumental, not commercial, and it cannot allow the extraneous considerations of commercial publication to frustrate it. Its purpose is to make material available to the few who are concerned, not to make profitable sales to the many. Whether it may show a financial loss is unimportant. Its "profit" is in the communication of findings to those who are engaged in similar experiments, in order that research and development may be unified into one vast and intercommunicating organism. Science is a social enterprise, and publication is the means whereby creative conversation can continue unabated within the community of scientists.

This attitude is as foreign to religion as are the ideas of the application of experimentation, trial and error procedures, testing of hypotheses, and all that goes with the scientific method. Thus the denominational publishing agencies of even the liberal movements seldom function to effect this process of intercommunication. A beginning has been made through the "Packets" of the agencies of education and extension in the Unitarian Universalist denomination, but it is much too indecisive and incomplete an agency and is prejudiced by being adulterated with promotional concerns.

Through the Meeting House Press all our various projects are made available to the world outside the Meeting House in Boston. *Hymns of Humanity, Anthems of Humanity, Festival Services,* and *Readings for the Celebration of Life* permit the materials we develop and test in our own celebration to be used and tested in the services of religious fellowships anywhere in the world. They find their way, by what paths I do not know, into Methodist and other services, as well as into liberal societies. The publishing of a book of this kind is the sending of an emissary, or many emissaries, on a journey. But one never knows where a book may go. It is, in a sense, a free agent, and can pass into many unlikely lands, and hands, and find responsive readers where one would never have guessed them to be. Publication sets one's findings free to find their own cohorts, releasing them from the limitation of one's own will and imagination. They then can make their own way in the world and talk for themselves.

Even in our short life we have seen the results of such communication. A dozen or more churches have changed their style and arrangement of architecture because of the influence of our experiments in "religion in the round" and symbolism. The distribution of the festival services has contributed to similar efforts elsewhere. Above all, the publication of hymns, anthems, and readings feeds into the very bloodstream of the expression of religion; as we have already noted, many of these materials have been incorporated in at least two hymnals published by the denomination. From these some will find their way into the hymnals of other movements.

The publication of this book is the full practice of this precept, for in it, to the best of our ability, we are attempting to make a full report and assessment of the Meeting House Project up to this time. Now that the project is going into another operational phase, that of putting its major efforts into the usage of a symbolic complex rather than its construction, continuing publication will be necessary. It will probably entail the use of recordings and films as well as printing, and other media. Experimentation demands the invention of "languages" into which to translate its findings, and inventions in the means of recording and transmitting its conclusions, as well as inventiveness in the making of the experiments themselves.

THE WORKING FAMILY

The best designation we have found for the operation of the Meeting House Project is that of a "family work project." Religious movements in their service activities have developed the "work project" agency, wherein a group of people assemble to work together for a time in various fields, sometimes in a mental institution, in a slum area, in a settlement house, in a refugee settlement, in educational projects. They make a contribution to service work in time, effort, and companionship, rather than just in money or used clothing. The Peace Corps is an extension of this kind of practice.

The Meeting House Project is a continuous "work project" in which the members of the society create and sustain the experimental process. Every Friday evening is set aside as "work night" and often many jobs will be in process, such as building a pipe organ, photographing art works, cataloguing the library, secretarial work, working on press publications, janitorial work, painting and remodeling the building, building furniture, and assembling the open hymnal for the next service. Different persons have found tasks congenial to themselves within the project and have assumed these as more or less their province. At the close of the evening there are sandwiches and coffee, and the whole evening is as much a social event as a work session. The same values of fellowship inhere in this as have been discovered in the denominationally sponsored work projects. The finest kind of fellowship develops when people work together at jobs in which they profoundly believe.

Over the years an incalculable amount of work has been accomplished in this way. It has stabilized our financial structure, as well as made possible the experiments, since much of what is done by the work group is labor that the conventionally operated society hires members of the professional staff to do for it. By doing these things ourselves, we have freed what financial resources we had to purchase materials and to finance the unavoidable expenditures in the projects. Since ordinarily the largest expenditures in an operation are the labor costs rather than the material costs, this strategy has allowed us to accomplish many things that would have been exorbitantly expensive if we had hired professionals.

Among such labors are the printing, folding, collating, and binding, and the wrapping, mailing, and bookkeeping in the press operation; the designing and making of the symbols; the remodeling and rearrangement of the pews; the laying of linoleum and the polar projection map; the painting of the mural; the making of bookcases and other furniture, including dozens of mantels and picture frames; the building of display cases, the arrangement of the art works, and the matting of prints; the janitorial work; photography; cataloguing of record and book libraries; preparing and serving of parish dinners and coffee hours; secretarial work; making up the hymnals and keeping the files of materials in order; continual repainting and refurbishing of the plant; furnishing all our own instrumental and vocal music; doing all our own teaching in religious education; making drapes for the windows; designing and making lampshades for the auditorium; remodeling a portion of the building into an apartment; removing an old pipe organ from the Meeting House, moving a new pipe organ from another site, and installing it in the Meeting House — and this is only a partial list. It has been this kind of group labor that has made the project possible.

A continual study and preparation program has accompanied the project, for we have had to learn the history, theory, and method of what we were doing as we went along. An adult

352

study group has met each week. The subjects under consideration have been varied, but among them have been the study of
anthropology, archaeology, world religions, with the use of
films, slides, books, and visiting lecturers. By this means we
have educated ourselves in the history, folkways, and beliefs
of the religions of mankind, even as we were attempting to
assemble them into a religion for one world. We have continuously studied and reviewed the symbols and art works as we
have assembled them. The regular religious services, through
the addresses and the discussion periods that follow, have also
been an educational and conversational method whereby group
understanding and cross-fertilization of ideas and opinions have
been accomplished. At one time we had a series of international
dinners, wherein we sampled the foods of the various world
cultures and brought in related speakers and films to accompany them.

This bare listing of activities must fail almost completely to
convey what has happened within the organic processes of the
group involved, but perhaps there is no way of communicating
such long and gradual accumulations of meaning and experience. This inability has created problems in human relations
in the developing of a society.

The first problem is one of transiency. Many of the people
who were quite active in the project in early years have moved
to all parts of the country, taking with them the experience and
"know-how" they had acquired working with us. The new
people who came in did not have the experience of the earlier
developments. Only a small core have been with the project
from the beginning, and they are the indispensable human
structure on which the project has depended. For such a project is an experience even more than it is a product, and what
it is, in many of its dimensions, can be known only by those who
have worked within it; some things are known only from the
inside. There has been a problem of maintaining morale, when
"old hands" have moved elsewhere. Often, as in building a
choir, just as we have developed a chorus that knows the repertoire of new anthems and the ways of our services, some of its
members move on, and the work of several years collapses. In
a fluid society there is only a partial continuity of the human

353

component of such a project, which places heavy burdens on the few who stay on and makes unrealistic demands on those who come into the work after it has been years in developing.

The problem is more severe for this kind of project than it would be for laboratories, orchestras, faculties, and such social assemblies, where trained personnel can be hired to replace members who retire and move on. Since we have no funds, we must rely on those who voluntarily join the group and desire to work in it. They may or may not replace the talents and abilities of those who have left. Therefore the group is in a position of continually making shift with what talent and personnel it has, and the extraordinary thing is that we have been able to find so many able and versatile persons to carry on the work. At times it has seemed as if some uncanny process were operating to bring in a person of just the skills and interests that were needed in the next development. Adjustment has also been made possible by the willingness of those involved to work at many different tasks. If there was no one in the group already trained for a new work demand, we simply set about training ourselves in the needed skills whether we had any previous experience or not. Some of the most exceptional contributions have been made by persons who went through this kind of "on the job" training. Of course, several times it has been exasperating to have discovered how to do a certain task just when it was over. We have gone through the laborious, and often painful, process of developing new skills and experience, and when they were finally in hand, there was nothing further on which to apply them.

The greatest difficulty, as we have observed elsewhere, is that the longer the project continues, the greater is that accumulation of "difference" between our program with the setting of our celebrations and that of conventional religious organizations. Those of us who have grown up with the project have adjusted to its new ways gradually over many years. But a newcomer is asked to accept and digest the whole thing as a *fait accompli*. At times it seems harder to involve new people now than it was earlier, and this is at least one of the reasons.

Thus the project continues to be experimental in its group process as well as in its other aspects. We are testing to see

354

whether an experimental religious society can survive and develop, as well as to see whether a religious group can experiment. Probably the most interesting experiment of all is the one that we are doing on ourselves.

THE SERVICES

What is the function of the temple in a religion for one world? This matter has been introduced in general terms in previous chapters, but here we will consider the use of the particular temple structure that has been developed in the Meeting House Project. It is an assembly of symbols, works of art, musical instruments, books, furniture, arranged into an over-all shape which is itself a symbol. The architecture in this case is extraneous, for the building was not designed to embody and reinforce the other elements which it houses. This is the main handicap of such an experiment, until it can leave the shell into which it crawled as a homeless hermit crab and build its own native structure.

The temple assembly conducts its own "service" for anyone who enters it. It should be a place of meditation and personal communion for any individual who seeks what it offers, as well as operate as a setting for group celebrations. We have sought to create an artistic and symbolic fullness to which a person can come to refresh his sense of the human situation and of his own significance in the universe and in humanity. We know that the Meeting House does so function, at least for some people. The symbols and the art of the world religions, the symbolic presentations of the atom, the earth, and the galaxy, the scrolls and books of the world scriptures, the general symbolic arrangement, can and do evoke the sense of belonging and that "shock of rightness" that occurs when a symbol or an analogy, as in poetry, clarifies and enhances the reality of which it speaks.

I have seen people come into the Meeting House auditorium and get its import in an immediate reaction of recognition. I have seen others who were disturbed and puzzled by it, and others who seemed to have no reaction at all. But there have been sufficient affirmations of what this temple construct can bring to those who enter it to prove that it possesses consider-

355

able validity. This affirmation is not simply subjective. The works of art and symbols have proved their meaning and power to the people of the cultures that produced them over centuries, and often for millennia. A one-world culture has advanced sufficiently so that there is no doubt that the people reared in one culture are capable of responding to the cultural productions of people in far-off lands. The only question of any considerable merit here is whether people can have a "religious" response to such a collaboration of world symbols and art. Enough people have affirmed their response to the temple for us to be confident that this approach has substantial validity. We shall not know how much until a great architectural expression of the idea is built to incorporate this approach to art and symbolism within itself. Only then will its full potential impact be realizable.

Just as the temple is the setting for personal meditation, so it operates as a surrounding symbolic milieu for any and all assemblies that gather in it, whether these be religious celebrations or not. It is our theory that this is the adequate and just setting for all serious human considerations and activities — drama, music, dance, forums, and the like, as well as worship. We have had testimony that it is. Other organizations have made use of the room for gatherings. One college uses it for assemblies, and I have learned that many of the students have responded to the meaning of the room, even though the events they were attending had no direct relationship to it.

One affirmation of its effectiveness came in a way quite unexpected. We were conducting a forum on the abolition of capital punishment, and the speaker was a well-known penologist of Episcopalian background. She prefaced her remarks by saying that this setting, among the symbols of humanity and love of the world's religions, was the proper setting to consider the matter of man's inhumanity to man in the practice of the death penalty. If this setting is as universal as we believe it is, it will provide the background for the consideration of all subjects and problems. Such has been the intention in building it: not that the services and events conducted in it shall necessarily be novel, although we hope some will be that too, but that it will bring the orientation of a religion of one world to whatever topic is the focus of the gathering within it. It becomes the expressive, and at the same time the tacit, background for all considerations.

But it is in the considerations of world brotherhood and understanding that it operates most effectively. It must find its own native forms and uses, and a few of these have developed in our services. One is the use of the recorded music and the writings and teachings of the world religions in the services. When a service presents as background music the religious music of India, this is quite fitting when the art and symbols and books of India are an inherent adornment of the temple itself. The room encourages the increasing assumption of a world orientation as to the subjects and materials of the services. Some liberal congregations have series of services on the world religions, but they come as something special. In our setting such services can and do occur at any time. The setting makes a service on India as "normal" as a service on Boston or Christianity.

A few devices have developed that make use of the facilities. We have mentioned using the recorded music of a culture to serve as background music for readings from that culture. At times we will use a series of related readings from several cultures, with their respective background music, giving a world setting to the issue at hand. We have made a beginning at adapting and paraphrasing the literature of world religions for readings, hymns, and anthems, and more of this will be done. It has also been mentioned that we can "swing the circle" so that the setting to which the service is oriented will be the center of one particular religion. In a service on Islam the congregation faced the side of the room where the Moslem center is located, and a spotlight singled out that center, whereas the others were in a dim light.

In the festival services the setting achieves its maximum impact. The three seasonal festivals, autumn, mid-winter, and spring, have received the major emphasis, but it is also possible to develop festival services about great persons and issues, and on particular cultures and religions. In this setting all kinds of music, the dance, ceremonies, rituals, and drama are made feasible.

The manner in which the setting functions can best be illustrated by reference to the Mid-Winter Festival and the Spring Festival. In the Mid-Winter Festival the theme is light, a common symbol in many religions at the time of the winter solstice and the longest night of the year. The focus of the service moves from center to center around the room, and as it advances the temple lamp in front of each center is lighted and votive lamps are lighted on each of the mantels. The printed program contains descriptions of the mid-winter festivals in the various cultures, and the recorded music, poetry, and legends of each religion are touched upon in turn, using individual readers, a singing choir, and a speaking choir. The symbols of each of the religions are brought in and hung upon an evergreen bower in the circle. When the full circle has been completed, the lights in the room are turned out, and the people sit surrounded by the temple lamps and votive lights on the centers of the world religions, symbols of one common festival of lights celebrated by humanity in the darkness of mid-winter.

Then the direction of the festival turns upon nature itself. The construction of the atom is lighted, symbolizing the basic light and energy within matter itself, then the mural of the galaxy, with a reading about the turning of the seasons and the swinging of the great spiral, and the service ends with the lighting of the Christmas tree, returning to the universal symbol of the tree of life.

In the Spring Festival much the same general pattern is followed, of moving from center to center around the circle, only this time the unifying symbol is a May-pole set in the very center of the room. The children carry streamers from the pole to attach to each center in turn, until the entire room is one May-pole, with everyone sitting under the streamers. Then the children wind the May-pole in a dance. Spring songs, poems, and legends are the materials of the service.

In the Fall Festival a different approach is taken. The Jewish Festival of Booths is used as the basis of the service, and the harvest festivals of the other lands are related to it. A booth is built, similar to those erected in Jewish synagogues, except that it is adorned with art and symbols from several religions, not just Judaism. The bulk of the readings are taken from the Jewish festival, but in the last part of the service the children bring fruits of the harvest from the centers in various parts of the world — wheat from Islam, rice from China, corn from the Americas, and apples from New England — and the music and legends of other lands are woven into the Jewish background. Thus the Jewish festival provides the theme for a one-world celebration.

We have made two attempts at festival services on universal themes: "The World Is One" and "Voices of Peace." The possibilities for such festivals are limitless. We hope in time to treat many themes in different ways, experimenting to discover the most effective ways to conduct celebrations for a religion for one world. One thing we know already: many generations, many centuries will be necessary before the poetry and ritual of the celebrations of this emerging religion can accumulate in lore and develop their own inherent modes. All the religions of yesterday will contribute their themes and ideals and manners to this new religion, but it will develop in ways which the past cannot prophesy. All we can do at present is to make fumbling forays into this new realm. We can express it as it exists for us now, but what it will grow into we cannot imagine. What follower of Gautama 2,500 years ago could have imagined the thousands of temples, the countless sutras, the variant philosophies and rituals that constitute Buddhism today? What disciple of Jesus 2,000 years ago could have foretold the equally widespread and variant growth of Christianity? Religions develop in their own uncontrollable and unpredictable ways. A drop of rain falling on the eastern slope of a mountain in Montana cannot predict the great Mississippi and the ocean into which it will flow.

THE DANCE PROJECT

Some elements of a project of this kind evolve slowly. From the beginning we have hoped that one day we would be able to weave the dance into our services. A few attempts had been made in the use of folk dancing, which had proved quite delightful, but no person or group had come forward to make it possible to present serious dance themes of a truly artistic nature. But after fifteen years of waiting, the project has taken shape this past year.

Mr. and Mrs. Albert Pesso, who conduct a dance school and have professional experience in leading dance groups, have interested themselves in the Meeting House. Using a dance group made up of their students, they have provided the dance elements in the Mid-Winter and Spring Festivals of which we have dreamed. The festivals had been designed for the dance, and they finally demonstrated that through the dance religious celebrations can be virtually "brought to life." Without the flow and movement of dance and the drama, ritual is static.

In the Mid-Winter Festival a dance sequence was provided in the first passage from primitive man, the major ballet was in the center of the service, and the sequence at the close, relating to the atom, the galaxy, and the tree of life, was also expressed in dance. The May-pole dance theme of the Spring Festival is natural for this treatment. We hope in time to develop a festival service with dance as its main theme, to be called "The Dance of Life."

A beginning has been made in the direction of a dance school connected with the Meeting House, in which a permanent dance troupe will be developed, oriented to the purpose of expressing the themes of a religion for one world through the dance. The ultimate goal would be to associate dancers from many of the world cultures with it. If we allow ourselves to daydream, we can imagine a time when choral groups, dramatic groups, and instrumental groups will be active at the Meeting House, to give a rich cultural expression to this religious idealism. As of now, the Pessos are conducting a beginners' group as a part of the educational program. What it will grow into we can only hope.

When religious celebrations become "natural and human" and lose their magical and supernatural import and function, they must seek another area of effectiveness and rationale. This can be found in the creativity and delight of artistic expression, where the performance is designed to elicit its own meanings and satisfactions, such as we find in concerts, the theater, and ballet. But when the arts are separated from the temple, they are likely to be reduced to the function of entertainment. When they are returned to the temple, they may speak again to the issues of religious dedication and aspiration. In the past the dance, drama, painting, sculpture, architecture, and music have found the temple to be their native and most profound and creative dwelling place. Perhaps in a religion for one world they will again find it so.

RELIGIOUS EDUCATION FOR ONE WORLD

The education of children in the Meeting House Project has been handicapped by the lack of a large number of children, which characterizes many churches located in the center city of large urban areas. The children are mostly in the suburbs and seek their church schools closer to home. But the same philosophy has prevailed in the educational program as in the Meeting House as a whole.

On the theoretical level, it is more instructive to refer to the experience of the educational program developed in the First Unitarian Society in Madison, Wisconsin, in the four years before I came to Boston. There, under the dynamic and creative direction of Mrs. Helen Groves, an experiment in a new kind of curriculum and study process was undertaken, the aim being to introduce the growing child to the religious history of the human race.

During the period before the child entered the first grade of the public schools — that is, until about the age of six — the program was that of an enlightened nursery school, with the emphasis on the world and the home and neighborhood in which the child lived, his relation to that world and to his fellow creatures. No effort was made at introducing the one-world theme.

The following years, taking the child through high school, were divided into three four-year periods, grades 1 to 4, 5 through 8, and 9 through 12. The strategy was to have the entire school engage in the same general study at the same time, on three different levels. The first group would study mainly folk stories, books about the children of other lands, and materials adjusted to their level of understanding and appreciation. The second group moved to another level of approach, that of geography, exploring the ways other peoples live, work, and worship. Here again materials were kept within the range of interest and comprehension of the age group. The third group, the high-schoolers, made a more adult study of the teachers and philosophies and moral systems of the various world religions. Since all the classes were studying the same culture at the same time, there was a good deal of interchange and cooperation between the several groups, such as often occurred in the one-room schoolhouse. The older children would often help out with the projects of the younger children.

The general scheme was as follows: The first year began with the very early development of Chinese religion, proceeding through its long history and joining it with the religion of Japan in its later stages. The second year repeated the process with the cultures of India and Islam. The third year did the same with Egypt and Judaism, and the fourth year with Christianity, developing into contemporary naturalism and liberalism as practiced within their own religious society. The theory was that if the child had made this cycle three different times, on three different levels of maturity, interest, and materials, he would at the end have a fairly adequate insight into the religious history of humanity. Our goal was to make the child religiously literate on a one-world level.

We wondered where we would get the substance for such a program but discovered that this was no considerable problem. Even twenty years ago a good public library had an abundance of materials suitable to all age levels on the peoples and religions of the world. Most of the materials had been produced by the secular press. As I recall, we had recourse to religious presses only for works on Judaism and Christianity, and for the few books with a comparative religion approach produced by our own liberal publishing agency, Beacon Press. Our problem was one of selection; there was more good material than we could utilize. I am sure the abundance of such publications for children has greatly increased since then.

The one criticism I have with our procedure, looking back on it from this distance in time, is that one section should have been devoted to primitive man, beginning with Stone Age man and the Bushman and bringing the story of man's religions up to the Neolithic revolution. Also, the accumulating knowledge of Sumer, Babylonia, and Assyria should be added to that of Egypt. But two decades have not altered my basic judgment that the outline of the procedure was sound.

One resource readily at hand in Madison was the group of foreign students at the University of Wisconsin. Each year students from the cultures being studied would serve as teachers in the school, so that personal and human elements were added to the study. One project I remember was that of kite-flying, supervised by two Japanese students.

After I had left, and under a new administration, the study program was discontinued, but not until the four-year cycle had been completed at least once. We were convinced it would have worked even better on successive turns. The thesis was that all the various theological ideas and moral principles could be taken up as they occurred in man's religious development, and that by this process the student could, over a twelve-year period and at several levels, explore the likenesses and differences of man's religious ideas and practices.

We had no difficulty in maintaining the interest and involvement of the children. The study tied in with and supplemented their public school studies at every point. Since the public schools intentionally avoid the study and discussion of religion, because of the principle of separation of church and state, we believed that this was the best way to complete their education in the area of religious understanding.

Two basic principles were involved. The first was the free-mind principle of religious liberalism. We wished to give the children a thorough religious education without indoctrinating them, or imposing an authoritarian set of beliefs and ideals upon them. We believed that if we introduced them to the various theological and philosophical religious systems, and helped them to understand the idealism of the various religions, they would then best be able to choose their own beliefs and ideals for themselves. We would not, of course, refrain from expressing our own convictions as adults, but we would give the child the convictions of others also, and do the best we could to furnish him with an arena of experience and understanding in which his own choice could operate with enlightenment.

363

The other principle was embodied in our conviction that we must now become citizens of one world, and that all the religions on the human scene were as necessary for concern and study as the religions of our own city and country, and the religion of our own society. We hoped that if we encouraged our children to understand and appreciate the people of other lands they might find it easier to think and feel about them as brothers.

This program was proposed to the then Unitarian denomination, but it never met with official approval, and it has never again been tried in the form we attempted at Madison. The idea has grown, and other liberal societies have begun to have "area study" programs in different cultures. Whether the educational goals envisaged can be attained will not be demonstrated unless some society adopts such a study program and practices it until a generation of children have grown up under its influence.

THE FUTURE

What is the future of the Meeting House Project? No one knows. It has been said that nothing can stop an idea whose time has come. The time has come for the idea of a religion of one world to be announced and to be projected in experimental models, but no one knows how long we must wait until it is established in any strength around the world. Local attempts to establish it will lead fragile and precarious lives until its time has come.

The Meeting House Project will continue in its insecure, hand-to-mouth, year-to-year existence as long as it can. It will move now into a more concentrated activity in creating festival services, and the literary, artistic, musical, liturgical materials for such services. Ground is already broken for major efforts in hymns, anthems, and readings. In the latter, paraphrases are being made of writings from the world religions, and the second volume of *Readings for the Celebration of Life* will be published in a few years. A third volume, derived from the writings of poets, novelists, dramatists, and philosophers of recent times, is also planned. We are already in movement in the dance and expect to make advances in the use of dramatics. Initial plans are laid to experiment with the use of slides and films.

There are many inviting avenues in social action. We are at present engaged in activity in the field of fair housing practices. The service agencies of our movement are active in cultural and scientific exchange between countries, in foreign student projects, in service projects overseas. We hope to encourage even more imagination in these areas, related to bringing people from other lands to our own country to teach us, as well as to sending our teachers to them.

The next logical step in the project is one that we have no prospect at the moment of being able to take. That is the application of our experiments in art and symbolism to the building of a new temple structure. We seem to be fated to continue within an old and handsome building, but one to which we must adapt in an always imperfect and unsatisfactory manner. On this level, we have demonstrated how other societies that must stay in their old buildings for various reasons might adapt their structures to this new purpose. The lesson is a practical and instructive one. But the more exciting venture would be to build a new temple.

Here we envisage a domed structure, making imaginative use of the functional aspects of the observatory, perhaps related to a triangular, spire-like form. Frank Lloyd Wright has theorized that the two basic forms, the triangle and the circle, complement each other. The triangle is dynamic, a symbol of movement and cleaving, as in the arrowhead. The circle and dome are more serene, encompassing. Life manifests both themes. Perhaps the two motifs could be combined in one structure, or in two structures set adjacent to each other.

As to the use of art and symbolism, the practices of the past offer ready solutions. The symbols could be carved upon or painted upon the structure itself, both inside and outside. Statuary can be made part of the architecture. We have envisaged four large murals in the main hall of the building, depicting the rise of religion in four major areas. This could be shown in several ways. The major contemporary world religions, Hindu, Buddhist, Moslem, and Christian, could be featured. In this case it would be interesting to have the four

365

murals painted by artists from the four cultures, with their differing styles native to the area being depicted. Another approach would be to use the religious development in primitive man, in early civilization (Egypt, Sumer, Babylonia), in the Orient, and in the Occident.

The themes for symbolizing a religion for one world are as plentiful as the concept is inclusive. A possible future project in the Meeting House may take the form of four non-objective murals on the themes of energy, life, the arts, and science and technology. These would be located on both sides of the arches on opposite ends of the auditorium. Sculpture can be used in many ways — in niches, as carvings upon the building itself, or as free pieces set in favorable locations about the building, even as it is used in the Meeting House now. A project that is exciting to contemplate is a temple that used sculpture on the exterior, as is often done in Gothic and Hindu temples, but to have the sculpture relate to all the world religions rather than just to one. This would be a project to demand the full creativity of both architects and sculptors.

Thus we can daydream, imagining a time when the musical resources of a community might be marshaled to put on a truly religious performance in such a temple of, for example, Hindemith's *When Lilacs Last in the Dooryard Bloomed,* or another work of equal scope based on a one-world theme. There is no theoretical reason why a great temple of universal religion could not have a full range of creative activities. Each evening there could be a quiet service, with the music, teachings, and poetry of man's religious heritage. Programs of dance, drama, films, lectures, and forums could take place in the temple setting. Creative group activities in the arts, in social action, in education could proceed in smaller rooms of the building. This is what we shall attempt to fulfill at the Meeting House in the future, even though we inhabit an architectural shell previously occupied by Baptists, African Methodist Episcopals, and Albanian Orthodox. Our predecessors, taken together, were somewhat prophetic of our present intentions.

Even though we have no prospect ourselves of being able to build the new temple, new ventures are proceeding in other parts of the country. In such widely separated spots as Denver,

Colorado, Van Nuys, California, southern New Jersey, Schenectady, New York, new buildings of contemporary design have been built in the round, and in some of them exciting innovations in the use of art, drama, and music are taking place. In San Jose, California, and in Gloucester, Massachusetts, old buildings are being rearranged and the use of art and symbols is developing. A general renaissance is occurring in Protestant, Catholic, and Jewish church architecture. The use of circular and domed structures is becoming frequent, and the use of art and symbolism is increasing, with contemporary treatments and materials in sculpture, painting, and stained glass. Although the latter tend to adopt traditional symbols and rituals to new designs and materials, rather than make any striking change in basic symbols or themes, there is an indication that these movements are more and more aware of the demands of one world. But how the traditional religions will develop in facing the challenge and needs of the one-world situation is not our problem here. All we can say is that some of them seem to realize that they cannot forever escape this confrontation.

We have described the means whereby we have attained the goals, which are now the Meeting House as it exists. All these achieved goals will in turn become the means for struggling to bring to actuality those further goals that still, and in some form will forever, elude our grasp and accomplishment. There is no final achievement, no final destination in life and growth, and we wish none. The future is just as problematical and precarious as the past. We have come this far. We will go on as far as we can, and then we will leave it for others to take it on from there. We cannot be sure, as was Moses, that the land ahead is promised, but it is promising.

Notes on the Plates

1. The Charles Street Meeting House. The Charles Street Meeting House was built in 1807, designed by Ascher Benjamin. It is a landmark of Federalist architecture. The interior, however, was remodeled around 1850, and has lost all the characteristics of the New England Meeting House style. This pen drawing is by Wittingham.

2. The Charles Street Meeting House, interior. This shows the auditorium when the project was only a few years old, after the bookcase and the sound system had been installed, and the symbol project begun.

3. The Charles Street Meeting House, interior. The auditorium in 1963, at the time of this writing.

4. The Charles Street Meeting House, interior. A close-up view of the auditorium, with the center circle and the mural, bookcase, sound system, and symbol arrangement. See also pp. 62, 65, 86-88, 90-94, 110, 271-279, 315-318, 321-331, 356-360.

5. The Great Nebula in Andromeda. One of the astronomical photographs from which the mural of the nebula was painted. See also pp. 65, 315-317.

6. The Polar Projection Map. This polar projection map of the earth, the symbol of one world, is inlaid in the very center of the auditorium. See also pp. 326-327.

7. The Constructivist Sculpture of the Atom. The sculpture

369

by Mr. Jack Burnham, the microcosm, with the mural of the nebula, the macrocosm, in the background. See also pp. 65, 318-321, 328.

8. The Bookcase. The bookcase, housing the reproductions of the bibles of humanity, with the lamp and the stellar globe. See also pp. 14, 43, 125-134, 238, 305-309.

9. The Sound System. The sound system, with the large and small circles. See also pp. 309-314, 345.

10. The Bookcase of Original Bibles. This bookcase, at the opposite side of the auditorium from the bookcase in plate 8, houses the original scrolls and books from the world religions, rather than English translations. See also pp. 305-309.

11. Winding the Maypole. Scene from the Spring Festival, which culminates in the winding of the maypole, after the streamers have been taken to the various centers. See also pp. 359-361.

12. Dance Sequence in Spring Festival. Episodes in the festival service danced by a group under the direction of Mr. and Mrs. Albert Pesso. See also pp. 359-361.

13. Theatre in the Round. A scene from the play "The Blind Men" of Michel de Ghelderode, as performed in the auditorium. See also pp. 325, 329.

14. Textile: Scene from Ramayana. A temple hanging, polychrome, representing a scene from the Indian epic, The Ramayana, showing Tama and his wife Sita with Laksmana. This depicts Rama's brother arriving at the forest where Rama will live for twelve years. One of four large corner hangings representing the four major living religions, in this case, Hinduism. See also p. 339.

15. Tapestry Fragment. This portion of a much larger tapestry is the second corner hanging, representing Christianity. Its provenance is unknown. It contains the admixture of classical and Christian elements that is typical of the Renaissance. At the top center is Christ the King, to his right Solomon, and to his left David. Below these figures on the left side are Pallas Athene, goddess of the civic arts, of war and culture, and Longinus, philosopher and critic. On the right side are Voluptas, goddess of pleasure, and Diana, goddess of the woods and the chase. The figure at the bottom may be a knight.

16. Kirman Rug. The third corner hanging, representing Islam, is a Persian Kirman rug of the *mille fleurs* design, a formal pattern of branches, foliage, flowers and birds. It is related to the garden and tree of life designs. The rug features the design of the gateway to the mosque, which is the dominant motif in the Islamic prayer rug.

17. Buddhist Tapestry. This Buddhist tapestry shows Buddha at the top, seated in the mountains, while below him are four of his *arhats,* or disciples. One is accompanied by a lion, a second by a tiger, and in the center an elephant has rolled over on one of the disciples, while another is attempting to dislodge him. Around the arch are dragons, and a motif of dragons and phoenix birds decorate the bottom border. There is no provenance on this work, but it is likely Chinese of the 19th century.

18. Memorial Statue, New Ireland. This *Malanggane* carving is an example of Melanesian tribal art from New Ireland, just northeast of New Guinea. The dead are represented by elaborately carved statues of a unique open-work design. The dead are remembered in ceremonies with dances using *Malanggane* masks. This art is associated with a cult of the sun and moon, and often carries sun and moon symbols.

19. Stone Churinga, Australia.

The churinga is one of the most wide-spread of all primitive sacred objects. Objects similar to churingas were found among the Magdalenians, and the Azilian culture that followed in Spain and France produced pebbles painted with dots, bars and wavy lines that must have had magical uses.

This stone churinga comes from the Australian aborigines. Wooden churingas, or bull-roarers, are attached to a thong and whirled around the head. The roaring noise they make warns the women and girls away from taboo ceremonies, such as the initiation rights for a boy. They vary in size from an inch in diameter to seven feet. The designs that cover them are totem signs, and designate them as the dwelling place of the spirits of their ancestors. They are kept hidden in sacred storehouses, caves or crevices in the rock, and must never be seen by the women. The young man may not receive his personal churinga until several years after his initiation, and it represents the spirit force of his totemic father.

The churingas are decorated with a vocabulary of signs, concentric circles, U within U figures, parallel, straight, curved and spiral lines, rows and panels of dots, tracks of birds and animals, diamonds and squares. There are many totems, and each has its traditional arrangement of these elements. Each pattern tells the story of the clan's spiritual ancestors. The same elements can represent different things in different totems. The spirals and concentric circles may represent the principle features of the myth, the ancestor, the places where he camped and waged battle with a rival. On one churinga they may represent a frog, on another a tree, a waterhole, or some other totem. The same elements may represent different things on different totems. See also p. 108.

20. Sulka Shield, New Britain. These shields, carved in relief and painted, are among the most striking art from Melanesian New Britain, which lies between New Ireland and New Guinea. The edges of the shield are laced with cane; the colors are black, white, earthen red, and blue-green.

21. Australian Aborigine Shield. Objects such as this shield and the churinga (see above) are the only sculpture of the Australian Bushmen. Although they are carved with stone tools out of very hard wood, there is an amazing control of design, abstraction, and sophistication. These shields are used in rituals as well as for protection.

22. Wooden Hanger, New Guinea. This wooden hanger, with a carved face on each side, and the body carved with an abstract design and painted, comes from the Sepik River area of New Guinea. The carved masks representing ancestors are the most important of religious objects. Sacred objects are kept in a "ghost house" to which only men initiated into the ceremonies and the cults are admitted.

23. Wayang Puppets, Java. The dramas enacted in the Wayang puppet theatre of Java often relate back to Hindu myths and epics. There are three types of puppets, *wayang golek*, carved in the round, with movable arms, and costumes (center and left); *wayang keliti*, flat figures carved in wood (right); and *wayang purva*, shadow puppets cut out of leather, their shadows being projected onto a white screen. The puppets represent a vast cast of characters, good spirits, demons, historical personages, and mythological figures.

24. Easter Island Ancestral Figure. This is the traditional ghost-man, the *moai-kava-kava*, of Easter Island. These figures are carved according to a strict convention, with long ears, hooked noses, and with their ribs protruding. In skill of carving and design, they represent one of the highest artistic achievements of Polynesia.

25. Ibid., side view.

26. Buddhist Arhat, Japan. A monochrome painting on paper of a Buddhist Arhat, one of the original disciples of Buddha. Each of the disciples, in accord with tradition, has an identifying characteristic, such as the lion which accompanies this arhat. We have no provenance on this painting, but from its condition it would seem to have some age.

27. Japanese Lamp. A hanging lamp is a part of each of the centers of the world religions, and its lighting is one of the rituals of the festival services.

28. Hotei, Japan. This wood carving of Hotei, the Japanese god of good luck, is the central figure on the Japanese center. See also pp. 102-104, 114.

29. Monjusri, Japan. Monjusri, one of the major Boddhisattvas, has the chief attribute of enlightenment. He is shown in this line painting with the sacred jewel, the symbol of enlightenment in his head-dress, holding a sutra in his hand.

30. Chinese Lamp. This is the lamp that hangs in front of the Chinese center.

31. Bronze Ku. This archaic Chinese ceremonial vessel is from the Chou Dynasty, 1250 B.C. This bronze culture flourished from 1500 B.C., during the Shang, Chou and Han dynasties, and produced some of the most powerful and beautiful vessels in the history of man's religious art. See also p. 80.

32. Jade Pi Disc. This jade Pi disc, symbol of the heavens, is 15 inches in diameter, and in the Han style. Estimates of its age rate from Han to late Tang or early Sung. A great deal has been written about the archaic jade symbols that accompanied the bronze vessels (see above), most of it theory and conjecture. It does seem clear that the Pi disc was a sun symbol, generalized into a symbol for the heavens. It is paired against the *tsun,* a square jade symbol of the earth (not shown).

The Pi disc stands on the bookcase beneath the mural of the nebula, with the *tsun* to its right and the cosmic disc (see below) to the left. Thus these three archaic Chinese jades, one of them dating back over three millenia, together with the mural taken from a contemporary astronomical photograph, give a dimension of cosmic symbolism to our temple. The Pi disc is 15 inches in diameter, of light gray jade. See also pp. 40-41, 333.

33. Jade Cosmic Disc. This archaic Chinese jade is known as a symbol of the cosmos, and of man's relation to the heavens. The notches that appear on the three segments traditionally represent the "seven governors," the sun, the moon, and the five planets. There is a theory that it was used as an astronomical instrument.

34. Chinese Kwan Yin. This statue of Kwan Yin, in grey limestone, shows the Bodhisattva holding a rosary and a sutra. Kwan Yin derives from the merger of the Hindu god Aviloketesvara, and the Buddhist Padmapani, with a Chinese mother-goddess. She has over eighty attributes, but she is mainly known as a goddess of motherhood and mercy. The sutra would identify her in this case in her attribute as goddess of learning and enlightenment.

35. Flower Goddess. A polychrome painting on paper, mounted on a silk scroll, of a Flower Goddess offering lotus petals, from Jehol circa the late 15th century, from a collection of paintings owned by the Meeting House of various gods and goddesses of the Buddhist and Taoist pantheon. This is the painting that hangs at the Chinese center.

36. Landscape. A monochrome painting on paper, showing a sage with his retinue contemplating nature, the mountain, mist, trees and waterfall. This painting is typical of the nature mysticism of Chang and Zen Buddhism, and is probably a Japanese painting adapted from a Chinese model. See also pp. 58, 147.

37. Marichi, Tibetan Bronze. A gilt bronze statuette of Marichi, goddess of the dawn, Tibetan, probably 19th century. She is shown with eight arms, and in two of her hands are symbols of the sun and moon. She has three heads, one that of a boar. Sometimes she is shown in a chariot drawn by seven boars. It is said that the goddess dwells among the stars that form the Dipper in the constellation of Ursa Major, and is worshipped by sailors. She is the central figure on the Tibetan center.

38. Krishna and Radha. Krishna, the Hindu god of love, is shown with his consort Radha. Krishna is an avatar, an incarnation of Vishnu, and is represented here in the flute-playing pose (*venu-gopala*). The flute, as usual, is left to the viewer's imagination. A cow and a peacock accompany the couple. North-central India, 18th-19th century, in copper. This group stands in the center of the Oriental side of the auditorium. See also pp. 114, 197.

39. Parvati, Bronze. This bronze statue of Parvati, 21 inches tall, is from South India, 17th century, and is the central figure on the Hindu center. Parvati is a consort of Shiva, his devoted and virtuous wife, in striking contrast to the other consorts of Shiva, the destroyer, such as Durga and Kali. This statue and others (Plates 38, 40, 42, 43, 61) are a portion of an extensive collection of Hindu and Buddhist and other art, given to the Charles Street Universalist Meeting House by Professor Samuel Eilenberg of New York. This statue of Parvati was given in memory of Guy LeCorneur.

40. Kali, Bronze. A bronze statue of Kali, South India, provincial in style, 18th century. Kali is the goddess of terror, of epidemics and cataclysms. She is a consort of Shiva, and more than any other of his many consorts, represents his power of destroyer.

41. Nandi, the Bull. This small stone statue of Nandi is of unknown provenance. The bull is a symbol of Shiva, and is worshipped among the Shaivas. Nandi probably relates back to the bull-worship of Mohenjo-Daro and Mesopotamia.

42. Lakshmi-Narashima. The lion-incarnation of Vishnu is represented seated with his consort, Lakshmi, on his left knee. South India, copper, 17th-18th century. This piece is worn by rubbing in worship. Vishnu assumed the form of man-lion for one of his mythological combats.

43. Lakshmi. Lakshmi is the consort of Vishnu, the goddess of motherhood, of the home, of wealth and good fortune, and as such one of the most popular of all Hindu deities. She is called

Padman (the lotus), and is the Hindu counterpart of Aphrodite. She is fabled to have risen from the milk-ocean when it was churned for ambrosia (see end papers). South India, copper, 18th-19th century.

44. Amida Buddha. The Japanese gilt-wood statue of Amida shows the Boddhisattva in a typical pose, seated on the cosmic lotus, with the hands in the *temborin-in* gesture composed of two wheels of the Law. See also pp. 104, 157, 245.

45. Chinese Kwan Yin. This white marble bas-relief carving of Kwan Yin is reputed to have come from a temple near Pekin.

46. Siamese Buddha. Bronze Buddha from Siam, undated, in the simple, austere style dating from the 14th century or later. The flame finial on the top of the head is missing. In the Buddhist center this Siamese statue represents the Buddhism of the Lesser Vehicle (Hinayana), the nontheistic Buddhism surviving mainly in Ceylon, Siam and Burma. The Japanese Amida Buddha (above), represents the theistic Buddhism of the Greater Vehicle (Mahayana) that developed in northern India and is now prevalent in China and Japan.

47. The Three Sages. In China and Japan the Three Sages, Confucius, Laotzu, and Buddha, are often pictured together. Sometimes they are shown drinking tea, each with a different expression, as an allegory that the same truth can appear differently to different persons. There is not the same need to be exclusive in one's religion in the Orient that we find in the West, and it was thought quite proper to give equal honor and reverence to all three of the Sages. This has been called Oriental Universalism. This Japanese monochrome painting on paper hangs in our center of Oriental Universalism, with statues of Confucius, Laotzu and Buddha on the mantle beneath. We have no provenance for the painting, so there is only our conjecture to confirm that it does represent the Three Sages. Groups of three figures, such as the Taoist Trinity of Yu Huang, Tao Chun, and Laotzu, are common in Oriental art. There are also the three Bodhisattvas, Manjusri, P'u Hsien, and Kwan Yin. See also p. 114, 158, 245.

48. Isis and Horus. This bronze statuette of Isis and Horus is the central figure on the Egyptian center. Horus, the Hawk, was identified with the Pharos of Egypt. The dead king was

Osiris, the father of Horus, who was the living Pharo. The religion that developed around the myth of Osiris, Isis and Horus was a powerful religious movement in Egypt for thousands of years. See also pp. 59-60, 114.

49. Bayaka Mask. This mask, used in circumcision rites of the Bayaka tribe of the Congo River area of Africa, has the typical elephant-like treatment of the nose, bulging eyes and stylized ears. These masks are highly stylized, surmounted by woven structures decorated with streamers, and heavy raffia ruffs and capes that cover the dancer.

50. Dan Mask. This is a mask of a secret society of the Dan tribe of Liberia. The secret society had a great many masks of widely varying form, each designating one of the positions within the tribe. This is an executioner's mask. The societies were self-contained, with their own laws and punishments. This mask was worn by the one chosen to carry out the tribal judgments. The power to execute lay in the mask, not in the wearer. The hair on the chin is said to have been taken from those executed. This mask profoundly illustrates the emotional power of African sculpture; it seems to exude a sense of terror. See also pp. 104-105, 114, 139.

51. Yoruba Statuette. Three pieces of Yoruba art are gathered in the African center, this statuette, a mask (Plate 57) and a stool (Plate 53). The scars on the cheeks of the statues and masks are said to represent marks of a leopard's claws. Ekun, the leopard, appears in their art, along with the ram and the dog. Statuettes like this represent sometimes ancestral figures, sometimes various gods and powers, and others are used as fetishes. See also p. 114.

52. Antelope Headpiece, Bambara. The Bambara antelope headpieces appear in two styles, the erect type used as model for the symbol (No. 19) and the horizontal type here shown.

53. Leopard Stool. The totem animal of the tribe is often used as in this stool. We have no provenance on this piece, and it is only a conjecture that it is Yoruba. This we have surmised because of the use of the leopard in Yoruba art, but we may be mistaken.

54. Statuette. We have no information as to the source of this statuette. Stylistic elements relate it to the Baule.

55. Ashanti Gold Weight. These small bronze works were used as counterweights in the weighing of gold dust. This bird is but one and three quarters inches in length, but has surprising sculptural quality.

56. Gouru Antelope Mask. The Gouro achieve a classical stylization in their antelope masks.

57. Yoruba Mask. The Yoruba mask, with the characteristic scarification on the cheeks, is worn on top of the head rather than over the face. The Yoruba are an agricultural people, and the masks are worn at large public festivals to propitiate the ancestors and promote prosperity.

58. Stone Head, Greece. This stone carving of a Greek god is believed to be a head of Zeus.

59. Tyche, City Goddess. A bronze Hellenistic statuette of Tyche, who is the goddess of the city. On her head is a crown in the shape of the wall of a city.

60. Brass Vase. The use of calligraphic inscriptions on this brass vase, possibly from Syria, is typical of Islamic cultures. Often the inscription is a quotation from the Koran.

61. Page from the Koran. This page is Turkish, from a manuscript Koran of the seventeenth century or earlier. The body of the text is a beautiful Nashki, while the bold inscriptions which run across each page are written in the style known as Tsuluts, called by the Persians Rogha. Arabic is always the language employed in transcribing the Koran, from Morocco to the Philippine Islands. See also pp. 57-58, 136, 157, 308.

62. The Jewish Center. This plate shows a typical center arrangement, with a lamp suspended in front, in this case a brass Sabbath Lamp, German, of the 18th century. The woodcut by Joseph Gropper shows the blowing of the Shofar Horn at the Day of Atonement. The Ceremonial Plates and Hannukah Lamp are described below. See also pp. 57, 135-136, 158, 297-298, 308-309, 313.

63. Megillahs and Torah Pointer. The Megillah is a scroll of the Book of Esther which is often performed as a drama in the Purim ceremonies. The scroll at the top is archaic in form, made of deer skin, from Yemen. The smaller scroll, on parchment in a silver case, is European, 19th century. A silver

Torah pointer lies beside another, smaller, Megillah case.

64. Sabbath Lamp. The Sabbath is inaugurated by the kindling of the Sabbath lights. In the western countries of Europe oil was typically used until the eighteenth century, when the lamps such as this became so much the mark of a Jewish home that it was called *Judenstern* (Jewish Star).

65. Seven Branched Menorah. The seven branch candlestick is established by traditions in the Old Testament, and is the oldest visible mark of identification of Judaism. It was one of the ritual objects in the Temple in Jerusalem. The Menorah is a conventionalization of the shape of the tree of life. This candlestick is of steel, German, of the late 19th century.

66. Silver Ceremonial Plate. This plate shows David with his harp, and altars. This, and the pieces in the next two plates, are from the Near East, or possibly North Africa.

67. Silver Ceremonial Plate of Moses and the Ten Commandments.

68. Silver Torah Finials. Torah headpieces adorn the poles on which the scroll is wound. Called *Rimmonim*. They are the oldest of the silver ornaments of the Torah.

69. Two Silver Kiddush Cups. The Kiddush (Sanctification) at the beginning of the Sabbath consists of two blessings, one on the holiness of the Sabbath and the other over a cup of wine. The Kiddush ceremony occurs in the synagogue as well as the home. The cup to the left is from the Near East, the one to the right from Europe.

70. Hannukah Menorah for the Home. This brass Hannukah lamp has eight cups for oil and a bracket for the lighter candle. Hannukah, the Feast of Dedication, is celebrated for eight days as a Festival of Lights at the time of the winter solstice. The two deer relate to other baroque animals adapted to Jewish ceremonial art, similar to the use of two rampant lions. The two twisted columns were shaped after ancient columns preserved in St. Peter's of Rome, relating to the two sacred pillars in Solomon's temple.

71. Hannukah Menorah. The use of candles began to replace the use of oil lamps in the nineteenth century. Hannukah candlesticks (Menorah) with eight candles plus the lighter candles, are used in both the homes and the synagogues.

72. Torah and Torah Cover. A Polish Torah, over 100 years old. On the Torah Cover are the Crown of David, the Lions of Judah, the Ten Commandments, and the Tree of Life.

73. Statue of St. Anne, Mary and Jesus. This painted wooden statue is French provincial, provisionally dated as the 15th century. It shows St. Anne, the mother of Mary, with Mary on her knee, and Mary holds the baby Jesus on her lap. This is the central figure in the Christian center.

74. The Christian Center. The picture on the Christian center is an aquatint by Rouault from the *Misere* series. A votive lamp hangs in front of the center. To the left is a Russian Icon of Mary and the infant Jesus, in the center the statue described above (Plate 73), and to the right a Mexican Christ (see below, Plate 76). See also pp. 56, 114, 245.

75. Christian Votive Lamp, Brass.

76. Mexican Statue of Jesus. This Mexican carving of Jesus, once used in a Mexican Catholic Church, has lost its polychrome, is blackened by time and smoke, and the right side is eaten away, but it still has dignity and devotional power.

77. American Indian Center. The theme of the center is the agricultural religion based on maize, that exemplifies the importance of this grain to the people of the Americas. The hanging is a Navaho Yeibichai rug of the corn maidens. *Yeibichai* refers to the Night Way chant and dance ceremonials, which include initiation rites for the boys and girls. In the center is a terra cotta reproduction of a basalt statue of the Corn Goddess of the Aztecs. The other two pieces are described below. See also pp. 141-142.

78. Mixtec Corn God. A terra cotta effigy vase of the Corn God from the Mixtec culture of South Central Mexico that was earlier than and contemporary to the Aztecs.

79. Mayan Corn God. A mold-made terra cotta statuette of a Mayan Corn God. He holds ears of corn in his hands.

80. Eskimo Mask. Eskimo Ceremonial Mask from Nunvak Island, probably representing the moon. Attached to the mask with feathers are wood carvings of hands, feet, birds, fish, otters. The two rings are reputed to symbolize the real world, in the inner ring, and the world above us, in the outer ring. The masks represent both good and evil spirits. This mask was the gift of Mr. and Mrs. J. Ray Shute, who contributed their collection of American Indian art to the Meeting House, and subsidized the purchase of other works.

81. Guerrero Stone Figure. This statuette from the State of Guerrero in Southwest Mexico, standing 13 inches tall, is one of the largest and most impressive of its kind.

82. Mayan Figure. Mold-made terra cotta figure, reputedly of Mayan origin.

83. Totonac Smiling Goddess. Characteristic "smiling goddess" of the Vera Cruz area. She holds an ear of corn in her hand.

84. Figure of Woman. This polychrome terra cotta figure of a woman is characteristic of the art of the Nyarit and Jalisco areas of Western Mexico.

85. Stone Figure. This stone figure, carved from tufa stone, is from Costa Rica.

86. Chimu Effigy Pot. Peruvian Chimu effigy vase of a male and female figure, which also acts as a whistle. The Chimu black pottery style had a long history through two eras, and continued to thrive throughout the Inca period up to the conquest.

87. Nazca Effigy Vase. The Nazca culture on the coast of southern Peru existed from 400-1000 A. D. This polychrome vase is in typical Nazca style. The back of the figure is covered with serpents.

88. Mochica Vase. The Mochica culture was contemporary with the Nazca on the northern coast of Peru. Mochica pottery takes many forms, human, vegetable, and a great variety of bird and animal forms.

89. Nazca Bowl. Nazca bowl depicting the "cat god" which is common in many areas of Peruvian art and culture.

90. Etching, Self Portrait, Kaethe Kollwitz. Klipstein No. 106. See also pp. 112-113, 344.

91. Woodcut, The Volunteers, Kaethe Kollwitz. Klipstein No. 178. This is the second work in the "War" series, which was Kollwitz' protest against war, following her experience in the First World War, and the death of her son in its early stages.

92. Etching, Mother with Dead Child, Kaethe Kollwitz. Klipstein No. 72. The themes of motherhood and the sickness and

381

death of children occur often in Kollwitz' work. The artist used her son Hans as a model for this etching.

93. **Etching, The Prisoners, Kaethe Kollwitz.** Klipstein No. 98. This is the last etching in the series on the "Peasants War." It shows the prisoners tied and herded together after the defeat of their rebellion. The artist's first great series of prints was on "The Weavers Revolt," and this series on the Peasants War followed. The poverty and oppression suffered by the lower classes was a constant theme in her art.

94. **Lithograph, The Survivors, Kaethe Kollwitz.** Klipstein No. 184. This lithograph, showing the survivors of war, the orphans, widows, the aged and the maimed, was created for use as a relief poster.

95. **The Unitarian Meeting House, Madison, Wis.** The exterior of the church designed by Frank Lloyd Wright, showing the prow-like shape of the auditorium and its roof. The educational wing lies to the right, with the entrance to the left. See also pp. 280, 322-323, 366.

96. **Ibid.** An interior view, showing the seating arrangement of the auditorium, with the pulpit and choir loft in the front.

97. **Church of the First Unitarian Society, Schenectady, N. Y.** Interior. This building, designed by Edward Durell Stone, features a successful treatment of "religion in the round." The use of symbols can be seen, and painting on the walls to the side. There is also an outside sculpture court, and a fully equipped sound system.

98. **Ibid.** Exterior view, showing the pool and fountain, the dome, and the design of intersecting circles on both the exterior and interior walls.

99. **Ibid.** Interior view showing the social area that surrounds the circular seating area under the dome.

100. **Proposed Building for Unitarian-Universalist Church in Van Nuys, California.** Drawings by the architect, Frank F. Ehrenthal, for a new church building. The circular auditorium is designed in order to make it suitable for dance and dramatics, and is capable of many different re-arrangements, such as for church services and church dinners. This sketch illustrates its use for a dramatic performance of theatre in the round.

382

101. Ibid. Exterior view, with educational wing to the left. The structure at the top of the dome is functional, to provide space for air conditioning, lighting facilities, etc.

102. Ibid. Diagram showing a seating arrangement for theatre or services.

103. Plan for a Unitarian Meetingplace. This cross-section view shows the plans for a church in a suburban area, done as a thesis subject by R. Dean Meredith.

104. Ibid. Floorplans for the basement and the auditorium, showing an effective use of a circular temple structure, and seating in the round.

105. Sketch for a Center of World Religion.

Is there a further step toward creating a religion for one world that might be taken in the near future, going beyond the efforts of small fellowships such as the Charles Street Meeting House? This sketch gives the merest indication of what is at present merely a "pipe dream," and yet it has certain practical aspects that make it possible of achievement. The proposal is to create a center of the world religions.

It might be created anywhere, but it would seem apt to put it near the United Nations Headquarters in New York. The basic idea is to create a park, in which would be located temples of the major living world religions. Each temple would have its own setting, surrounded by trees and gardens, and thus be a unit in itself, but all the temples would be within the same park, connected by roads and paths, thus symbolically demonstrating the variety and the unity of the world religions. These temples would be active parishes, and could draw their membership from personnel at the United Nations, and people of that faith in the area.

Nations and religious movements could be invited to build their own temple in the park, or better, to move an historic temple of their religion to the park. India, for example, might choose to move and restore one of the many ruined Hindu temples in that country.

In the center of the park, with all the other temples radiating from it, would be a Temple of Humanity, decorated with the art and symbols of all the world religions, ancient and modern. In this temple the representatives of all religions could come together, to celebrate those common ideals and aspirations they all hold, and each would have its own distinctive temple related to this universal central structure.

Of one thing I am sure, nothing is to be gained by a negative spirit of iconoclasm in moving toward a religion for one world. We do not wish to destroy the past, nor the values and beauties inherent in the many religions now on the world scene, but to enhance and celebrate them. Such a center for world religion would gather together the temples of humanity, in all their uniqueness and distinctiveness, and provide places for the practice of the celebrations of these religions. But it would also stress the relatedness of the religious spirit in all peoples. The Temple of Humanity in the center of the park would be a prophesy of a future condition of world unity, on the religious as well as on the political and humanitarian level. At present both exist, the particularity of the various cultural faiths, and the striving toward world brotherhood and fellowship. Perhaps such a center of world religions would dramatize the best in our present condition, as well as a dream for tomorrow.

Note: The sketch for a Temple of Humanity is intended only to suggest a symbolic approach to a temple structure for a religion for one world, not a structurally feasible solution of the problems. The author is no architect. The two motifs, the dome and the spire, are the symbols of the thrust of aspiration and achievement, and the serenity and inclusion of the inevitable return to the earth and the enfolding universe. If these could be included organically in one structure, with the girders of the spire cleaving through the dome, perhaps, both within and without, these two principles would be dramatized in the very structure of the building. The height of the spire has been truncated because of space. It might soar higher in the air, with an eternal flame burning at its apex, to symbolize the never ending hope and vision of humanity.

END PAPERS

The Churning of the Milk Ocean.

This Javanese painting depicts the ancient Hindu myth

of "The Churning of the Milk Ocean." The gods, who had been weakened by a curse, sought help from Vishnu, who said that only ambrosia, the cream of the milk-ocean could help them. The gods could not accomplish the task themselves, so they sought the aid of the Asuras, the enemies of the gods, promising them a share of the ambrosia. They used the great serpent Vasuki as a whip, with the gods holding one end and the Asuras the other. As the churning proceeded, the fourteen precious things came to the surface of the ocean, including the ambrosia. After the churning the gods and the Asuras both drank of the ambrosia, and the gods were sufficiently strengthened to put the Asuras to flight. Among the fourteen precious things that came from the churning were the moon, the Parijata tree, the elephant, the cow, the Asparas, and the goddess Lakshmi.

The picture is chosen for the end papers as a suggestion that perhaps if all the religious forces in the world can co-operate in building one world (both the gods and the enemies of the gods, so-called), perhaps such further precious things as peace, understanding and prosperity for all might result.

THE PLATES

THE PLATES

UNIVERSALIST
MEETING HOUSE
·BEACON HILL·

1

2

3

4

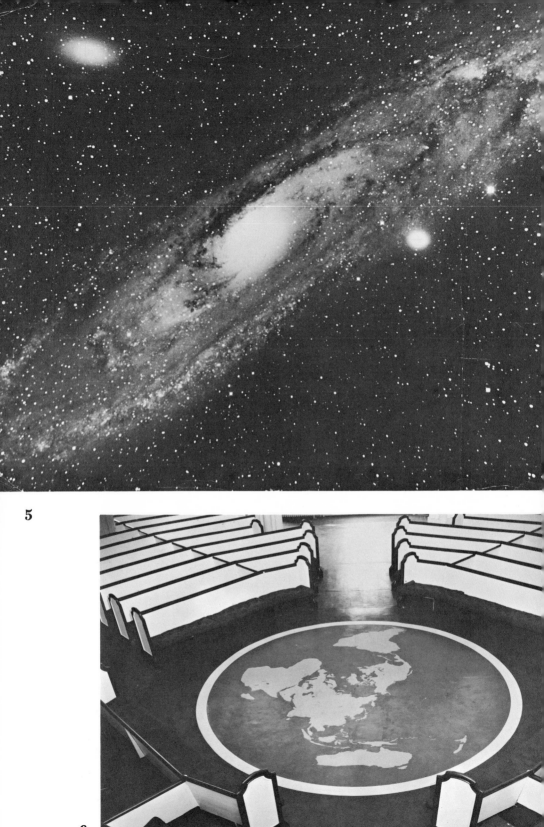

5

6

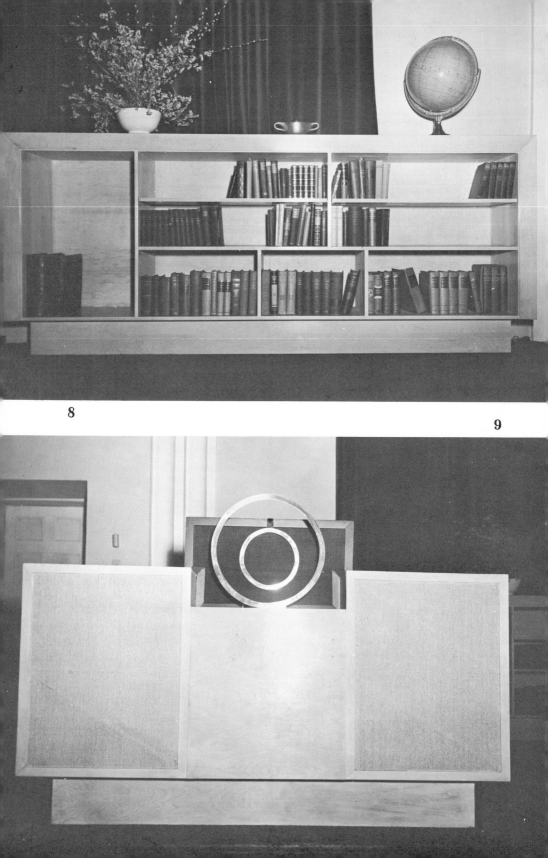

8

9

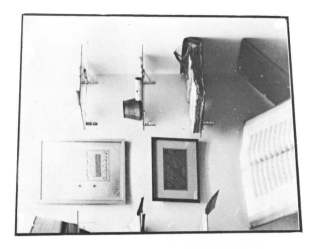

10

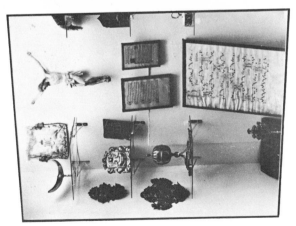

11

12

லிதாபிராட்டமானைகபடித்
தகொடுத்தபடிஸ்ரீராமலை
வேண்ட

14

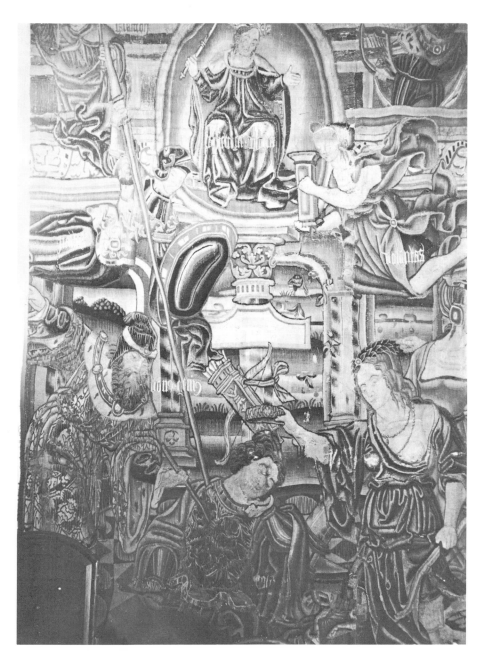

15

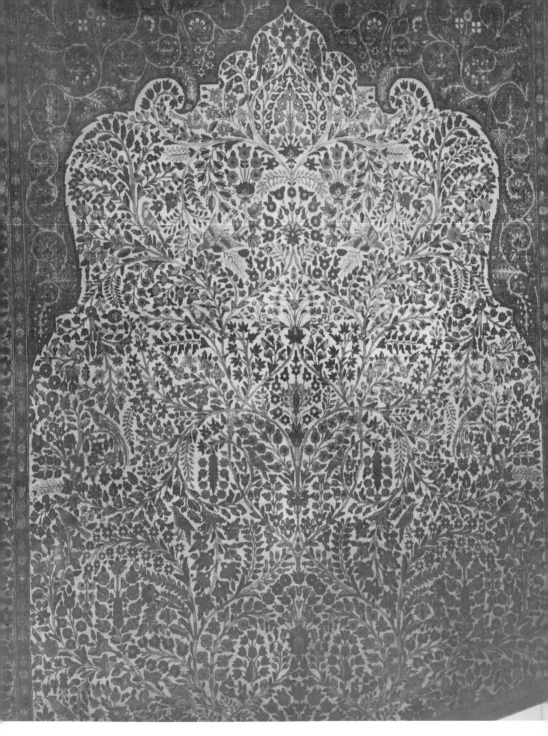

16

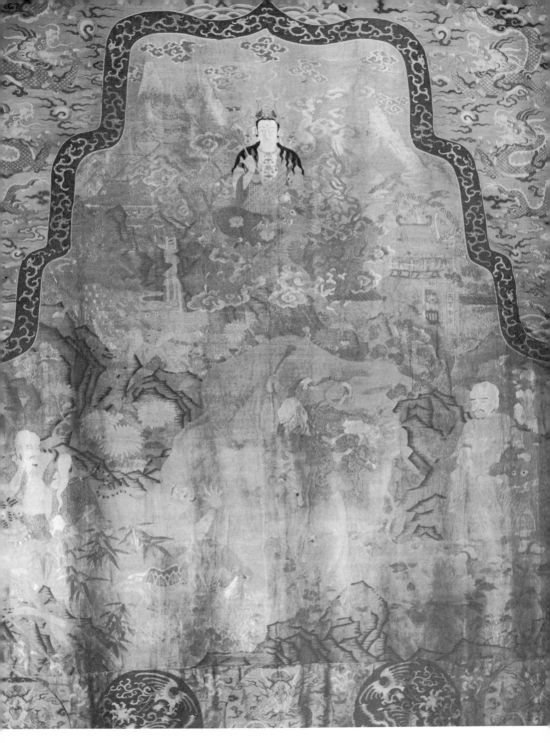

17

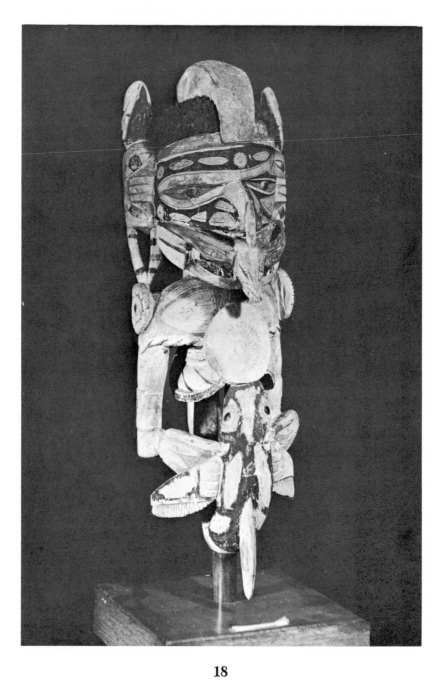

18

19

20

21

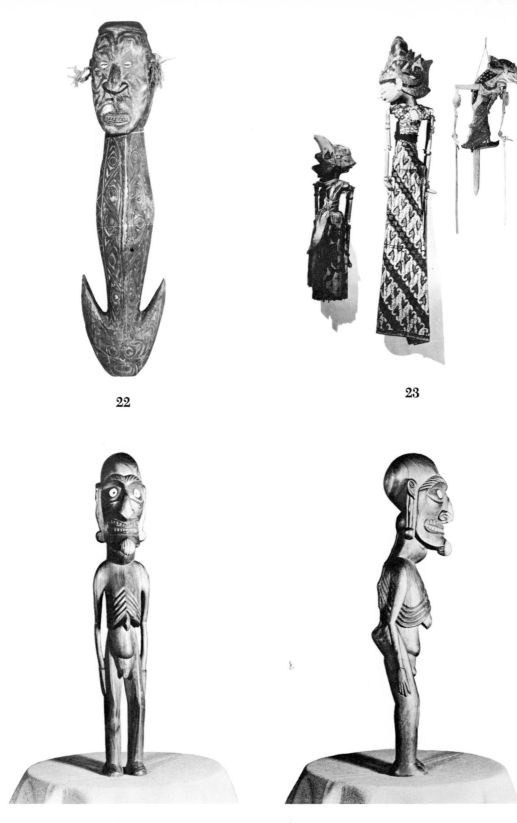

22

23

24

25

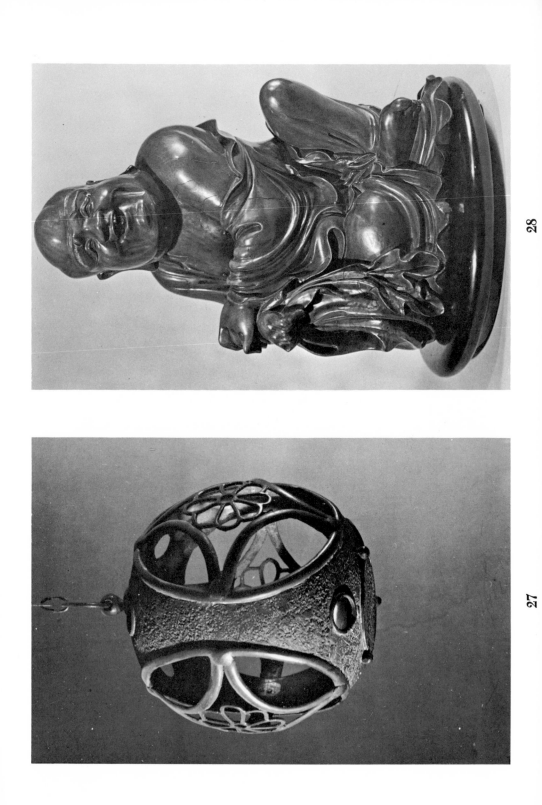

27   28

29

◄ 30

31

◄ 32

33

34

35

36

37

38

39

40

41

42

43

44

▼ 45

47

48

49

50

51

52

53

54

55

56

57

58

59

61

60

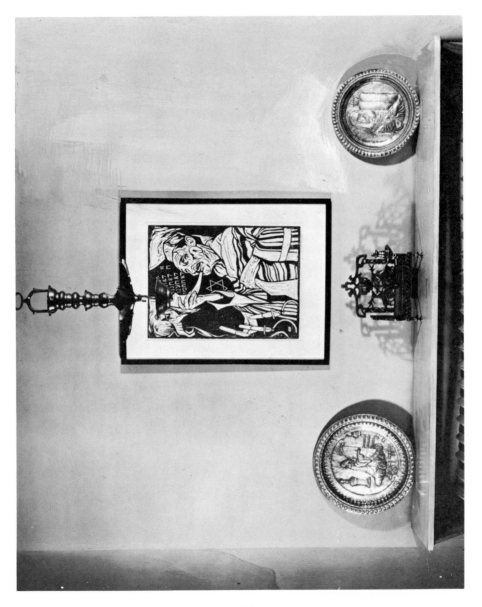

62

63

64

65

66

67

68

69

70

71

72

73

74

75

76

77

78

79

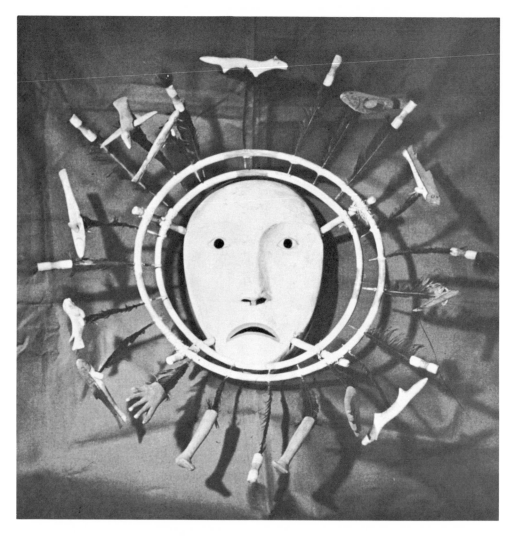

80

81

82

83

84

85

86   87

88   89

90

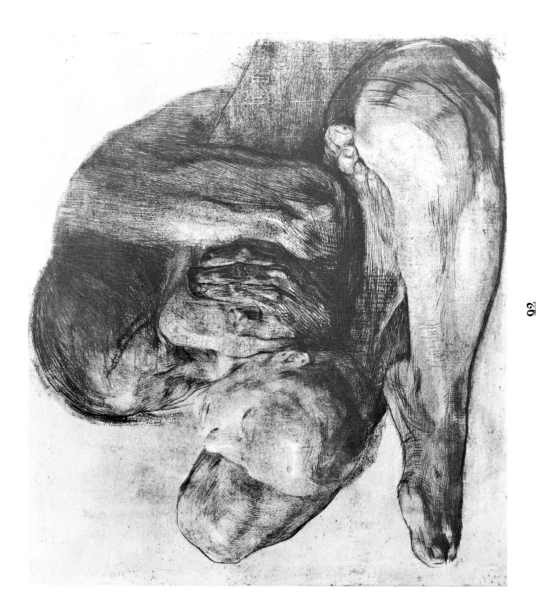

98

99

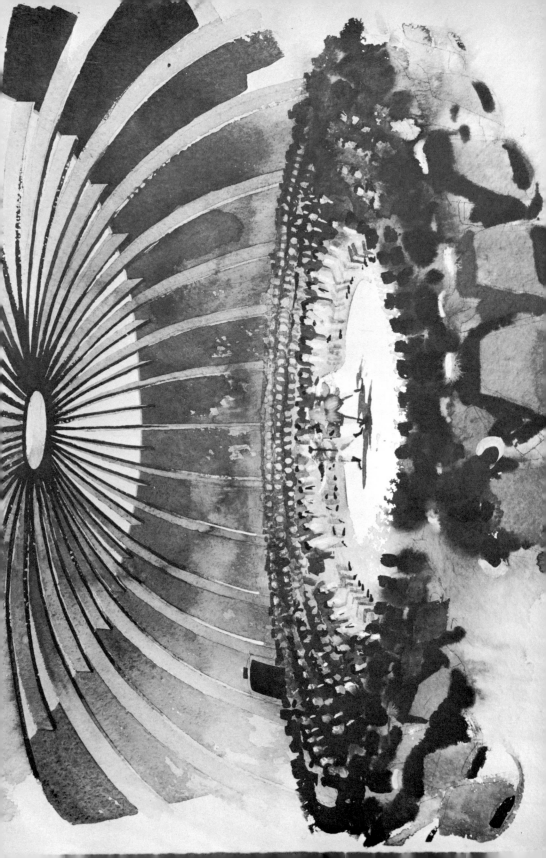

101

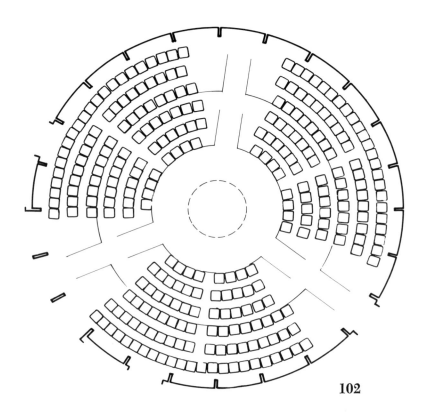

102

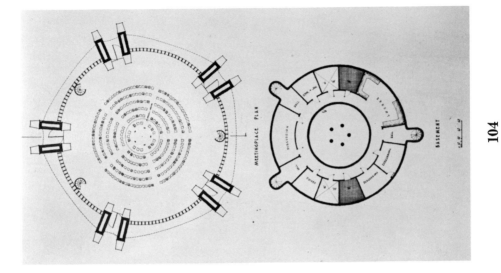

MEETINGPLACE PLAN

BASEMENT

104

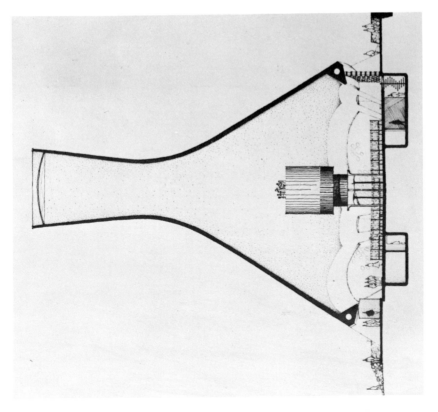

103

105

The Symbols

THE CIRCLE

The circle has been chosen as the basic symbol for a universal religion, for a religion for one world. It is a symbol of unity, of eternity, of holiness, of the universe, the sun, the moon, and the earth. Since the circle is found in the galaxy as well as in the globular shape of stars and planets, it is a natural symbol that only needs to be adapted from nature. The circle is not only used as an individual symbol, but in "religion in the round" the circle becomes the symbolic shape that the temple and the assembly assumes. See also pp. 40-41, 64-65, 275, 324-330, 332-333, 367-368.

THE CIRCLE AND CROSS

This symbol is very ancient, going far back into pre-history. Many meanings have been attributed to it. It is here used as a symbol of the earth. The cross within the circle is said to designate the four quarters of the earth or the four rivers in the Garden of Eden. One modification of the symbol is used in the Celtic Cross, which, interestingly in relation to the symbolization of the earth, is often entwined with vine and foliage decoration. The meanings found in the separate symbols of the circle and the cross can be implied to this one symbol that combines the two.

THE FIRE WHEEL

The progress of the sun across the heavens has been symbolized in many ways, and symbols of the sun are associated in one way or another with the symbols for many other things. The reason is, of course, that the sun is such a dominant and important part of the human environment. Early man saw the sun as a wheel of fire that rolled in an arc across the sky. This he symbolized in many wheel forms, in the disc, and in the swastika and triskelion.

The sun symbol here presented was taken from a stone carving coming from stone age Scandinavia. The radiating fires of the sun are dramatically presented by conventionalized flames. See also p. 38.

454

CHURINGA — DARAMULUM

This symbol consists of the Australian churinga, or "bull-roarer," with the figure representing Daramulum, a semi-human deity, superimposed upon it. The history and meaning of the churinga is described in the notes for Plate 19, pp. 371-372. See also p. 108.

THE TORII GATE

The Torii gate stands at the entrance to the precincts of Shinto shrines. Sometimes there are several Torii in succession leading up to the shrine. Without it no shrine is complete. The Torii probably had their origin in the two or threefold fences, poetically called *yaegaki* (eightfold fences) which encircled the ancient dwellings of some nobility. Accordingly the presence of many Torii on the single shrine pathway represent the gates to the several fences. Originally the Torii were very simple and primitive, of two upright pillars and two horizontal beams, usually of unpainted straight round timber. Different and more ornate styles developed in time, some built of stone or metal. The great Torii of Itukusima Shrine stands in the water of the inland sea, fifty-three feet high and seventy-three feet across, adding greatly to the charm of the island on which the shrine is located.

THE TORTOISE

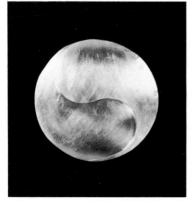

Kame, the tortoise, is a Shinto symbol of longevity. The tortoise is pictured accompanying both Jurojin and Kukurokujiu, two of the Seven Gods of Good Luck, both of whom stand for longevity.

In China the tortoise was one of the four animals symbolizing the four quarters of the earth. It was emblematic of the earth and of longevity, strength, endurance and sagacity. The dome-like back of the tortoise represents the dome of the sky, marked with the constellations of the heavens, and is essentially Yang. The lower shell is marked with the lines relating to the earth and is Yin in nature.

YANG AND YIN

One of the oldest Chinese symbols is the T'ai Chi, the Creative Principle or Origin of all things, the Yang and Yin. This represents the male and female elements, the duality from which all existence is derived. Yang represented the positive elements, heaven, sun, light, masculinity, and Yin the passive elements, such as the earth, moon, darkness, and femininity. Yang was active, warm, hard, dry, bright, procreative, steadfast, the essence of sunlight and fire, the south side of a hill, the north bank of a river. Yin was cold, wet, soft, dark, mysterious, secret, changeable, cloudy, dim, quiescent, the essence of shadow and water, the shade on the north side of the hill and the south bank of a river.

Through the intercourse of Yang and Yin all things come into being, including heaven which is Yang, and earth which is Yin. Yang and Yin are not really opposites, for they are in basic accord, complementary. When they work together in harmony they are always good.

456

THE TAO

This ideograph of the Tao is used as the symbol of Taoism, one of the oldest philosophies and religions of China. Its teachings are found in the Tao Te Ching and in Chuang-tse. The Tao is by nature undefinable, for it is that which permeates all things, the way or the road of nature. The aim of life is to attain harmony with the Tao. A person must flow as water flows, without assertion or struggle, and thus he will find the common level of life. Taoism counselled a kind of anarchy, government by not governing. One must conquer by not contending or striving.

The way of the Tao is to be in harmony with the laws of nature, which simply is the way it is, unconditioned, uncaused, the unity that underlies all seeming diversity. One must keep an infant heart, by yielding, unresistant, ungrasping. Quietism and serenity are the marks of the Taoist sage.

Tao is the Ultimate Reality, existing before time and higher than heaven, the principle or law of nature, eternal, unchanging, all-pervading. It is the principle or law at the root of all events, through which all nature is ordered and controlled. It pervades, harmonizes and influences all things. Its quiet but all-effective action is the model on which all human activity should be patterned.

Taoism, as a popular religion, degenerated from this philosophical and mystical beginning, and became a system of magic to ward off evil spirits. With the coming of Buddhism, this popular Taoism took on many of its symbols, manners and institutional behaviors. See also pp. 114, 150.

457

LI

This ideograph, Li, designates ceremonials, customary morality, rites, rules of good manners, proper conduct, and propriety, the essential virtues of Confucianism. Etiquette and ceremonial was the way of promoting harmoniousness. Confucius did not favor empty and lavish show. He said, "In ceremonials, it is better to be simple than lavish; in the rites of mourning, heartfelt distress is better than observance of detail." Emphasis was laid on the basic meanings of ceremonial and music rather than on their outer forms of presentation.

The meaning of the word li was very inclusive, denoting much more than etiquette, but rather the entire body of usages and customs, political and social insitutions. Says Fung Yu-lan, "All the rules for everything pertaining to human conduct may be included under the term li." In the concept of li lies the basis for the conservatism and the traditionalism that is the essence of Confucianism, as against the mysticism and the spontaneity that are the essence of Taoism. These two concepts of Li and Tao represent the two complementary sides of the Chinese culture and personality.

K'UNG FU TZU

This ideograph, K'ung Fu Tzu, is the name of the Chinese philosopher and moralist which we have latinized as Confucius. He is pre-eminently the image of the Chinese sage, the first great teacher, scholar, and literary anthologist in Chinese history. The compilations that are credited to him became the basis for Chinese education for two thousand years, and his moral teachings provided an essential character to Chinese government and social behavior. This ideograph is used as a symbol of the Chinese sage, and thereby a symbol of the ideals of character and achievement which he embodies. See also pp. 114, 158, 245.

THE LOTUS

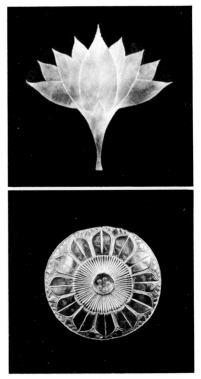

The lotus is one of the richest and most universal of all symbols. It was widely used in Egypt, where it was a symbol of the reproductive power of nature. It was also used by Assyrians, Persians, Arabs, and by the Greeks who dedicated it to the Nymphs.

Its best known use is in the religious symbolism of Hinduism and Buddhism. At the beginning of creation, the cosmic waters grew a thousand petalled lotus of pure gold, the womb of the universe. From it issued Brahma, the creator-god, and then all the creatures of the world. The lotus goddess is the goddess of moisture, of the earth, the Mother Goddess. The Lotus Goddess is Shri Lakshmi, and she bestows health, long life, prosperity, offspring, and fame, as the beloved wife of Vishnu, the sustainer-god. Her earliest appearance is at Mohenjo-Daro, 2,500 B.C., as a goddess with a lotus in her hair.

In Buddhism the Bodhisattva Padmapani (Lotus in Hand) takes over the role of the Lotus Goddess. The lotus pedestal, the lotus of the world, becomes the symbol of Buddhist enlightenment, upon which various Buddha figures are seated. It represents purity and perfection, because it grows out of the mud but is not defiled. The petals of the lotus also resemble the spokes of a wheel, so the flower becomes associated with the wheel of reincarnation. It was one of the "Eight Treasures" or auspicious signs inscribed upon the sole of the foot of the Buddha.

In China the Taoists considered the lotus an emblem of summer and fruitfulness, of purity, and of many children. Its relation with water had a spiritual significance for Taoists, who related the flow of water to the way of the Tao. The early Buddhist visitors to China commented on the similar symbolic use of the lotus in China, and in later centuries this symbolism merged, and the lotus became a pervasive symbol in Chinese culture and religion.

The lotus has different meanings, depending on its stage of growth. We have adopted its use as a half-opened flower, and in its fully opened state.

THE SACRED JEWEL

The Sanskrit word *mani* stands for jewel or pearl. The pearl is an emblem of purity, and stands for enlightenment, for the truth of the Buddha and the Law. It is a symbol of the Buddha and the Doctrine. In Japan the Three Jewels (tri-ratna), standing for the Buddha, the Law, and the Community, are greatly prized. They appear as one pearl in painting, with a fire halo, and in sculpture as one pearl surmounted by a three-pointed flame. In Esoteric doctrine it stands for the *manas* or sixth sense, and is "the glorious vesture of the soul, the radiant vehicle of the divine essence which, united with matter, forms man." The jewel also is supposed to have the power to grant wishes. The Boddhisattva Nyo-i-Kannon is a granter of desires; she holds the jewel in one hand or between her two hands. The jewel often appears in the forehead and in the hair of Amitahba Buddha. Hindus and Buddhists use words or phrases, called *mantras,* as aids to meditation. The best known is the Tibetan mantra, *"om mani padme hum,"* translated as "Ah! The jewel is in the lotus." It assists in attaining enlightenment and escaping the wheel of rebirth.

THE WHEEL OF THE LAW

The wheel is a symbol common to both Hinduism and Buddhism. It appears on some temples as the Wheel of the Sun. As the Wheel of Life it symbolizes the principle of reincarnation, the eternal cycle of birth and rebirth. In Buddhism the wheel symbolizes the Law of the Buddha and the circle of perfection which comes in the exercise of the wisdom of Buddha and the attainment of his vows. In hand symbolism the circle is made by joining the thumb and index finger.

As a sun symbol the wheel symbolized the movement of the sun across the sky, and thus it becomes a symbol of time. In India before Buddhism the wheel stood for the king who caused the wheel of life to turn. This meaning is re-interpreted in Buddhism, where Buddha is the one who causes the wheel of the Law to turn. The wheel has two meanings, that of destroying evil as it rolls across the earth, and of giving light, referring back to its origin as a sun symbol. The wheel is closely associated with the lotus, which, when it is fully opened, also stands for the sun, the divine birth, and the purity of the law. It is divided into eight petals, which relate to the eight spokes of the wheel, and symbolize the noble eight-fold path of Buddhist doctrine. The hub of the wheel is the "secret pivot of the world" around which everything must turn.

SHRI-YANTRA

The Shri-Yantra is a cosmic diagram of the Hindus. It seems like little more than a complex geometrical design, but Zimmer says that it was used as an aid in meditation, giving in visual form a diagram of "the logic-shattering paradox of eternity and time." He says that this symbol contains the whole meaning of the Hindu world of myth. A yantra is an instrument to stimulate the imagination and contemplation of the worshipper.

The Shri-Yantra consists of a square outer frame broken in a regular pattern, enclosing an arrangement of concentric circles and conventionalized lotus petals, and in the center a design of nine interpenetrating triangles.

The Shri-Yantra design is widely used in the Lamaistic Buddhism of Tibet, in temple decorations and in paintings with a Buddha figure in the center. Possibly the most spectacular use of the Cosmic Yantra is that of the three dimensional plan of the great Buddhist temple at Borobudur in Java. It was designed with a square base and arranged in seven planes, rising in a flattened spheroid form, recalling the shapes of the early stupas. The pilgrim reached the summit by walking around and around the stupa, past bas-relief sculptures depicting the life of the Buddha. At the summit he reached Kailasa, the center of the Cosmic Yantra where Gautama Buddha sat calling earth to his enlightenment. Thus the creators of Borobudur symbolized the highest insight of the devout Buddhist. See also p. 80.

461

THE DISC OF ATEN

The disc was the Egyptian symbol for Aten, the highest of all the deities. This is a modern version of the sun disc, not one, as far as I know, that is found in Egyptian art. There it is often pictured with rays emanating from the disc, each ending in a small hand which sometimes bestow the ankh. Aten was life itself, and the bestower of life, from whence come action, intelligence and joy. At first Aten was alone in the universe; all the other gods descended from him. See also pp. 40, 41, 65, 74.

THE CRUX ANSATA

The crux ansata or the ankh, is the Egyptian symbol for life, and in time it became one of the cross symbols of early Christianity. It is the Egyptian ideograph meaning "to live, living." It is often carried by the gods, seemingly as an intrument to awaken the dead to new life. In a carving from the twelfth dynasty the goddess Anuke-t holds the ankh, "the Key of Life," to the nostrils of King Usertesen III, with the inscription: "I give unto thee life, stability, and purity, like Ra for ever."

ANCESTOR GUARDIAN FIGURE

The African tribal religions have few symbols as such. We have selected objects of tribal art that adapted themselves to use as symbols. The function of these guardian figures is to protect the ancestor's bones, which are placed in baskets into the midst of which the base of the figure is inserted. The figures are made of wood and covered with metal sheets of copper or brass. The face is so arranged as to show the frontal view and profiles of the hair dressing at the same time. The treatment is stylized, but it represents a person's head surrounded by an elaborate hair dressing. They come from the Bakota tribe of the Gabun.

ANTELOPE HEADPIECE

The best known of the Bambara sculptures are their antelopes. They are the property and dance equipment of the associations of young men in the villages, and the rituals are mainly concerned with the increase of agriculture. The antelope headpieces are employed in dances just before the rainy season. They are worn attached to a basket-cap out into the fields to accompany those who work. They return to the village in pairs, one male and one female, and execute a dance accompanied by an orchestra of drums and watched by the whole population. With jumps and leaps and sudden turns they imitate the play of two antelopes, propitiating the spirits of the earth that have been disturbed by the farmers' activities.

THE BULL OF SUMERIA

This symbol of the bull was taken from the decoration of a harp found in a Sumerian grave from 3,500 B. C. There seems to have been some ritualistic convention that gave the bull a beard. In Sumeria Enlil, the god of the storm and of fertility, had the form of the bull. His spouse was Ninlil, the cow or mother goddess. Their union caused the waters of the Tigris and Euphrates to overflow, fertilizing the land. The bull god and the king shared the title "Wild Bull," and the kings wore bull-horned headdresses as a symbol of their divine appointment and power.

In Egypt Ptah, the Creator, was symbolized as a bull, as was the Norse god Thor. The bull was a common symbol in ancient India; as Nandi the bull is now a form of Shiva, and is held sacred. The bull also was important in Crete, and was related to Zeus and the bull-God Dionysus in Greece. Some of the significance and ritual of bull-worship still continues in the bull fights of Spain. See also p. 105.

THE TREE OF LIFE

The Tree of Life is so widespread in usage that it comes close to being a universal symbol. The design we have used is the sacred tree of Assyria. It is sometimes shown being fertilized by griffin demons with a date blossom. It is composed of different elements. In the center is a palm rising toward the crown at the top. What seem to be branches on the sides have been interpreted as representing undulating water courses such as irrigation canals, with palmettes growing at the sides where the canals meet. The plant forms are marked by a chevron pattern which differentiates them from the canals.

It has been suggested that the beginning of the tree of life may have been in the reed pillars used as posts of the gates of cattle byres by early Mesopotamian farmers. In Sumeria they stand apart as sacred pillars. The columns of Egyptian temples developed from such pillars made of reeds. They became a symbol of the Mother Goddess as the Gate of a sanctuary which is conceived as her body. Such pillars guarded temple gates in Syria and Palestine. Peasants in Anatolia and Syria still have their sacred trees. See also pp. 65, 75-76.

THE SCARAB

This symbol of the scarab, or beetle, is taken from an ancient Babylonian design. It appears everywhere in Egyptian art, especially as an amulet, used to ward off danger, and to help assure immortality. Before the journey to heaven a dying man would hold the scarab amulet above his breast as a passport.

The Egyptian ideograph of the scarab means "sun at dawn." An Egyptian beetle lays its eggs in dung, which it rolls into a ball with its hind legs. This ball was likened to the globe of the sun god. The sun was represented as a beetle rolling its egg across the sky, symbolizing the sun god Khepera. The scarab is essentially a symbol of resurrection and immortality.

SACRED FIRE OF ZOROASTRIANISM

In Zoroastrianism the spiritual world is linked with the material. Each of the Bounteous Immortals came to be identified with physical elements, Wholeness with water, Right-Mindedness with the earth, and Truth with fire. The celestial fire of the stars, which is always victorious over darkness, has its symbol in the inextinguishable fire on the altar, which also served the Persian kings as an image of their enduring power. Ahura Mazda dwelt on high in endless light, and Ahriman dwelt below in endless darkness. This symbol was derived from a Zoroastrian fire altar which was pictured on an ancient coin.

MITHRA

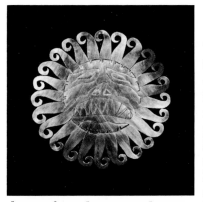

Mithra was an ancient god of the Vedic hymns, as well as the hymns of the Avestas of Iran. Mithra was a god of light, the protector of truth. He is the light that dissipates the darkness and restores happiness and life to earth, providing the heat that makes nature fertile. He scatters the waters of the sky and causes the plants to grow. In Zoroastrianism Mithra became a lesser deity, but in time he developed into the hero of a salvation cult, one of the "mystery religions." It wasn't until the end of the first century that Mithraism became known in Rome, where it became popular in the army, which spread it over all the Empire. At the end of the second century Mithra became one of the favorite gods of the Roman aristocracy and the imperial court. The struggle for control of the Roman Empire that waged between Christianity and Mithraism was finally won by the Christians, but Julian the Apostate, the last of the pagan Caesars, was one of Mithra's followers. See also p. 323.

THE CRESCENT

Islam has no specific symbols. The crescent is a natural symbol of the moon, and as the symbol of Diana and other moon goddesses, it is a common symbol in the Near East where Islam arose. In pre-Turkish times the crescent was used as an ornament on the minarets of mosques and on flags. It was the military and religious symbol of the Ottoman Turks beginning in the thirteenth century, and appears on banners as a symbol of the Ottoman Empire. It has been suggested that it symbolizes the new moon that heralds the sacred month of Ramadan. See also p. 74.

THE STAR OF DAVID

The six pointed star is called the Star of Creation, or the Star of David. It is also known as a necromancer's symbol, the knot of Solomon, and some Jewish scholars claim that it is therefore a magic and secular symbol, and not a sacred symbol. Symbols are capable of almost infinite re-interpretation, and the *Mogen David*, or Shield of David as it is also called, has been given various spiritual meanings, and is a common decoration on synagogues, Menorahs, and other sacramental objects.

THE TABLETS OF THE LAW

The symbol designating the Tablets of the Law, the ten commandments handed down by Jehovah to Moses on Mount Sinai, is often found on synagogues and on ceremonial objects. The tablets of the law symbolize the law of God, which is contained for the Jews in the Torah, the Pentateuch or the five Books of Moses.

466

THE LATIN CROSS

The use of the cross for the crucifixion of criminals and political offenders was common in Roman times, and after the crucifixion of Jesus, the cross became the central symbol of Christianity. But it was already a very ancient symbol, being used in many forms in many places. Within Christianity the cross occurs in hundreds of versions. We have chosen five of the most representative versions.

The Latin Cross is the most common, and bears the shape reputed to the cross on which Jesus was crucified. The upright arm is much longer than the other. It symbolizes the Passion and the Atonement. Sometimes five red marks or jewels are placed on the cross to represent the five wounds, and sometimes the crown of thorns hangs upon it.

THE GREEK CROSS

The Greek Cross, or the Cross of St. George, has four equal arms, and it is used more often as a symbol of the church than as a symbol of the crucifixion. A chalice cover in the Meeting House collection is in the form of a Greek cross. This is the most common form of the cross in the ancient world. It appears on a Kassite seal of 1750 B. C., where it is associated with the Sun-god. It appears in Egyptian art at Thebes.

THE PAPAL CROSS

The Papal Cross has three bars. The Patriarchal Cross or Cross of Lorraine has two bars, and a third and longer bar is added below them for the Papal Cross. It distinguished the Western or Roman Church from the Byzantine Church of the East. The top bar is said to indicate the scroll which was nailed to the cross, and which was inscribed in Hebrew, Greek, and Latin.

467

THE ORTHODOX CROSS

The Orthodox Cross exists in two versions, with three bars, the lower bar shorter than the middle bar. It is said to represent the footrest. The lower bar is commonly slanted. The cross did not become the dominant emblem of Christianity until the Fourth century. The early Christians assigned magical powers to the cross, using it as a sign to make themselves known to one another.

THE CELTIC CROSS

The Celtic or Iona Cross has a circle at the crossing. It was apparently originated by the Celtic speaking peoples of the British Isles. It often appears adorned with leaves and flowers. Some of the finest products of the Anglo Saxons were stone crosses, found in towns, markets, roadsides and cemeteries. See also pp. 74-75.

THE BEARDED SERPENT

This image of the Bearded Serpent is used as a symbol of Zeus and of Greek Mythology. At a March festival, Zeus was honored with the added title of Meilichios, which shows that he had taken on the title and attributes of the aboriginal god Meilichios, a huge, bearded snake. The snake was, for early man, a symbol of the underworld, since he came up from holes in the ground. There would seem to have been some conflict in joining the rites of a sky god such as Zeus with those of an underworld deity like Meilichios. The old snake relief carvings were dedicated to Zeus. The name

468

Meilichios means "easily entreated." His cult was connected with the fertility of the soil. This March festival was a day of feasting, of making merry with one's kin, and giving presents to children.

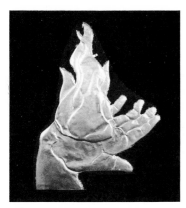

THE HAND AND FLAME

We have adapted the hand and flame as a symbol of the Promethean myth, in which Prometheus stole fire from Mount Olympus to give it to man. Thus it is a symbol of man gaining control over the powers of nature. The taming of fire by stone age man, which seems to have gone back to Pekin man about 500,000 B. C., was one of man's earliest achievements in his control over nature, which led in time to modern technology, science, and civilization. See also pp. 115-124.

THE FASCES

The Fasces is a Roman symbol of government. Bundles of elm or birch rods, from which the head of an axe projected, were fastened together by a red strap. As an emblem of authority, they were carried by lictors, in the left hand and on the left shoulder, before the higher Roman magistrates, and at the funeral of a magistrate, behind the bier. The fasces represented the power over life and limb possessed by the rulers. Within the precincts of the city of Rome the axe was removed, in recognition of the right of appeal to the people in a matter of life or death; outside Rome, however, each consul retained the axe.

The Fasces has been interpreted to mean that, whereas it is easy to break one rod alone, if many rods are bound together they are impossible to break. Thus a people bound together under common law and agreement are powerful in their civic action, their law, and before the onslaught of an enemy.

THE HAMMER OF THOR

This symbol of Thor's Hammer came from an amulet from Uppland, Sweden. In Old Norse it is called Mjollnir, the magic hammer that always returned to him after he had cast it as a thunderbolt. Thor was the god of strength in Norway and Iceland, the defender, the god of war, the protector from disease.

The hammer has a long history as a symbol. It occurs in ancient Crete, associated with the Mother-goddess, in the form of the sacred double axes. The Cretan bull cult, symbolizing the father-god, was closely associated with the mother-goddess. The images of the bull have a sacred double axe between the horns. The axe appears also in Hittite and Syrian art associated with the bull. The thunderbolt was also the weapon of Zeus, who was a god of the sky, of thunder and lightning, as was Thor.

The symbolism continues to our own time in the gavel, a symbol of authority in the hand of the judge, the chairman, and the auctioneer. The auctioneer speaks of things being sold "under the hammer."

The name of the Scandinavian god Thor is identical with the name for thunder used by all Teutonic people. He is defined thus: "Thor who is thunder and lightning presides in the air; he rules over winds and rain, fair weather, and fruitful seasons." He is "the strong one of the gods, the friend of man, the hurler, the noisy one, the giant-killer."

The hammer was a sacred symbol, used in consecrations and blessings. It was made by the dwarf Sindri, and Thor could use it only when he wore his iron gloves. However hard he smote, it never failed him; if he threw it, it would never miss. With the hammer Thor slew monsters and giants and forced Loki to keep silent. Germanic peoples believed a thunderbolt accompanied the lightning, a black wedge which buried itself in the earth, the hammer of Thor. See also p. 75.

THE CELTIC SWASTIKA

This Celtic and Druidic symbol is a swastika made from two S forms. In *The Migration of Symbols* D'Alviella gives a whole chapter to the migrations and transformations of the swastika or gammadion. It seems to have been an Aryan symbol, probably originating in the Danube area, travelling from there to Thrace, Greece and Italy. "It seems to have been introduced into Germany, Denmark, Sweden, Norway and Iceland, in the same manner in which the runic writing was brought from the Danube valley to the shores of the Baltic and the ocean. It may have penetrated into Gaul, and from there into England and Ireland."

The meaning of the swastika is a matter of conjecture. It often occurs with the solar disc. Its branches may symbolize the rays of the sun in motion, from which it may have come to symbolize astronomical movement in general, that of the moon and the stars as well as the sun.

SACRIFICIAL KNIFE

The Indians of South America had no symbolism as such, since they did not develop even a hieroglyphic writing, as did the Mayans and Aztecs. They did use animals symbolically, such as the "cat-god" and the condor. In seeking something that would act as a symbol for these people, we were attracted to this sacrificial knife, with a head decorating its handle. Thus it serves two purposes, to symbolize the religions of South America, and also to symbolize sacrifice, which is one of the oldest ritual practices of man's religious behavior. The provenance given was Columbia.

THE BAT

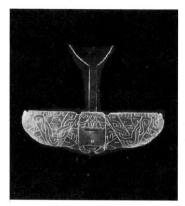

This symbol of a vampire bat is taken from a jade pendant from Costa Rica. Camazotz is known at the Death Bat or Ruler of the Bats, a dread and potent deity among the Mayans, and, as the vampire, feared and propitiated far into South America. In the Meeting House symbol collection it represents Central America and stands for death.

The bat has called forth strikingly similar responses in other parts of the world. In Egypt it symbolizes black magic, darkness, madness and rapacity, and in Babylon evil spirits and ghosts. In Medieval Europe it typified death, misfortune and witchcraft. But in China and Japan it is the courier of heavenly blessings, a bringer of good fortune and long life, and is supposed to live for 1000 years. It is a symbol of nocturnal activities and transmigrations, and is associated with the peach in Chinese art.

THE CALENDAR DISC

This is a symbol of Aztec religion and of the theme of time and the seasons in human religion. A gigantic Aztec calendar stone was discovered beneath the foundations of the cathedral in Mexico City in 1790, buried since 1521. It was twelve feet high and weighed twenty-four tons. It is a symbol of the infinity of the Aztec universe. The face of the Sun god Tonatiuh is in the center, with the names of the twenty days encircling it. It is filled with symbols of previous world epochs, and of heaven.

Time and the calendar were basic to the whole life of the Aztec people. There were two calendars, a ritualistic one of 260 days, and a solar calendar of 360 days plus five uncounted days, "the empty *nemontemi*." The ritual calendar was magical and sacred and ancient, for it had been used by the Mayans for 1500 years. The end of each solar year was a threat, as was the end of each 52 year cycle. No one knows why the Mayans and the Aztecs were so obsessed with the passage of time, but the entire life of the tribe was organized to avert the wrath of the gods and the threat of disaster at the end of each cycle.

THE THUNDERBIRD

This design of the Thunderbird comes from the Navaho Indians, where it is the symbol for rain and happiness. The Thunderbird is a mythical bird causing lighting and thunder, often a supernatural eagle, who is the spirit or god of thunder. The Thunderbird is a deity all over North America, from Mexico to Alaska. The Eagle Dance was one of the chief ceremonies of the Plains Indians.

On the North Pacific Coast, the Thunderbird was supreme, like the other thunder gods Jupiter and Thor. The Thunderbird lived alone in the pristine world. He swooped down from the clouds, flew over the waters, touched them with the tips of his wings, and the earth rose from the bottom of the sea, floating on the water. He is usually helpful to man, who must invoke and worship him. It is believed the Thunderbird casts thunderbolts at the whales and captures them.

MANITO, THE GREAT SPIRIT

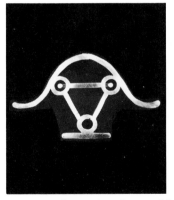

The Algonquin Indians believed in a Great Spirit who dwelt in the western skies, named Kitshi Manito, who had created everything, the heaven and the earth and all creatures. He created one man and one woman, and through them all of humanity. Hoffman, who lived with the Ojibwas in 1877, wrote: "The Ojibwa believe in a multiplicity of spirits, or man idos, which inhabit all space and every conscious object in nature. These man idos, in turn, are subservient to superior ones, either of a charitable or benevolent character, or those which are malignant and agressive. The chief or superior man ido is termed Ki'tshi Man'ido — Great Spirit."

Some students believe the manito refers to any spirit or daemon, good or bad, or to an ancestral figure favorably disposed to his children,

473

but that the Indians had no idea of a Great Spirit or Creator over all other manitos. They attribute this concept to the teaching of Christian missionaries, which turned the manito idea into the meaning of God.

The manito of greatest authority among the Algonquins was Michaba, but he was far from a supreme spirit. He was the "great hare," originator of exorcising and the arts of the medicine man, who ruled the winds, and guarded his people. He is called "the hare that made the moon," and is even said to have created the earth. In time manito came to be a general term, and was used to denote the personal guardian spirits of some Western tribes. It may be that this is the source of the symbol of Manito as a bison.

THE BEAR

The bear is one of the chief totem animals of the Northwest Coast American Indians. It undoubtedly derives from the bear festivals and ceremonials of Siberia and Northern Europe. The Laplanders call a slain male bear "sacred man," and a slain female bear "sacred virgin." They cook the bear meat in a special hut to which the women are not admitted and sing and celebrate for three days.

The myth of the Bear developed three main forms, the Bear Mother relating to a berry picker kidnapped by grizzlies, the Grizzly Bear slain by the Copper-Canoeman, and the Grizzly Bear of the Sea. They relate to Asiatic ideas of the union of a human being and a god, the self-sacrifice of a supernatural being, the ceremonial eating of a supernatural being, and the seeking of atonement through rituals and offerings. The myths are elaborate, and form the themes of the carvings and paintings of the Haidas and other Northwest Coast tribes.

The symbol of the bear stands in our collection for the religion of the Northwest Coast Indians, and as an example of totemism, a religious theme widespread in primitive and tribal cultures.

THE SPIRAL

The spiral occurs in Neolithic art on pottery and in stone carving. It appeared even earlier in the Magdalenian times. It occurs on archaic Chinese pottery and in Europe, and was carried westward by the megalithic movement from Malta all the way to Ireland, where it decorates the passage-graves. Its symbolic meaning was probably that of endlessness, of eternity.

The spiral occurs in Hindu art in the form of the cosmic serpent, Ananta, the Endless One, who is the couch and canopy of Vishnu, the Lord of Life. In the philosophy of Yoga the cosmic spiral force is known as Maha-kundali, the Great Coiled One, which has its seat in the human body.

In his essay on "Circles" Emerson writes: "The life of man is a self-evolving circle, which, from a ring imperceptably small, rushes on all sides outwards to new and larger circles and that without end." In the Meeting House Project the spiral stands for growth and evolution. See also pp. 27, 28, 65.

THE ATOM

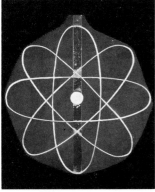

The diagram of the atom is the symbol of matter and energy. Such diagrams are an outgrowth of modern physics, in an attempt to make their theories objective and understandable. Such a diagram does not convey an accurate representation of the structure and activity of the atom; indeed no pictorial representation could. So it must be taken simply as a symbol, with only a rough suggestion of the nature of reality.

Atomic physics has furnished the basis for a new kind of philosophical materialism, wherein matter is equated with energy, and the old dualisms between matter and spirit seem meaningless. In the circle we have a symbol of the universe, the macrocosm, and in the atom we have the opposite pole of reality, the microcosm. These two symbols relate to the mural of Andromeda and the construction of the atom that form the poles of the symbolism in the Meeting House. See also pp. 65, 318-321.

MAN AS MICROCOSMOS

This symbolic representation of man as microcosmos was taken from the works of Agrippa, von Nettesheim, Heinrich Cornelius, a German physician of the sixteenth century. His interest in magic involved him in trouble with the Church. In the diagrams the symbol of Mars is at the head, Venus and Jupiter at the hands, and Juno and Saturn at the feet. The sun appears at the navel and the moon at the crotch. Within the circle are the lines of a cross and a five-pointed star. As a microcosm, man or human nature is seen as an epitome of the universe as a whole.

This diagram has obvious relations to astrology which flourished in Europe up to the seventeenth century, and still lingers on in some circles. We do not ascribe to the magical or astrological implications of this symbol, but since astrology is the early form of astronomy, just as alchemy is the early form of chemistry, we do think that this symbol presents an interesting and vivid image of the relation of man to the solar system and to the universe. Under the interpretation of man as an offspring of nature, and from the point of view of modern science, through biophysics and biochemistry, man can still be interpreted as a microcosm, as the universe in miniature. The idea of microcosm, a comparison of man's frame and members with the parts of the universe (macrocosm) and nature, came from the Greek philosophers, and to the Jews through Neo-Platonism, and was much favored by the Kabbalists.

MAN

The design for this symbol was taken from a copper sheet figure in the shape of a man that was found in India, and which has been dated as about 1000 B. C., or later in the first millenium B. C. It was chosen because, in a very simple and diagrammatic form, it gives a symbolization of man.

THE LYRE

The Lyre is the symbol of music, taken from a Greek design. It was used by the Greeks to accompany singing and recitation, and was associated with Apollo, the god of music, and especially with his son Orpheus. Orpheus came from Thrace in northern Greece, and appeared as a magical musician, whose music had power over the wild and untamed things in nature. Upon the death of his wife, Eurydice, Orpheus followed her down into Hades. He so affected the gods of the underworld with his music that they allowed her to return with him, on condition that she should walk behind him and Orpheus should not look back. He did look back, however, and she became a ghost again and returned to Hades.

The lyre appears to have been invented in Babylonia or Assyria, and to have moved from there into Egypt, and thence into Greec.

THE SICKLE AND WHEAT

Wheat was possibly the first plant that man domesticated, and its cultivation marked the beginning of the Neolithic revolution in the Near East. The first sickles were made of stone, or of microliths set in a strip of bone or wood. Since the sickle was probably used to harvest wild grasses before agriculture began, the sickle well may be man's first agricultural tool. This combination of the sickle and spears of wheat has long been a symbol of agriculture. See also p. 65.

THE CORNUCOPIA

The cornucopia, the horn of plenty, is a symbol of abundance and of harvest. It is known as the horn of Amalthea, the nurse of Zeus, who has been depicted as a goat which suckled the god and was set by him among the stars, or turned into a nymph. The horn of Amalthea was one of the goat's horns, which had the magical power to be filled with water or whatever was its owner's wish. It is often associated with local deities such as river gods, and with such personifications as Abundance, and the goddess Fortuna. See also p. 65.

THE HAND AND THE HAMMER

Man is differentiated from other animals by being a tool user. His long journey upward to civilization seems to have begun when he invented the hand axe, which was little more than a stone held in his fist. It took him another hundred thousand years to improve on this first tool by the invention of a handle for it. This became in time a weapon for battle and the hunt, an axe for chopping, an adze and a hoe. Thus the hand holding the hammer is the fitting symbol for labor. See also p. 65.

THE COGWHEEL

The first revolution in man's ability to provide food and goods was that of agriculture. The second was the coming of technology, the industrial revolution, with the greatly increased development and use of machinery. The cogwheel is a typical element of the machine, and has come to be used as a symbol of technology. See also p. 65.

478

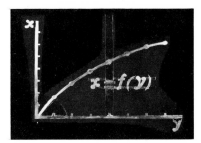

X EQUALS THE FUNCTION OF Y

This mathematical equation has been described as the most typical of the equations of scientific procedure. It is used as a symbol of scientific investigation, and as a symbol of the relation of mathematics to science. See also p. 206.

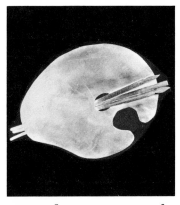

BRUSHES AND PALETTE

This symbol of art is simply composed of the essential tools of the painter's craft. This is an ancient and universal device in the creation of symbolism. The stone axe of stone age man was one of the first symbols. In tribal societies impractical imitations of tools and weapons are used ceremonially and symbolically. In early China ceremonial blades were made of jade. Thus the use of the cogwheel and the brushes and palette as symbols of technology and art grows out of very ancient tradition.

THE CLASPED HANDS
OF BROTHERHOOD

This symbol comes from Asia Minor where it is the symbol of union and brotherhood. This symbol persists into our own times in the handshake of greeting and welcome. The hand is an old symbol, the raised hand of blessing, the outstretched hand, a sign of offering, and the laying on of hands, a symbol of the passing of divine power in the ordination of priests. Buddhism contains a complex vocabulary of hand symbols. The clasped hands, as a symbol of fellowship now, has almost universal understanding and usage. See also p. 64.

479

CIRCLE AND PINE TREES
OF COOPERATION

Often generalized emotions and ideas, such as love and cooperation, have rarely been converted into symbolic form. We have searched for years for a fitting symbol of love, but have been determined not to settle for the sentimentalized symbol of the heart pierced by an arrow. The only symbol for cooperation which we have been able to find is that of the circle enclosing two pine trees, which is a symbol used by the cooperative movement in America. Whether it was invented by them, or has an older history, we do not know. Since it is a graceful and effective symbol we have adapted it from them to represent this basic and essential attitude in human society. See also p. 64.

THE LAMP OF KNOWLEDGE

In literature and art the lamp is a symbol of learning, sharing the symbolism of light and fire with the torch as a symbol of truth. The lamp is also a symbol of the home and of the altar, where it stands for divinity. Originally the lamp was a vessel for holding oil that could be burned through a wick, made from shell or stone. Its use extends far back into the old stone age, and it has been one of the richest and most suggestive of all man's symbols.

The lamp was used on the altars of oracles in Egypt and Greece. Whoever wished to consult the oracle went in the evening and filled the lamps and lit them, and left some coins on the altar. Lamps were also placed on tombs in memory of the deceased. See also pp. 327, 334, 359.

THE SWORD AND SCALES

The sword and scales as a symbol of Justice goes back to Roman usage. Justice, when personified, was pictured as the Roman goddess Justitia, holding sword and scales. Sometimes she is blindfolded as a symbol of impartiality. Themis is the Greek goddess who is the counterpart of Justitia. Maat was the goddess of justice in Egypt, and the scales are used as an ideograph for justice. In Egyptian art they occur in scenes where the dead are coming before Osiris for judgment. Scales for weighing originated in pre-dynastic Egypt as early as 5000 B. C.

THE LAUREL WREATH

Branches of the laurel tree were used by the ancient Greeks to crown the winners of the Pythian games, at Delphi, of which the god Apollo was the patron. Myths ascribed the origin of the games to Apollo as a celebration of his victory over the Python, and they formed one of the four great Panhellenic festivals. They emphasized musical and dramatic contests, for which the prizes were palm branches and laurel crowns. The laurel wreath came to be used as a mark of distinction for certain offices, functions, and academic honors.

THE CADUCEUS

The Caduceus appears in Greek mythology as the staff of Hermes, the messenger of the gods. It is a winged rod on which two serpents are entwined. It probably was originally a solar symbol, and the Greek tradition has it given to Hermes by Apollo. Homer says it was a rod of gold that "charms the eyes of men and calls them from their slumbers." It lures the dead to Hades, and can bring them back to life. It changes all that it touches to gold. It seems to have been related to the

481

winged globe of Egypt and Assyria, and the rod may recall the tree of life in simple form. In its use by Hermes it refers to industry and commerce.

The snake was sacred to Aesculapius, legendary Greek physician, and a version of the Caduceus with but one snake related to him. Since 1600 the rod with two snakes entwined has replaced the former version, and the Caduceus has become a symbol of the physician and of healing. See also p. 65.

THE OWL

The owl seems to have become a symbol for wisdom because of the bird's appearance of solemnity. The owl also symbolizes solitude, and is pictured in paintings of hermits. One of its most common appearances is in paintings of St. Jerome as a hermit in the desert praying or writing, while a crucifix, a skull, and an owl are nearby, symbolizing the wisdom of the saint. Greek priests carried a stuffed owl as a badge of their profession. Athena, the goddess of Athens, was associated with the intellectual attainments of its people. The owl is her bird, and the owl appears on early vases as human-headed, spinning, or armed. On a vase in the Louvre the owl is armed with a shield and spear, and there are a series of plaques in which an owl with human arms is spinning wool. Although the owl is an ominous bird in much folklore, it is often considered to be an omen of good fortune.

THE TORCH

The torch shares in the symbolism of light and fire, which is one of the oldest and richest of all symbols. It is used as a symbol of knowledge and freedom. Since it lights up the darkness it is a natural symbol of illumination and enlightenment. It also carries the allusion of passing knowledge from one person to another in learning, with one torch being lighted from another in a torch race. The torch is associated with freedom, as is enlightenment, and is held aloft by our own dominant symbol of freedom, the Statue of Liberty in New York

Harbor. In Christianity the torch is a symbol of Christ as the Light of the World.

In Greece the torch was used in fire rituals in agricultural festivals, perhaps to represent the sun in sympathetic magic. The torch was identified with Demeter, and her "torch day" was doubtless to purify the land and ward off pestilence from the crops.

In Athens a torch race was featured in festivals in honor of various gods. It was first held in honor of Prometheus, the fire-bringer, at whose altar the competitors lit their torches. Victory rested with the team whose lighted torch first reached the goal, an altar on which a fire was kindled by the torch. It seems to have originated in the need to carry fire from one altar to another with great speed, when the fire on an altar had become contaminated. In Greece and Rome the torch was used in wedding processions, and also in funeral processions, where it was used to light the pyre on which the corpse was burned. See also p. 64.

THE TRISKELION

There is no doubt that the triskelion, a symbol formed by the same process as the swastika, represented the solar movement. It is frequently seen on coins from Asia Minor in the form here used, consisting of three legs bent, as in the act of running. It appears with the sun in the center between the three legs. It also occurs with the crescent, symbolizing the circular course and the phases of the moon. The triskelion was used by the Greeks as a symbol of progress.

DOVE AND OLIVE BRANCH

The dove and olive branch has been a traditional symbol of peace. With the Greeks it was a symbol of rescue, whereas the dove and laurel branch symbolized peace. The source of the symbol probably goes back to the Old Testament legend of the flood, where Noah sent out a dove from the ark, which brought back an olive branch to show that the flood had receded, and that God had made his peace with man. In the law of Moses the dove was declared to be pure for this reason and was used as an offering of purification after the birth of a child. In the New Testament the dove is used as a symbol of the Holy Spirit, when it comes to alight upon Jesus at his baptism by John the Baptist. In Greek mythology the dove was sacred to Aphrodite. The snake was an embodiment of chthonian divinity in Egypt and Greece, and the dove is the vehicle of the divine spirit. In Crete doves settle on the person of the goddess or were offered as votaries. Doves are also perched on the axes, trees and shrines of the altars. They probably represent the original dwelling place of the goddess as a spirit of the sky. See also pp. 64, 67, 74.

UNITED NATIONS SYMBOL

The symbol designed for the United Nations demonstrates that the creation and use of symbols still continues in human society. Using the ancient symbol of peace, the olive wreath, to circle a polar-projection diagram of the earth, the result is a beautiful and significant symbol of one world united in peace. We have included it in our collection of symbols because we believe that a religion for one world is a direct counterpart of the expression of political and social universalism in the United Nations. The world united in international law and cooperation, to the end of making war no longer necessary to settle international disputes, is certainly a religious ideal of high order. See also pp. 21, 61, 64, 67, 68, 101.